P9-ARU-867

WITHDRAWN

MYTHOLOGIES OF VIOLENCE IN POSTMODERN MEDIA

Mythologies of Violence in Postmodern Media

Edited by

Christopher Sharrett

 WAYNE STATE UNIVERSITY PRESS   DETROIT

Library of Congress Cataloging-in-Publication Data

Mythologies of violence in postmodern media / edited by Christopher
    Sharrett.
        p.   cm.—(Contemporary film and television series)
    Includes bibliographical references and index.
        ISBN 0-8143-2742-7 (pbk : alk. paper)   ISBN 0-8143-2879-2
        1. Violence in motion pictures.   2. Violence on television.
    I. Sharrett, Christopher.   II. Series.
    PN 1995.9.V5M98   1999
    791.43'655—dc21   99-24232

Grateful acknowledgment is made to the University of Texas Press for
permission to reprint Martin Rubin's "The Grayness of Darkness: *The
Honeymoon Killers* and Its Impact on Psychokiller Cinema," which first
appeared in *Velvet Light Trap* 30 (1992): 48–64, and to the editors of
CineAction, for permission to reprint Annalee Newitz's "Serial Killers,
True Crime, and Economic Performance Anxiety" and Ken Morrison's
"The Technology of Homicide: Constructions of Evidence and Truth in the
American Murder Film," both published in issue 38.

Contents

6

Acknowledgments

Obviously a critical anthology is a collective effort, but I wish to acknowledge some people beyond my contributors who were crucial to this book's realization.

Sid Gottlieb offered enormous technical assistance, his usual critical acuity, and most especially his warm friendship. Along with their brilliant essays, Bill Luhr and Barry Grant helped this book with comments on its scope and shape. Krin Gabbard assisted me by reading portions of the book early in its production. Peter Lehman offered incisive criticisms that helped give the book its current form. The friendship and intelligence of David Curtis and Elaine Davis will always be important to me. Vincent Salandria, Marty Schotz, Ben Schotz, Steve Jones, Joan Mellen, Mike Morrissey, Gaeton Fonzi, Ray Marcus, Bob Dean, Fletcher Prouty, and Jim Douglass dazzle me with their penetrating view of the circumstances of our current world; I so much value their camaraderie.

A number of colleagues at the Columbia University Seminar on Cinema and Interdisciplinary Interpretation supported me with their friendship and comments on subjects relevant to this book, especially Martha Nochimson, David Sterritt, Jackie Reich, Pam Grace, Louise Spence, and Steve Elworth. Many colleagues at Seton Hall University were similarly helpful through their good humor and rich intellectual sustenance, including Larry Greene, Judith Stark, Gisela Webb, William

7

ACKNOWLEDGMENTS

Sales, David Abalos, Elizabeth Milliken, Rev. Lawrence Frizzell, Marla Powers, Jeff Levy, Philip Kayal, David Black, Amy Kiste Nyberg, and the faculty of the Department of Communication. Donald McKenna, chair of the department, has been very important to me and to this project. He has shown unflagging sensitivity, support, and concern for both.

Terry Geesken and Mary Corliss of the Museum of Modern Art Film Stills Archive were very helpful and enormously cordial in providing images for this book. Susan Morrison of *Cineaction* also gave me important assistance.

I am grateful to Patricia Erens for her advocacy and insights. Jennifer Backer of Wayne State University Press could not have been a more supportive or effective editor. Alison Reeves, Kathleen Wilson, and Alice Nigoghosian were most professional in making this book happen.

This book, like virtually everything else I do, owes a great deal to the presence of my wife, Joan Hubbard.

Christopher Sharrett

January 1999

INTRODUCTION

CHRISTOPHER SHARRETT

The topic of violence in the arts and in society has seldom been as rife in public debate as in the last several decades of twentieth-century America. Approaching the subject of violence, even when the focus is narrowed to its representation in film, media, and mass culture (as in the case of this anthology), poses some daunting challenges for the critic. It seems the tendency of much postmodern media criticism to remove itself from the activity of society, the "real world," to focus on lived experience solely as "text" and "discourse." Such an approach is often regarded as cynical, "academic" in the worst sense (i.e., irrelevant to public debate and public concern), and a particularly amoral stance when the subject becomes something as charged as the omnipresence of violence in American life. For many, doing otherwise almost necessitates becoming involved in empirical data, usually for the purpose of "proving" how media violence affects social behavior, always with a distinct ideological agenda hiding behind the facade of empirical observation, statistics, and "objectivity."

This critical anthology is not a social science effort in demonstrating, even tentatively, the causes of violence in contemporary civilization. These essays are concerned with "mythologies of violence" in media since the authors share a critical/theoretical attitude, despite different methodologies, that looks at the violent image not as a given function of human nature, but as an artifact embodying ideological assumptions. These assumptions and the images they generate have complex functions within society, making difficult any pat conclusions about the impact of violence on the subject. What becomes clear is the extraordinary preeminence of the violent image in the extreme alienation of late twentieth-century America.

There is an obvious qualification to that statement. What these essays undertake, it seems to me, is a mapping of the mediascape that demonstrates the importance of the violent image in furthering an atomized society that has been in the making since colonial forces took possession of this nation. With the reach of the supranational corporate state, whose nexus is still the United States, my contributors find it important to concern themselves with the violent image as it appears in the international arena.

The term "mythologies" is not used in any Jungian sense suggestive of the archetypal, mystical, or the endemic presence of violence within humanity. Rather, the concern of the contributors herein is the discussion of various forms of mythic speech as developed by cultural and language theorists and current forms of cultural studies. Contrary to Jung and his followers, the contributors suggest that far from being endemic to human society, mythic speech is an operation of ideology, a series of narratives that conflate nature with culture, tending to have us assume that certain attributes are given and immutable. Therefore, mythic tales (of heroes, of conquest) reflect universal, transcendent truths necessary to the advancement of civilization.

Despite this, it would be disingenuous for a book of this type not to avail itself of some hard data and take notice of the world "out there," wherein the concern about the violent image and the culture of violence in general is so profound. In many respects the current debate about violence in society contains all the difficulties of postmodern civilization; art and life are frequently commingled as social scientists and media pundits use catch phrases from pop criticism and even motion pictures to explain complex social phenomena. While the media are frequently pointed to as culprits in fostering a climate of violence, little effort is made to determine what exactly the media are, the political and economic interests they represent, and the ideological assumptions they perpetuate. While institutions such as the American Academy of Pediatrics insist that "media violence can lead to aggressive behavior in children," pointing to "over 1,000 studies that confirm this link,"[1] a contextualization of the violent image within the history of American representation, framed by some sense of American political economy, is invariably missing.

10

Similarly, such a contextualization is missing from the horrific media vignettes describing the schoolyard gun play in Littleton, Colorado, Jonesboro, Arkansas, and Springfield, Oregon, and countless other sites of the late 1990s where it would seem Richard Slotkin's "gunfighter nation" has come home to roost. The loss of affect among some of the youngsters participating in these shootings seems correlated with a devaluation of the human subject and the increased sense of no future that is a hallmark of late capitalist society, yet killing from ambush and taking what one wants is as old as the nation. As Barry Keith Grant suggests early in this anthology, it may be unwise to dissociate contemporary serial violence and shooting sprees from an earlier American violence that gave us the Leatherstocking Tales and the nineteenth-century gunslingers who were valorized by twentieth-century film and television, an issue developed in the book's afterword. At the earliest stages of this nation's history, a profound anti-intellectualism was perhaps best evidenced in the quick recourse to the gun. Indeed, the Indian removal policies of the last century were effectuated against a backdrop of public discourse that decried "book larnin' " (associated with the Old World) and preferred action. The Civil War, always a subject for film and television rhapsody, was in part about the scrapping of political debate in favor of bloodletting. This is not to say that violence and its representations are about the slow dumbing-down of America or a hostility to reason alone. Rather, the preeminence of the violent image seems concurrent with a basic distaste for democratic discourse and the ascendance of a perceived elitist need to manufacture public consent, in Walter Lippmann's phrase. The hyperviolence of the post-1960s cinema seems to have flowed logically from this attitude, and from the barbarism of the Vietnam War, the political assassinations of the 1960s, the scrapping of the social contract at Watergate, the devaluation of human labor with the rise of cybernetics and the migration of capital, and the reduction of the population to mere spectators as it becomes alienated from the political process.

Instead of being encouraged to appreciate such a context, we are faced with an eternal present, as politicians and media commentators argue that violent acts are aberrant, unrepresentative of authentic American experience and ambition. Referring to the 1998 lynching of James Byrd, a middle-aged black citizen of Jasper, Texas, President Clinton remarked, "This is not what America is about." Is it not? Given the history of race relations in this country, particularly after the rollback in social/economic justice and racial tolerance of the Reagan-Bush-Clinton epoch, such an assertion seems at the least ahistorical, and in fact risible.

11

These events are framed by other media moments that are less involved in making a spectacle of or trivializing violence than in showing the peculiar convergence of politics and show business that is often the sum of political discourse in postmodern America, while nevertheless making us understand something about the lionization of violence in America. In a riposte to those who condemn the availability of firearms in the United States after a number of gun murders involving juveniles, the National Rifle Association held a convention in spring 1998, during which it elected actor Charlton Heston as its new president. Heston made a remark that is something like a challenge, thirty years after the fact, to Malcolm X's admonition about those who offer problems and those who offer solutions to social injustice problems. Heston said to vacillating, peacemonger gun owners: "Get together or get out of the way." Heston's exhortation is perfectly in keeping with an American apocalyptic consciousness that sees violence as the first rather than the last resort in the protection of dominant interests. Perhaps there is no irony in Heston's remarks coinciding with the release of the blockbuster disaster film *Armageddon* (1998), the prelude to which contains a voice-over narration by Heston, an actor firmly associated with the great patriarchs of Western culture, informing us that an asteroid brought about the end of the dinosaurs, and that "it will happen again . . . the only question is when." Apocalyptic rhetoric informs discourse today almost as much as during the era of the Puritan fathers, whose jeremiads warned of God's vengeance when the divine contract for conquest of the new golden land should be neglected or violated.

The apocalyptic views again resurgent in discourse cut across much of the spectrum, from disaster-fixated commercial entertainment media to the born-again rhetoric prominent in state power that represents formidable sectors of corporate power, much of it located in a publicly subsidized weapons industry. The belief in violence as aberration is a prominent aspect of American ideology. In the wake of the political assassinations and the social and economic rebellion of the 1960s, Arthur Schlesinger complained of a "pornography of violence" in culture (he was apparently unaware the phrase had been used in the *Partisan Review*).[2] There is an obvious moralistic conflation here of the erotic with violence, but certainly not on the order of, say, J. G. Ballard's *Crash* (1998). On the contrary, the pornography Schlesinger spoke of equates the sexual image with sin, and the violent image with an awful blemish, a gratuitous and indulgent act that has no place in the American character. The easy availability of guns, and not the assumptions of those who manufacture, advocate for, and use them, is also a feature

12

of the delimited liberal public discourse that prefers not examining the American world view.

The criminal and the violent act also serve the politics of scape-goating. Richard Nixon pronounced Charles Manson "guilty" before the case went to the jury, and Manson's prosecutor spoke of Manson as "the evilest man who ever lived" as the bombs were falling over Cambodia. The demonization of the criminal, who is presented as an excrescence of society, has never been more baldly asserted as such by commercial representation, as Elayne Rapping argues in her essay on "cop TV." Perhaps the fetish status of the criminal sociopath, a subject discussed in this anthology, is about recognizing the serial killer/mass murderer not as social rebel or folk hero (as often suggested in gore film fanzines of the last two decades) but as the most genuine representative of American life. If Manson was the "dark side of Aquarius," he was also, as he argued with fractured eloquence, a pure product of America that America needs simultaneously to destroy through propitiatory ritual, and, as if out of guilty conscience, make sacrosanct.

In the 1980s and 1990s, it became standard practice for state figures to scapegoat the media for the tidal wave of violence associated with late capitalist society, as New Deal policy, and even a general spirit of good will and altruism associated with a rudimentary social contract, came to a close. Consequently, the attempted murder of Reagan had us looking at John Hinckley's interest in Jodie Foster and *Taxi Driver* (1976) and away from the Hinckley family's associations with the Bush family. Teen violence and suicide were caused by heavy metal music and images of the devil in rock video. The 1996 documentary *Paradise Lost* is instructive. A grisly murder in the deep South is blamed on three teenage boys, not on the reactionary and abusive parent who was most likely the killer, largely because one of the boys read books on Aleister Crowley and liked rock musicians who wore bizarre stage makeup. And while Bush pummeled Iraq with a devastating air armada, the talk shows were filled with hand-wringing about the popularity of serial killer movies. There is perhaps no irony in the regular invocation of God that circumscribes the Persian Gulf War, the scapegoating of children, the murder of women at abortion clinics. Jane Caputi's essay in this book emphasizes the centrality of Western, patriarchal theologies to the primacy of bloodletting in generating meaning.

As suggested, the contributors to this anthology are concerned with demonstrating how shifting mythic and ideological imperatives within the uses of violence attempt to construct audience conscious-ness and world view in service of political-economic assumptions. The contributors are largely in agreement that there is more continuity than discontinuity in the importance of violent representation to various phases of American (and now transnational) capitalist/patriarchal ideology as they survey the era now thought of as postmodernity.

The first section of this book focuses on the primacy and valorization of bloodletting within postmodern representational practices. Grant's essay, with its suggestive subtitle taken from a prescient moment of modern poetry, acts as a preamble to this section. Grant charts the violent mediascape from Hitchcock's landmark *Psycho* (1960) to the controversial bestseller by Bret Easton Ellis, *American Psycho* (1991), noting that while the latter (and media fads like "serial killer trading cards") suggest that Fredric Jameson's flattening of affect has occurred within the presentation and acceptance of violent imagery and narrative in postmodernity, it is crucial to appreciate this representation within the legacy of American culture and ideology.

Martin Rubin argues that the modest film *The Honeymoon Killers* (1971) not only marks the beginning of the psychokiller cinema, but also suggests that the new, affectless attitude toward violence contained in this original work says much about the break-up of social consensus and the end of the bogus liberal, humanist values that dominated the American scene just before the Vietnam invasion.

Annalee Newitz applies a distinct economic strategy to her analysis of the serial killer cinema, arguing that the violent characterizations of films like *Henry: Portrait of a Serial Killer* (1990) and others in this phase of filmmaking coincide with a recognition within the independent cinema of the post-industrial subject strictly as producer and consumer. The "body count" of this cinema is a caustic rebuke to an atomized society of consumption in which cravings are constructed so as never to be fulfilled.

Mark Pizzato presents a close and well-documented reading of the case of serial killer and cannibal Jeffrey Dahmer. Using dramatic theory, anthropology, and psychoanalysis, Pizzato notes how the accounts of Dahmer's crimes, and in particular the media frenzy of his trial, functioned as vicarious thrill and religious ritual for the spectator-consumer, but in ways that showed the inefficacy of cathartic sacrificial ritual in postmodern society.

Philip L. Simpson closes out this section with a discussion of the apocalyptic turn in such 1990s films as *Seven* (1996) *Kalifornia* (1993) and *Natural Born Killers* (1994), arguing the ways by which the apocalyptic rhetoric of these works necessarily reinstates a religious/mystical view of violence and social disintegration briefly challenged in the 1970s by films such as *Badlands* and *A Clockwork Orange.*

The next section of the book is concerned with the importance of gender construction to the implementation of ideological agendas in violent narrative. Jane Caputi argues that such seemingly disparate films as *Forrest Gump* (1994) and *Seven* are united by a theology of violence that is in fact the dominant patriarchal theology of the West, demanding the subjugation and murder of women, nature, and at last life itself. Her critical strategy involves an adversarial gesture—she offers the film *Follow Me Home* (1996), with its non-white, non-patriarchal spiritual vision, as a riposte to the violent cosmology that is the currency of Hollywood cinema and Western art.

Frank P. Tomasulo's piece on Martin Scorsese's pivotal film *Raging Bull* (1980) suggests that this complex and contradictory work inaugurates the cinema of the "angry white male." It is very much in step with the beginning of the Reagan era, embodying many of the class, gender, and racial biases present within a vengeful and resurgent late capitalist culture. Yet much of the reaction of *Raging Bull* is covered over by hip, postmodernist stylistics, including anti-illusionist devices and the exposure of the cinematic apparatus to the spectator. Implicit in Tomasulo's argument is a question: Do the presentational, anti-illusionist stylistics lauded by radical modernist art now serve to give a fresh patina to reactionary ideas within postmodern artistic practice?

Mark Gallagher's article on the incorporation of melodrama into the action film uses James Cameron's *True Lies* (1994) for its model of explanation. Gallagher argues that the use of conventions from supposedly "female" genres like melodrama assist the action thriller in reconciling the hyper-violence of the Arnold Schwarzenegger-style blockbuster with the "family values" insisted upon in neoconservative capitalist culture.

William Luhr closes this section with a meditation on the extremely reactionary films directed by and starring Mel Gibson. Luhr points to the atavistic, religious conservatism of Gibson's work, with its resurrection of the old-fashioned charismatic, supremely competent epic hero in narratives that depict vicious homophobia, anti-feminism, and hysterical castration anxiety. Luhr's essay makes apparent that the reactionary climate of the final decade of twentieth-century representation often forgoes a slick "new democratic" burnish in favor of a rather medieval intolerance.

The third section unites visual theory with cultural analysis, with a concern for understanding how the postmodern media apparatus functions as policeman/penal authority, and how the technical depictions of violent images have changed with recent transformations in

15

consciousness, representational practice, and ideological demand in the last quarter-century.

Elayne Rapping opens this section with an application of Michel Foucault's theories to tabloid television shows like *COPS*. Rapping argues that the postmodern media panopticon suggests much about the rightward drift of social policy, viewing the criminal not strictly as a Foucauldian subject to be pathologized, controlled, and treated, but as a post-Foucauldian, incorrigible, and subhuman Other to be demonized, contained, and destroyed.

Susan Crutchfield explores how slasher films' depictions of the blind touch encode a powerful mimetic critique of the visual simulation that saturates and defines the representational and ideological predicament of postmodernity. Through discussions of blind characters in *Peeping Tom* (1960) and *Proof* (1991), she argues that the slasher film pathologizes tactile contact in the slasher character's "finishing touch," and violently denigrates tactility in the blind character's "touching scene," all in the interest of assuaging anxieties about the physiological and cultural vulnerability of vision.

Ken Morrison traces the trajectory of violence from the modern to the postmodern with his concept of the "technology of homicide," which he applies to our changing perception of the dead or wounded body within representation. He studies the shower murder in *Psycho* and Kennedy's fatal head wound as portrayed in Oliver Stone's *JFK* (1991) to explain how psychiatry, law, science, and conspiracy have been marshalled (inadequately) in these and other films to explain violent action, without accounting for the value and currency that the violent image continues to have outside of real, lived experience.

The final section of this book looks at the transnational, corporate reach of the American image industry and its violent ethos, as well as inflections on violence in some national cinemas demonstrating that the late capitalist era is not "post-colonial," but colonialist under new economic and cultural manifestations of authority. This section also looks at the changing nature and status of the Other, domestically and internationally, and at peculiar uses of the violent image within pop media fads.

Ilsa J. Bick opens this section with an analysis of the ways in which the popular TV show *The X-Files* suggests a profound collective trauma about which the public seems to be in a state of denial. While *The X-Files* explores a desolate American landscape, it does so by way of an insistent repression of history and denial of a pandemic psychological crisis as it takes on, obliquely, the death of the family, the Holocaust, political and serial murder, sexual violence (especially the violation of the female body), and child abuse. This series, Bick argues, is very much in tune with postmodernity's disingenuousness in replacing historical consciousness with fractal, subjectivist, hallucinatory, conspiratorial fictions that seem to pass for a new skepticism, one that obtains legitimacy from the sophomoric postmodernist acknowledgment of the slipperiness of truth.

Lianne McLarty then applies Slotkin's and René Girard's theories to a reexamination of the Other, this time as configured in the alien invasion films of the 1990s. She argues that the alien is suffused with all the qualities of the racial and sexual Other of traditional American mythology and folklore, and has to some degree taken the place of this previous Other, which is no longer permissible in the mediascape.

Julian Stringer studies the "Category 3" films of postmodern Hong Kong, exploring the ways by which sex and violence in these exploitation films suggest the economic, gender, and national anxieties of China, post-Tiananmen Square, particularly as Hong Kong enters fully into the postmodern, transnational corporate arena.

Jane Smith examines the recent popular films of New Zealand, in particular *Broken English* (1996), *The Piano* (1993), and *Once Were Warriors* (1995), arguing that the often grisly violent domestic melodramas at the center of these films tend to elide or overwhelm the nascent historical lessons the films contain about the real politics of corporate neocolonialism. In many of the popular New Zealand films, Smith argues, the personal does not really become the political, and the knocked-around female does not always equate with knocked-around New Zealand and its exploited Maori population.

Tony Williams closes the book with his essay on popular Hong Kong director John Woo's first American film, *Hard Target* (1993). While confronting resistance from the corporatized Hollywood system, Woo fashions a narrative that may be a summary of the neoconservative, late capitalist environment, with its tale of the poor being literally hunted down by the rich. Woo, already established by the popular press as a "master of screen violence," has a virtue lost on this press, as it was lost on those directors previously awarded the dubious title (Sam Peckinpah and Sergio Leone). Woo's moralism and humanism stand at the center of his ironic and critical action films.

My afterword offers several theorizations about violence and postmodern ideology. I continue the argument touched on in this introduction concerning the continuity of current tendencies of the violent image with American ideology, particularly since the push in American expansionism of the nineteenth century. I discuss the ideas of Slotkin, Bataille, and

Girard, three theorists whose reflections on violence have become central to numerous disciplines. I am concerned chiefly with applying their divergent, yet often complementary, notions of the role of violence in generating meaning to an understanding of this function to conceptions of value and social cohesion in the exceptionally atomized postmodern condition. It seems to me that while scapegoating and the continued persecution of the Other, ideas important to the work of Slotkin and Girard, are still paramount in the reunification of a disintegrating social order, such notions have been sufficiently exposed in public discourse as to render them steadily useless as myths uniting a civilization, yet they are played out, rather desperately, for their own sake. Such a tendency has been visible since the Holocaust, when sacrificial mythology was continued for itself rather than for any ultimate ideological agenda, even when its function in uniting components of a barbaric Self became ineffectual (Auschwitz was given a top priority by the Nazis even as the Third Reich ran out of food, fuel oil, and the basic staples needed to preserve the legitimacy of the ruling order). This moment was a harbinger of what was in store for the West through its insistence on a mythic rather than a historical perception of reality. Invoking the Holocaust, of course, raises the question of why this book is focused chiefly on American violence. Violence is certainly not peculiar to America, but violence in American culture seems peculiarly instructive, since it seems to signify the end product of European notions of progress that led to the development of the United States. At the end of this century, violence appears to be about the unraveling of American myth and ritual, of the national self-concept. In postmodernity, sacrificial ritual has devolved into free-form violence and "gaming," which seems a rebuke to a modernist thinker such as Bataille, who held that the excessive sacrificial gestures of primitive society might serve as a rebuke to the production-oriented capitalist societies of the industrial world.

Every anthology wants to be as comprehensive as possible, and the reader will no doubt notice gaps; these have not gone unnoticed by me and my contributors. A director such as Quentin Tarantino, whose work seems synonymous with postmodern portrayals of violence in genre film, seems underrepresented. A good deal has already been written on Tarantino, and the shallowness of much of the commentary may suggest something of the shallowness of his punk-nihilist-film-fan sensibility and his incessant allusionism. With the exception of *Reservoir Dogs* (1992), which seems to explore the gay politics nascent within the male-oriented action films of a director such as Howard Hawks, Tarantino's films are made trivial by his obsession with the kitsch of the postwar culture industry, particularly that of the 1970s.

On the other hand, the authors and I note with some regret that there are no discussions of Abel Ferrara, an innovative artist whose grisly and dolorous films (*King of New York* [1990], *Bad Lieutenant* [1992], *The Addiction* [1996], and *The Funeral* [1997]) are concerned with the impoverishment and suicidal direction of the American experience. The later films of Martin Scorsese (*Goodfellas* [1990], *Casino* [1996]) continue the project begun with *Mean Streets* (1973) and *Taxi Driver* of using late twentieth-century American urban society as a metonym for the failed American civilizing experience. Scorsese's Mafia films appear to be about a rather banal id unleashed, as Scorsese forgoes the operatics of Francis Ford Coppola in describing, in often absurdist tones that mock Coppola's high seriousness, the waste, excess, and disintegration of America. Similarly, Michael Mann's crime epic *Heat* (1995) seems worthy of discussion (it has been virtually ignored critically). Its sense of the male group performing a futile last stand against a glacial Los Angeles landscape of Prozac, cable television, computers, and collapsing families seems a fine illustration of male culture's anguished eulogy for itself, simultaneous with an insistence on violence as a retort to the postmodern world that has dissolved male privilege. Perhaps these suggestions will prod others to undertake further study.

As suggested, it is the concern of this book to place violent representation in a political/social framework and to make such an approach assist a systemic, structural account of violence in the image culture and in social interaction. Historical and structural analysis that conjoins, for example, psychoanalysis to ideology is disturbing to many, since it does not provide the comfort of treating the violent act as aberrant, as the product of this or that permissiveness or exposure to the wrong cultural product. Scapegoating has become as central to our official public discourse about social ills as it is to the marginalization and destruction of undesirable human beings (the poor, minorities). The tendency to avoid in-depth historical analysis of this milieu is not surprising, and it follows axiomatically from the continued repression of history in capitalist culture. Such a critical approach is, however, mandatory in the academic and public discourse about violence. It is hoped that this project can play some role in furthering this larger discourse.

Notes

1. "Media Violence," AAP Committee on Communications, *Pediatrics* 95.6 (June 1995).

2. Arthur Schlesinger, Jr., *Violence: America in the Sixties* (New York: Signet, 1968), 53. The phrase was initially used by Geoffry Gorer, "The Erotic Myth of America," *Partisan Review* (July–August 1950).

Part I

Gore Culture

1

AMERICAN PSYCHO/SIS:
THE PURE PRODUCTS OF
AMERICA GO CRAZY

BARRY KEITH GRANT

In the 1980s, the Talking Heads asked the timely musical question, "Psycho killer, qu'est que c'est?" It seems that this question has been particularly significant for us since the late 1950s, as there has been a veritable explosion of real and fictional mass murderers and serial killers in contemporary popular culture. The subject has become a considerable media mini-industry, sometimes given its own discrete section in bookstores—a clear indication that this type of story has attained generic status. Even the medium of trading cards has developed its own corner of the market, producing several "collectible" series featuring the "best" serial killers, complete with seasonal statistics. In 1991, Jonathan Demme's *The Silence of the Lambs* won several Academy Awards and brought serial killing squarely into the mainstream. In short, as Martin Rubin has noted, "fin-de-siècle America seems especially obsessed with the figure of the modern multiple murderer."[1]

Just as in the 1930s Busby Berkeley understood that thirty-three pairs of breasts were more appealing to the male viewer than one pair, so multiple and serial murders offer a convenient solution to the narrative problem of providing increasing doses of violence for consumers already accustomed to considerable violence in both the real world and cultural texts. Nevertheless, the structural repetitions inherent in the act of serial killing seem to echo the repetition compulsion in our own intensive

23

consumption of narratives about it. Further, it is the *manner* in which their gruesome acts are today represented that I find of particular interest, for many of these works share a distinctive stylistic strategy in their depiction of violence that marks a considerable change over previous representations. In the postmodern procession of simulacra, traditional images of violence have lost their affective power, and consequently have been replaced by a more "neutral" style.

Alfred Hitchcock's *Psycho* (1960), of course, is the film that can be said to have inaugurated the contemporary cinema's treatment of violence.[2] The film's modern mixture of black comedy and body horror initiated the character of popular culture's recent interest in serial killers, in which the killers are at once frightening and funny, revered and reviled. Released in 1960, the movie was based on Robert Bloch's novel of the same name, itself based in part on the real-life exploits of Ed Gein, whose grisly killing and flaying of victims in rural Wisconsin was discovered in 1957. Harold Schechter notes that a wave of Gein jokes swept the region after the public revelations about his ghoulish habits, and that numerous marketing tie-ins followed, such as t-shirts emblazoned with "Ed Gein Lives" in letters of little bones.[3] Virtually every real mass murderer since Gein has been the object of intense tabloid coverage, as well as the subject of a movie and/or book. And most of these works, from *Bonnie and Clyde* (1967), *The Boston Strangler* (1968), and *In Cold Blood* (1968) on, have achieved some degree of commercial and/or cult success.

Large-scale violence has always been part of the American psyche, ever since the first European settlers began to wrest the land away from natives. The lengthy campaign was once called, for ideological purposes of expansionism, "manifest destiny," but now we might call it "ethnic cleansing." Beginning with the Puritan settlers, Americans created a cultural myth—so pervasive in the American psyche that it has been termed the national "monomyth"[4]— of a communal Eden that must be redeemed by what Richard Slotkin calls a "regeneration through violence."[5] D. H. Lawrence was indeed accurate when, in his discussion of Fenimore Cooper's Hawkeye, the first American mythic hero, he speculated that "The essential American soul is hard, isolate, stoic, and a killer."[6]

This is not to suggest, however, the absence of compelling explanations for our *current* interest in these stories. Marxist critics see such violence as representative of the importation into personal relations of the conditions of alienated labor, intensified within late capitalism. In a discussion of real serial killers, Annalee Newitz persuasively relates work and economic status to the repetitiveness of the act of serial killing, emphasizing a resemblance between alienated workers and the killers, who "kill after reaching a point where they begin to confuse living people with the inanimate objects they produce and consume as workers."[7] These killers, she claims, may be understood as acting out the enraged confusion with which Americans have come to regard the decline of their postwar economic and social productivity.

A similar interpretation informs parts of Robin Wood's extremely influential analysis of contemporary horror cinema. As he notes, it is no coincidence that the four films he describes as the most "intense" works of post-*Psycho* horror—*Night of the Living Dead* (1968), *Raw Meat* (a.k.a. *Death Line*, 1973), *The Texas Chainsaw Massacre* (1974), and *The Hills Have Eyes* (1977)—share the motif of cannibalism, for, he argues, "Cannibalism represents the ultimate in possessiveness, hence the logical end of human relations under capitalism."[8] The intensity of these films is profoundly disturbing, claims Wood, because they offer an uncompromising apocalyptic vision that does not easily fit into the dominant ideology. This potential leftist critique distinguishes for Wood "progressive" horror from the more common, pervasive "reactionary wing."

Bret Easton Ellis's novel *American Psycho* (1991) is as disturbing a critique of dominant ideology as any of these movies and works in ways similar to the best of them. In fact, one might argue that it continues the tradition of progressive horror which in the 1990s, with rare exceptions like *The People under the Stairs* (1991) and *Candyman* (1992), has been largely abandoned by the genre which, for the most part, has succumbed to pastiche, sequelitis, and mindless gore. The novel is fascinating as a particular instance of contemporary violent horror, but it also provides the perfect touchstone for a contemporary consideration of general representations of violence. Its depictions of horrific violence crystallize so well the nature of postmodern violence that it is, as Wood has said of its namesake, *Psycho*, "one of the key works of our age."[9]

American Psycho is a first-person chronicle by a rich investment executive who is also a psychotic serial killer. The plot is nicely summed up by the blurb on the back of the paperback edition: "Patrick Bateman is handsome, well-educated, intelligent. He works by day on Wall Street, earning a fortune to complement the one he was born with. His nights he spends in ways we cannot begin to fathom. He is 26 years old and living his own American Dream." This description of Bateman's activities is indeed significant, for the book emphasizes his craziness as an extension of capitalist values. Indeed, it is a prime example of a recent cycle of

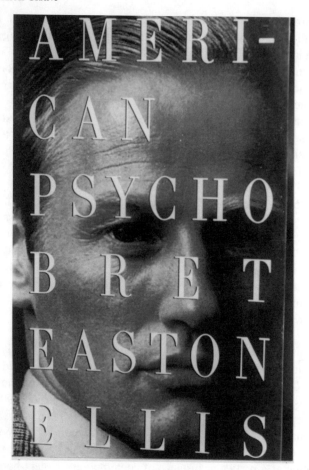

Yuppie monsters and the death of affect: *American Psycho* (Vintage, 1990).

horror that I have elsewhere termed "yuppie horror," a distinct group of movies (e.g., *Fatal Attraction,* 1987; *Pacific Heights,* 1990; *The Hand That Rocks the Cradle,* 1992) employing horror's conventions but which address contemporary economic rather than supernatural fears.[10]

The evil of yuppie monsters, unlike the monsters of classic horror films, is *not* expressed through horrifying appearance, but rather, by just the opposite. Hence the devilish charm of Michael Keaton in *Pacific Heights* or of Rob Lowe in *Bad Influence* (1990). As someone acutely observes of corporate competition in *The Temp* (1993), "They still stab you in the back as much as in the 80s, only now they smile when they do it." This is certainly true of the handsome and charismatic Bateman in *American Psycho*. At one point he casually remarks that he has a .357 magnum barely concealed beneath his Giorgio Armani overcoat; at another, that he has "a knife with a serrated blade in the pocket of his Valentino jacket."[11] He lives in a swank penthouse apartment that, to paraphrase the advertising hook for *Alien* (1979), affords him a private luxury space where no one can hear you scream. In the light of day, Bateman sends his bloody clothes and linen to be dry-cleaned, openly complaining when his Soprani jacket comes back with flecks of "someone's blood on it" (81). His female victims likely would have thought twice about entering a deserted alley with a man they just met, but not, it seems, an upscale condo. In short, the executive privilege and freedom of action granted Bateman by his position of wealth serve as a constant reminder of the horrifying inequality generated by both class and racial difference in America.

On the margins of his world, appearing periodically, are the homeless and indigent, who for him represent the horror of career failure he fears most. At one point Bateman coolly punctures the eyes of a black panhandler, a literal act of appropriating the gaze of the Other. Cannibalism is given the same graphic but metaphoric function in *American Psycho* as in the progressive horror film. Thus Bateman kills one of his perceived rivals for handling an account he wants and then "consumes" the man's body by dissolving it in a tub of acid. More literally, he chews, bites, and eats parts of his numerous female victims.

Most of Bateman's victims are female. They are dispatched in increasingly gruesome and graphic ways, and—make no mistake—these scenes are graphically depicted and intensely revolting. But it is precisely here that the book links its critique of capitalism to patriarchy. Certainly, there is no question that in the real world women are overwhelmingly the victims of serial killers. Any analysis of serial killing is incomplete without considering the dynamics of power in regard to gender, race, and class. In the case of *American Psycho,* the emphasis on the details of female victimization work to present a disturbing picture of a besieged white phallocentrism. Bate*man*'s mutilations of women are grotesquely graphic exaggerations, overtly monstrous depictions, of the treatment of women within patriarchy. Thus, when he candidly reveals to some of his bar-hopping executive buddies that he has a large pipe with which he batters women, their response is to laughingly chide Bateman for boasting about the size of his penis (325).

The progressive thrust of *American Psycho,* particularly in terms of its gender issues, becomes especially clear in relation to its namesake, *Psycho.* (Let us not forget it was Hitchcock, after all, who said that a sure way to create suspense was to "torture the women!") Ellis's book, like Hitchcock's film, works to implicate the reader through the manipulation of the processes of identification. In both cases, we are gradually moved, even before we realize it, inside the psychotic killer's consciousness. Just as Norman is first introduced as a nice, polite boy who cleans up after his mother, Bateman is similarly described as "the boy next door," and we inevitably like him because he is the only one who censures the anti-semitic discussion taking place among his friends (37–38). In short, whether by Bates or Bateman, *we* are baited by the text.

Yet there is a crucial difference between the two works. Hitchcock, even while getting us to identify with Norman, ultimately positions us outside the violent acts Norman perpetrates, both physically, by giving us a different point of view than that of Marion, and morally, by representing the shower murder, through abrupt montage and Bernard Herrmann's piercing violin score, as shocking. This external perspective is taken to the extreme in the killing of the detective Arbogast, when the camera retreats to a vantage point in a corner of the ceiling. Ellis, however, keeps readers thoroughly immersed—entrapped—in the perspective of the narrator, particularly by his unwavering employment of a bland tone of narration. This lack of affect is characteristic of Bateman, not Ellis, and whether the events being described are gruesomely violent or boringly banal, the narrative perspective remains stubbornly true to Bateman's values, not ours.

The book's many connections to *Psycho* are important because they underscore the novel's value as ideological critique. *Psycho* is acknowledged as the pivotal work in the development of the progressive horror film; more than any other single movie, it is responsible for establishing the genre's recent fascination with the horror of the normal. Set in contemporary motel rooms, family homes, and bathrooms complete with toilets, *Psycho* forever relocated the site of horror from its traditional Gothic setting to the more mundane world of the viewer.

The same theme informs *American Psycho*. But because the book addresses these issues in such a graphic, uncompromising manner, it has been widely vilified. The eleventh-hour decision by Simon and Schuster, Ellis's first publisher, not to publish it on grounds of taste was covered widely by the media. Condemned by the popular press as pornographic, anti-feminist, sick, and dangerous, it was scorned in a manner reminiscent of horror and exploitation cinema before these forms became critically fashionable, even for feminist critics such as Carol Clover.[12] The novel's reception seems a vivid demonstration of Wood's assertion that truly progressive works of horror are not, or at least not easily, recuperable into the dominant ideology.

Perhaps the most controversial aspect of the book is the flat, zero-degree tone in which it is narrated. It may be the perfect example of what Fredric Jameson calls "the waning of affect," the "flatness or depth-lessness" that characterizes postmodern art.[13] As Vicky Lebeau acutely observes, recalling earlier comments about the work of J. G. Ballard, the book seems to lack either purpose or pleasure; it presents itself as neither social criticism nor pornography, and so offers no convenient liberal rationale for its consumption.[14] Indeed, it was just this lack of moral purpose that invited the explicit wrath of reviewers. Whereas in *Psycho* Norman's relationship with his mother explains everything, at least according to the psychiatrist, in *American Psycho* Patrick's visit to his mother, the only scene involving his familial past, uncovers nothing. In the end, Bateman himself concludes that his narrative is purposeless: "I gain no deeper knowledge about myself, no new understanding can be extracted from my telling. There has been no reason for me to tell you any of this. This confession has meant *nothing*" (377). Therefore, for many, the book's extreme sexist violence can only be gratuitous.

But while Bateman is incapable of articulating an easy moral lesson for the reader, the style of his narration offers a forceful one. For Bateman is nothing more than a complete product of popular culture, his imagination both limited and shaped by it. One might regard him as Steven Shaviro does Drew Barrymore's infernal teenager in the yuppie horror movie *Poison Ivy* (1992). Her crime, writes Shaviro, is

> finally just that she *over*invests in the glamorous images of familial togeth-erness, paternal authority, and suburban affluence that have proliferated so abundantly and so sickeningly in post-Reagan America. She simply takes these media images "at their word," enacting them in her own flesh, on the level of lived reality.[15]

Similarly, Bateman, recalling Wood's phrase, is himself merely "the logical end of human relations under capitalism"—an unforgettable object lesson that, as William Carlos Williams had so presciently put it, "the pure products of America go crazy."[16]

Bateman's narration is full of annoying passages about consumerism that, in Brechtian fashion, interrupt and punctuate his story. They are like the intolerably long tracking shots in what Brian Henderson calls the "non-bourgeois" style of middle-period Godard, wherein depth as a primary component of bourgeois illusionism is drained from the images to create what Henderson emphasizes is a visual flatness that corresponds to the characters' lack of moral depth.[17] As Bateman himself observes, "Surface, surface, surface was all that anyone found meaning in" (375). The dull chapter of the book titled "Morning" consists entirely of Bateman's shower, shave, and dressing rituals, complete with a catalogue of brand names and consumer wisdom culled from advertising. Twice the narrative halts completely as Bateman offers five-page reviews of real records by Genesis and Whitney Houston, set-pieces that brilliantly replicate the impressionistic, pseudo-intellectual discourse of pop music magazines like *Rolling Stone*.

Every time a character enters the scene Bateman gives us a lengthy description devoted to every item of his or her apparel, complete with brand names, what real shops in New York City the items come from, and retail prices. One of the book's many dark jokes is that while Bateman gives us such details, neither he nor any of his friends are able to correctly identify acquaintances by name, always confusing one person for another. Ironically, nobody notices that the people Bateman has killed are missing because they are virtually interchangeable, all wearing the same trendy upscale fashionwear and mouthing the same inane banter—"clucking their thick tongues oh so delicately," as Norman Bates would say. Like their possessions, they are themselves things—things for which Bateman, like any good capitalist manufacturer, has planned obsolescence.

The joke upon this other joke is that our tedium in reading these consumer litanies is relieved only when something—that is to say, something violent—happens. This response only implicates us further in Bateman's heinous acts, much the way that Hitchcock encourages us to become emotional "accomplices" first to Marion and then to Norman in *Psycho*. But in *American Psycho* we are accomplices in a more fundamental way, because we are made to confront the loathsomeness of the popular culture into which we frequently and fervently escape. Thus Bateman's very perception is structured by the technical conventions of popular movies. He often describes what he sees—"the film of his vision," as he puts it (239)—by employing such cinematic terms as pans (5), dissolves (8), slow motion (114), and even jump zooms (292).

His erotic encounters, most of which inevitably turn violent and fatal, are set up in emulation of scenarios from pornographic movies. Bateman claims, in fact, to prefer pornography to romantic sex because it is "less complicated" (264). Only the technology he employs is complex; for example, as he carefully relates on one occasion, he uses a Sony palm-sized Handycam or "a Minox LX ultra-miniature camera that takes 9.5mm film, has a 15mm f/3.5 lens, an exposure meter and a built-in neutral density filter" (304). Some of his victims are tortured while forced to watch videos of previous victims, scenes which inevitably recall Michael Powell's *Peeping Tom* (1960), *Psycho*'s evil twin and a film as condemned in its time as Ellis's novel today. Bateman directs the action in his scenarios with a careful manipulation of the gaze, enamored of and taking to the literal extreme "the frenzy of the visible."[18]

Bateman's sexuality and desire, like everything else about him, is thoroughly determined by consumer culture. He moves without transition from masturbating to fantasies of real women to poster models wearing Calvin Klein halter tops—emblematic images of postmodern masculine "desire" insofar as they all become "products" for consumption (24). In other words, Bateman victimizes women because popular culture does so routinely. The book's tone is flat because its point is that, in the end, Bateman's actions are, surprisingly enough, *unexceptional.*

The protagonist in Walker Percy's 1961 novel *The Movie-goer* (interestingly, another investment executive) is also influenced by films. But Percy's character clearly sees the disparity between his own life and the movies; as he observes, "Other people, so I have read, treasure memorable moments in their lives: the time one climbed the Parthenon at sunrise, the summer night one met a lonely girl in Central Park and achieved with her a sweet and natural relationship, as they say in books. I, too, once met a girl in Central Park, but it is not much to remember. What I remember is the time John Wayne killed three men with a carbine as he was falling to the dusty street in *Stagecoach*."[19] This narrator prefers the masculine ego-ideal constructed by Hollywood, yet although his own identity may suffer by comparison, it is still distinct. Thirty years later, in the postmodern era, this distinction between the real and the representation collapses. Compare Bateman's description of one of his sexual encounters: "I am so used to imagining everything happening the way it occurs in movies, visualizing things falling somehow into the shape of events on a screen, that I almost hear the swelling of an orchestra, can almost hallucinate the camera panning low around us, fireworks bursting in slow motion overhead, the 70 mm image of her lips parting and the subsequent murmur of 'I want you' in Dolby sound" (265).

In one of the final chapters, "Chase, Manhattan," a slam-bang, shoot-'em-up passage in the mold of an action movie in which Bateman is almost caught by the police, we are not sure whether we are inside a pulp fiction fantasy on his part or not. If we are, have we been there all along? Where does the "real" New York City end and Bateman's imaginary one begin? Like *Total Recall* (1990), *American Psycho* situates us within a Baudrillardian dilemma, a postmodern nightmare of the simulacrum which simulates the condition it describes in our very experience of it. Bateman, then, as evil as he may be, is himself a victim possessed by what Jean Baudrillard would call "the evil demon of images."[20]

The novel's postmodern media critique is intimately connected to the book's treatment of violence. Since everyone else in *American Psycho* is, like Bateman himself, an image, then to commit violence is simply to enter the image flow that marks contemporary consciousness and to cast oneself as a star in a world with others who are assigned supporting roles as victims.

Beverle Houston argues that while cinema sutures its viewer with a dream of plenitude, television "insists upon the reformulation of desire."[21] Because televisual flow shifts between different kinds of narrative and spectatorial address—between shows, commercials, and that abject category, "infommercials"—desire is repeatedly interrupted, blocked, and renewed. As Houston puts it, the particular nature of the televisual flow repeatedly opens "the gap of desire" for consumption.[22] The result is that the televisual subject becomes a serial viewer, perpetually watching, never fully satisfied.

Video, because it gives us the technological means of making our own movies and projecting our own image, is now perhaps more graphic proof of our postmodern fragmentation than the technology of grassroots political liberation it was once heralded to be. In a culture where interior life is diminished and disparaged at every turn, where the physical is everywhere privileged over the spiritual, watching ourselves in home videos—seeing our images *out there,* on the television set, itself a palpable *thing* occupying space—confirms our presence, our being in the world. Further, video is the theater where identity, as many postmodern theorists would argue, inevitably becomes performance. It provides us with the stage on which we may strut and fret—or whatever. Video offers us a technological schizophrenia wherein we may identify with ourselves, creating a narcissistic feedback loop that cancels out other subjects, who become mere bit players.

According to Newitz, many serial killers are motivated in part by a desire for media fame. She claims that "they kill precisely in order to see themselves mass produced as simulations in the newspapers and television reports about themselves."[23] In movies, Caesar Enrico Bandello speaks of himself in the third person when hearing a radio news report about Little Caesar, Arthur Penn's Bonnie Parker and Clyde Barrow are concerned about their coverage in the local newspapers, and the charismatic serial killer of *Man Bites Dog* (1991) is obsessed with the making of a cinema verite documentary about his life. In many recent serial killer movies, it is video that figures specifically, especially during sequences of violence. *Natural Born Killers* (1994), for example, is structured around video, both in form as well as content. The outlaw couple use video as a means of documenting their exploits, and the film's style is marked as an interplay of cinematic and video images. The "I Love Mallory" sequence vividly demonstrates that the very consciousness of the characters, if not of viewers, is shaped by video; a subjective memory from Mallory's point of view, it recalls her first meeting Mickey as a scene out of a sitcom. In the most chilling sequence in John McNaughton's *Henry: Portrait of a Serial Killer* (1990), loosely based on the life of Henry Lee Lucas, the most prolific serial killer known, Henry and his accomplice Ottis arbitrarily break into a family home and kill the family members while videotaping their actions, which are choreographed for the camera. Like them, we see the event as video, which they watch repeatedly, replaying the "good parts." In these movies, video is the most pervasive signifier of postmodern alienation, and it is no coincidence that movies like *Henry* employ a "zero-degree" tone similar to *American Psycho*. Through this rhetorical trope, cinema may be valorizing itself at the expense of video, but it also conveys the nature of our postmodern ennui.

In British detective fiction murder represents a violent intrusion into the orderly bourgeois world, a shock perfectly captured by the striking image of a blood stain on the drawing room carpet. Now, however, a dead body on the carpet is less a horrifying reminder of civilization's fragile veneer than, as a character says about a corpse in the Scottish thriller *Shallow Grave* (1995), simply a matter of logistics. The scene in *Pulp Fiction* (1994) where two hapless hit men must deal with the splattered blood and brains of their dead hostage Marvin demonstrates that today we are more likely to laugh at blood on the upholstery than to be shocked.

Contemporary texts tend to depict violence as insignificant fact rather than consequential act. The strongest response these films elicit is a bemused detachment, which has given rise to one of the major conventions of the contemporary action/adventure film, wherein the hero dispatches some body or bodies, often in a bloody and graphic manner, with an off-hand pithy remark. Arnold Schwarzenegger, in particular, has perfected this device. His "hasta la vista, baby" became something of a cultural mantra after the release of *Terminator 2: Judgment Day* (1991). Schwarzenegger has established a persona as phallic uebermensch that is at once serious and comic, an image that sustains the different pleasures offered by the serious action of *Predator* (1987) as well as the self-parodic *The Last Action Hero* (1993).

Such representations may not be entirely surprising in a culture where American bomber pilots tell reporters that watching their payload exploding over Iraqi civilians is like being at Disneyland, or in the age of drive-by shootings and random terrorist attacks—some of which are perpetrated not by foreign "extremists" but by our fellow Americans. It is no wonder that popular culture deals so frequently with serial or multiple murders and murderers, or that these acts often occur randomly in a universe that seems absurd. In *American Psycho,* Bateman expresses this view perfectly in his thoughts about a woman who has survived a date with him:

> She's lucky, even though there is no real reasoning behind the luck. . . . Maybe the glass of Scharffenberger has deadened my impulse or maybe it's simply that I don't want to ruin this particular Alexander Julian suit by having the bitch spray her blood all over it. Whatever happens, the useless fact remains: Patricia will stay alive, and this victory requires no skill, no leaps of the imagination, no ingenuity on anyone's part. This is simply how the world, *my* world, moves. (77)

The seemingly pervasive yet arbitrary nature of so much contemporary violence is emphasized in many texts as the "inexplicable" actions of apparently normal folks who suddenly engage in paroxysms of mass carnage—violent variations of what André Gide called *l'act gratuit.* By 1968, the besieged farmhouses in both *Night of the Living Dead* and the film version of *In Cold Blood* showed that this inexplicable violence reached beyond the inner city to the rural heartland. In the same year, Peter Bogdanovich's *Targets* (1968) offered no explanation for the all-American boy who calmly gathers high-powered rifle, ammo, and candy bars, settles in behind the screen of a drive-in cinema, and begins picking off people in their cars, much like Charles Whitman had done on a Texas university campus only two years earlier. Tellingly, the movie-within-the-movie in *Targets* features classic horror star Boris Karloff as a classic horror star who wants to retire because horror films can no longer match the horrors of everyday life.

One day in January 1979, Brenda Spencer, a seventeen-year-old San Diego girl, randomly shot eleven passersby, killing two. The reason, she told the police and the media, was that "I don't like Mondays." For the Boomtown Rats, in their song of the same name, this inadequate explanation quickly became a metaphor of the stultifying banality of

34

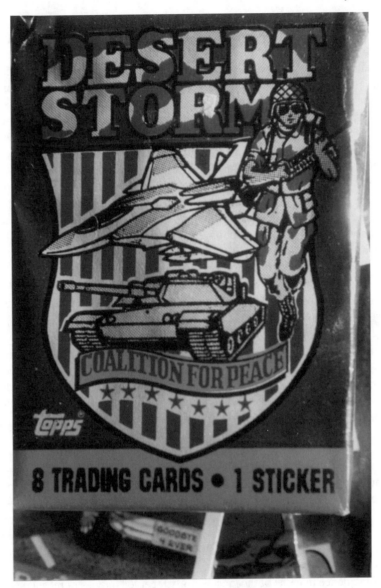

Pop culture and official violence: Desert Storm trading cards (Topps, Inc., 1990).

contemporary bourgeois life. Indeed, such a mixture of inexplicable action and banal context constitutes the discursive logic and, presumably, fundamental appeal of many of the various series of True Crime trading

35

cards. For example, as one card in the "True Crime #5: Strange Crime Stories" series tells us, Joseph Fallet, age sixty-one, of Harrison City, Pennsylvania, one day in August 1992 killed his wife of twenty years, stabbing her 161 times, because he had become enraged by her habit of putting the fresh vegetables in front of the milk on the refrigerator shelf.[24] The implication is that the violence on Fallet's part was inexplicably excessive—and so "incomprehensible"—as a response to his wife's trivial housekeeping habits. This depiction of randomness may be an indication of our failure to fathom the violent depths of the human soul—what John Fraser in his book *Violence in the Arts* calls a "schizophrenic unreachableness"[25]—but the marked increase of such events in recent years suggests that it is a compelling index of the contemporary sensibility more than it is a universal condition. Violence is now perceived as a common occurrence, part of the fabric of daily life.

For many contemporary texts, since violence is no longer thought to be remarkable, it is presented *un*remarkably. Like *American Psycho,* many recent films treat violence by "flattening" it. This tone characterizes such youth movies as, for example, *Juice* (1992), *Menace II Society* (1993), and *Kids* (1995). These movies share a depiction of young people responding to violence with an indifference that infects the films' styles. *River's Edge* (1989), with its factually based story of a group of teenagers who respond without concern to the death of one of their peers, her body left stretched out on the grass of the town's river bank, is explicitly about the failure today of blood on the carpet to shock.

Because violence is no longer redemptive or cathartic, but commonplace, it is this "senseless," "meaningless" violence that now seems meaningful to us. As one of the killers says in the obligatory explanation scene in Wes Craven's recent *Scream* (1997), "It's the millennium— motives are incidental." Perhaps the recent pop cultural phenomenon of "dumbing down"—as in movies such as *Dumb and Dumber* and *Airheads* (both 1994), and the *Beavis and Butthead* television show— is symptomatic of our failure to make "meaning" of it all. It is no coincidence that one of the most warmly received movies of recent years was *Forrest Gump* (1994). The film was so popular precisely because it comforted us in the knowledge that we are all simpletons who cannot possibly comprehend the complex workings of our modern world. After all, when James Oliver Huberty, a nice citizen, one day in December 1983 walked into a McDonald's and killed twenty-one people, what else can we do but throw up our hands and accede to Norman Bates's assertion that "we all go a little mad sometimes." This is exactly the premise of *Falling Down* (1993), and its most famous scene, of Michael Douglas trying to get breakfast his way in a Whammyburger restaurant, is a clear reference to Huberty.

The first words of *American Psycho* are "abandon all hope, ye who enter here" (3). For in such a world as these works depict, physical, violent action—in sharp distinction to both traditional American fiction and classic Hollywood cinema—cannot be truly heroic, because it cannot be moral, because nothing is especially meaningful. The contemporary action movie is merely the other side of the same coin. Full of the stuff of heroic action, but performed by undifferentiated Steven Seagals and Jean-Claude Van Dammes, it is violence without character, and the action is reduced to mere gestures of heroism.

Literary critic Marius Bewley once observed that in Fenimore Cooper's *Leatherstocking Tales* action serves as "the intensified motion of life in which the spiritual and moral faculties of men are no less engaged than their physical selves."[26] In other words, the characters' physical, often violent actions always expressed an ethical vision, and were the concrete expression of it. "First be sure you're right, then go ahead," in the plain words of Disney's Davy Crockett, pop icon of 1950s banality. The embodiment of ethics in the physical world is the informing principle of what Richard Chase calls the American Romance, which is manifest most famously in the virtuous "code" of the western hero.[27] This was a reassuring mythic vision, for when the guns of the classic western hero were fired, it was never arbitrary or impulsive, but always for a reason, one that in the end served communal rather than individual goals. Inevitably, we felt a righteous identification with the hero. But this mythic optimism is hardly possible in a world shaped by the defeatist, determinist philosophy of John in *River's Edge,* whose view of life is that "you do shit, it's done, and then you die."

Already in 1974 John Fraser referred to such multiple killers as Charles Starkweather and Charles Manson as "quintessentially modern examples of anomie and alienation."[28] Significantly, in Quentin Tarantino's *Pulp Fiction,* which perhaps stands in relation to the contemporary action cinema as *Psycho* does to the modern horror film, the narrative structure is a fractured one that offers the spectator no stable position of identification. (It is no coincidence that *Pulp Fiction* acknowledges *Psycho* in the scene where boxer Butch Coolidge, attempting to flee town, sees Marcellus walk across the street in front of his car, just as Marion Crane sees her boss as she is driving out of Phoenix.) But if Hitchcock put us in the driver's seat along with Marion, Tarantino puts us in the back seat of the hit men's car along with their captive at the moment when he is accidentally shot point blank. In this one moment, splatter becomes emblematic of the postmodern condition, translating our eroded subjectivity into the graphics of the fractured head.

These works I have been discussing are, certainly, as the droogs of *A Clockwork Orange* (1971) would describe them, "real horrorshow." But just as Anthony Burgess's novel complicates issues of both the representation and the reception of violence, so my point is not simply to lament the decline of moral values in these newer representations. Such complaint is common enough and was articulated at least as far back as George Orwell's 1944 analysis of British crime fiction, wherein he blamed the influence of "Americanization" for both the erosion of the genre's traditionally clear moral order and the trend toward passages of graphic sadism.[29]

For Fraser, the artistic use of violence involves eliciting a shock of recognition in the viewer, akin to the method of Artaud's theater of cruelty. Certainly, not all of the works I have been discussing are truly progressive, although they do demythify violence by revealing it for the inglorious, brute force that it always is. But some of them do work in a profoundly moral way insofar as they shock us by *not* shocking us—more precisely, by refusing to employ the conventional stylistic markers of "shock" exactly when we would expect them to do so. Given the pervasiveness of violence in contemporary culture, some of these texts seem aware of the need for new strategies to challenge viewers. They also offer a vivid demonstration of Martin Rubin's observation that "the interrelated discourses of liberal humanism, scientific rationalism, and expressive realism, though appropriate for the postwar problem film were . . . inadequate to convey the emerging popular mythology of modern multiple murder."[30] The failure of these traditional discourses is itself the theme of *Kalifornia* (1993) and *Copycat* (1995), in which bourgeois characters who have the hubris to write sociological treatises on serial killers are personally confronted by real ones whose actions they can neither comprehend nor contain.

Bruce Kawin has argued that the experience of horror is like "a visit to the land of the dead, with the difference that this Charon will eventually take you home."[31] Some new works of horror take us across the Styx but then, however, refuse to ferry us back again. The last sentence of *American Psycho* is, tellingly, "this is not an exit" (395). In forcing us to confront such violence so directly, without the traditionally obligatory but hypocritical moral distance, texts such as Ellis's go beyond the "therapeutic" quality some critics have imputed to classic horror, to bring us up sharply against the institutionalized horrors of contemporary culture to which many of us have become desensitized. In this theater of cruelty, as in the real world, we are left to find our own way back from the land of the dead.

Notes

1. Martin Rubin, "The Grayness of Darkness: *The Honeymoon Killers* and Its Impact on Psychokiller Cinema," *Velvet Light Trap* 30 (1992): 20 (reprinted herein).

2. See, for example, Robin Wood, "An Introduction to the American Horror Film," in *American Nightmare: Essays on the Horror Film,* ed. Robin Wood and Richard Lippe (Toronto: Festival of Festivals, 1979), 19.

3. Harold Schechter, *Deviant: The Shocking True Story of the Original "Psycho"* (New York: Pocket Books, 1989), 272.

4. Richard Jewett and John Shelton Lawrence, *The American Monomyth* (Garden City, N.Y.: Anchor Doubleday, 1977).

5. Richard Slotkin, *Regeneration through Violence: The Mythology of the American Frontier, 1600–1860* (Middletown, Conn.: Wesleyan University Press, 1973).

6. D. H. Lawrence, *Studies in Classic American Literature* (New York: Penguin, 1970), 68.

7. Annalee Newitz, "Serial Killers, True Crime, and Economic Performance Anxiety," *CineAction* 38 (1995): 41 (reprinted herein).

8. Wood, "Introduction," 21.

9. Robin Wood, *Hitchcock's Films* (London and New York: Zwemmer/ Barnes, 1965), 122.

10. Barry Keith Grant, "Rich and Strange: The Yuppie Horror Film," *Journal of Film and Video* 48.1–2 (Spring/Summer 1996): 4–16.

11. Bret Easton Ellis, *American Psycho* (New York: Vintage, 1991), 347, 52. Subsequent references appear parenthetically in the text.

12. The novel has been equally shunned in academic discourse, there being only one serious discussion of *American Psycho,* albeit a brief one, that I know of: Vicky Lebeau's *Lost Angels: Psychoanalysis and Cinema* (London and New York: Routledge, 1995).

13. Fredric Jameson, *Postmodernism, or the Cultural Logic of Late Capitalism* (Durham: Duke University Press, 1992), 16.

14. Lebeau, *Lost Angels,* 129.

15. Steven Shaviro, *The Cinematic Body* (Minneapolis: University of Minnesota Press, 1993), 263.

16. William Carlos Williams, "To Elsie," in *The Collected Earlier Poems of William Carlos Williams* (New York: New Directions, 1951), 270–72.

17. Brian Henderson, "Towards a Non-Bourgeois Camera Style," in *Movies and Methods,* ed. Bill Nichols (Berkeley: University of California Press, 1976), 422–38.

18. See Linda Williams's pioneering work on pornographic film, *Hard Core: Power, Pleasure, and "The Frenzy of the Visible"* (Berkeley: University of California Press, 1989).

19. Walker Percy, *The Movie-goer* (New York: Penguin, 1961), 12.

20. Jean Baudrillard, *The Evil Demon of Images* (Sydney, Australia: Power Institute of Fine Arts, 1987).

21. Beverle Houston, "[Re]Viewing Television: The Metapsychology of Endless Consumption," in *American Television: New Directions in History and Theory,* ed. Nick Browne (Switzerland: Harwood Academic Publishing, 1994), 81.

22. Ibid., 82.

23. Newitz, "Serial Killers," 45.

24. *True Crime #5* (Forestville, Calif.: Eclipse Comics, 1992).

25. John Fraser, *Violence in the Arts* (London: Cambridge University Press, 1974), 23.

26. Marius Bewley, *The Eccentric Design: Form in the Classic American Novel* (New York: Columbia University Press, 1963), 73.

27. Richard Chase, *The American Novel and Its Tradition* (Garden City, N.Y.: Anchor Doubleday, 1957), vii–xii.

28. Fraser, *Violence in the Arts,* 22.

29. George Orwell, "Raffles and Miss Blandish," *Critical Essays* (London: Secker and Warburg, 1960), 171–73.

30. Rubin, "The Grayness of Darkness," 50.

31. Bruce Kawin, "Children of the Night," in *Film Genre Reader,* ed. Barry Keith Grant (Austin: University of Texas Press, 1986), 237.

2

The Grayness of Darkness: The Honeymoon Killers and Its Impact on Psychokiller Cinema

Martin Rubin

"No sense makes sense."

—Charles Manson[1]

"Negativity can only be described in terms of its *operations,* and not by any means in terms of a graspable entity. . . . Negativity does not so much indicate oppositions as combine negations with a resultant unforeseeability. It disperses what it undercuts and turns into a proliferating offshoot of what has been negated."

—Sanford Budick and Wolfgang Iser[2]

Jamie Gumb Superstar

The resounding critical and commercial success of *The Silence of the Lambs* (1991) has confirmed the status of the psychokiller as superstar. Jonathan Demme's revisionist cop thriller features not one but two of the sanguinary celebrities: debonair man-eater Hannibal Lecter and transvestite woman-skinner Jamie Gumb. It is a tribute to Jodie Foster's screen presence that her dogged, down-to-earth heroine was not blown away by the double-barreled media blast—first over the showy performance of Anthony Hopkins as Lecter, then over the alleged homophobic fallout from the Gumb character.

Of course, Lecter and Gumb are just two of the legion of murderers who have possessed filmmakers' and filmgoers' imaginations in the post–Norman Bates era.[3] This modern-day demonology ranges from the real-life killers of *In Cold Blood* (1967), *Helter Skelter* (1976), and *The Executioner's Song* (1982), to the fictional psychopaths in *Dirty Harry* (1971), *Manhunter* (1986), *Relentless* (1989), and *The Silence of the Lambs,* to the semi-supernaturalized stalkers, slashers, and splatterers who have bubbled up from the collective id in numerable recent slaughter sagas.

Every era has its preferred nightmares, and this dark side can shed light on some of the era's most troubling tensions (e.g., gangster films in the 1930s, film noir in the 1940s, science fiction in the 1950s, horror in the 1970s). Millennial America has been obsessed with the figure of the modern multiple murderer (especially the serial killer)—an obsession that began stirring in the 1950s and 1960s but has gathered much momentum in recent years. As often happens when exploitation-susceptible subject matter is involved, the strongest expressions of popular nightmares are not always tasteful or critically recognized.

The pivot of this article is *The Honeymoon Killers* (1970), a low-budget "exploitation" film that represented a genuine breakthrough in the treatment of psychopathic violence on the screen. A remarkable experience in its own right, it has been followed by a small group of like-minded films, some with significant cult reputations (*Badlands* [1973], *Henry: Portrait of a Serial Killer* [1990]), some fairly obscure (*The Boys Next Door* [1985], *Murder One* [1988]). For almost thirty years these films have provided an especially effective variation on our recent fascination with multiple murder, and they offer an illuminating angle of approach to the historical and cultural contexts that have shaped that fascination.

The term "without apparent motive" is often applied to modern multiple murderers.[4] But it is not quite precise or comprehensive enough; modern multiple murderers often do reveal motives, apparent or otherwise.[5] However, there is an enigmatic aura surrounding modern multiple murderers that endows them with special menace. Although lack of motivation does not sufficiently distinguish multiple murder from other types of homicide, these killers embody a more crucial cause-and-effect dysfunction occurring on another level, one that involves style and appearance more than motivation. The modern multiple murderer frequently confounds notions of a "criminal type" or behavioral predictability. Typical statements used to describe modern multiple murderers include "the All-American boy" (applied to Charles Whitman), "voted most likely to succeed" (Herbert Mullin, an especially demented multiple murderer of the 1970s), and "the nicest boy in Wolcott" (Kansas family killer Lowell Lee Andrews).[6] The modern multiple murderer's monstrous actions often emanate from a bland and unimpressive agent.

A crucial distinction must be drawn between the current concept of the modern multiple murderer and an earlier model, the traditional compulsive killer. The modern multiple murderer incorporates elements of the latter but is not the same. Traditional compulsive killers (like the characters played by Peter Lorre in *M* [1931], Laird Cregar in *Hangover*

Square [1945], Anthony Perkins in *Psycho* [1960], and Carl Boehm in *Peeping Tom* [1960]) are presented as tortured souls who are driven by internal demons. Although these killers may appear bland on the outside, their psychology contains a monstrous alter ego more in keeping with the monstrous acts they commit. Their deviance ultimately "makes sense."

The modern multiple murderer, on the other hand, often seems to exhibit an equally bland psychology beneath his bland exterior. Although a sense of internal compulsion may be present, this drive seems less flamboyant, anguish-ridden, soul-centered, and more stolid, detached, machinelike. Typically opaque banalities from the lore of modern multitude include: "Well, the time had come, and I did what I had to do" (Lowell Lee Andrews); "I had a job to do, and I was doing it" (David "Son of Sam" Berkowitz), and "I just wondered how it would feel to shoot grandma" (Edmund Kemper).[7] The monstrousness of the crimes seems excessive in terms of both the external and internal sides of the murderer's personality. This results in an alienating sense of excess and disproportion—a schizophrenic disconnection between the murderer and his murders.

THE PROBLEM WITH PROBLEM FILMS

The Sniper (1952) is perhaps the first Hollywood film to attempt to deal seriously with a serial killer on a clinical level, regarding him not as an embodiment of abstract evil but as a problem to be examined and understood. Produced under the Stanley Kramer banner, *The Sniper* takes a liberal approach to the subject. The protagonist is Eddie (Eduard Franz), a disturbed young man who expresses his mother-motivated hatred of women by picking them off with a long-range rifle.

In addition to carrying on the tradition of the postwar social problem film (e.g., *Crossfire* [1947], *Gentleman's Agreement* [1947], *Home of the Brave* [1949]), *The Sniper* borrows much of its style and underlying assumptions from the semi-documentary crime film (e.g., *The House on 92nd Street* [1945], *Call Northside 777* [1948], *The Naked City* [1948]), including location-shooting, an emphasis on facts, and a reliance on scientific procedures. Like those films, it projects a faith in rationality and social authority. The police are viewed as dedicated and effective, even if their methods are a little old-fashioned. The necessary modernization is provided by a police psychiatrist (Richard Kiley) who serves as the voice of reason. Whereas the veteran police detective (Adolphe Menjou) is baffled by this newfangled type of murder, Kiley's character knows all the answers. He neatly pigeonholes the disruptive irrationality of the serial "sex-killer": such killers "run to a pattern," fit into "water-tight compartments," and "stay in their own grooves." Milking the significance of every clue available, this psychiatric Sherlock deduces an impressively accurate profile of the still-unknown killer-at-large.

Such faith in rationality is reflected in the form of the film. *The Sniper* presents a world that is highly expressive and charged with significance. Deep, intricate spaces provide an appropriate expression of psychological complexity. Magnified shadows; flickering firelight; whirling amusement-park rides; an atmospheric soundtrack of sirens, foghorns, and trolley bells; and priapic towers and chimneys all serve to convey Eddie's psychological quirks, insecurities, and changing moods. *The Sniper* portrays an eloquent world, eminently readable, filled with signs to be deciphered and connections to be made. This is also true of *The Silence of the Lambs,* which likewise presents a richly meaningful environment, cluttered with signs and portents. These allusions may be arcane and bizarre—in fact, they are all the more compelling *because* they are arcane and bizarre. But they are ultimately decipherable and lead to a rationally revealed truth, with the oracular Lecter acting as gatekeeper, slyly tossing out clues and riddles.

Despite its commitment to a liberal/rationalist viewpoint, *The Sniper* does not present such attitudes in a simple manner. Outside of the omniscient psychiatrist, the film is relatively discreet in its message elements. It refrains from overexplicit analysis of the killer. The conjectures of the psychiatrist, although not discounted, are left unconfirmed, and there are no flashbacks or *Psycho*-style postmortems to smother Eddie's disturbing deeds in explanations. A pioneer treatment of a difficult subject, *The Sniper* searches a little too hard for conventional connections, but it restrains itself from filling in all the blanks.

Such restraint is largely absent from another landmark of psychokiller cinema, the critically acclaimed *In Cold Blood* (1967), adapted from Truman Capote's account of the spree killing of a rural family by two ex-cons, Dick Hickock and Perry Smith. Despite its title, the film is anything but cold-blooded. Writer-director Richard Brooks overbakes the material in the hot air of excessive explaining and editorializing. Much of the film's considerable weight is expended upon ponderous ironies (an insurance salesman cheerily wishes Mr. Clutter "a very long and healthy life" on the evening before his murder) and editing (Mr. Clutter dunks his face in a bathroom sink, and the scene cuts to Smith raising his face from a sink in a bus station lavatory). Such devices dilute the estranging impact of the murders by imposing a familiar pattern of fatalism on them. Brooks also encumbers the film with flashbacks to "explain" the Smith character, including a Rosebud-like revelation just before he takes the final drop.

In Cold Blood is less disquieting than noisy: windshield wipers thrash, trains and trucks roar, amplified heartbeats pound, and, in the film's corniest touch, a Bible wielded by a prosecutor booms shut like a clap of Jehovah's thunder. The Clutter home is unnecessarily embellished with Charles Addams atmospherics, such as howling wind and gloomy lighting—the inhabitants are, after all, guilty of nothing more serious than being ordinary. The hangman in the execution scene is depicted as a Gothic apparition, his grizzled face enfolded in shadow beneath a rumpled hat; one half-expects him to be assisted by Boris Karloff, dragging a clubfoot. The film's most effective sequences are those that play against this predominant tone of doom-laden portentousness: Hickock's giddy check-bouncing spree in Kansas City and the ruefully ironic treasure hunt for soda bottles in the Nevada desert.

In Cold Blood careens clumsily between Gothic and cinema-verité styles, and it ultimately runs for cover into the reassuring discourse of the social problem film. This, along with its overwrought search for explanations and connections, are like distress signals sent up from a sinking ship. The interrelated discourses of liberal humanism, scientific rationalism, and expressive realism, though appropriate for the postwar social problem film, were inadequate in conveying the emerging popular mythology of modern multiple murder.

THEY'RE FAT AND BALDING . . . THEY'RE IN LOVE . . . AND THEY KILL PEOPLE

From start to finish, *The Honeymoon Killers* is a profoundly unsettling movie.[8] The first shot shows a hearse as it rushes toward a hospital, opening the film on a note of unresolved urgency; the vehicle's pressing errand is not shown, and we never hear of it again. The next shot shifts our attention to a startling off-screen pop and a mysterious puff of smoke emerging in a hospital corridor. A disorienting camera movement pulls *away* from the mystifying event, then swivels to discover the imposing personage of nurse Martha Beck, who bursts out of a doorway and barrels down the hall like a stupendous Valkyrie. The opening scene (like the rest of this grisly tale) is accompanied by the stately strains of Gustave Mahler.

The Honeymoon Killers is based on the lurid "Lonely Hearts Murders" case of the late 1940s. Through a correspondence club, Martha Beck, a hefty nurse living in Florida, met Raymond Fernandez, a New

45

York con-man who used the club as a means of swindling love-starved middle-aged women. Ray and Martha fell in love and, apparently at Martha's instigation, began murdering as well as bilking Ray's victims. Although the motives for Ray and Martha's crimes are to some extent conventional (robbery, jealousy), the film's emphasis is on their estranging, psychopathic qualities.[9] Its unconventional presentation of psychopathic violence points toward innovative possibilities for treating serial murder, mass murder, and other forms of modern multiple murder; this links *The Honeymoon Killers* much more strongly to the films featured in the next section of this article than to those described in the previous one.

At the end of *The Honeymoon Killers,* an overlay informs us that Martha Beck and Ray Fernandez were executed at Sing-Sing Prison on March 8, 1951. Despite this factual wrap-up, an opening "this is a true story" statement, and cinema verité-like, black-and-white camerawork, the film's stripped-down style dispenses with period details (car models, dress styles, props, and so on). Although this lack of period authenticity undoubtedly serves low-budget exigencies, it has other functions as well. As noted in the above discussions of *The Sniper* and *In Cold Blood,* the parameters of expressive realism that usually define mainstream cinema have seemed inadequate to deal with such massively estranging subject matter as modern multiple murder, because they almost inevitably diminish the material, containing it within familiar discourses of liberalism, plausibility, and verisimilitude. *The Honeymoon Killers* contains strong currents of documentary realism, but it pushes them to the point where they erode the balance of realism and expressionism that provides a basic framework for Hollywood style.

The most impressive example of this is the film's lighting, in which budget limitations result in stylistic dissonance. Very fast film stock appears to have been used, evidently to compensate for the limited lighting resources. With little or no fill lighting, the lighting becomes unbalanced in strikingly discrepant ways. The main characters are often cast into near-silhouette, while the backgrounds shimmer behind them. Isolated strong light sources (lamps, exposed light bulbs, sunlit windows) become overexposed, flooding many shots with a frosty incandescence that obliterates large areas of the image. Such nuances inevitably suffer on videotape, and I urge interested readers to seek out a celluloid version of this remarkable exercise in low-budget style. On tape, the overexposed backgrounds appear merely washed-out, losing much of their wintry quality and the gradational border regions between barely discernible image and luminous blankness—a treacherous perceptual precipice, where visibility drops off into nihility.

Similar dissonances are produced by the film's use of music. It would be too narrow to read the Mahler score as simply a textbook example of contrapuntalism, in the manner of the toe-tapping "ultraviolence" of "Singin' in the Rain" in *A Clockwork Orange* (1971) or the jaunty melody that accompanies Mr. Memory's poignant death scene in *The 39 Steps* (1935). Better comparisons are the abrupt austerity of Michel Legrand's score in Godard's prostitution drama *Vivre Sa Vie* (1962), or the incongruous jazz in Ichikawa's Genroku saga *An Actor's Revenge* (1963). In other words, the effect is not so much irony as *displacement*—a fluctuating overlay of multiple contexts upon the events depicted.

To a certain extent, the Mahler music does clash with the sordid banality of the events and characters, but it also activates some unsettling interpretations of those elements. At times, the grave tempo matches Martha's pace as she walks toward the camera, transforming her weighty tread into a stately, operatic procession. This effect gives Martha the aura of a character who is fulfilling her destiny with a self-conscious grandeur that is impressive as well as absurd. Bursts of Mahler also bestow a purifying detachment upon some of the film's most brutal passages.

Mahler's music catapults us outside the often unbearable events and at the same time plunges us inside the main characters' (especially Martha's) inflated and distorted interpretations of those events. The music neither endorses the characters' views through straight expression nor dismisses them through easy irony. Instead, the music's precise misalignment brings out this subjective dimension, which collides with other intractable elements in the film, such as the hideousness of the murders, the vulgarity of the victims. *The Honeymoon Killers* reaches toward a pluralistic style in which elements weave along adjacent tracks, instead of being contained in ambiguity or a fixed hierarchy.

This idea of unstable and contradictory tensions also applies to the presentation of the film's characters. Martha and Ray sorely lack the cinematic glamor of Bonnie and Clyde. Played by Tony LoBianco as a Ricky Ricardo gone-to-seed, Ray is a balding lady-killer whose transparent smarminess could be overlooked by only the most undiscerning ladies. Martha (Shirley Stoler) is self-indulgent, vicious, and bigoted (fired by a Jewish supervisor, she huffs, "I'm not so sure Hitler wasn't right about you people!"). She insists on accompanying Ray on all his romantic sorties—a ludicrous arrangement, because she flies into jealous rages whenever he starts buttering up the victims. She and Ray pose as brother

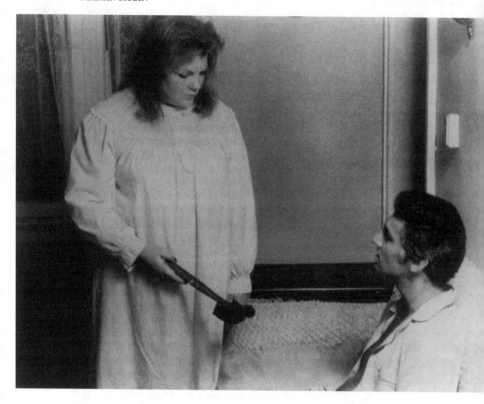

The banality of violence: *The Honeymoon Killers* (Warren Steibel Films, 1971).

and sister, despite their absurdly disparate appearances and accents (the swarthy Ray speaks with a heavy Hispanic accent).

Martha's weight and appetites provide another fertile source of humor. At one point, Ray leaves her alone in a hotel room with a box of chocolates to pacify her. An extreme close-up follows her plump forefinger as it browses over the diagrammed menu, hovering deceptively between nut nougat and chocolate caramel before swooping down to snare an unsuspecting chocolate truffle. The scene then discreetly dissolves to Martha snoozing contentedly amid a pile of empty candy wrappers.

There are two factors that keep Ray and Martha from being unsympathetically grotesque. One is the undeniable sincerity of their passion for each other. When Ray gets too friendly with one of his victims at a lakeside setting, Martha ruins the whole scheme with an impulsive suicide attempt in which she wades into the water and struggles to

48

submerge her bulk beneath it. Rather than getting angry, Ray swims to the rescue, frantically apologizing and embracing her. The film ends on a note of triumphant romanticism. Awaiting trial, Martha seems less anxious about the verdict than about Ray's feelings toward her. She then receives a jailhouse letter that resoundingly reaffirms his devotion: "You are the one and only woman I will ever love, now and beyond the grave."

The other factor is the general banality of the society to which Ray and Martha constitute a menace. There is none of the sanctimoniousness that surrounds the portrayal of the victimized Clutter family in *In Cold Blood*. Instead, *The Honeymoon Killers* presents a putrescent version of Norman Rockwell's America: a kitschy wasteland filled with uninspiring patriotism, meager dreams, and tawdry decor. At one point Ray and Martha try to live a normal life by buying a house in Valley Stream. The film does not bother to dwell on predictable shots of suburban vacuity. We just see Ray moping by an overlit window that obscures the void outside; he observes glumly, "They call this place Valley Stream. What a joke!"

Such drab normalcy attains its most vivid expression in Ray and Martha's victims. These decaying dowagers are all petty, simpering, miserly, and/or wincingly trite in varying degrees. The first one is a loud New Jersey schoolteacher who chortles "America the Beautiful" in the bathtub; Martha retaliates by bellowing "Battle Hymn of the Republic" as she makes love to Ray within his unwitting bride's earshot. Another victim is so patriotic that she holds a party on Lincoln's birthday, complete with cake and candles.

Janet Fay, however, really takes the cake: a twittering cheapskate whose prized possessions are two paintings of Jesus and whose favorite expression is "Isn't that cu-ute!" She magnanimously offers to treat Ray and Martha to a cafeteria meal, then nervously clucks, "My, a dollar eighty-five for a veal cutlet. . . . But have whatever you want, don't let me influence you." "I'll have the veal cutlet," Martha declares firmly. After Janet's murder, Martha tosses the Jesus paintings into the woman's basement grave and, in an appallingly funny moment, sneers, "Now, isn't that *cu-ute!*"

What prevents *The Honeymoon Killers* from being completely heartless is the discomfiting vulnerability of the victims and the undiluted horror of their deaths. Janet is the victim of Ray and Martha's first hands-on murder (a previous bride died of poisoning). The camera moves in close, building tension as the woman begs on her knees and Martha raises a hammer. A cut to a long shot deceptively releases the tension a split-second before Martha brains Janet with the hammer. A moment of

49

stunned silence follows in which the characters are frozen in a ghastly tableau that marks the point of no return. The victim has to be finished off, and she is slowly, messily strangled with a scarf. Martha, ever the helpful nurse, hands the hammer to Ray and advises him to use it as a deadly tourniquet.

Although a film of limited stylistic development, *The Honeymoon Killers* negotiates a difficult path between self-indulgent exploitation and debilitating good taste. Its saving grace is its contradictoriness, which prevents it from settling into the positions of condescension that characterize the work of Terrence Malick and David Lynch. It is difficult to disengage the film's grotesque hilarity from its horrific violence. Are the victims to be pitied or despised? Are the murderers hideous or tragic? Monstrous or banal? On the other hand, Ray and Martha do not congeal into a cliché like "the banality of evil"—they are not quite banal nor evil enough.

The Honeymoon Killers is an exercise in purposeful confusion. Much of its power derives from its ability to arouse a mixture of strongly conflicting responses without refining them or sorting them out. Intensely involving and intensely estranging, it is a film that ruins complacency.

FILMS FROM BENEATH THE FLOORBOARDS

As noted earlier, *The Honeymoon Killers* was followed by a handful of films that played variations on the strategies it pioneered. Released irregularly over the last twenty years, this group of films (which I will refer to as *The Honeymoon Killers et al.*) seem too scattered to form even a modest-sized subgenre. Perhaps sub-subgenre would be a more appropriate label, befitting their bargain-basement budgets and under-the-floorboards subversiveness.

Badlands: The elusive Terrence Malick made his directing debut with this critically acclaimed post-mortem on exhausted rebel mythologies (the 1950s juvenile delinquent, the 1960s outlaw). A South Dakota punk named Kit (Martin Sheen) falls for baton-twirling, fifteen-year-old Holly (Sissy Spacek), shoots her disapproving father, and takes her along on a desultory murder spree.

The Boys Next Door: Penelope Spheeris's post-punk paraphrasing of the 1949 film-noir classic *Gun Crazy* received limited release and largely negative response. Roy (Maxwell Caulfield) and Bo (Charlie Sheen), two blanked-out buddies on the road to nowhere, commemorate their high school graduation with a string of pointless murders. Bo, the more sensitive of the pair, finally kills Roy to prevent further bloodshed.

Murder One: This deep sleeper by Graeme Campbell was consigned to the more obscure corners of the video market. Two half-brothers escape from a Maryland prison. They take along a black fellow-inmate and their complaisant kid brother Billy (Henry Thomas). Their flight takes them through a Deep South heartland populated by "god-fearin', tractor-ridin', beef-eatin' farmers," several of whom they slaughter before being captured in West Virginia.

Henry: Portrait of a Serial Killer: A cause célèbre of the X-rating controversy, John McNaughton's first fictional feature has been almost too widely acclaimed to be considered a cult film. A stolid Chicago-based psychopath (Michael Rooker) carries out a series of brutal murders, mostly of women. He acquires a cretinous partner named Ottis and is attracted to Ottis's sympathetic sister, Becky. Both end up dead and dismembered, and Henry moves on to new hunting grounds.

Although each of these films centers on a case of multiple murder, this factor is not the primary one that groups them together and gives them their particular power. Just as important are the stylistic and structural devices they use to present their story, position the spectator, and position themselves in relation to other films.

The films are typically patterned on real-life precedents and include prominent prefatory statements along the lines of "This is a true story."[10] However, an appearance of factuality seems more important than an actual adherence to the facts, which are often handled loosely and even disdainfully. The factual veneer functions not so much to support a style of documentary authenticity as to enter into a system of tension and contradiction with other elements of the film.

As noted above, other film treatments of "senseless" multiple murder have been diluted by the normalizing influence of conventional expressive realism. Unlike films such as *The Sniper, In Cold Blood,* and *The Silence of the Lambs,* which attempt to "get inside" the subject matter through those means, *The Honeymoon Killers et al.* pursue a style of studied disassociation that hinders such access. There is a certain numbness to their styles, signaling a crisis of conventional means of expressivity.

An exemplary passage occurs in *Murder One.* The film's cruelest scenes involve a woman who stumbles onto a murder scene. Paralyzed by terror and incomprehension, she is raped repeatedly and then meets a miserable death, shot in the head as she huddles naked and dazed in a misty, puddle-pocked field. These brutal events are presented neither with supposedly alienating bluntness nor with conspicuous, suggestive obliqueness (which might simply be a case of reverse emphasis). Instead, the film maintains a rigorous denial of emphasis. The woman is shown,

51

generally toward the bottom of the frame, not prominently enough to be an object of spectacle but not indirectly enough either to mitigate the horror or to enhance it through suggestiveness. The scrupulous flatness with which atrocity is depicted here compares favorably with Jean-Luc Godard's war film *Les Carabiniers* (1963) or, on the literary side, Flannery O'Connor's short story "A Good Man Is Hard to Find," an important precursor of the films under discussion.

This general anti-expressiveness is sometimes augmented with specific devices that trouble the creation of a homogeneous realism. Examples include the unbalanced lighting and "inappropriate" Mahler music in *The Honeymoon Killers* (*Badlands* uses music by Carl Orff in a somewhat similar way); the woefully inadequate commentary provided by Holly's cliché-choked voice-over in *Badlands;* the comparable but more sporadic narration of Billy in *Murder One;* the soundtrack stylizations that punctuate *Henry: Portrait of a Serial Killer* (overamplified ambient sounds, distorted aural flashbacks, odd synchronizations of sound effects and music score).

In *The Honeymoon Killers et al.,* suspense leading up to violence is generally avoided in favor of arbitrary suddenness or flat inevitability. A celebrated example of the latter approach is the scene in *Henry: Portrait of a Serial Killer* wherein the murder of a family is seen retrospectively on videotape as the killers view it at their leisure. These films contain a scarcity of climactic, cathartic shootouts and/or executions, in contrast to *Bonnie and Clyde* (1967), *In Cold Blood, The Silence of the Lambs,* and so on. The characters just seem to wind down, overcome by exhaustion and inertia. Martha wearily turns in herself and her lover to the police in *The Honeymoon Killers.* Kit shoots out his own tire and waits for the law to catch up in *Badlands.* The exhausted, unresisting fugitives are apprehended while asleep in *Murder One.* Henry is not even caught in *Henry: Portrait of a Serial Killer;* he simply dumps a corpse-stuffed suitcase by the roadside and drives off.

The films end with the main characters in a limbo of disconnection and suspension. Martha sits motionless beneath an American flag in *The Honeymoon Killers.* Kit and Holly float through cottony clouds in *Badlands.* Bo is waltzed off by the police in ethereal slow-motion in *The Boys Next Door.* Billy has the sensation of watching himself in a movie as he and his comrades are led away (again, in slow motion) in *Murder One.* Henry simply disappears at the end of *Henry: Portrait of a Serial Killer.*

Finally, these films are centered on a position with which it is difficult to sympathize but from which we cannot distance ourselves. Their inaccessible protagonists stand in contrast to the ambivalently sympathetic outlaws and psychopaths of *Gun Crazy, Peeping Tom, Psycho,* and *Bonnie and Clyde.* On the other hand, the films are not centered on the side of normality, with the inscrutable killer positioned as an external threat, as in *Cape Fear* (1962, 1991), *Experiment in Terror* (1962), *Sleeping with the Enemy* (1991), and the most characteristic stalker/slasher movies. In *The Honeymoon Killers et al.,* we remain at nearly all times on the killers' side of the narrative. The realm of "normal values" is not only distant but is often regarded by the criminal protagonists with a sneering disdain that the films' actions make it difficult to discredit entirely.

The spectator is maintained in a untenable position between complicity and detachment, passivity and revulsion. A paradigm for this position is provided by Sissy Spacek's character in *Badlands* and Henry Thomas's character in *Murder One:* a reluctant though voluntary passenger "along for the ride," neither a bystander nor a full-fledged participant in the crimes that transpire. In an analogous way, it is difficult for the spectator to find a place to stand in regard to these films.[11]

In the face of their intolerable subject matter, *The Honeymoon Killers et al.* adopt a certain attitude of refusal: refusal to express, refusal to resolve themselves, refusal to admit categorization. To a great extent, they are defined by what they are not and what they fail to be. In fact, much of these films' force and relevance derive from the way they fall through the cracks. They incompletely fill gaps left by moribund or decadent genres, and they lodge in the margins of other, more vital genres. They are by no means outside of genre; instead, they hover around a wide range of generic contexts without settling comfortably into any of them.

For example, *The Honeymoon Killers et al.* are like *gangster films* because they feature monstrous criminal protagonists, but their protagonists lack the stature of the gangster anti-hero. They are comparable to *film noir* in the way they expose the underside of their era's strained optimism, but their blunt, austere style is virtually the inverse of noir. Their factual and documentary elements place them closer to *semi-documentary crime films,* but they lack the positivist, rationalist spirit of those films. In terms of the characters and violence they portray, they resemble *compulsive-killer studies* such as *Psycho* and *Peeping Tom,* but they do not share those films' semi-expressionist stylistics and emphasis on the characters' interior lives. Their bleak vision of a decayed, criminal-infested society resembles that of *cop-avenger films* in the *Dirty Harry* mold, but they ignore the police hero and tell the story from the criminal's side of the law. Their remorseless killers link them to *stalker/slasher films,* but they do not focus on the victims, and (with the possible exception of *Henry*) they do not mythicize the killer figure.

These are difficult films, because they are difficult to pin down in a number of ways. In the piece cited at the head of this article, Budick and Iser describe negativity as an aesthetic route that can be used for approaching the "unsayable." This negativity exists only in its operation, its play, its oscillation—not as a position, but as a constant loss of position.[12] There are certain affinities between such concepts and the operations encountered in *The Honeymoon Killers et al.* These films become exercises in instability, creating a series of slippages from one "anti-" position to another, and this contributes to their unsettling, negativist quality. They say "no," not in thunder (a privilege Herman Melville once claimed for himself and kindred spirit Nathaniel Hawthorne), not in a defiant roar, but in a sullen muttering, a dissonant and elusive crepitation. It is precisely such qualities that enable these films to burrow so insinuatingly into the dirty corners of recent American history and also to connect with more general, long-standing trends in American culture.

AMERICAN HISTORY, AMERICAN VIOLENCE, AMERICAN PSYCHOS

The late 1960s saw a marked increase in the consciousness of violence in America, spurred by such highly visible phenomena as war, urban riots, assassinations, political demonstrations, and the suppression of those demonstrations. One manifestation of this consciousness was a quantum leap in the depiction of screen violence, spearheaded by such films as *Bonnie and Clyde, The Wild Bunch* (1969), and *Night of the Living Dead* (1968). Another manifestation was a rash of published reflections on the subject of violence. This was a vintage season for studies, anthologies, editorials, and commission reports on America the Violent. Included in this trend were a number of major scholarly analyses of the role of violence in American history.[13]

Most of these analyses concur that the American tradition of violence has been significant, but overlooked, and usually perpetrated by conservative rather than radical forces.[14] It has been implemented mainly by the members of the established order against perceived troublemakers, undesirables, and outsiders. At the same time, it has been largely localized and decentralized, directed not against the dominant class or central governmental institutions but against racial (African Americans, Asians, Native Americans), ethnic (the latest immigrant wave), political (Communists and other "agitators"), and economically marginalized groups (the "white trash" and frontier "scum" who were the primary targets of vigilante organizations—themselves a peculiarly American phenomenon).[15] This has resulted in a distinctive and paradoxical configuration of high violence *and* high stability in American history.[16] According to Richard Hofstadter, the United States has maintained a level of political stability comparable to Scandinavia and a level of civil violence comparable to Latin America.[17] In contrast to European traditions of violence, which are considered to be more directly related to protest, social change, and challenges to the central class structure, American violence has been perceived (somewhat too narrowly) as marginal and fragmented, subordinating class conflicts to culture-group conflicts and attacking the state only rarely and to a limited degree.[18]

It follows that especially marginalized and devalued modes of violence in America would include those with overt anti-establishment political content and, at the other extreme, apolitical acts of "irrational" violence. These two forms can have a reciprocal relationship: the suppression of the political mode is obscured by the sensationalism of the more easily discredited irrational mode. As J. Bowyer Bell and Ted Robert Gurr write, "Savage killers and madmen American society certainly has, but violent revolutionaries, no."[19]

These depoliticized visions of American violence are closely related to a certain model for interpreting American history, commonly known as the "consensus" model. As opposed to the conflict-based model, it envisions American history as an idealistic progression wherein class, politics, and other social divisions are subsumed into a greater commonality.[20] The consensus approach was especially prevalent during the 1950s as an instrument of American self-image in the cold war global arena. It also reflected the centrist temper of domestic politics in the postwar era, with depression-era radicalism widely purged, and liberal/conservative factionalism moderated under the bipartisan banners of anti-Communism and welfare-state entrenchment. This period represented the high-water mark of the consensus school of American historians, sociologists, and political scientists.[21] The title of Daniel Bell's 1960 collection *The End of Ideology* provided a catchy, if oversimplified, slogan for the movement.[22]

But ideology, far from being at an end, came back into American society with a vengeance. The late 1960s witnessed an atypically intense and widespread incidence of political violence, often directed against central power structures and public institutions (the federal government, the military-industrial complex). These disturbances marked the breakdown of the centrist equilibrium of postwar American politics and placed a severe strain on the anti-ideological ideology that had supported it. The "consensus" honeymoon was over, killed by the eruption of its own internal conflicts.

It was during this period of political violence, the breakdown of centrist consensus, and the oncoming rightward realignment that the figure of the modern multiple murderer crystallized in American popular mythology. Richard Maxwell Brown points out that the year 1966 (the threshold of the decade's political activism) was marked by a heightened public consciousness of "free-lance multiple murder," with the sensational crimes of Richard Speck and Charles Whitman occurring within a few weeks of each other.[23]

As indicated above, American popular mythology has normally been far more receptive to savage killers and madmen than to violent political revolutionaries. In the 1960s, the spectral figure of the savage killer rose up alongside the emergent violent revolutionary, walked next to him for a while, then nudged him aside and stalked on alone into the imaginations of post-1960s America. Charles Manson can be seen as a key transitional figure in these terms. He and his cult encapsulated the devolvement from a 1960s image of political/countercultural violence (as evidenced by their murder-scene graffiti, "DEATH TO THE PIGS," "POLITICAL PIGGY") to a more depoliticized, dismissible image of senseless butchery inflicted by demoniac outsiders. The violence of the 1960s, along with the images of internal conflict with which it challenged consensus assumptions, was blocked, turned in on itself, divested of its political dimensions, and diverted into forms that seemed solipsistic, gratuitous, and irrational.

As might be expected, recent years have produced many analyses of the multiple-murder "epidemic," with explanations that include genetic and physiological determinism (Joel Norris, *Serial Killers,* 1988), the sexist foundations of patriarchal culture (Deborah Cameron and Elizabeth Frazer, *The Lust to Kill,* 1987), the experiential gratifications of the crime itself (Jack Katz, *Seductions of Crime,* 1988), and the pernicious influences of Marxism, existential philosophy, and liberal permissiveness (Colin Wilson and Donald Seaman, *The Serial Killers,* 1990). One of the most interesting interpretations is provided by Canadian anthropologist Elliot Leyton in his book *Compulsive Killers: The Story of Modern Multiple Murder* (1986), which analyzes these crimes primarily in terms of their social content.

According to Leyton's thesis, the marginalized violence of the modern multiple murderer can be seen as a crazy mirror that both reflects the dominant violence of American culture and distorts certain aspects of it.[24] The violence of multiple murderers is essentially conservative (like the dominant violence), but it is directed from below rather than above. In Leyton's view, multiple murderers challenge not the established social order, but their own exclusion from it. The most common profile of this type of criminal is a male on the border between the lower and middle classes whose insecure social status drives him to select victims from the group that excludes or oppresses him. There is often only a small but crucial difference in status between the killer and his victims, who represent the rung that is just out of reach. The killer's career becomes "a kind of personal and primitive class war."[25]

Although his focus seems somewhat selective, Leyton's approach is noteworthy for centering on class rather than sexual motivations, and it applies remarkably well to some of the most notorious modern multiple murderers (e.g., David Berkowitz, Ted Bundy, Albert DeSalvo, Edward Kemper, Charlie Starkweather). It could justly be said that class, even more than sex, is the Great Repressed in American culture. America's cherished credos of individualism and economic mobility have made its less "successful" individuals especially vulnerable to expressions of frustration through violence.[26] Leyton, like the political scientist James Chowning Davies, sees the upheavals of the 1960s as reflecting increased tensions between aroused expectations and the failure to achieve them.[27] The rise of class-conscious multiple murderers is just one statistically small but mythically potent manifestation of those tensions.

More so than other films on the subject, *The Honeymoon Killers et al.* embody the general issues described by Leyton. With the notable exception of *Henry: Portrait of a Serial Killer,* they tend to play down sexual factors in favor of social factors. In comparison with compulsive-killer films from *M* to *The Silence of Lambs, The Honeymoon Killers et al.* contain relatively few instances of sadistic rape or murder. To an even greater extent than Leyton describes, the criminals in these films are more concerned with status than sex. They tend to be highly conscious of their excluded status, which they acknowledge with a derisive irony that can be literally devastating. Ray and Martha's sorry attempt to blend into suburbia in *The Honeymoon Killers* has already been noted. In *The Boys Next Door,* when Bo expresses mild regret over a sweet-faced teenage girl Roy has just blasted into oblivion, Roy sourly ripostes, "What were you going to do—ask her out?" In a similar vein, when the fugitives' car breaks down in *Murder One,* one of them asks, "What the hell are we supposed to do—wait for Triple A?" (Instead, they kill a passing motorist and take his car.) In *Henry: Portrait of a Serial Killer,* the Chicago-based Henry is accosted with the civic watchword, "How 'bout those Bears?" "Fuck the Bears," Henry growls. In *Badlands,* most of the irony is supplied by the spectator rather than by the criminal couple, who clumsily mimic the values of the status group to which they aspire.

In addition, these films define the murderers' social status more narrowly than Leyton does. The murderers in *The Honeymoon Killers et al.* could nearly all be categorized under the heading of "white trash." Interestingly, this is the same group that has traditionally borne the brunt of "establishment violence" in American history, going back to the vigilante committees of the Old West and various "citizens' groups" like the Ku Klux Klan.[28] To a certain extent, this pattern represents a classic ideological inversion: the victimized group is perceived as the victimizer, and vice versa.

ORCHIDS AND WEEDS

The Silence of the Lambs points to an additional crucial difference between *The Honeymoon Killers et al.* and other films dealing with modern multiple murder. Although *Lambs* is conscientiously revisionist in its enlightened treatment of the heroine and its restrained presentation of violence, it is more conventional in the mystification and extravagance that characterize the depiction of its two multiple murderers. Lecter and Gumb are loaded with gimmicks, gothicisms, and colorful psychological quirks. Gumb is not only a cross dresser but also a dungeon master, skinner, seamster, rhymester, breeder of exotic Asian moths, and headline-grabbing serial killer with a modus operandi almost as cluttered as the decor of his hillbilly-gothic domicile. Lecter is a Nietzschean anthropophagus, psychiatrist, and psychopath, as well as a talented amateur painter, virtual telepathist, Mabuse-like manipulator, and Houdini-class escape artist. His first appearance—set in a dungeon bathed in lurid red light and resounding with ominous machine-hums—is given a portentous build-up worthy of the white whale in *Moby Dick* or the mother ship in *Close Encounters of the Third Kind* (1977). Like most films on the subject, *The Silence of the Lambs* cultivates the exotic orchids of psychokillerdom; *The Honeymoon Killers et al.* confine themselves to the weeds.

No representation of a crime is entirely innocent. The concept of criminality is important in drawing the boundaries of a social order and its concepts of normality. In *Discipline and Punish,* his masterful analysis of the evolution of modern penology and criminology, Michel Foucault points out how the criminal class serves a very useful function in the constitution of the authority structure of a society, for instance, by co-opting potentially more disruptive forms of illegality, and by justifying the use of policing apparatuses with broad political applications.[29]

In many recent cop-avenger and psychokiller films, the extraordinary nature of the multiple murderer necessitates extraordinary law enforcement figures to contain him. The "superpsycho" and the "supercop" become two sides of the same coin. Although *The Silence of the Lambs* takes an unusually sophisticated approach to these issues, it is a variation rather than an alternative to the pattern. It presents a fallible and demystified law enforcement figure as the protagonist, but behind her stands a law enforcement agency that contains many of the characteristics excluded so carefully from the heroine. *The Silence of the Lambs* balances its superpsychos not with supercops but with a super institution: the FBI, depicted as an organization of dedicated professionals with a quietly overwhelming arsenal of high-tech communications, octopus-like aerial connections, and elaborate profiling and surveillance systems. These types of weapons easily can be turned to other, less commendable, more covert and political uses (and, in the FBI's history, often have been). Whatever the intentions of its makers may have been, *The Silence of the Lambs,* by trafficking in super criminals and super organizations, opens a Pandora's box of exalted institutional power that other elements in the film do not sufficiently counteract.

One of the most admirable qualities of *The Honeymoon Killers et al.* is the way they demystify rather than exoticize the mythically loaded figure of the modern multiple murderer.[30] The gothicism that surrounds other screen psychos is either heavily downplayed or uncomfortably complicated in these films. As suggested earlier, an especially disturbing set of implications arising from modern multiple murder emphasizes not exoticism and classification but ordinariness and decategorization. *The Honeymoon Killers et al.* have tended to maximize such implications.

In various ways and to varying degrees, these five films have demonstrated uncommon and often unexpected stylistic integrity through their cultivation of unresolved tensions and contradictions, their elusiveness of genre, their departures from conventional schemes of expressiveness and identification, and their somewhat paradoxical mix of austere stylistics and lurid subject matter. These strategies have enabled *The Honeymoon Killers et al.* to infiltrate the type of inherently difficult material easily diluted by more mainstream approaches. The films' oblique, unstable perspective has also brought out with unusual vividness some of the historical patterns and underlying issues that have converged around the figure of the multiple murderer. These include the suppression of class in American ideology, the power relations involved in labeling and representing criminality, the interrelated roles of devalued (anti-establishment) and hidden (establishment) violence in American history, and the disavowal of internalized conflict in consensus politics.

The Honeymoon Killers, as the first in this small but potent group of films, appeared at the end of the 1960s, when the centrist consensus was in crisis and the era of overtly ideological violence hit a brick wall of political reaction. Operating from their position on the margins, opportunistically straddling borderlines and slipping from one side to another, these films touch upon stress points and contradictions in the maintenance of the American Dream that have become especially strained in the post-1960s era. Through their negativity and stylistic dysphasia, they indicate spots where such contradictions become unspeakable, producing unspeakable acts and signaling the unspeakability of certain concepts that represent gaps in American ideology: the concept of conflict in a "consensus" society, of exclusion in a "pluralistic" society, of class in a "classless" society, of failure in a "land of opportunity." In *The Honeymoon Killers et al.,* some of these submerged tensions are brought to the surface and spewed back in an especially violent, disturbing, and revolting (but not revolutionary) form.

These bleak, nasty little films have preferred not to join in our current version of the "era of good feeling," serving instead to keep alive an endangered spirit of negation. Their stunted, visceral nihilism has certain affinities to the punk movement, and, like punk, they represent a limited (though demonstrative) response to social frustration. But, as we drift through the superficially placid doldrums of recent American history, with repression and complacency ascendant on the right, left, and center, such gray continuations of the grand American tradition of nay-saying blackness seem more valuable than ever. "For all men who say yes, lie," said Herman Melville. Just say no.

Notes

1. Quoted in Vincent Bugliosi with Curt Gentry, *Helter Skelter: The True Story of the Manson Murders* (New York: W. W. Norton, 1974; paperback ed., Toronto: Bantam, 1975), 155.

2. Sanford Budick and Wolfgang Iser, *Languages of the Unsayable: The Play of Negativity in Literature and Literary Theory* (New York: Columbia University Press, 1989), xii–xiii, xv.

3. Some terminological distinctions: "Serial murder" refers to a series of compulsive but furtive homicides committed periodically over a long stretch of time—Albert DeSalvo (the "Boston Strangler"), Ted Bundy, and Jeffrey Dahmer

are well-known examples. "Mass murder" denotes a blatant, often suicidal outburst in which many lives are taken on one occasion (e.g., Charles Whitman, the Texas tower killer; George Hennard, the Luby's Cafeteria killer). A variation is the "spree killing," in which a murderous rampage extends sporadically for a period ranging from several hours to several days, without the overtly suicidal, "last-stand" qualities of the mass murder (e.g., the Starkweather/Fugate spree of 1958). Another variation is the "family killing," in which the murderer's violence is directed primarily against members of his own family (e.g., James Ruppert, perpetrator of the 1975 "Easter Sunday Massacre" in Hamilton, Ohio). For the sake of regularization, I am using the term "modern multiple murder" to refer to all of these types collectively—a usage borrowed from Elliot Leyton's *Compulsive Killers: The Story of Modern Multiple Murder.*

4. See, for example, Ronald M. Holmes and James De Burger, *Serial Murder,* (Newbury Park: Sage, 1988), 24, 36; Jack Katz, *Seductions of Crime* (New York: Basic, 1988), 288; John M. Macdonald, *The Murderer and His Victim,* 2d ed. (Springfield: Charles C. Thomas, 1986), 106; Gwynn Nettler, *Killing One Another,* vol. 2: *Criminal Careers* (Cincinnati: Anderson, 1982), 187; Joel Norris, *Serial Killers* (New York: Doubleday, 1988), 16; Colin Wilson and Donald Seaman, *The Serial Killers: A Study in the Psychology of Violence* (New York: Carol, 1990), 10–15.

5. For example, some notable cases of multiple murder (Gary Gilmore; Dick Hickock and Perry Smith) were committed in the course of robberies. In many other cases, motives of deviant sexuality and displaced personal vengeance are all too apparent.

6. Jack Levin and James Alan Fox, *Mass Murder: America's Growing Menace* (New York: Plenum, 1985; paperback ed., New York: Berkeley, 1991), 14; Donald T. Lunde, *Murder and Madness* (San Francisco Book Co., 1976), 69; John Godwin, *Murder U.S.A.: The Ways We Kill Each Other* (New York: Ballantine, 1978), 36.

7. Godwin, *Murder U.S.A.,* 36; Leyton, *Compulsive Killers,* 152, 39. The contrast between the modern multiple murderer and the traditional compulsive killer is sometimes represented within a single work—notably, the pairing of Perry Smith (traditional compulsive killer) and Dick Hickock (modern multiple murderer) in *In Cold Blood. The Silence of the Lambs* presents a similar (though not quite as pure) contrast between Jamie Gumb (traditional) and Hannibal Lecter (modern).

8. Martin Scorsese, the initial director of *The Honeymoon Killers,* was removed after a week's shooting. The film was completed by Leonard Kastle, who had written the screenplay. As far as I can determine, *The Honeymoon Killers* represents Kastle's only screen credit. The rest of his artistic activity has been in the field of musical composition, including songs, orchestral works, and two full-scale operas. Kastle also has a strong interest in Herman Melville; he has orchestrated a Melville poem, written an opera (*The Pariahs*) with a Melvillesque whaling subject, and owned a dog named "Moby Dick."

9. The term "psychopath" refers to a general inability on the part of a deviant/criminal/murderer to experience "normal" feelings of empathy and remorse. John Godwin describes the condition as "a lobotomy of the moral sense" (*Murder U.S.A.,* 300). The equivalent term "sociopath" has become more fashionable in recent years. This is because many professionals in the field are committed to a termino-

logical tightrope-walk in which they must maintain that most multiple murderers are emotionally dysfunctional but nevertheless legally sane. "Psychopathic" sounds too much like "psychotic" and so threatens that fine but all-important distinction. As Levin and Fox write in *Mass Murder,* "The sociopath is bad not mad, crafty not crazy" (xxiv). Some writers have questioned the entire concept of psychopathy as an example of interest-serving categorization (or "labeling," as it is commonly termed in criminology and other branches of deviance study). For an acerbic overview of this issue, see Michael Hakeem, "The Assumption That Crime Is a Product of Individual Characteristics: A Prime Example from Psychiatry," in *Theoretical Methods in Criminology,* ed. Robert F. Meier (Beverly Hills: Sage, 1985), 197–221.

10. *Badlands* is based on the highly publicized 1958 Nebraska murder spree of Charlie Starkweather and Caril Fugate, *Murder One* on a less widely known spree that panicked Georgia in 1973, and *Henry: Portrait of a Serial Killer* on the career of prolific murderer Henry Lee Lucas. *The Boys Next Door* is the only one of the group without a specific factual prototype. To compensate, it begins with the most elaborate of these fact-invoking prefaces, featuring a roll call of infamous multiple murderers.

11. Not surprisingly, the two best-received films in the batch are those which dilute this aspect the most. In *Badlands,* Spacek's voice-over is allowed to dominate the film too much, placing the spectator in a sustained position of dramatic irony. Though similar in some respects, the sparer narration of Billy in *Murder One* is more effectively disorienting, serving as an intermittent inflection rather than to set a consistent tone. *Henry: Portrait of a Serial Killer* is simplified by the monolithic presentation of Henry himself. He is easily the most awesome of these protagonists, at times approaching the superhuman stature of such bogeymen as Jason Voorhees (*Friday the 13th*) and Michael Myers (*Halloween*). The results are too much like a typical slasher movie; the film does not establish enough distance between Henry's power and its own fascination with that power.

12. Budick and Iser, *Languages of the Unsayable,* xi–xxi.

13. Examples include: Richard Maxwell Brown, ed., *American Violence* (Englewood Cliffs, N.J.: Prentice-Hall, 1970); Richard Maxwell Brown, *Strain of Violence: Historical Studies of American Violence and Vigilantism* (New York: Oxford University Press, 1975); Hugh Davis Graham and Ted Robert Gurr, eds., *Violence in America: Historical and Comparative Perspectives: A Report to the National Commission on the Causes and Prevention of Violence,* 2 vols. (Washington: Government Printing Office, 1969; rev. ed., Beverly Hills: Sage, 1979); Hugh Davis Graham, *Violence: The Crisis of American Confidence* (Baltimore: Johns Hopkins University Press, 1971); Ted Robert Gurr, *Why Men Rebel* (Princeton: Princeton University Press, 1970); Richard Hofstadter and Michael Wallace, eds., *American Violence: A Documentary History* (New York: Knopf, 1970; Vintage, 1971); Lynne B. Iglitzin, *Violent Conflict in American Society* (San Francisco: Chandler, 1972); Richard E. Rubinstein, *Rebels in Eden: Mass Political Violence in the United States* (Boston: Little, Brown, 1970); Thomas Rose, ed., *Violence in America* (New York: Vintage, 1970); Arthur Schlesinger, Jr., *Violence: America in the Sixties* (New York: NAL, 1968); Michael Wallace, "The Uses of Violence in American History," *The*

American Scholar 41 (Winter 1970–71): 81–102. The Graham and Gurr anthology is especially useful.

14. J. Bowyer Bell and Ted Robert Gurr, "Terrorism and Revolution in America," in *Violence in America: Historical and Comparative Perspectives,* 333, 343; Richard Maxwell Brown, "Historical Patterns of American Violence," in ibid., 20; Hugh Davis Graham, "The Paradox of American Violence," in ibid., 482–85; Richard Hofstadter, "Reflections on Violence in the United States," in *American Violence,* 3–11, 30, 37–39; Iglitzin, *Violent Conflict in American Society,* 1–2; Richard E. Libman-Rubinstein, "Group Violence in America: Its Structure and Limitations," in *Violence in America: Historical and Comparative Perspectives,* 442–47; Rose, *Violence in America,* xix–xx; Bernard Sternsher, *Consensus, Conflict, and American Historians* (Bloomington: Indiana University Press, 1973), 216–18.

15. Richard Maxwell Brown, "The American Vigilante Tradition," in *Violence in America: Historical and Comparative Perspectives,* 174; Brown, "Historical Patterns," 31; Graham, 482; Hofstadter, 20.

16. Graham, 475.

17. Hofstadter, 10–11.

18. Graham, 483–85; Hofstadter, 13; Libman-Rubinstein, "Group Violence in America," 445, 449.

19. Bell and Gurr, "Terrorism and Revolution in America," 345.

20. Graham, 476; Iglitzin, *Violent Conflict in American Society,* 1; Libman-Rubinstein, "Group Violence in America," 437; Rose, *Violence in America,* xx.

21. Key works in this diverse movement include Daniel J. Boorstin, *The Genius of American Politics* (Chicago: University of Chicago Press, 1953); Louis Hartz, *The Liberal Tradition in America: An Interpretation of American Political Thought since the Revolution* (New York: Harcourt, Brace, 1955); Talcott Parsons, *The Social System* (New York: Free Press, 1951); David M. Potter, *People of Plenty: Economic Abundance and the American Character* (Chicago: University of Chicago Press, 1954).

22. Daniel Bell, *The End of Ideology: On the Exhaustion of Political Ideas in the Fifties* (New York: Free Press, 1960).

23. Brown, "Historical Patterns," 28.

24. Virtually all writers on the subject see modern multiple murder as an overwhelmingly (though not exclusively) American phenomenon.

25. Leyton, *Compulsive Killers,* 23–31, 137.

26. Deborah Cameron and Elizabeth Frazer, *The Lust to Kill: A Feminist Investigation of Sexual Murder* (New York: New York University Press, 1987), 159; Graham, 480–81; Nettler, *Killing One Another,* 273–79.

27. Leyton, *Compulsive Killers,* 286. Davies, in his book *When Men Revolt and Why* (New York: Free Press, 1971), formulated the well-known "J-curve" theory, which states that social upheaval is most likely to occur when a prolonged period of rising expectations is followed by a sharp reversal.

28. As Richard Maxwell Brown points out, it was poor whites, rather than blacks and other racial minorities, who were the primary targets of these groups (even the KKK). Brown, "The American Vigilante Tradition," 159–61; Brown, "Historical Patterns," 35.

29. Michel Foucault, *Discipline and Punish: The Birth of the Prison,* trans. Alan Sheridan (New York: Vintage, 1979), 271–92.

30. Even Henry, although given some questionably superhuman aspects, is for the most part resoundingly banal. His modus operandi, philosophy, and wardrobe are all quite perfunctory in comparison with those of Gumb and Lecter.

3

SERIAL KILLERS, TRUE CRIME, AND ECONOMIC PERFORMANCE ANXIETY

ANNALEE NEWITZ

Torture. Dismemberment. Rape. Cannibalism. Incest. Murder. His crimes make Ted Bundy and Charles Manson sound like choirboys! . . . Complete with never before published photos including artwork by Lucas himself!
—*from a blurb on* Henry Lee Lucas: A Biography of the Serial Killer, *by Joel Norris*

For Americans, serial killers like Henry Lee Lucas and Ted Bundy are media celebrities. This is so widely known, and so generally condemned, that Oliver Stone recently made an entire movie, *Natural Born Killers* (1994), based on the critique of serial killer celebrity. Like Norman Mailer's 1979 "true life novel" *The Executioner's Song,* *Natural Born Killers* focuses—often ironically—on the promotion and popularization of charismatic young Americans who murder people and commit other violent crimes. For Mailer and Stone, the murderers themselves are less problematic than the media industry which makes them famous: Stone ends his film with Mickey (one of the killers) telling a tabloid TV reporter that the reporter is the morally bereft "Frankenstein" who made him possible in the first place. Mickey and his wife Mallory then shoot the reporter, filming it all on a portable TV camera.

In movies like *Natural Born Killers,* Americans look critically at their pleasure in murder as much as they celebrate murder itself. One might make a similar observation about the obsession with O. J. Simpson's murder trial. Although the trial consistently made front page news, op-ed pieces—and even feature stories—blasted Americans for "sinking to a new low" in their love of exploitation and sensationalism. One might say that there is often something like social criticism going on when Americans consume stories about murder. This social criticism

65

has a specific historical context: serial killers and stories about them are associated with the period beginning roughly near the end of the 1950s.[1] What might the culture and society of post-1950s America have to do with the eruption of a new kind of homicidal pathology? And what exactly is it about the narratives of serial killers which makes them so seductive, particularly when their seductiveness is so easily and quickly criticized? I suggest that the serial killer—in both allegory and reality—acts out the enraged confusion with which Americans have come to regard their postwar economic and social productivity.

TRUE CRIME

Hitchcock's film *Psycho* (1960) is often cited as the original serial killer narrative, which spawned an entire genre of serial killer or "slasher" films popular throughout the 1970s, 1980s, and 1990s.[2] However, the film *Psycho* is itself based upon an original narrative, the life story of Ed Gein,[3] who in 1957 was discovered to have killed and ritualistically mutilated two elderly women who reminded him of his dead mother. Gein, like *Psycho*'s Norman Bates, was a seemingly ordinary and shy man who lived an isolated life in a rural American town. While Hitchcock's shocking ending to *Psycho* introduced Americans to cross-dressing, Gein had already done Hitchcock one better in the shock department. Rather than dressing up in his mother's clothing, he dressed up in her cured and preserved skin. Decades later, audiences finally got treated to a dose of Gein's "true" crimes in *The Silence of the Lambs,* which won awards for best picture, best actor (Anthony Hopkins), best actress (Jodie Foster), and best director (Jonathan Demme) at the 1991 Academy Awards. In homage to both *Psycho* and Gein, Demme directed a film about a serial killer who wears the skins of his female victims. It was at this moment— when the cinematic serial killer's crimes were at their most shocking and "true"—that the serial killer achieved the status of allegorical figure in what powerful cultural institutions like the Motion Picture Academy name "art."

Because fictional representations of serial killers are often based on the biographies of actual killers, one might say the serial-killer narrative spans the genres of both fiction and nonfiction. Biographical portraits of famous serial killers are available to consumers of the popular genre known as "true crime." Interestingly enough, bookstores often place the true-crime books next to the sociology books.[4] True crime seems to consider itself the nonfictional counterpart—and theory of— fictional narratives about crime and criminality. Criminological and

The serial killer narrative as social allegory: *The Silence of the Lambs* (Orion Pictures, 1990).

true-crime accounts of serial killers agree on the demographics and personality characteristics of serial killers. Joel Norris, a psychobiologist and author of many true-crime accounts of serial murder, writes in his trade paperback *Serial Killers* that most serial killers are white men under forty.[5] His point is reiterated in a scholarly textbook on the topic, Eric W. Hickey's *Serial Murderers and Their Victims.* Hickey notes that "in this study, males were responsible for 88% of all serial murder cases . . . male offenders tended to be in their late 20s . . . 85% of male offenders were white."[6] A great deal of overlap exists between popular true crime, and what might be called authentic criminology. Indeed, Hickey introduces his book by acknowledging the contributions true-crime authors such as Ann Rule (a former police officer) have made in his field.

True-crime authors and criminologists postulate that serial killers' psychopathology allows them to function "normally" in most situations; many are able to hide their periodic moments of homicidal psychosis. Most are drifters who commit similar crimes in a number of regions over a period of time. The most noteworthy and characteristic aspect of serial killing is the relative randomness of the victims. Serial killers are rarely acquainted with the people they kill, and for this reason serial killings are sometimes called "stranger murders."[7] Serial killers are also known as "recreational killers" or "lust killers,"[8] indicating the degree to which their acts are associated with the pursuit of leisure and sexual desire. Often in true-crime books we find a kind of self-reflexive cultural analysis of American masculine identity gone awry.

Masculinity, as Lynne Segal has observed, is an identity constituted by a reaction against what is perceived to be "feminine" or "other" in human beings. That is, for a man to identify himself as masculine, there must exist a series of identities which he refuses to claim as his own. He projects these identities onto subordinated "others," which in an American context are most often women, children, and ethnic or sexual minority groups. The "other" is generally associated with vulnerability, passivity, domesticity, and emotionality, while the man is free of them. "No one can be [masculine] without constantly doing violence to many of the most basic human attributes," Segal writes.[9] To maintain his identity, in other words, he must commit a kind of psychic violence to himself; he excises and disavows a portion of his feelings and social experiences. One can see where this feminist analysis of serial killing might go: the serial killer kills off the "feminine vulnerability" in himself when he kills women, and thus proves himself a man. While this reading is a good start, both true-crime literature and its subjects are more complex than that— men sometimes kill other men, and women sometimes do the killing themselves. While clearly there is a deep connection between cultural constructions of masculinity and serial murder—as true-crime authors almost unanimously acknowledge—it may not be enough to understand this kind of violence simply in terms of gendered hierarchies.

As Mark Seltzer points out in his discussion of serialized violence, masculinity is also associated with dominant modes of economic production and reproduction.[10] Seltzer draws a connection between repetitive male violence and "machine culture," which he links to the bureaucracies of industrialized mass production and information processing. In other words, he offers us a way of understanding masculine violence in terms of the kind of work men do in a bureaucratic capitalist culture. This work is repetitious, blurs the boundaries between what is natural and artificial, and takes place in a consumer-oriented economy. Seltzer's analysis suggests that serialized violence may be a social corollary to working conditions under consumer capitalism. Indeed, the American "ideal" of masculinity is based as much upon what it means to be economically productive as it is upon a repudiation of femininity. The man who makes a great deal of money is seen as more potent, more masculine than the man who, for example, teaches writing and composition for a living.

Keeping this in mind, I want to take a look at what Ted Bundy referred to in a series of interviews as his "professional job,"[11] kidnapping, raping, and murdering women. Bundy's effort to achieve "normal" masculinity was profoundly dependent upon his sense of himself as a successful worker. Ann Rule, his former colleague and biographer, reports that during the time he was murdering women in Colorado, Utah, and Seattle, Bundy was pursuing—rather successfully—a career in law and politics. He volunteered with the Republican party, served on various local committees for the prevention of violent crimes, and matriculated as a law student at the University of Utah. With a bachelor's degree in psychology, he also did a good deal of social work, such as volunteering with Rule at a suicide-prevention hotline in Seattle. His background, as Rule puts it, was "stultifyingly middle-class,"[12] and Bundy was ambitiously pursuing both economic and social upward mobility.

In her biography of Bundy, *The Stranger Beside Me,* Rule is explicit about the relationship between Bundy's crimes and his desire to be upper class. His victims resembled each other quite closely: all were conventionally beautiful and "feminine," all had long hair parted in the middle, and all of them tended to be middle- to upper-middle-class. His final killing spree in Tallahassee, Florida, took place in a prestigious sorority house, a virtual factory for the production of upwardly mobile women. Moreover, Rule and other commentators on Bundy's crimes have noted that Bundy began killing women shortly after being rejected by Stephanie Brooks, a wealthy woman he dated for a year in college, who wore her long dark hair parted in the middle. Rule believes that Bundy felt Brooks "outclassed him,"[13] and his subsequent murders of women who resembled her would seem to indicate that his victims were chosen not just for their gendered characteristics, but for their apparent class backgrounds as well. One might say that Bundy, rather than "marrying up," killed "up."

Ultimately, Bundy's crimes got him the best job of his law career: his own case. When on trial in Colorado and Florida, Bundy acted as his own defense attorney and spent vast amounts of time and energy in law libraries working on his own defense. His state-appointed lawyers served as "counsel" for the most part, and Bundy became famous for discrediting his attorneys, asking that the state reassign him different ones, and generally making a nuisance of himself in court and out with his requests for special treatment and delays. At one point during his Florida trial, he was witness, defendant, and defense attorney all at once. Of course, Bundy was not the only one making a career out of his murders. Rule herself, a single mother of four trying to make ends meet on a police officer's salary and the money she got writing articles for true-crime magazines, got her first big break when she realized that she was acquainted with Ted Bundy from their work at the suicide-prevention hotline. Because she knew him, Rule was able to scoop the story and get exclusive interviews with the recently apprehended killer. One of the most fascinating aspects of *The Stranger Beside Me* is Rule's personal story of her growing fame and success as she writes the book. Her concerns about money, writing, and raising her family are interwoven with Bundy's life story, which often echoes—perversely—her own. Both Bundy and Rule desired professional success, and both used crime to get it.

HOMO ECONOMICUS

Economic identity, especially after World War II, is associated with the ability to produce efficiently, but more notably with the ability to consume. Juliet Schor describes what economists of this period dub "homo economicus," or economic man:

> The most important personality trait of homo economicus is that he can never be satiated. He will always prefer more to less. Although he can become tired of any particular good, there is never a point at which having more goods overall will make him worse off. And because more will always make him better off, his desires are infinite.[14]

His desire is to consume infinitely, and, as a result, he must work infinitely as well. Indeed, the premise of Schor's book *The Overworked American* is precisely that homo economicus must essentially become a workaholic in order to support his consumer habits. Serial killers, in real life and in Hollywood, often seem trapped in what Schor calls the "treadmill" effect of consumer capitalism, where the American Dream is dominated by a frantic desire to work hard enough to maintain it. For these serial killers, the act of murder stands in for their inability to stop working and consuming. They kill after reaching a point where they begin to confuse living people with the inanimate objects they produce and consume as workers.

Tim Cahill named his biography of serial killer John Wayne Gacy *Buried Dreams* in ironic reference to the American Dream of prosperity and political success for which Gacy longed. Gacy had nearly achieved that success when he was caught; he had even had his picture taken with then-First Lady Rosalyn Carter after he organized a large civic parade. Cahill repeatedly calls Gacy a workaholic, and Gacy's criminal acts did indeed become notorious because they appeared to proceed directly from the kind of work—contracting—he did for a living. When Gacy was finally arrested, he gave a series of voluntary statements about his crimes. He admitted to killing over thirty boys and claimed that many were buried in the crawl space under his home. Later, Gacy drew a concise map of where each of the graves was located. They had been laid out with the precision of a contractor, in such a way as to conserve space and utilize every foot of the crawl space available. Gacy had a tendency to kill his young employees; they had often been told to dig trenches in his crawl space for "laying pipes," which led to reports about how Gacy had his victims dig their own graves. Gacy, one might say, did not always make a distinction between people and commodities. He used his skills as a contractor both to produce buildings and to dispose of dead bodies in a systematic way. The dead bodies produced by his criminal acts were literally *built into* the structure of the house he had produced while working as a contractor.

Jeffrey Dahmer, another notorious serial killer, seemed to see little difference between the men he murdered and the kind of work he did at a chocolate factory. Dahmer's modus operandi was to kill men in his apartment, dismember them, and dissolve their body parts in a fifty-gallon drum of acid he kept for that purpose. He occasionally ate parts of his victims' bodies. At work, Dahmer stirred liquid chocolate in large drums. Essentially, Dahmer was treating his victims just as he treated the commodity he produced at the chocolate factory: sometimes he

71

stirred them into large drums of liquid, and sometimes he ate them.[15] But Dahmer, as his biographer Don Davis explains, was an utter failure as a worker; although his family was middle-class, Dahmer himself was downwardly mobile. He went from the army to factory jobs in Milwaukee. Interestingly, Davis draws a parallel between the economic depression in Dahmer's birthplace of Akron, Ohio, to Dahmer's own social alienation and emotional depression. He writes, "In the same way that Akron cannot keep its young [workers], Jeffrey Dahmer had a hard time keeping friends."[16] Just as we find a correspondence between Gacy's overwork and murder, we also find an inverse one between Dahmer's underemployment and murder. Ultimately, what matters here is that true-crime biographers frequently link serial murder to economic conditions no matter what those conditions might be.

Dahmer once stated that part of what motivated his homicidal behavior was a fear of abandonment. This fear of abandonment is usually associated with interpersonal relationships, but it can also relate to the economic relationship between workers and commodities. In a capitalist culture, the commodity is an object that appears to abandon the workers who make it. Marx has called this process "alienation": workers find themselves alienated from what they produce because they do not own the means of production, nor do they own the products of their labor.[17] Therefore, it would appear that the mass production of commodities is a kind of mass abandonment, for nothing that workers create while on the job belongs properly to them—they cannot keep what they make.

We can see the logic of alienation at work in the biography of Henry Lee Lucas. Lucas, a drifter famous for killing hundreds of people in the South, reported to biographer Joel Norris that the abuse he suffered as a child gave him the sense that he was essentially alienated from his own life because he had never felt he owned or loved anything. He said:

> I was worth nothing. Everything I had was destroyed. My mother, if I had a pony she'd kill it. . . . She wouldn't allow me to love nothin'. . . . She wanted me to do what she said and that's it. That is, make sure the wood is in, the water's in, make sure the fires are kept up. . . . Work! That's it![18]

Here Lucas connects his sense that he was deprived of emotional sustenance to his having to perform endless work for his mother in their rural home. Lucas was experiencing a version of alienated labor, although his position as a child in his mother's home would have made his situation more psychologically traumatic. Indeed, because his mother worked at home as a prostitute, one might say that Lucas never learned to distinguish between emotional alienation and economic alienation. His mother was a commodity (she sold her body for money) and also an abusive, neglectful parent. He later murdered her. For Lucas, then, people and commodities were intertwined sources of pain and alienation.

Karl Marx referred to capital as "dead labor" in order to metaphorically represent how value is produced and measured in a commodity culture. This metaphor is useful here as well, for it serves to define the performance of economic and psychological identity we find in the serial killer's repeated acts of murder. Marx writes that "Capital is dead labor. . . . The time during which the laborer works, is the time during which the capitalist consumes the labor-power he has purchased of him. If the laborer consumes his disposable time for himself, he robs the capitalist."[19] Capital is "dead labor" because it is the index by which the worker's value is measured and consumed by a capitalist employer over time. When a person is working, he is experiencing what might be called "dead time" because at work, the worker belongs to his employer, the capitalist. His work time is dead for him. Moreover, what he produces at work is also dead to him, because he does not own it. Ultimately, the worker experiences himself as "dead" while working, for nothing he does at work enriches his life in any way. However, he does gain his salary, which is paid to him in money—he is therefore rewarded economically for being "dead." His worth as a human being is measured for him in terms of how long he is willing to perform his "dead labor" to get money. Marx continues his analysis by pointing out that the worker in capitalism is just another commodity which can be purchased and used. He is—figuratively—merely an object among objects, rather than a subject with agency and self-determination. One might say that the message capitalism sends to workers is this: The longer you stay dead, the more you'll get paid. And, as a corollary: the more death you make, the more you'll be paid as well.

One of the basic and painful contradictions a worker must face is that his source of social power is also the source of his degradation as a subject. That is, his work may give him power, but the price he pays is the "death" of his subjectivity, or various parts of his subjectivity over time. When this contradiction becomes too much for him to bear, he may develop a psychopathology which compels him to literalize Marx's metaphoric notion of "dead labor" by killing people who represent it. Murder is, for these men, a way of projecting onto others the destructive feelings inspired in the workplace. This logic is particularly clear in Gacy's case, as he converted his employees (dead labor) into dead people. Dahmer and Lucas, on the other hand, killed and consumed people as if they were commodities. Indeed, Lucas felt he could only possess and love people if they were dead; he reported to Norris that most of the sex he had was with the bodies of women he had killed.

But as the epithet "recreational killer" suggests, serial killing is supposed to take place outside the realm of work, during leisure or family time. Henri Lefebvre theorized that as bourgeois society developed, work became more rigidly delineated from leisure at the same time that it also became segregated from family life. Hence, Lefebvre, notes, "family life became separate from productive activity. And so did leisure."[20] If we consider serial killing a pathological form of recreation, it is logical that we might find serial killing also represented as a pathological extension of family relations. Narratives that portray fathers, mothers, and even children as serial killers are quite common (for example, *The Bad Seed, The Other*). When seemingly ordinary fathers become serial killers, their pathological transformation is often caused by their discovery that family life is as difficult and demanding as work.[21] Lefebvre's contention that capitalism sets up families and leisure in opposition to labor helps explain why a man who wishes to escape from work might hope to find a safe haven in his family. What seems to convert these fathers into murderers is the realization that work does not end when they come home to their wives and children.

The Stepfather (1987), a "sleeper" horror film followed by two sequels, demonstrates the congruence between fatherhood and work, as well as one man's unsuccessful effort to escape both. The movie opens with Jerry, the serial killer, altering his appearance and identity after having brutally murdered his family. Jerry is, we discover, not just a serial killer, but a serial father. His modus operandi is to move from family to family, marrying women with children, all of whom he kills once they "disappoint" him. Jerry facilitates his movement from one family to the next by quitting his job and getting a new one somewhere else; hence, he murders the family he is leaving behind only after he is sure he will be employed afterward. His ability to repeatedly murder his family is, in other words, contingent upon his ability to find work in a place far enough away from the scene of his crime that he will not easily be noticed.

Having gotten a job as a real estate agent, Jerry quickly ingratiates himself with a new family. Once this occurs, we see Jerry and his new family almost entirely from the point of view of his teenage stepdaughter, Stephanie. Stephanie seems to sense that Jerry is dangerous, particularly because she sees him fly into a violent rage, throwing his carpentry tools around and talking to himself when he believes no one is watching. Jerry is equally suspicious of Stephanie. Her problems at school force him to confront the fact that his family is not perfect, although he continues to pretend it is. When Stephanie is expelled for starting a fight with another student in art class, Jerry insists that "girls don't get expelled." Later, he nearly beats up Stephanie's boyfriend when the boyfriend kisses her goodnight, insisting that the young man is "trying to rape her." His alternately dismissive and aggressive responses to Stephanie finally alarm her mother, who yells at him for not making an effort to talk to her first about how to raise Stephanie. It is at this point that his new family becomes too much work for Jerry. In response to his wife's desire to discuss their family, he says menacingly, "I'm taking care of it." His wife asks, "By yourself?" Jerry nods. This response is key to understanding Jerry's murders in the context of American economic identity, which is deeply connected to a "do it yourself" ethos.

At a company barbecue, Jerry says to his fellow real estate agents, "I truly believe that what I sell is the American Dream." Part of the American Dream, of course, is individualism. At work, Jerry is able to be the ultimate autonomous individual; even as he plots to kill his present family, the free market always provides him with an opportunity to rebuild himself, get a new identity, and find a new place to raise a family. That is, the free market is what allows Jerry to individuate himself from his family before he murders them. His comment to his wife about how he can fix their family "by himself" tips us off to his main problem with family life. Family life is work that relies upon social interdependence, rather than individualism. As much as he desires family life—he returns to it again and again—his training as an individual in the free market makes it impossible for him to perform his work in the home.

But why is the father's rejection of family life represented with such brutal violence in serial killer narratives? Charles Derber, referring to the Menendez brothers, famous for murdering their millionaire parents, concludes that their "pathology was that they allowed themselves to be socialized so completely." For Derber, the Menendez brothers are a version of Jerry—their act of violence was a logical extension of the behavior they observed growing up in a family which valued making money above all else.[22] In other words, the problem with the Menendez family—and Jerry's failure as a father—might be that ideals of the marketplace have fully invaded the home. Rules intended to regulate economic exchange serve instead to regulate socialization within the family. For example, the individual who must aggressively compete with other individuals "works" within the economic sphere, but within the domestic sphere this ruthless pursuit of autonomy and promotion disrupts family work. Violence erupts in the serial killer narrative when family life tends to resist complete assimilation into economic life; a character like Jerry exhibits murderous violence when he must compromise his status as an autonomous individual. In attempting to organize the family by economic principles, he is left with seemingly no choice but to destroy it entirely and move on to the next one.

Photographic Production

Describing how the term "serial killer" originated to categorize people who murder repeatedly for seemingly no reason, FBI veteran and ex-army CID (Criminal Investigation Division) colonel Robert Ressler writes:

> I think what was . . . in my mind were the serial adventures we used to see on Saturday at the movies (the one I liked best was *The Phantom*). Each week, you'd be lured back to see another episode, because at the end of each one there was a cliff-hanger. In dramatic terms, this wasn't a satisfactory ending, because it increased, not lessened the tension. The same dissatisfaction occurs in the minds of serial killers. The very act of killing leaves the murderer hanging, because it isn't as perfect as his fantasy.[23]

This diagnosis is familiar to any consumer of the serial killer narrative, in which we are often told (most famously by serial killer psychiatrist Hannibal Lecter in *The Silence of the Lambs*) that the killer is acting out, or creating, some kind of fantasy in his murders. What is interesting here is the way Ressler, who studies serial killers, is himself participating in the same type of serialized, unsatisfying fantasy. When he came up with the name "serial killer," it was *he* who was thinking about adventure serials like *The Phantom*. Along these same lines, we might postulate that the pleasure an American audience gets out of consuming serial killer narratives is in the way serialized homicidal crimes seem so well-adapted to the mass cultural form.

As Guy Debord points out in *Society of the Spectacle,* late capitalism sells us images as often as it sells us goods. Similarly, Jean Baudrillard's *Simulations* addresses the way everyday reality in late capitalism is permeated by "simulacra," objects and events that exist only as reproductions and have no proper original version. Simulacra grow out of a culture in which mass production and the mass media have altered the way people interpret reality. People are increasingly unable—and unwilling—to maintain a distinction between reality and what is fictional, or simulated, in mass-produced images and things. A culture of simulation encourages people to understand all objects (including other people) as simultaneously fictional and real. Furthermore, simulacra always seem to come in a series of reproductions precisely because fiction in late capitalism is associated with mass production. If homo economicus confuses himself with commodities, Baudrillard's discussion of commodity culture serves to explain why contemporary murder could involve a series of acts designed to make their instigator—and their object—into simulations. In fact, Joel Black's fascinating analysis of celebrity murderers in *The Aesthetics of Murder* suggests that the fantasy many killers are after is one of media fame; they kill precisely in order to see themselves mass produced as simulations in the newspapers and television reports about them.[24]

Several films and novels about serial killers suggest a connection between image production and murderous acts. In the movie *The Eyes of Laura Mars* (1978), for example, a fashion photographer, Laura Mars, has a telepathic link to the mind of a serial killer. She views murders through his eyes and then duplicates several of the murder scenes in her highly successful photographs of models who appear to be wounding or killing each other. Famous for her provocative photography, she is indebted to a serial killer for her inspiration.

In Dennis Cooper's novel *Frisk*—made into a film shown at the 1995 San Francisco Lesbian and Gay Film Festival—we see a similar narrative in which an artist simulates murder.[25] Dennis, the novel's point-of-view character, tells the story of his obsessive fantasies about having sexual relations with beautiful, dead men. Throughout most of the novel, the reader is unsure whether Dennis is actually killing men, or if he is merely writing a novel about doing it. Finally, we discover that his descriptions of murdering young men in Holland are actually a series of letters he has been writing and sending to his old lovers, two brothers named Julien and Kevin.

The violence of serial killers, it would seem, is associated in particular with the aesthetics of photographs or film. In *Frisk*, we discover that Dennis traces his fascination with eroticized dead bodies back to a series of "snuff" photographs he saw as a teenager in the back room of a magazine shop. *Frisk* begins and ends with short sections titled only with the symbol for infinity. Each is a description of the snuff photographs; in the opening section, we are unsure of whether the boy in the photographs is actually dead, and in the closing section we know that what appears to be a wound in his anus is "actually a glop of paint, ink, makeup, tape, cotton, tissue, and papier-mâché sculpted to suggest the inside of a human body . . . you can see the fingerprints of the person or persons who made it."[26] Dennis's quest, it turns out, has been to recreate those photographs he saw as a teenager. Once Julien and Kevin answer his letters, the three of them photograph a willing young man, and the result is the description we get in the last section of the book (quoted above). The whole process, however, is dependent upon Dennis's having seen images of a (possibly) dead boy—just as Laura's photographs are dependent upon her having seen actual murders taking place.

Not surprisingly, these fantasy images of murder have their true-crime counterparts. Ressler's book, *Whoever Fights Monsters,* is like other true-crime narratives in that it features a series of photographs in the middle of the book, much like a centerfold. These photographs are of Ressler himself, the serial killers he interviewed, many of their victims, the crime scenes, and the law enforcement officers on various cases. Other books—such as Norris's *Henry Lee Lucas*—include photographs of the victims' dead bodies. Such photographs add to the scientific, or ethnographic, feel of true crime, but they are also clearly for sensationalist entertainment purposes. They seem to ask: Can we read "evil" in this criminal's face? Can we imagine what it must feel like to be murdered when we look at the dead, mutilated, and naked bodies of his victims? Asking these questions, we are invited to engage in simulation on our own, inseparable from the "truth" of true crime.

Private Parts (1972) is a cult film in which a photographer's work is inextricable from his murderous acts, which involve killing beautiful young women who find him attractive. We discover that George, the photographer, is actually a woman whose mother essentially forced her to become a man because she thinks all women are whores. George lives in her mother's hotel, where she photographs beautiful women whom she later kills with a hypodermic. Her particular ritual, which is acted out in detail during several scenes, is to attach a photograph of her victim's face to a transparent, blow-up sex doll filled with water. When she gets excited enough, she uses a hypodermic to inject the doll with her own blood in an obvious reference to the act of ejaculation. In order for George to have a sexual relationship with anyone, it would seem, they must be converted into a photograph and blood must be shed. Furthermore, George's obsession with photography and murder is linked to her own desire to pass as a man. Although the photographic image is often understood to reproduce "reality," George must constantly confront the contradiction between realistic images and reality itself. While she *appears* to be a man, she in fact is not. Her murders are a way to maintain her sense of herself as a man, and to keep her masculine appearance intact. It is only when a woman is dead or in a photograph that she cannot discover the difference between George-the-male image and George-the-female body.

George—like many serial killers—is torn apart by a desire to appear masculine and, more importantly, productive. Serial killers are represented as people who long desperately to appear ordinary on the outside. They are intriguing because they succeed at seeming normal while engaging repeatedly in highly deviant, antisocial acts. We can understand the serial killer's identity in terms of a desire to be consumed as if he were a photographic image which does not have anything "real" or "truthful" behind it.[27] The serial killer wishes to be looked upon as if he has nothing to hide, as if his normal image conceals nothing, so that he may do his "work" as efficiently as possible. However, people who consume the serial killer image in narrative enjoy it precisely for the opposite reason: they know the image is not real, and are thus given the chance to feel as if they have outsmarted their own simulated culture. Viewers of photographic images generally do not expect a photograph to hide or alter any aspect of reality; they expect reality to be revealed in it. But viewers of the serial killer image can "know better," and that is the hook.

I will close my analysis with a discussion of two movies in which serial killers try to convert themselves into photographic or film images that an audience can "see through." Both *Martin* (1978) and *Henry: Portrait of a Serial Killer* (1990) hinge on the audience's ability to get at the "truth" of the killer's image and understand him for the criminal that he is. In George Romero's *Martin,* the teenage protagonist Martin believes that he is a vampire, having been told so by his religiously crazed grandfather. More than anything, Martin wants to convince himself and others that he is, indeed, like the monsters he has seen sucking blood in the movies. Martin "becomes" a vampire by murdering people and drinking their blood, and then he calls a radio talk show and describes his "vampiric" deeds. To embody the vampire image, in other words, he must act like one and—importantly—publicize his acts in the mass media. Unlike Martin, his grandfather, and some of Martin's companions, the audience of *Martin* is generally led to believe that he is not a vampire. He requires a syringe full of drugs to subdue his victims and kills them human-style, with a razor. We are also given plenty of clues, such as Martin's strange home environment and his sexual uncertainties, that indicate Martin's many reasons to be mentally unbalanced. While there remains some doubt about Martin's "true" nature, it seems fairly clear that this is a movie portraying a person who *seems* like a vampire—so much so that his grandfather finally kills him by driving a stake through his heart. Part of the pleasure in watching this film is in knowing the "truth" about Martin's crimes; he is not a vampire, but a serial killer.

Henry: Portrait of a Serial Killer, loosely based on the life of Henry Lee Lucas and his partner Ottis Toole, is about a prolific killer who feigns an image of normalcy and consumes movies of his own murderous acts. One of the most graphic and disturbing points in the film comes when Henry and Ottis shoot home movies of themselves torturing and killing a family. Subsequently, they watch it and drink beer, joking around with the remote control. Earlier in the film, after Henry and Ottis murder two prostitutes, we discover that Henry views all human relations as a matter of life and death; for him, killing is an ordinary response to human interaction. "[Killing] is always the same and always different," he says, "It's either you or them—one way or the other." The pseudo-documentary style of the film calls attention to Henry's "normal" act; the grainy photography and cinema verité acting invite audiences to see it as artfully constructed. In some ways, *Henry* is actually a boring narrative; although its content is often gruesome and terrifying, we are always returned to scenes of characters eating dinner or playing cards in a most mundane manner.

What appears to be ordinary in this film turns out to be both realistic and fake at the same time. Henry's "normal" facade conceals his violence and brutality. But the docu-drama artificiality of *Henry*'s realism works to enhance our sense that Henry and Ottis's ordinariness is sheer performance, and thus utterly extraordinary. While an audience can see through Henry's "ordinary guy" act, doubts about what is ordinary remain. Just as *Martin* encourages an audience to ask if in fact Martin's vampiric image might not be reality, *Henry* offers us the possibility that serial killing might indeed be more normal (or, at least, common) than we think. Even when an audience is offered a way to deconstruct images in these movies, there remains a kind of escape hatch for simulation. One can believe and not believe in these serial killer images at the same time. And ultimately, this escape hatch provides a way for audiences to ignore the critical aspects of these narratives as they apply to economic relations under postwar capitalism.

In Sheila Isenberg's *Women Who Love Men Who Kill,* women who have fallen in love with convicted killers describe their love for these men as a function of their confinement. That is, they enjoy their lovers' violent histories precisely because these men are cordoned off from normal life.[28] I think we can understand an audience's response to serial killer narratives in much the same way. While their content calls into question what Americans conceive of as a productive and normal life under capitalism, these narratives are also separate from most consumers' daily lives by their exceptional violence. An audience may be able to accept a comparison between serial murder and capitalism precisely because serial murder is—

The killer ordinary and terrifying: *Henry: Portrait of a Serial Killer* (Maijack Productions, 1986).

for most consumers—an outlandish, distant problem. Popular true crime and mass culture are able to connect economics to death precisely because that connection is so well-contained by the crimes that construct it.

What is the truth of true crime? It may indeed be the reality of material life in capitalism, where people are encouraged both literally and figuratively to make and buy dead labor. But as long as that truth is leashed to simulated crimes in pop culture, it will be very hard for audiences to venture beyond their criticism of murder stories to a larger criticism of capitalist production itself.

Notes

1. See Eric W. Hickey, *Serial Murderers and Their Victims* (Pacific Grove: Brooks and Cole, 1991), 74–77. He notes that the past twenty-five years have seen a dramatic increase in serial killing, especially the 1970s.

2. See, for example, Andrew Tudor's discussion of the popularity of "psycho" movies after 1960 in *Monsters and Mad Scientists* (Oxford and Cambridge: Blackwell, 1989), 185–209.

3. More accurately, Hitchcock based *Psycho* on a novel by Robert Bloch which was inspired by Ed Gein's life story. For an account of Gein's crimes, see Harold Schechter, *Deviant* (New York: Pocket Books, 1989).

4. I found this to be the case in both a local Berkeley bookstore, Cody's Books, and in the corporate bookstore chain Barnes and Noble. In fact, Cody's had placed true crime on a few shelves in between a section called sociology and a section called Marxism and labor. I suspect—based purely on anecdotal evidence—that this is a peculiarly American configuration. Once, shopping for true crime in Cody's, I began chatting with another patron who was visiting from Scotland. She was stocking up on true-crime books because, she said, American bookstores had the best selections she had ever seen.

5. Joel Norris, *Serial Killers* (New York: Anchor Books, 1988), 47–58.

6. Hickey, *Serial Murderers and Their Victims,* 133.

7. Robert Ressler and Tom Shachtman, *Whoever Fights Monsters* (New York: St. Martin's Press, 1992), 153.

8. Norris, *Serial Killers,* 15.

9. Lynne Segal, *Slow Motion: Changing Masculinities, Changing Men* (New Brunswick, N.J.: Rutgers University Press, 1990), 114.

10. Mark Seltzer, "Serial Killers (1)," *Differences* 5.1 (Spring 1993).

11. In *The Stranger Beside Me* (New York: Signet, 1980), investigative reporter Ann Rule describes the way Bundy, watching the news with his neighbors after the Sigma Chi sorority killings in Florida, told them that he was sure the murders were a "professional job" (282). Bundy was convicted of murdering two women at the Sigma Chi sorority and severely beating two others. At his Florida trial, his neighbors' testimony regarding this comment about the "professional" nature of these killings was discussed at length to indicate the extent of Bundy's "character disorder."

12. Ibid., 12.

13. Ibid. This is from Rule's reconstruction of Bundy's early life, and is not a direct quote from Bundy himself.

14. Juliet Schor, *The Overworked American* (New York: Basic Books, 1992), 136.

15. For information on the Dahmer crimes, see Joel Norris, *Jeffrey Dahmer* (New York: Pinnacle, 1992); and Don Davis, *The Milwaukee Murders* (New York: St. Martin's Press, 1991).

16. Davis, *The Milwaukee Murders,* 23.

17. Karl Marx, "Economic and Philosophic Manuscripts of 1844," in *The Marx-Engels Reader,* ed. Robert C. Tucker (London and New York: Norton, 1972), 71–74.

18. Quoted in Joel Norris, *Henry Lee Lucas* (New York: Zebra, 1991), 36.

19. Karl Marx, *Capital* (New York: New World, originally published in 1867), 224.

20. Henri Lefebvre, *Critique of Everyday Life, Vol. I* (New York and London: Verso, originally published in 1947), 31.

21. Because I am looking primarily at masculinity here, I will focus only on

serial killer fathers, rather than mothers and children. It is worth noting, however, that often when women and children kill, it seems to be because family life is too much work for them to bear as well, although in rape-revenge movies like *Ms. 45,* the motive is less clearly related to economic concerns.

22. Charles Derber, *Money, Murder and the American Dream* (Winchester, Mass.: Faber and Faber, 1992), 37. I would add that Derber wrote this chapter before the widely publicized trial of the Menendez brothers, in which they attributed their actions to childhood sexual and psychological abuse. At the time Derber's book went to press, media coverage of the case emphasized the brothers' desire to inherit their father's financial empire as a possible motivation for the murders.

23. Ressler and Shachtman, *Whoever Fights Monsters,* 33.

24. Joel Black, *The Aesthetics of Murder* (Baltimore: Johns Hopkins University Press, 1991), 135–65.

25. Directed by Todd Verow, and produced by Marcus Hu.

26. Dennis Cooper, *Frisk* (New York: Grove, 1991), 128.

27. The idea of becoming an image is, in contemporary America (and the West) intimately bound up with becoming a commodity-object.

28. Sheila Isenberg, *Women Who Love Men Who Kill* (New York: Dell, 1991), 126–29. Here Isenberg compares these relationships to the ideal of "courtly love," in which romance is confined to the emotional realm.

4

JEFFREY DAHMER AND MEDIA CANNIBALISM: THE LURE AND FAILURE OF SACRIFICE

MARK PIZZATO

It may be a truism that violence sells, but its stock has risen exponentially in recent decades. Despite congressional concern with TV and film violence, despite decades of studies on anxiety levels of TV watchers, despite explicit copycat crimes, the myth-making media continues to magnify news events, as stations and networks compete for Nielsen ratings that, however inaccurate, determine the value of commercial time slots. In this postmodern Aristotelian rite, the sympathies and fears of a mass audience are lured to the screen for tentative catharsis as police, lawyers, and reporters give partial solutions to a particular crime. But then the fear-mongering begins again with each new tragic plot, victim, and villain. Slick commercial lures are juxtaposed with fearful figures and legal dramas, to give further cathartic hope through the spectator's purchasing power. As we become more anxious about our vulnerability to violent crime all around us, we can temporarily purge our fears by possessing the products that frame the news. Yet our anxieties are recast nightly. The ritual violence that gave birth to ancient drama—the agony of a tragic hero on stage, evoking sympathy, fear, and catharsis in the audience—is replayed, though in a very different form, by the hypertheater of the postmodern simulacrum, from television to the marketplace.

Today's "home theater" of television has become the primary vehicle for staging dramatic identity and violence. Even when displaying news events rather than fictional shows, television involves its audience in a framework of meaning that is both ritual and theatrical. As ritual, television focuses the order of the day and week, especially when regular programming is interrupted to create the collective rite of passage through a "live" historic event, such as the televised trials of Jeffrey Dahmer and O. J. Simpson. Through its fictional dramas and its dramatic magnification of certain slices of life, television invites spectators to identify their personal desires and fears with the mythic dimension of violent characters and crimes presented on screen. Television thus creates a theater of mimetic catharsis in Aristotelian terms by shaping the representation of life, evoking the participation of audience emotions, and purging— or sparking the repetition of—violent impulses, personal and social. Of course, one cannot completely define the complex play of media images within the millions of minds of the mass audience. Yet various theories of theatrical violence, from ancient to modern, can illuminate the paradigms being repeated, with historical and technological variations, in the ritual of television today, where life imitates art, and both crime and courtroom play more and more to the camera and its *agora*.

Over a hundred years ago, Friedrich Nietzsche developed a theory of the ritual effect of violence in ancient Greek theater, which may speak as much to the romantic paradigms in the emergence of our century's mass dramatic media as to the birth of theater prior to Aristotle. In Nietzsche's view, the terror of individual mortality was evoked not only by the mimetic actor and his drama, but also by the medium of a ritual chorus, singing and dancing in the orchestra circle, between the stage and the audience. (The orchestra space of choral performance began in the ritual threshing floor of the *agora,* the Greek marketplace, prior to the invention of the *theatron,* cut into the temple hillside with an altar at the center of the orchestra circle.) It took the collective Dionysian terror of chorus and audience to create a transcendent vision upon the actor's Apollonian mask, an artful illusion to cover, yet engage, the common pain of existence.[1] In today's home theater of the TV screen, the beautiful faces of news reporters and anchors, aligned with attractive commercial images, are the Apollonian masks that give us the illusion of controlling our fears. But such transcendent illusions also demand that certain Dionysian demons act out the sacrificial desires and fears of the mass audience—for *sparagmos* and *omophagia* (the Dionysian rituals of animal dismemberment and "eating raw")— somewhere off screen.

Jeffrey Dahmer, police photograph.

Violence sells in the media today because it is also in us, not just in the criminal element of our society, but also behind the Apollonian masks that we put on, mirroring the stars idolized on screen. Violent characters shock the mass audience even more if they wear a mask of normalcy, rupturing the Apollonian surface of "real life." Serial killer Jeffrey Dahmer's 1992 insanity trial epitomized the mystery of violence behind a handsome, yet common, face. How could a middle-American, middle-class family (Dahmer's father holds a Ph.D. in chemistry) produce such a monster? Despite his Dionysian revelries, involving seventeen dead male lovers, painted skull relics, preserved genitalia, experiments in cannibalism, and plans to build a satanic altar with reassembled skeletons, Dahmer was designated "legally sane" by a Milwaukee jury.[2] In 1994 his father's memoir was published, adding to the trial's gruesome details a parent's guilt-ridden speculations.

Later that same year, Dahmer was murdered in prison by a fellow inmate, as if the choral rage of many in the mass audience had found a surrogate actor to execute vengeance in a state that lacks a death penalty. In psychotheatrical terms, the media's restaging of Dahmer's serial killing and the televising of his enigmatic presence in court raised his performance of personal, necrophilic rites to a mythic, sacrificial dimension, engaging the audience at a primal place of violence: through the collective heritage of Western theater's "birth" out of Dionysian ritual sacrifice, yet also through the cannibalistic experience of early infancy, lingering within current unconscious memories, and lurking behind the ego masks of the consumer dream screen.[3] Spectators who participated in this theater (becoming Dahmer's Nietzschean, yet postmodern chorus) glimpsed the Dionysian shattering of their own individual egos through the choral medium of television and the details of Dahmer's crimes, perceiving in themselves, if only for a moment, an eviscerating sense of loss, vulnerability, and vengeance. Dahmer's execution in prison became the final act of a revenge tragedy that involved the mass audience as chorus.

Dahmer killed, he said, to keep his male lovers from leaving him. He dissected their bodies, making art works and relics, to gain power precisely where he was fatally wounded (like the repetition compulsion of the Aristotelian hero's *hamartia*). Today's mass audience is drawn toward the restaging of mythic criminals, in news and fiction, in order to experience some degree of primal, ritual violence—like Dahmer in his private acts and passions—from extreme ego vulnerability to ecstatic creative power. If Dahmer's necrophilic rites were powerfully addictive (as his lawyer and expert witnesses argued), repeating and escalating from adolescent experiments in taxidermy to adult murder and mutilation, then he serves as an exemplary warning about our normal addiction to TV illusions. It is not too much violence on television that is dangerous, but the way we submit to the screen, gaining the illusion of remote control, which traps us in the televisual ritual.

The term "serial killer" was coined in the 1970s by FBI agent Robert Ressler through his memory of cinema's narcotic effect when he was a child: "In my mind were the serial adventures we used to see on Saturday at the movies (the one I liked best was *The Phantom*). Each week you'd be lured back to see another episode, because at the end there was a cliff-hanger. In dramatic terms there wasn't a satisfactory ending because it increased, not lessened the tension. The same dissatisfaction occurs in the minds of serial killers."[4] But serial television today has greatly increased the addictive tension of dramatized violence, partial climax, and delayed catharsis—not only through cliff-hanger endings, but also by commercial interruptions. In her comparison of cinema and television, Beverle Houston finds that television is "more directly linked to consumption, which it promotes by shattering the imaginary possibility over and over, repeatedly reopening the gap of desire. Television sets up an obsessive acting-out of desire, which the spectator tries to assuage by consuming the television text itself in its unique promise."[5] As we buy images and cling to beloved products, which temporarily fill the hollowness of our egos, we fulfill a certain role in the addictive televisual apparatus, continuing the serial cannibalism (the *sparagmos* and *omophagia*) of the media marketplace.[6] Dahmer fulfilled his role by giving us contemporary necrophilic rites and a mythic, yet normal, face as extensions of our desire. We fulfill another role—lost in the millions of eyes watching him on television, we still participate to some degree in the recreation of his transcendent acts.

This essay proposes a theatrical and psychoanalytic view of this recent criminal star of the news media, who exemplifies the sublimated cannibalism of our consumer culture. Like the props of victims' body parts that Dahmer saved and (according to his confessions) tasted in his Milwaukee apartment, pieces of his mythic character were idolized and consumed by a mass audience, through the dissection and fetishization rituals of the television and print media. Perhaps this essay merely perpetuates such cannibalizing of a mythic Jeffrey Dahmer. But if we carefully consider the acute pain and rage within his psyche, we may sense a similar rage simmering in all of us—and better perceive the sacrifices that we make in the media marketplace.

THE DESIRES OF THE AUDIENCE

According to psychoanalyst Jacques Lacan, human subjectivity (*manque-à-être,* lack-of-being or want-to-be) is created by insatiable desire, the desire of the Other, which is more than that of any "other" person.[7] Thus, in the hypertheater of postmodern life, a sense of "audience" becomes omnipresent, as the Other's desire demands symptomatic actions from each individual, through various social influences and personal memories, even when one is alone. The hidden theater of Dahmer's criminal activity was edged with influential spectators (personal and social aspects of the Other): inside his psyche, in the immediate characters around him, and in the media's regard for prior serial killers, manifesting and stimulating the taste of a "mass audience" for new Jack-the-Ripper figures. Despite such audience desires, Dahmer was still the main actor in his serial killing and necrophilic activities. And yet, like his victims and their families, Dahmer suffered in his role. His monstrous character and addictive fate developed not only through many incidents and choices in his private life, but also through the public demand for news figures of mythic stature to represent the social unconscious. As Dahmer acted out his desperate desire to control other bodies, moving from the dissection of animals to the drugging, lobotomizing, killing, dissecting, and eating of humans, he came more and more under the control of the Other's desire—of the devilish, perverse impulses within our common social order. Dahmer's life in that sense was "scripted." He answered a casting call to wear the mask of the media figure he eventually became, embodying the desire of the Other, of the mass audience.

The mystery play of Dahmer, as perverse martyr, from his arrest and insanity trial to his assassination in prison, shows him to be both villain and victim, guilty and innocent—a tragic hero (a common-man Oedipus) facing the horrifying fate of his own history,[8] and a scapegoat (in René Girard's sense) catharticly absorbing and purging public pity and fear.[9] This was the crux of his insanity trial: not the fact that Dahmer killed, but the problem of how to interpret him. Though he was found sane by a Milwaukee jury and sentenced to fifteen consecutive life terms,[10] the plot changed two years later with Dahmer's death in prison at the hands of a fellow inmate. Yet, his unofficial executioner, while rescripting the drama's end, also answered a casting call of the mass audience: to act out a final twist in Dahmer's fate, by realizing the Other's desire for sacrificial revenge.

> He died of massive head injuries, suffered sometime between 7:50 and 8:10 A.M., when he was found in a pool of blood in a toilet area next to the prison gym.[11]

Given his fame for fetishizing male body parts and his problems with the disposal of the rest of his victims' bodies, this execution near a gym and toilet was an apt symbolic end for Dahmer.[12] It also offered the mass audience a sacrificial climax, beyond the judicial sentence and the lack of a death penalty in the state of Wisconsin. "I've heard it on the streets," reported a former neighbor of Dahmer at the news of his death, "young black men saying they wished they could get their hands on him. There was too much hate for him to live."[13] (Most of Dahmer's victims were young black males.) Inez Thomas, a relative of one of the victims, applauded the revised ending as exemplary: "It shows today that he paid for what he did to these kids."[14] But the most enlightening comment came from Rita Isbell, the sister of one of Dahmer's last victims. At his trial two years earlier, she had screamed a death threat and lunged at him in the courtroom—a scene prominently replayed in the TV news at the time. Upon the announcement of his death, Isbell said she had been getting phone calls for the past two years from the serial killer's prison inmates, promising that he would be "taken care of."[15] Whether or not those calls came from prisoners connected with Dahmer's murder, the performance of his execution was probably influenced by earlier media scenes and audience reactions: from the initial disclosure of his crimes and ritual props, to the creation of his mythic mask, to the failure of the courtroom ritual to give enough poetic justice, to the vengeful rage acted out by Isbell, across the judicial frame, as a sudden Dionysian expression of the violent desires in the TV audience.

There was some speculation while Dahmer was still alive that a made-for-TV movie about the Milwaukee cannibal's life might be created. However, Dahmer never sold his "true story" to Hollywood,[16] although his victims' families sued to get any money he might receive and were awarded up to eighty million potential dollars.[17] If an authorized Dahmer movie had been made, the families of his victims would have found a financially happy ending to their tragic roles, through the further voyeurism of the mass audience. But without the Hollywood deal, the family members and their lawyers had to look for another way to profit from the media's gaze by somehow cannibalizing Dahmer's (and their lost loved ones') remains.

The victims' families recognized the value of certain ordinary objects that were turned into sacred relics through Dahmer's rituals and his televised trial. They wanted to possess the remains from his crimes in exchange for the body parts of their loved ones that Dahmer had fetishized. These surrogate objects would then be offered to other consumers. "The families want to auction off some 312 items, including a 55-gallon vat he used to decompose the bodies; the refrigerator where he stored hearts; a saw, a hammer and his toothbrush. Tom Jacobson, the lawyer for the families, said the auction could bring more than $100,000."[18] Jacobson was also quoted as saying, in a final coup de grace: "I think his death makes the stuff even more valuable." Of course, the reason certain collectors might have given so much for the Dahmer collection— the refrigerator where he stored human hearts, the saw and hammer he used to dismember bodies, even the toothbrush that cleaned his cannibal teeth—was the prior fetishization of such props and the consumption of his cannibal drama by a mass audience. Dahmer's death made his apartment remains "more valuable" because of the aura they gained in the consummation of the Other's desire. And yet, the celebration in the news media of that final act in the Dahmer drama also shows the perpetuation of sacrificial desire, which was at the heart of Dahmer's crimes.

A rehearsal of Dahmer's execution occurred in July of 1994, when an inmate tried to slash Dahmer's throat but failed to kill him. At the end of

November, the inmate arrested for the successful assassination, Christopher Scarver, received praise from the relatives of Dahmer's victims, appropriate to the dramatic act and the Thanksgiving season. "He's my hero," said Jamie Hagan. "I want to send him a thank you note."[19] Scarver was already serving a first-degree murder sentence, like Dahmer. Scarver (if he committed the deed)[20] not only pleased the media audience by acting out the Other's desire, he also fulfilled Dahmer's own death wish.[21] With the help of Scarver (or his stunt double, as in Genet's *Deathwatch*),[22] Dahmer played out the final act of his drama, as both villain who deserved the ultimate punishment and as tragic hero who faced the horror of his own character and fate. Dahmer's death was a final ritual passage, beyond the inadequate catharsis of his repetitive acts of violence.[23] For the rest of us, though, who remain in this mortal coil and media theater, one serial killer's death is not enough to purge the mass audience's fixation with such figures. A closer look at the Dahmer drama, moving back through his father's memories toward earlier scenes of Jeffrey's childhood, might provide a better view of the sacrificial desires that we continue to share.

LIKE FATHER . . .

Just seven months before Dahmer's death in prison, the media theatrics of his 1992 insanity trial were reinvoked by the publication of his father's memoir, *A Father's Story*. To help publicize the book, both Lionel and Jeffrey Dahmer appeared on NBC's *Dateline* on March 8, 1994. During his network interview with Stone Phillips, the son summarized his desire to kill (in a line reminiscent of Genet's drama): "My only objective was to find the best-looking guy that I could. I went to bathhouses. I went to bars, shopping malls."[24] Such shopping around for beautiful bodies to fetishize and consume shows Dahmer's horrifying deeds reflecting the everyday theatrics of market forces. Dahmer's method for finding his victims suggests that the commerical TV spectator shares a sense of the killer's desire when using the remote control, cutting between beautiful body parts on screen, cutting out fetish images to imitate or buy—to "incorporate"[25] through consumer culture and the home theater.

The shock of Dahmer's drama is all the greater because his life began in what appeared to be a normal home. But the common conflicts in the Dahmer household, pushed to certain extremes, are precisely what the father analyzes in his memoir—to ask how different he and his family were from us and ours. Through this question Lionel Dahmer also suggests the indirect complicity of a mass media audience, through the TV set at the center of the home. "In addition to whatever my genetic contribution was, the violence and crime in our society and in the media had a great influence on my son, as well as on the countless other children who are exposed to the glorification of violence that they watch in movies and television."[26] This might seem an easy excuse for the father of a multiple murderer. But the crucial issue of media violence in relation to Dahmer's rites of sacrifice deserves further consideration. I would like the reader to consider two opposing theatrical approaches in viewing the details of Dahmer's life via his father's memoir: Bertolt Brecht's alienation-effect and Antonin Artaud's theater of cruelty.

Brecht's approach to performance stresses critical thought about societal connections, by revealing the mechanisms of theater, especially the gaps between actor and character, and between character and audience, to demystify the tragic hero and distance the spectator from emotional union with the play.[27] Regarding Dahmer's case, one might try, in Brechtian fashion, to separate the criminal actor, who developed out of a specific home and media environment, from the mythic character the media later made of him. But one must realize that the earlier Dahmer actor is also a characterization, (re)produced by his insanity trial confessions and father's memoir. Each detail given by Jeffrey or Lionel Dahmer is a performance of their characters for the media gaze. This distancing of earlier Dahmer actors from their eventual celebrity characters, while alienating the mass audience from Dahmer's childhood and crimes, also involves a certain closeness, bringing the viewer, as well as the society and the media, directly into the scene. Whether or not one finds the real Jeffrey Dahmer in his father's memoir, one finds the figures of a shared social pathology, as they struggle to find a personal ritual cure.

However, such a personal connection to a serial killer and his father relates more to Artaud's sense of alienation affect, rather than Brecht's effect. Artaud theorized a passionate communion between spectators and the cruel sufferings of characters on stage, through which an audience would be personally transformed.[28] If we also to take an Artaudian angle on the Dahmer show, we might identify with the father, as he relates his haunted memories and troubled ties to the son.[29] Though merely reading (about) the Dahmer memoir, the present audience could apply various shades of critical Brechtian distance and sympathetic Artaudian intimacy, while reimagining Lionel Dahmer's struggle to connect memories of his child with the media figure of Milwaukee cannibal. This should provide a more complete view of the cruel communion and alienating theatricality of mass-media cannibalism, in the context of family life.[30]

In his memoir, Lionel Dahmer realizes that he played a specific media role before and during his son's insanity trial. "My only task was to 'appear' to be his father, to wait patiently for his trial, then to occupy my assigned place in the courtroom, as powerless, and in a sense, as utterly faceless, as the male mannequin Jeff had stashed in the dark closet of his bedroom in West Allis."[31] The father sensed that he was being used by the media just as his son was—and just as the stolen mannequin and actual human bodies were used by his son—as stage prop and "faceless" actor for the voyeuristic, fetishistic, and cannibalistic *jouissance* of the mass audience. That is not to say that he or Jeffrey suffered as innocently as Dahmer's victims and their families. But this Brechtian/Artaudian view does show that we in the mass audience are not simply innocent victims either. We who watched contributed to the judicial rite and prison sacrifice of Dahmer and helped to create the mythic scapegoat—idolized beyond his pathetic addictions—as a new ideal for future serial killers to imitate or beat.[32]

Lionel Dahmer denies that he ever sexually abused his son, despite such claims by a guest on the *Phil Donahue Show*. Yet the father admits that his media role changed after that show: "Suddenly, I was no longer cast in the role of devoted and long-suffering father, but as a dreadful and perverse father. . . . I was the accused, rather than the father of the accused, an agent in my son's crimes."[33] Whatever the degree of actual sexual abuse in the Dahmer family (or neighborhood),[34] the father of Jeffrey Dahmer did play the role of actor as well as spectator, not only in the media's casting call, but also in his son's early life, as the memoir confesses. Lionel Dahmer even speculates at parallels between his own perverse desires and those of his son. They both, says the father, "dreamed repeatedly of murder."[35] In fact, Lionel Dahmer describes being caught in the grip of a certain memory, from the age of eight to his early twenties, that he had "murdered someone."[36] Unable to recall the specifics of this repeated nightmare once he awoke, Lionel Dahmer was nevertheless haunted by his own desire to kill:

> Even though I had no vision of the crime itself, no physical details, no slaughtered bodies, no weapons, no blood-spattered rooms, I nonetheless could not shake myself from the conviction that I had brutally and wantonly killed someone. The sensation would last no more than a minute or so, but during that awful interval, when I would literally hang between fantasy and reality, I would be terrified at what I might have done. I would feel lost, as if I had gone out of control, and in that instant, done something horrible.

In a psychotheatrical sense, Jeffrey Dahmer's desire to kill was not solely his own. He was performing the desire of the Other (the Other in his head and in our society) when he killed and played with his victims' bodies. That desire came to him at least partly through his father, through innumerable points of contact between them as the son grew up, and even before he was born. The father, as a conscious and unconscious actor in the child's life, thus became a spectral spectator within his mind as he killed, part of the desiring Other applauding (and horrified by) his son's crimes. Perhaps Lionel Dahmer did not himself cross the line "between fantasy and reality" in his dreams of murder—or in any scene of sexual abuse. But he did "hang" at the edge of actual murder in his memory of desire—like the mass audience watching his son and remembering his deeds through the televised trial.

Dahmer was the main actor in his cruel drama. He made many incremental and escalating choices as a child and adult: to kill animals, to cut up their bodies, to play with a stolen mannequin, and eventually to kill and toy with human bodies. But in crossing from fantasy to reality (in what Lacan calls a *passage à l'acte,* a temporary ritual "cure" and self-punishment for psychic pain),[37] Dahmer stepped into a character created by the Other, by the internal audience of his unconscious desires and the external audience of family, society, and media.[38] Once he had crossed that liminal threshold, rehearsing his perverse rites again and again, Dahmer became fatally overpowered by the role as much as his victims were by him—repeating the offense in order to purge, yet thereby compounding the guilt. Eventually, with the full disclosure of such ritual power, Lionel Dahmer was also forced to face his role and publicly confess, though the media and mass audience were allowed to celebrate their role without a corresponding guilt.

CONTROLLING THE BODY, AS SPECTATOR AND ACTOR, CONTROLLED BY THE RITE

Lionel Dahmer's empathy for his son leads him to interpret a common fear and desire between them, which the rest of us watching might also confess to sharing, although our cathartic reactions may differ widely. In his memoir, Lionel Dahmer identifies with his son's "dread of people leaving him" and his desire "to 'keep' people permanently, to hold them fixedly within his grasp."[39] First, the father summarizes the plot of his son's drama, from perverse fantasy to criminal reality, including cannibalism. Then Lionel Dahmer sees himself in Jeffrey's character: "I had the same extreme fear of abandonment, a fear so deep that it had generated a great deal of otherwise inexplicable behavior." Thus, he implicitly asks us to look into the mirror of Jeffrey Dahmer's character as well.

As spectator at the insanity trial, full of sympathy and terror, the father realized further evidence tying his own character to this tragic flaw in his monstrous son.[40] He recalled certain wounds in his own character when he was a young boy, such as the "profound sense of isolation and abandonment" when his mother went to the hospital for an operation, and a "severe stuttering problem" that he developed shortly thereafter.[41] Although he credits "special classes" and his "dear father's dedication" for curing his childhood stutter, Lionel Dahmer's also describes later symptoms, which more directly affected his family and now seem to parallel his son's vices:

> I had relentlessly clung to a first marriage that was deeply wounded. I had clung to routines and habits of thought. To guide my behavior, I had clung to highly defined personal roles. It struck me that I had clung to all these things because they had given me a profound sense of permanence, of something I could "keep."[42]

Such "clinging" to personal roles and rituals (which also involved body-building, pranks with small explosives, and Ph.D. work in chemistry) might seem a far cry from his son's eventual cannibalism. But Lionel Dahmer's new vision of himself, through fear of and pity for his son, shows a potential cathartic bridge for all of us in the serial killer's audience: from our common existential alienation (Lacanian *manque à être*) to the father's confession of clinging to certain roles, to the apparently normal face of Jeffrey Dahmer at the trial, to the horrors within his character and memories.

Lionel Dahmer's memoir restages a specific scene of his own some-what normal clinging as parallel to his son's "psychotic need for control."[43] The father, as a young boy, had playfully hypnotized a young girl in his bedroom by candle light. "I intended to cast a spell over her, so that I could control her entirely."[44] All he did was command her to breathe deeply and lift her arms over her head—a cute, childish "experiment."[45] Yet such an act has now changed in his memory, becoming less innocent given his son's later experiments. "She obeyed instantly," says the father. "I remember that I felt exhilarated as I watched her, felt truly powerful, truly in command of another human being." This directorial power over the actor's body was taken even further by his son, expressing a perverse Dionysian side to the father's Apollonian mask as scientist.[46] Jeffrey Dahmer eventually "hatched a crude scientific scheme for lobotomizing" his male lovers. As his father, the chemist, calmly relates: "My son drilled holes in their skulls and poured muriatic acid into their brains."[47] When these experimental zombies failed to survive (though one did live for two days), Jeffrey's next step, according to Lionel Dahmer, was to use the dead bodies of his victims as hypnotic toys, as the perfect actors and props: "bodies he could deflesh and eviscerate, preserving certain parts and devouring others, but always in order to live out his need for complete control."

The great power of film and television today, to control actors' bodies and spectators' perceptions, might also be reflected in the macabre light of the Dahmer drama. The loss of self and of those we love is something experienced by and threatening to all of us. But it is only in certain extraordinary actor-directors, like Jeffrey Dahmer, that we might glimpse the cannibalistic desire in our mimetic arts. Theater, film, and television also turn the lost mortal body into a ritual prop for cathartic consumption—if only through the eyes and ears and imagination, not, of course, the mouth. Yet, we are in danger of becoming more and more "addicted" to television and movies,[48] like Dahmer to his violent fantasies and rituals.[49] Television in particular gives us not only the physical thrill of imaginary action, but also the illusion of personal power over so many faces and body parts and channels—in "remote control"—as we submit our bodies to the control of that ritual act and its lens.

APPROPRIATE PROPS AND MASKS

There is a crucial difference between imagining Dahmer's crimes, or fictionally acting out his cannibalism on stage (as in Reza Abdoh's *The Law of Remains*),[50] and actually performing the brutal crimes. But there is also a common human desire in Dahmer's lifelong *passage à l'acte*, as he created progressively more addictive ritual scenarios from childhood to adulthood, acting out his sexual fantasies, and eventually graduating from animal to human dissection. Even the censoring of "revolting" details in the Dahmer drama by some agents of the media shows the power of his abjection to touch ours.[51] Dahmer, as a postmodern cannibal, epitomizes the hollowness of communion in the media simulacrum, through his desperate attempts to make consumption more real. He fashioned a powerfully perverse sense of self by ritually controlling the loss of his loved ones by destroying, dismembering, and eating them (or saving their parts). With these bloody props and the power he felt through their possession, Dahmer masked from himself the abyss of loneliness within. He thus wore various layers of personal and social masks: the private illusion of power in his violent rituals; the normal, anonymous face he showed in public while practicing his secret rites;[52] and the mythic character that he eventually acquired in the media limelight.

97

These Dahmer masks illustrate the lure to impersonate, to participate in fantasy, to use others as props—to temporarily fill the lack of being in being human (Lacan), intensified by postmodern life and media.

Looking back at his son's childhood, Lionel Dahmer also remarks that the aggression building within Jeffrey was masked by a passive act.[53] Unfortunately for Dahmer's victims and their families, the extreme lack of being fueling the violence beneath his passive mask was not perceived by the father (or by other patriarchal authorities) until after multiple murders. "I look at his face, particularly in photographs taken during the trial, and I see no feeling in him whatsoever, no emotion, only a terrible vacancy in his eyes."[54] Dahmer's normal, somewhat handsome face and dispassionate tone of voice were the tools for his serial killing as well as his courtroom and media masquerade. Dahmer lured his homosexual victims into his violent rituals, and lured his father and the police away from them, by wearing appropriate masks and performing credible lies. The father's memoir confesses his failure to interpret the inner sacrificial theater through the outer familial one. Yet it also shows, in retrospect, a symptomatic trail of fetish props, from Jeffrey's early experimental confusion to his later ritual certainty.

Lionel Dahmer remembers searching under his house in 1964, when his son was just four years old, to find the source of "an unbearable odor."[55] He found "a large pile of bones, the remains of various small rodents which had probably been killed by the civets that populated the general area." According to Lionel Dahmer, the chemist, these civets and their "feast" were the source of the smell "that had invaded the house." His prodigious son then imitated and extended his father's fascination (and perhaps his mother's concern) with the bones of the civets' victims. After the father emerged from under the house with a bucket of the bones, "white, dry, and completely fleshless, since they had been picked clean by the civets," little Jeffrey began a *fort/da* game—like the one Freud observed in his own grandson—as a way of controlling the pain of maternal absence through ritual repetition, acting out presence and absence with a prop.[56] Yet the young Dahmer's game, in his father's memory, seems a prelude to more extreme play: the later necrophilic and cannibal rites that also caused a terrible smell in other theaters, in his grandmother's house, and in his own apartment building:

> He had taken a great many of the bones from the bucket and was staring at them intently. From time to time, he would pick a few of them up, then let them fall with a brittle, crackling sound that seemed to fascinate him. Over and over, he would pick up a fistful of bones, then let them drop back into the pile that remained on the bare ground.[57]

These bones, at the liminal edge between nature (civet invaders) and culture (house with foul smells), may have come to symbolize, within Jeffrey's developing unconscious,[58] the lure of violent passions inside (beneath) his parents' house as they fought their way toward an eventual divorce. His playing with the bones of the civets' victims (as a four-year-old) parallels his later play with the bones of small animals (as a teenager),[59] and with the bones of his own human victims (as an adult), which he defleshed and saved as fetish props. These cannibalistic memorabilia and personal art works eventually became public props, too, as forensic evidence and media relics.[60] "A two-drawer file cabinet contained three skulls that had been spray painted with a gray 'granite-like texture' paint."[61] Three "skeletonized bodies" were also found in a plastic storage drum. The words Lionel Dahmer recalls his child saying, as he played with the bones, thus become prophetic lines for his later theater of absurdity. "He seemed oddly thrilled by the sound they made. 'Like fiddlesticks,' he said. Then he laughed and walked away."[62]

This incident, says the father, "was once nothing more than a rather sweet memory of my little boy, but now it has the foretaste of his doom."[63] Dahmer was certainly not doomed at the age of four to become a serial killer. Yet this scripting, by his father's memoir, of an early scene involving the "foretaste" of his later cannibalism shows how a sweet memory of childhood play—with a pun on nonsense ("fiddlesticks")—might be re-viewed as a theatrical and musical prelude to later acts. Perhaps the scene also played a significant role in the serial actor's developing chain of fetish props, conscious and unconscious,[64] as he gradually ritualized the non-sense of mortality, and the ab-sense evoked by his parents' divorce (and his mother's rejection of him), shortly before his first murder at the age of eighteen.

The ritual props of the adult Jeffrey Dahmer came to play an impor-tant role in the uncanny fascination of the mass media with his abject cannibalism. They can be seen, too, as reflecting the illusions of daily communion that millions of spectators feel, as "mass audience," with their TV sets. Beautiful body parts, eroticized through fictional and journalistic violence, are the imaginary manna that temporarily fill the psychic emptiness of those watching. Yet such fetishes fail to fulfill. They merely re-stimulate desire, perpetuating the rituals of TV (and cinema) spectatorship through commercial consumerism: the purchasing of props associated with one's favorite shows and stars. Possessing the object of desire in the advertising image means, as with Dahmer's props, being possessed by such rites. His bone play, as child and adult, shows, *in extremis,* our primal fascination with the drama of life and death (like that of tribal societies in saving and purifying human bones through cannibalism).[65] Thus, the Dahmer drama reminds us to keep asking, as media spectators, "who is being sacrificed and at what cost in our ordinary feast at the communal 'boob-tube'?"

The properties used in Dahmer's rituals were connected to his imaginary masks, the various personas he performed for the external and internal audience as he recarved his split subjectivity (Lacan) by carving up others' bodies in order to control his lovers and dispose of them without letting them leave him. In this sense he fashioned his perverse face of power immediately behind the normal mask of passivity, through the body parts he fetishized and consumed (somewhat like Hannibal Lecter's escape trick in the film *The Silence of the Lambs* [1991]). In a footnote to his analysis of the *fort/da* game, Freud reported that the child in question, playing with his mother's absence, also "found a method of making *himself* disappear. He had discovered his reflection in a full-length mirror which did not quite reach to the ground, so that by crouching down he could make his mirror-image 'gone'."[66] Dahmer, too, with his painted skulls and his own famous postmortem face, shows us the lure of the media mirror and its staged identifications, to control not only the desired other's threat of absence, but also our own *aphanisis* (fading).[67] Or rather, he shows the powerful compulsion to repeat this illusory mastery of the loss of self and other,[68] through ritual identification with certain characters (and ghosts of dead actors) on screen, whose appearance and disappearance we seem to physically direct through the remote control or cinema ticket even as we lose ourselves through such worship. Other props in the Dahmer drama further exemplify this worship and loss of self to media images: he saved photographs of his victims' remains,[69] showed a video of *The Exorcist* (1973) to at least one victim,[70] and imitated the sadistic emperor in *Return of the Jedi* (1983) by wearing yellow contact lenses.[71]

AN INSIDE-OUT CHEMISTRY

The various props in the Dahmer drama reveal paradoxical combinations of science and art, of violence and beauty. The young Jeffrey, in his father's memory, was fascinated not only with animal bones but also with viscera: "He seemed captivated by the gutted fish [when father and son went fishing together], staring intently at the brightly colored entrails."[72] This might seem a normal boyhood curiosity, in a beautiful scene of father-son bonding, if not for the props found in Dahmer's apartment some years later. "The kitchen area was void of food products. . . . The freezer portion of the refrigerator contained a human heart sectioned in three pieces and a large muscle mass contained in a ziplock plastic bag."[73] As Lionel Dahmer points out, his own "early obsession with fire had led to nothing more unusual than chemistry, to a life-long work in scientific research."[74] But Jeffrey's performative response to the fireworks between his parents (which the memoir also describes)—and to his father's scientific detachment and analysis—was to experiment more directly with sexuality, mortality, and disappearance.

"Not long after I'd discarded the animal remains I'd found beneath our house, I took Jeff to my chemistry laboratory for the first time. We walked from home, his hand in mine as we moved down the narrow dirt road."[75] This beautiful bonding scene from Dahmer's early childhood also led to certain precedents for his later violent acts. At the lab, says his father, "I showed Jeff as much as I could of my work, introducing him to what, for me, were the fascinations of chemistry." The son of the scientist "watched attentively" as the paper changed color in the acid-base litmus test, and "stared wonderingly as a beaker of phenolphthalein turned dark pink when I introduced ammonia into the solution." Later, this chemist's son would perform lobotomy experiments upon his victims, in order to control them sexually and prevent the loss of such lovers, drilling holes in their heads (while they were heavily tranquilized but still alive) and injecting acid into their brains.[76] He would also use acid to dispose of unwanted body parts after dissecting his victims.[77] Four large containers of muriatic acid were found in his apartment at the time of his arrest. The young Dahmer became infected by his father's love for chemistry, but transcribed that passion through his own sacrificial experiments: substituting certain props, liquid and solid, for more threatening human relations—as his father had done in avoiding Jeffrey's mentally ill mother by turning to solutions in the lab (which eventually led to the loss of his mother in the divorce process).[78] This double Dahmer scenario, of sacrificial substitution and transcendence by father and son, also parallels the general use of cinema and television by many Americans—a ritual escape into dramatic fantasy on screen as a way to ignore the real pain of daily drama at home. Yet, the escalation of Dahmer's brutal rites provides further warning signs, showing the return of the repressed, of the *agon* in his Oedipal drama, with great creative virulence.

Jeffrey Dahmer's own confessions reveal a perverse extension of the father's "work" in the son's later experiments with life and love. "He claimed that when he was 15 or 16, he had a compulsive interest in dissecting animals that he found dead on the road: 'I did it four or five times. I was going to keep their bones and make a statue out of them like a taxidermist, but I never got to it. The animals were mostly dogs or foxes.' "[79] Dahmer remembered stealing the head of a fetal pig he was dissecting at school, "and keeping the skull." He also set a dog's head on a stake in the woods. As a mature artist, Dahmer saved seven skulls (and painted three) from his human victims. He also planned to build a satanic temple with the human skeletons he had saved and cleaned.[80]

Lionel Dahmer claims ignorance, until the trial, of Jeffrey's teen play with animal bodies.[81] Years later, while the adult Jeffrey was living at his grandmother's house, she complained of "a horrible odor" in her garage. But Lionel Dahmer accepted his son's explanation of an "experiment with bleaches and muriatic acid" on a dead raccoon.[82] "I just wanted to see what the chemicals would do," said the masked serial killer. When questioned further, he added (according to the father's memory): "I know it's stupid, Dad, but I just like to experiment." Here Dahmer was clearly seeking paternal recognition, though hiding the fact that he was really experimenting on humans, not animals. The father's acceptance of the lie and "belief" in his son's (al)chemical theater[83] might have been all the more reason for Dahmer's extreme creativity through further ritual scenes

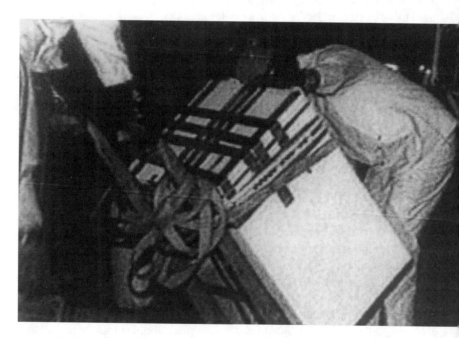

Media rituals and serial murder: police photo of Dahmer crime scene.

and props, in perverse imitation of the father's earlier desire to make chemical rather than marital solutions in his relationship with the mother. And yet, Dahmer's experimental rituals also responded to the desire of the Other beyond his immediate family, later revealed in the public fascination with *his* insides, via television and courtroom dissection.

At the time of the televised trial, the props in Dahmer's human sacrifices were judiciously dissected, as was his persona. His personal art works and scientific specimens, with the aid of his confessions, became forensic evidence,[84] but there was not much analysis of the parallels in certain childhood scenes, and even less of the concurrent metatheater in the media marketplace. In his interviews with an expert psychiatric witness (Dr. George Palermo), who later testified in his stead, Dahmer explained himself as a "loner" when a teenager, "envious of other boys," taking refuge in alcohol, marijuana, and magazine images. "When masturbating [daily] I would look at pictures of good-looking guys in magazines—trim with good muscle tone, youngish, not older than 30."[85] Through his early performance art work with animal corpses, Dahmer eventually developed such media-inspired masturbatory fantasies into a full-blown criminal theater. One of his earliest adult crimes was stealing a full-size mannequin from a department store, by taking the torso apart in the store and slipping each half into a bag, and thus taking it home to his grandmother's house, where it was eventually discovered by her "in Jeff's closet."[86] At the time, his father took this act as a curious prank, but by the time of the trial it seemed to the father to parallel Dahmer's later taking of human life and the taking apart of bodies in his apartment. Such parallel performances might thus be seen as playing upon (and to) the father's fetishizing of a well-built body, with the equipment he gave his teenage son to build up his muscles, just as the father had done himself as a teen.[87] But they also show an extremely perverse, yet uncannily appropriate response to the mass media's daily worship of beautiful body parts through violent drama on screen and eye-catching ads in magazine pages—like the pictures that inspired Dahmer's masturbatory envy.

There were also certain psycho-physical traumas in the serial killer's childhood that became crucial to the fatal plot of his personal theater and public fame. In his earliest years, while his mother had nightmares of being chased by a bear and sometimes, in actual fights with her husband, jabbed at him with a knife, Dahmer "fell victim to various infections."[88] He would cry all night with ear and throat pain, receiving so many injections for such problems that "his little buttocks were covered with injection lumps, and he began to lash out at the nurses and doctors."[89] Such vulnerability to infection was almost certainly affected by the stress

103

and violence at home, as his infant body absorbed the theater of cruelty within his mother and between his parents. His suffering, too, at the hands of medical authorities—and his lashing out—were early symptoms of his physical fear, vulnerability, and rage as an adult. "He enjoyed sodomizing people but abhorred the idea of being sodomized."[90] The adult Dahmer not only mimicked his father the chemist, he also transformed the doctors and nurses of his primal memories into his own characterization of Doctor Frankenstein, injecting acid into his lovers' brains to make them his zombies.

These early traumatic episodes at home and in the hospital climaxed with Dahmer's double hernia surgery at the age of four (in the year of the "fiddlesticks" bone play). The operation may have been necessary to cure a birth defect, but the experience was so painful for the child that he "asked Joyce [his mother] if the doctors had cut off his penis."[91] The father also remembers after that a "flattening of mood" that seemed "permanent." This was clearly a dramatic twist in the serial killer's earliest memories, given a particular prop found twenty-five years later at the crime scene. In a file drawer, forensic authorities discovered "desiccated genitalia that had been painted a Caucasian flesh tone."[92] Or, as a Milwaukee reporter put it: "Dahmer saved a penis from one victim and painted it flesh-colored so it would look natural."[93] This prop became one of the most significant in his final media theater, connecting his childhood trauma, his later impotency, and his necrophilic desires: "Dahmer could not get an erection if his partner was awake, only after he was unconscious."[94] It might also be (re)viewed as a general symbol relating the personal theatrics of serial killing to other expressions of patriarchal desire for phallic control in ordinary life,[95] especially given the fetishism encouraged by today's commercial media.

CRACKS IN THE TV PROSCENIUM

Daniel Dayan and Elihu Katz see live TV news events as approaching a communal catharsis, akin to medieval mystery plays.[96] Borrowing terms from anthropologist Victor Turner as well as from Freud, Dayan and Katz call mass-media events "liminal" moments of ritual passage and "sacrifice," in which journalists, as "priests," make the living room "sacred" through a certain degree of choral catharsis, "by the viewers' consciousness of the sheer size of the audience and by the 'oceanic' feeling of being immersed in it."[97] The Dahmer show trial certainly became a liminal event, with some degree of communal catharsis for those watching from "sacred" living rooms, guided in the rite by journalistic, judicial, and psychiatric priests on screen—especially in Milwaukee, where it was broadcast live on commercial television. "Local and nationally known psychiatrists and attorneys said that the city's gavel-to-gavel coverage of the trial had been cathartic, helping the community to face the horror loosed by Dahmer and to begin to heal."[98] But the lure of communal catharsis in the re-dramatizing of the Dahmer myth also provided a deceptive Apollonian screen, masking the Dionysian "horror" of Jeffrey Dahmer.

Dahmer's crimes were not performed in "reenactments" on screen, as is the fashion on *America's Most Wanted*. But a red dot in the corner of the screen (in the Milwaukee broadcast) warned—or alerted—spectators to the most perverse details of his confessions, as related by police and therapists on the witness stand. This red dot advertised, like an R or NC-17 movie rating (and similar labels on today's TV programs), the desirable danger of watching and listening at certain dramatic moments, despite the otherwise tedious courtroom details throughout the day-long broadcasts. For the courtroom show itself was not very dramatic. The tragic terror of the victims never appeared on screen, only an enigmatic photograph of each one smiling for the camera at some other point in his life. None of the photos taken by Dahmer of his victims was shown on TV, nor was the other evidence he left. Dahmer himself appeared in the courtroom in a mild-mannered mask, despite his claim of insanity, while witnesses read confession statements and used esoteric psychiatric terms. (Dr. Fred Berlin, an expert witness for the defense, became almost comical in his flustered fumbling with notes, which he had crammed into a suitcase.)[99] The sheer number of crimes and victims' names made the judicial ritual numbing and confusing to watch. Even the red-dot details were repeated over and over by various witnesses to Dahmer's confessions, through the seemingly endless questions of attorneys on either side, trying to spin the testimony their way or undermine the credibility of the other side's witnesses—until the legal game, rather than Dahmer's deeds, became the only *agon*(y).

While such courtroom rituals controlled the Dahmer drama, almost to the point of theatrical absurdity, there were entertaining and insightful moments of dark comedy and Dionysian climax, shattering the Apollonian mask of legal propriety and rationality. The usually expressionless Dahmer even laughed with his courtroom audience at the beginning of his trial, when his attorney, Gerald Boyle, held up a tabloid newspaper headline: "MILWAUKEE CANNIBAL KILLER EATS HIS CELLMATE."[100] But throughout most of the televised proceedings, Dahmer remained hidden behind his Apollonian mask and came across as a shy, handsome cannibal. According to one of the courtroom spectators, literature scholar Brian Masters, Dahmer "showed no signs of self-importance or diabolic character. He might also have been a spectator at the play rather than its principal actor." Yet Dahmer resisted the role of both spectator and spectacle. In fact, he took off his spectacles before entering the courtroom, because he did not want to see "what was going on or who might be looking at him."[101] Like a Brechtian actor (but for his own reasons), Dahmer distanced himself from the legal morality play, in which his mythic character starred. While he wore a mask of normality and poor vision to hide his shame from the Other's gaze, the sacrificial passions of his audience did break through the legal frame. At one cathartic point in the courtroom performance, the diabolic scapegoat merged with the emotionally distant body of the defendant through a certain spectator's unexpected action.

Though the victims' pain had been displaced by the legal process and psychological testimony, Judge Laurence Gram allowed one representative from each victim's family to address the court after the verdict and before the sentencing. Most of them politely expressed their personal feelings, but one, Rita Isbell (sister of victim Errol Lindsey), suddenly revealed the real *chora*[102] repressed by the symbolic order of the trial and its TV proscenium. "Whatever your name is, Satan. I'm mad. This is how you act when you are out of control. [*Voice rising*] I don't ever want to see my mother have to go through this again. Never, Jeffrey! [*Screaming*] I hate you motherfucker! I hate you!"[103] While screaming this, she rushed toward Dahmer and had to be restrained by the bailiffs. It seemed a pure act of rage, a Lacanian *passage à l'acte*. Yet her words also declared that she was acting for Dahmer, as well as the court and the TV audience—like Artaud's stage martyr "signaling through the flames," as well as Brecht's street-scene "demonstrator."[104] This is how *you* acted, how you suddenly became violent and killed my brother. You are not me, but I must become you in this moment to show the world who you really are, Satan. Because you have possessed me, too, with your evil rage.

Such homeopathic moments are rare in TV drama and when captured by the news camera are usually—like the Rodney King beating—repeated so often that their "live" cathartic power is beaten out of them. Yet Isbell's performance in court nearly upstaged the expected climax of the trial: a short speech given by Dahmer himself. But that speech also bore certain Dionysian insights. Speaking for the first time in court, Dahmer read from a previously composed script in a very undiabolic, unemotional voice. "This has never been a case of trying to get free," he explained. "Frankly, I wanted death." (Those of us watching at the time did not know his desire would be fulfilled, even without a Wisconsin death penalty, through the prison assassination two years later.) "I should have stayed with God," Dahmer reflected in his final statement. "I tried and failed and created a holocaust." Aware of his influential media stature, Dahmer said he had submitted to the trial process, rather than just pleading guilty, in order "to tell the world that if there are people out there with these disorders, maybe they can get help before they end up being hurt or hurting someone."[105] The mask of Dahmer thus turned into that of teacher and therapist, perhaps even of TV shaman, though not as spectacularly as Isbell's sudden character change and spontaneous *passage à l'acte*, which showed the passion for violence that the killer's courtroom mask hid.

Despite Dahmer's self-conscious statement of power about wanting to reach "the world" with his message, his final trial gesture exhibited a great loneliness in the role of serial killer. He was seeking another like him "out there" to confirm his own alien species of human being—someone in the TV audience hurting with him—with more than Aristotelian fear and pity. Dahmer's extraordinary alienation, shame, and drive for human contact were at the heart of his earlier murder, cannibalism, and necrophilia. His final statement explains how, while an active serial killer, he sought help for his affliction through faith in God, inspired by his pious Christian grandmother. But this potential cure for Dahmer's death-drive guilt backfired—leading to serial murder and cannibalism, his worldwide show trial, and the granting of his final wish in the toilet area of a prison gym.[106] Eventually, the only way Dahmer could connect with others, the only way he could make love to his victims and give a climax to his TV audience was through death, that of his victims and himself.

Dahmer's various taxidermic and cannibalistic experiments were attempts at a home-brewed, homeopathic cure for his extreme sense of alienation and violent vulnerability.[107] He made animal and human victims into science toys, zombies, and dead lovers as a way of keeping himself company, even though that separated him even more from live human contact. Similarly, our TV sets have become fantastic love objects, offering illusions of community and personal immortality through beautiful body parts on screen—substitutes for mere mortal connections.[108] While most of us do not directly re-enact the erotic and violent scenes that we see on television, we do daydream of them.[109] If left unanalyzed, the desires in such dreams, as manifestations of the personal and social unconscious, may also seek real-life expression with more destructive consequences, as in the Dahmer case.

Stanley Cavell relates the illusion of community in TV watching to the desire for, yet fear of that apparatus. He sees the TV spectator as "monitoring" rather than viewing the tube, plugged into the liveness of what millions of others are watching at that moment. Cavell explains the "fear of television" in the sacrifice of one's lifetime to the illusion of a live mass audience, so that we suffer a "loss of our humanity."[110] But I would argue that this lost humanity is not just the fault of television. Dramatic news events like the Dahmer trial demonstrate that we are already lacking as humans. While the TV-marketplace apparatus takes advantage of our emptiness and love of illusion,[111] we also contribute our specific desires. As spectators we co-create art, entertainment, commercials, and crime to cover the black hole of mortality and to "screen" our own violent emotions. The reality of Dahmer behind the mythic media mask hypostatizes our fear of, yet identification with the TV Other, reflecting the temptation to fetishize and consume commercial idols in ordinary life.[112] Unfortunately, we tend to see monsters like Dahmer as simply the Other, not as ourselves. We ought to take his crimes more to heart, rather than merely monitoring his drama, even if our cannibalism is regulated by commercial feeding frenzies, on screen and off, upon certain fashionable products or identities. Despite journalistic and judicial attempts to analyze the collective Dahmer nightmare, despite red-dot moments and violence ratings for many shows, despite parental-guidance warnings in "prime time," the reciprocal cannibalism of TV drama, commercials, and consumers will continue. So it is up to us, as members of the mass audience (especially those of us who are parents), to determine whether TV violence will lead to further mimetic addiction in the real world or, through the way we watch, to a more effective catharsis that purges the off-screen rage for sacrifice.

Notes

Parts of this essay were presented at the 1993 and 1995 National Conference of the Association for Theatre in Higher Education and published in the premiere issue of the online journal LIMEN (http://kali.murdoch.edu.au/limen/) as "Performance and Violence: Dahmer's Audiences." I want to thank Tullio Maranhão, Cecilia Farr, F. Granger Babcock, and Christopher Sharrett for their comments on earlier versions.

    1. Friedrich Nietzsche, *The Birth of Tragedy* (New York: Random House, 1976).

    2. Dahmer's jury voted 10 to 2 that he did not meet the requirements for "Not Guilty by Reason of Insanity" (NGRI). A unanimous decision was not needed.

For further details on the M'Naghten and American Law Institute criteria for such a ruling, along with the new alternative term, "Guilty but Mentally Ill" (GMI), see George B. Palermo and Richard D. Knudten, "The Insanity Plea in the Case of a Serial Killer," *International Journal of Offender Therapy and Comparative Criminology* 38.1 (1994): 3–16. Basically, Dahmer was judged not to have lacked, by virtue of insanity, "*substantial* capacity either to appreciate the criminality (wrongfulness) of his conduct or to conform with the requirements of the law" (8). This phrase, along with the "irresistible impulse" test (i.e., would he have committed the crime even with a "policeman at the elbow"?), was used often in the televised insanity trial, especially in the questioning of expert psychological witnesses. Palermo (hired by the court) testified as such a witness against Dahmer's plea of insanity, but his subsequent article, co-authored with Knudten, advocates the use of the GMI rather than the NGRI ruling. See also Anne C. Gresham, "The Insanity Plea: A Futile Defense for Serial Killers," *Law and Psychology Review* 17 (Spring 1993): 192–208, on the history of the NGRI defense, and the current pressures against it—through "community outrage," fear of early release, and the collective sense that "an actor deserves to be punished"—in cases like Dahmer's (204–6).

3. See Melanie Klein, *The Selected Works of Melanie Klein,* ed. Juliet Mitchell (New York: Macmillan, 1987), 180. "In states of frustration and anxiety the oral-sadistic and cannibalistic desires are reinforced, and then the infant feels that he has taken the nipple and the breast *in bits.*" See also 202: "destructive impulses against the object [the breast] stir up fear of retaliation." But it is not only the breast that the infant desires to cannibalize (and fears as cannibalistic): "In the early anal-sadistic stage the child . . . desires to get possession of the mother's faeces, by penetrating into her body, cutting it into pieces, devouring and destroying it." Cf. Julia Kristeva's sense of the "abject" in *Powers of Horror* (New York: Columbia University Press, 1982), and Jacques Lacan's view of the infant in the "mirror stage" experiencing its body as "fragmented," in sharp contrast with the ideal image of its self in the mirror, *Écrits: A Selection* (New York: Norton, 1977), 4–5.

4. Robert K. Ressler and Tom Shachtman, *Whoever Fights Monsters* (New York: St. Martin's, 1992), 29. When asked by both sides to testify in Dahmer's insanity trial, former FBI agent Ressler decided to work for the defense, since he sympathized so much with that tragic hero and his crimes. "After two days interviewing him, I felt only empathy for the tormented and twisted person who sat before me" (245–47).

5. Beverle Houston, "Viewing Television: The Metapsychology of Endless Consumption," *Quarterly Review of Film Studies* (Summer 1984): 184. See also Joyce Nelson, *The Perfect Machine* (Toronto: Between The Lines, 1987), 69–72, on the hypnotic effect of television, as it activates the emotional right hemisphere of the brain and "tunes out" the logical left, because the latter "becomes habituated to the scanning dot and . . . slows down and goes into alpha."

6. Cf. Doris-Louise Haineault and Jean-Yves Roy, *The Unconscious for Sale: Advertising, Psychoanalysis, and the Public* (Minneapolis: University of Minnesota Press, 1993). In applying a Lacanian critique to mass-media advertising, these Montreal psychoanalysts diagnose a perverse "stopgap answer" to our common

manque-à-être (want-to-be/lack-of-being). Advertising gives the illusion of an object (a fetish or *objet a*) that would fill the gap in our being, that would make us whole again, though it is always insufficient: "We consume in order to avoid what is intolerable about desire, in order to maintain the economy of our yawning gap" (184). Haineault and Roy describe this common addiction to advertising and consumption using terms that resonate with Dahmer's objectification of his victims' body parts: "In the same way, the necrophiliac avoids the fact that the other, still alive, should possess the power to get away. *And in that sense, we are all perverse.*"

7. See Jacques Lacan, *The Four Fundamental Concepts* (New York: Norton, 1981), 38, 158, 188, 204–5, 214–15, and translator's note on 278.

8. Cf. Arthur Miller, "Tragedy and the Common Man," in *The Theater Essays of Arthur Miller,* ed. Robert A. Miller (New York: Viking, 1978), 3–7. See also the comments of Dr. Judith Becker, a psychologist who interviewed Dahmer and testified as an "expert witness" for his side at the insanity trial: "Jeffrey Dahmer is a tragic figure. He in a sense was an incredibly lonely person who believed that nobody would elect to stay with him. He did not enjoy the act of murder. He felt so powerless that he found that [killing or making zombies] was the only way to have power." Qtd. in Scott Sleek, "Sexual Deviancy a Disorder, Not an Evil," *The American Psychological Association Monitor* 25.1 (January 1994): 32. See also Joel Norris, *Serial Killers: The Growing Menace* (New York: Doubleday, 1988), 20: "The serial murderer, unlike the traditional criminal, is addicted to his passion. . . . He is his ultimate victim."

9. René Girard, *Violence and the Sacred* (Baltimore: Johns Hopkins University Press, 1977).

10. Dahmer was sentenced to fifteen life terms, though he confessed to killing seventeen victims, because one murder was committed in Ohio, and another case lacked sufficient evidence (Palermo and Knudten, "The Insanity Plea," 7).

11. Don Terry, "Jeffrey Dahmer, Multiple Killer, Is Bludgeoned to Death in Prison," *New York Times,* Nov. 29, 1994, A1.

12. Body-building had also been an important ritual for the young Dahmer and for his father, Lionel, according to the latter's memoir. "As a young boy, I was almost the stereotype of the weak, skinny kid . . . the kid who finally decided that a 'great body' was what the girls wanted, and who then methodically went about the task of creating one, working out three times a day until the 'skinny kid' had been replaced by someone else." Lionel Dahmer, *A Father's Story* (New York: Morrow, 1994), 223–34. Then, when his son was sixteen, Lionel gave him "a Bullworker, for isometric exercises, and showed him how to use it" (79).

13. Carolyn Pesce, "Neighbors Agree: 'He Deserved It,' " *USA Today,* Nov. 29, 1994, 3A.

14. "Fellow Inmate in Custody in Dahmer Killing," *St. Paul Pioneer Press,* Nov. 29, 1994, 8A.

15. Terry, "Jeffrey Dahmer," A13.

16. At least one "unauthorized" movie about Dahmer's deeds was made for video viewing: *Jeffrey Dahmer: The Secret Life,* dir. Rick Bowen, with Carl Crew, Magnum Films, 1992. No secrets are revealed, however, and the film becomes increasingly tedious, showing a series of pick-up scenes, each ending in a quick eruption of violence, with less and less pornographic allure. The Dahmer character

stabs or strangles several victims, soaks a body in acid, fondles a skull, and offers "venison" to another victim. See Lance Loud's sarcastic review, "No Hatchet Job," *The Advocate,* Nov. 3, 1992, 93. After noting the director's acknowledgment of the influence of Hitchcock on his work, Loud describes this film as "ironically Hitchcockian—sort of. Actually, *Dahmer* is less *Psycho* and more sicko."

17. "For a Serial Killer, Money from around the World," *New York Times,* Mar. 7, 1994, late ed., A10. This article also reports that Dahmer, while in prison, had by that date "received more than $12,000 from letter-writers around the world," but the victims' families had not yet received any of their $80 million. See also David Grogan, "Cashing In," *People,* Aug. 8, 1994, 26–30, on Lionel Dahmer's failure to give any money to the families of his son's victims. The killer's father reportedly received a $150,000 advance for his book (29–30).

18. Terry, "Jeffrey Dahmer," A13. Robert Zaller has already suggested that the victims' families were "cannibalizing their kin in cashing in on the potential profits of the tale." "*American Psycho,* American Censorship, and the Dahmer Case," *Revue Française d'Études Américaines* 57 (July 1993): 323.

19. Jamie Hagan, qtd. in "Fellow Inmate in Custody," 8A.

20. See Don Terry, "Suspect in Dahmer Killing Said, 'I'm the Chosen One,' " *New York Times,* Nov. 30, 1994, A18. "Other inmates may have been in the area, but investigators would not say how many or how close they were to the attack." The end of Terry's article also suggests links between Dahmer's more famous trial and Scarver's own insanity trial and hallucinatory voices as possible motives for the murder of Dahmer.

21. At Dahmer's death, his attorney, Gerald Boyle, said he had warned the public what would happen if his client were denied the verdict of "Not Guilty by Reason of Insanity" and given a prison sentence instead of hospitalization. "Dahmer had a death wish, and I know that he didn't have the gumption to do it himself, so I had predicted that the day would come when he would be killed in prison," qtd. in "Fellow Inmate in Custody," 8A. See also Brian Masters, *The Shrine of Jeffrey Dahmer* (London: Hodder, 1993), 170. He quotes Dahmer as saying before his insanity trial: "Death would be preferable to what I'm facing."

22. Jean Genet, *The Maids and Deathwatch* (New York: Grove, 1954). In Genet's prison drama, *Deathwatch,* Lefranc kills Maurice, trying to become a great murderer like Green Eyes. "I want to take your place . . . your luminous place" (161). But Green Eyes, it seems, will get the credit anyway—as the Guard "leers" at him in the final stage direction (163).

23. See Norris, *Serial Killers,* 33, on the failure of the typical serial killer during each ritual murder to "achieve the emotional release he was trying to reach."

24. "A Yawning Loneliness and Ugly Urges Led to Unspeakable Crimes," *Minneapolis Star Tribune* Nov. 29, 1994, 9A. Cf. Kenneth A. Bennett, "Victim Selection in the Jeffrey Dahmer Slayings: An Example of Repetition in the Paraphilias?" *Journal of Forensic Sciences* 38.5 (September 1993): 1227–32.

25. Cf. Sigmund Freud's *New Introductory Lectures:* "Identification has been not unsuitably compared with the oral, cannibalistic incorporation of the other person." *The Standard Edition of the Complete Psychological Works of Sigmund Freud,* vol. 22 (London: Hogarth, 1953–74), 63.

26. Dahmer, *A Father's Story*, 252.

27. See *Brecht on Theatre*, trans. John Willett (London: Methuen, 1964), especially 91–102, 125–26, 143–45, 191–94. See also Robert Stam, "Television News and Its Spectator," *Regarding Television* (Los Angeles: American Film Institute, 1983), 37, on the pseudo-Brechtian alienation-effect of commercial TV.

28. See Antonin Artaud, *The Theatre and Its Double* (New York: Grove, 1958). See also Mark Pizzato, *Edges of Loss: From Modern Drama to Postmodern Theory* (Ann Arbor: University of Michigan Press, 1998).

29. Cf. (former theater critic) Frank Rich, "Loving Jeffrey Dahmer," *New York Times*, Mar. 17, 1994, late ed., A23: "But if we can't identify with the son, might we not with his caring, intelligent father?"

30. Unfortunately, space does not permit a close look at Jeffrey Dahmer's mother and paternal grandmother, though they play crucial roles in Lionel's memoir.

31. Dahmer, *A Father's Story*, 199.

32. Specific evidence for this audience involvement can be seen in the fan letters sent to Dahmer in prison, as summarized by his father (ibid., 238–41).

33. Ibid., 203–4.

34. Lionel Dahmer told a Milwaukee probation officer, after Jeffrey's arrest for child molestation (years before his serial killing was discovered), that his son had been molested when he was eight years old by a neighbor's child. Joel Norris, *Jeffrey Dahmer* (New York: Windsor, 1992), 63. But Lionel Dahmer does not describe this event in his memoir.

35. Ibid., 212.

36. Ibid., 213.

37. See Carolyn J. Dean, "Law and Sacrifice: Bataille, Lacan, and the Critique of the Subject," *Representations* 13 (Winter 1986): 42–62, especially 51–56, and *The Self and Its Pleasures* (Ithaca: Cornell University Press, 1993), 42–48.

38. Cf. Dean, "Law and Sacrifice," 55: "the criminal act, by shredding the veil of the symbolic, becomes a sort of tragedy, a theater of self-revelation in which it is the hero's downfall that reveals the essence of his character."

39. Dahmer, *A Father's Story*, 216.

40. See chapter 13 of Aristotle's *Poetics* on sympathy and fear for the hero's tragic flaw. Regarding my adaptation of Aristotle's theory of tragedy, cf. Joel Black, *The Aesthetics of Murder* (Baltimore: Johns Hopkins University Press, 1991), especially chapters 4 and 5, "Mimesis and Murder" and "Catharsis and Murder."

41. Dahmer, *A Father's Story*, 217.

42. Ibid., 218.

43. Ibid., 220. Cf. Masters, *The Shrine of Jeffrey Dahmer*, 154–73 (chapter 8, "The Question of Control"), though he focuses solely on Jeffrey, not on Lionel Dahmer.

44. Ibid., 222.

45. There is also a possible parallel between this performance of Lionel Dahmer's hypnotized actor (especially if his son ever heard the story told this way) and the posture in which Jeffrey photographed many of the dead bodies of his male victims: lying down with their arms raised over their heads. This posture is shown, too,

in a poster found on the wall of his apartment. See Jeffrey Jentzen et al., "Destructive Hostility," *American Journal of Forensic Medicine and Pathology* 15.4 (1994): 288.

46. Cf. Masters, *The Shrine of Jeffrey Dahmer,* 14–15, on the Dionysian in Dahmer and in all of us.

47. Dahmer, *A Father's Story,* 221.

48. Cf. Irving Schneider, "The Shows of Violence," in *Images in Our Souls: Cavell, Psychoanalysis, and Cinema,* ed. Joseph H. Smith and William Kerrigan (Baltimore: Johns Hopkins University Press, 1987), 145–46: "Anyone who has sat through a frightening or violent movie knows that it produces powerful visceral effects—all sorts of tightenings, churnings, and quickenings. These reactions may in fact be the equivalent of a drug high." See also Mark Seltzer, "Serial Killers (1)," *differences* 5.1 (1993): 113: "The logic of addiction in machine culture seems 'hard-wired' to the logic of the subject and its determination."

49. Cf. Michael Newton, *Serial Slaughter* (Port Townsend, WA: Loompanics, 1992), 77, 125–28, on the "addictive drug" of serial killing. Dahmer also had a drinking problem from an early age, which facilitated his eventual criminal rituals, as is common among serial killers. See Norris, *Serial Killers,* 233–34.

50. I attended a showing of Reza Abdoh's performance art piece, *The Law of Remains,* in Minneapolis in October 1992. Abdoh's "Dar a Luz" company enacted many scenes inspired by the Dahmer news story, including the eating of human flesh. One actor ate raw meat upon (seemingly out of) the naked body of another actor, lying in an aisle of the audience. For the script of this work, see *Plays for the End of the Century,* ed. Bonnie Marranca (Baltimore: Johns Hopkins University Press, 1996), 9–94.

51. According to *Editor and Publisher* Feb. 29, 1992 (125.9): 15, the *Chicago Sun-Times* "reprinted much of Dahmer's police confession . . . [but] omitted testimony that Dahmer had eaten a bicep and likened the taste to beef, because the detail was 'clearly revolting,' executive editor Mark Nadler said."

52. See Norris, *Serial Killers,* 219–20, on the "masks of sanity" of many serial killers.

53. Dahmer, *A Father's Story,* 89.

54. Ibid., 92.

55. Ibid., 52.

56. See Sigmund Freud, *Standard Edition* 18: 14–17, for his analysis of the child's game of throwing a toy away (and saying *fort,* "gone"), then pulling it back (and saying *da,* "here"). See also Lacan's description of the stage edge in this primal game: "For the game of the cotton-reel is the subject's answer to what the mother's absence has created at the frontier of his domain—the edge of his cradle—namely, a *ditch,* around which he can only play at jumping" (*The Four Fundamental Concepts,* 62).

57. Dahmer, *A Father's Story,* 52.

58. Cf. Richard Boothby, *Death and Desire* (New York: Routledge, 1991), 92: "The fact that the trauma exhibits a decidedly *scenic* character . . . elicits a regressive re-entrenchment of the ego's defenses along the fault lines laid down by the traumatizing experience."

59. See Masters, *The Shrine of Jeffrey Dahmer,* 36, on the "small hut" (near his parent's house in Bath, Ohio) where the teenage Dahmer kept small animal skeletons, a moth collection, and insects in formaldehyde. There Jeffrey also dissected a dead mole in front of his brother, David, and put the heart and liver in formaldehyde. The father's memoir makes no mention of this hut, where Jeffrey performed his early anatomic and chemical experiments.

60. Cf. Joyce Carol Oates, "I Had No Other Thrill or Happiness," *The New York Review of Books,* Mar. 24, 1994, 52. "The psychopathic serial killer is a deep fantasist of the imagination, his fixations cruel parodies of romantic love and his bizarre, brutal acts frequently related to cruel parodies of 'art.' "

61. Jeffrey Jentzen, George Palermo, L. Thomas Johnson, Khang-Cheng Ho, K. Alan Stormo, and John Teggatz, "Destructive Hostility: The Jeffrey Dahmer Case: A Psychiatric and Forensic Study of a Serial Killer," *American Journal of Forensic Medicine and Pathology* 15.4 (1994): 285.

62. Dahmer, *A Father's Story,* 52.

63. Ibid., 52–53.

64. See Lacan, *Écrits: A Selection,* 146–78, on "The Agency of the Letter in the Unconscious or Reason Since Freud."

65. Cf. Slavoj Zizek, *The Sublime Object of Ideology* (London: Verso, 1989), 207–9, on the Hegelian/Lacanian proposition, "the Spirit is a bone."

66. Freud, *Standard Edition* 18: 15n. 1.

67. The act of the child that Freud describes, at the age of one and a half, playing peekaboo in the mirror, would also correspond to Lacan's "drama" of the mirror stage (*Écrits: A Selection,* 1–7). On *aphanisis,* see Lacan, *The Four Fundamental Concepts,* 206–29, 236. For an application of Freud's *fort/da* theory to TV spectatorship, see John Fiske, *Television Culture* (London: Methuen, 1987), 231.

68. Cf. Ellie Ragland, *Essays on the Pleasures of Death* (London: Routledge, 1995), especially 86–87.

69. "Numerous Polaroid photographs of the victims in various stages of dissection and dismemberment were present about the house and most prominently contained within a drawer in the bedroom. These victims had also been photographed, both alive and in various poses after they had been killed" (Jentzen et al., "Destructive Hostility," 285).

70. Masters, *The Shrine of Jeffrey Dahmer,* 182, recounts the testimony of Tracy Edwards, Dahmer's last potential victim. In Edwards's description Dahmer seems to have mimicked both the possessed child and the devil-controlling priest while they watched the video together: "Watching the *Exorcist* film Dahmer began rocking back and forth and muttering. 'I couldn't understand what he was saying. The preacher in the film impressed him and he wanted to mimic him. He kept changing moods, was a different person from one moment to the next. He was transfixed by the movie.' " See also Dahmer, *A Father's Story,* 247, where Lionel lists some of the videos found in Jeffrey's apartment after his arrest: *Blade Runner, Star Wars, Hellbound, Exorcist III,* and several pornographic tapes.

71. Anne E. Schwartz, *The Man Who Could Not Kill Enough* (New York: Birch Lane, 1992), 195.

72. Dahmer, *A Father's Story,* 54.

73. Jentzen et al., "Destructive Hostility," 285.

74. Dahmer, *A Father's Story,* 54.

75. Ibid., 55.

76. See Schwartz, *The Man Who Could Not Kill Enough,* 200, for a brief account of this and also Jentzen et al., "Destructive Hostility," 285, for forensic confirmation in the evidence of several skulls found in Dahmer's apartment.

77. Jentzen et al., "Destructive Hostility," 287.

78. See Dahmer, *A Father's Story,* 31–32, where Lionel describes the psychological disturbances of his wife, Joyce, while she was pregnant with Jeffrey. "She found the slightest noise unbearable, and every odor, regardless of how ordinary, was insufferable to her." Such hypersensitive suffering led to continual fights between Joyce and Lionel: "She grew increasingly irritable at my refusal to complain to our neighbors." The father also confesses that he treated his wife's emotional problems "analytically, which is the way I always tend to think." Lionel distanced himself from Joyce's emotional and physical turmoil through his graduate study in analytical chemistry at Marquette University. "I was away from home for much of the day, particularly during the last two months of her pregnancy" (35). With this approach there was a notable worsening of her condition:

> She continued to suffer from long bouts of nausea; but now, a form of rigidity developed, one which none of the doctors who saw her was ever able to diagnose exactly. At times, her legs would lock tightly in place, and her whole body would grow rigid and begin to tremble. Her jaw would jerk to the right and take on a similarly frightening rigidity. During these strange seizures, her eyes would bulge like a frightened animal, and she would begin to salivate, literally frothing at the mouth. (33–34)

Whatever the physical root of his mother's epileptic performances, or the ways he later became conscious of them, a curious parallel developed in the theatrical symptoms of Jeffrey's own ritual practices: playing with dead animal bodies and making love to human stiffs (in his zombie experiments). Joyce Dahmer's seizures while pregnant also led to "injections of barbiturates and morphine" to relax her, which may have affected Jeffrey *in utero.* Cf. Norris, *Jeffrey Dahmer,* 60. Writing before the publication of Lionel Dahmer's memoir, Norris speculates that the "strong prescription medication," which Joyce also reportedly took for depression during her pregnancy, "may well have [given Jeffrey] a condition similar to Fetal Alcohol Syndrome, which may have impaired his ability to control his most violent urges."

79. Palermo and Knudten, "The Insanity Plea," 7–8.

80. Schwartz, *The Man Who Could Not Kill Enough,* 203–4. See also Jentzen et al., "Destructive Hostility," 285. What they mention as the "black art-deco style table upon which many of the victims had been photographed and dissected" is the same table Dahmer planned to use as his altar in his satanic temple (as yet unbuilt at the time of his arrest): "He planned to line up the skulls of ten victims on the table and position one full skeleton on each end of the table" (Schwartz, *The Man Who Could Not Kill Enough,* 204). Cf. Masters, *The Shrine of Jeffrey Dahmer,* 221–22.

115

81. Dahmer, *A Father's Story*, 80. Cf. Norris, *Jeffrey Dahmer*, 64–66, on neighborhood rumors about the young Dahmer's animal experiments, which makes the father's ignorance apparently willful. See also Masters, *The Shrine of Jeffrey Dahmer*, 36, on how much David Dahmer (Jeffrey's younger brother) and Eric Tyson (a neighborhood friend) knew about the "hut" near the family home in Ohio, where animal experiments were performed and taxidermic collections kept.

82. Dahmer, *A Father's Story*, 124–26.

83. Lionel Dahmer defends his ignorance by insisting that he searched the garage and found nothing "other than a thick, black liquid" that he took to be just ordinary "meat and vegetable matter" from his mother's garbage cans (*A Father's Story*, 126–27). But the memoir then admits: "I allowed myself to believe my son."

84. See Jentzen et al., "Destructive Hostility," 286: "Dahmer, himself, greatly facilitated the rapid identification of his victims."

85. Qtd. in Palermo and Knudten, "The Insanity Plea," 8.

86. Dahmer, *A Father's Story*, 119.

87. Ibid., 79.

88. Ibid., 45.

89. Ibid., 45–46.

90. Palermo and Knudten, "The Insanity Plea," 8.

91. Dahmer, *A Father's Story*, 58–59.

92. Jentzen et al., "Destructive Hostility," 285.

93. Schwartz, *The Man Who Could Not Kill Enough*, 200.

94. Ibid., 198.

95. In *The Lust to Kill: A Feminist Investigation of Sexual Murder* (New York: New York University Press, 1987), feminist authors Deborah Cameron and Elizabeth Frazer also point out the phallic, patriarchal theatrics in the general phenomenon of serial killing: "The motifs of that sexuality are *performance, penetration, conquest*" (169). See also 1, 23–25, 63, 166–70. In "American Psychos: The Serial Killer in Contemporary Fiction," *Journal of American Culture* 16.4 (1993), Jane Caputi goes even further in her gendering of serial killer motifs: "We must break the grip of the immortal ripper on our symbol system in a number of ways: . . . by making matter and women once again sacred; by deconstructing the myth of the eternal sex killer; and by conjuring immortal female power" (110). Caputi explicitly states that serial killing is symptomatic of "masculine domination and defeat of the feminine, even when the feminine is embodied by males [as victims]" (102). See also Jane Caputi, *The Age of Sex Crime* (Bowling Green: Bowling Green State University Popular Press, 1983), where she makes a similar argument (a decade earlier) that "serial sex murder is gynocide, sexually political murder, an extreme form of terrorism in the service of the patriarchal state" (198). Caputi's terms explicitly parallel those of Mary Daly, *Gyn/Ecology: The Metaethics of Radical Feminism* (Boston: Beacon Press, 1978).

96. Daniel Dayan and Elihu Katz, *Media Events: The Live Broadcast of History* (Cambridge, MA: Harvard University Press, 1992), 91.

97. Ibid., 104, 138, 192, 195, 197. Cf. Victor Turner, *From Ritual to Theatre:*

The Human Seriousness of Play (New York: PAJ Publications, 1982), especially "From Liminal to Liminoid, in Play, Flow, Ritual," 20–60.

98. Joan Ullman, "I carried it too far, that's for sure," *Psychology Today* 25.3 (May–June 1992): 31. See also the comment (in Ullman's report) from Gerald Boyle, Dahmer's attorney, that the televised trial and its " 'star professionals' had cleansed Milwaukee's image in the eyes of the 'state, the nation, and the world,' reassuring the great people of Milwaukee that this sort of thing can happen anywhere.' "

99. See Masters's account of Dr. Berlin in court: "appeared frivolous, chuckled too often, was too pleased with himself, . . . constantly scratched his eyebrow and nose and perspired too readily" (*The Shrine of Jeffrey Dahmer,* 185).

100. Schwartz, *The Man Who Could Not Kill Enough,* 191. After recounting this episode of trial comedy, which she witnessed, Schwartz then states: "I could see how so many were taken in by him."

101. Ibid., 177.

102. See Julia Kristeva, *Revolution in Poetic Language,* trans. Margaret Waller (New York: Columbia University Press, 1984), 25–28, 46–49, 152, and Kristeva, *The Powers of Horror,* 14–18, on the semiotic *chora* (Plato's "receptacle of becoming") as abject, repressed womb of language and psyche. Cf. Richard Schechner's use of the Bakhtinian "carnivalesque" in his performance study of street and media theater (Tiananmen Square, swimming in the Lincoln Memorial Reflecting Pool, the fall of the Berlin Wall, the King Zulu parade of Mardi Gras, spring break in Daytona Beach), in "Invasions Friendly and Unfriendly: The Dramaturgy of Direct Theater," *Critical Theory and Performance,* ed. Janelle G. Reinelt and Joseph R. Roach (Ann Arbor: University of Michigan Press, 1992), 88–106.

103. Qtd. in Schwartz, *The Man Who Could Not Kill Enough,* 216.

104. Artaud, *The Theatre and Its Double,* 13; Brecht, *Brecht on Theatre,* 121–28.

105. Qtd. in Schwartz, *The Man Who Could Not Kill Enough,* 216–18.

106. See Boothby, *Death and Desire,* 3–6, for a quick summary of the relation between Freud's "death drive" and guilt.

107. According to the testimony of psychologist Judith Becker, Dahmer "bought meat tenderizer, tenderized the heart, and ate it and the muscle meat. It gave him a sexual thrill while eating it. He felt that the man was a part of him and he internalized him. He reported having an erection while eating it." Qtd. in Schwartz, *The Man Who Could Not Kill Enough,* 205–6.

108. Cf. Herbert Blau, *The Audience* (Baltimore: Johns Hopkins University Press, 1990), especially chapter 5: "The Illusion of Alienation."

109. Cf. Mark Seltzer, "Serial Killers (II): The Pathological Public Sphere," *Critical Inquiry* (Autumn 1995): 141–49, on the "mimetic compulsion" of the serial killer in relation to his "abnormal normality." See also Seltzer, *Serial Killers: Life and Death in America's Wound Culture* (New York: Routledge, 1998).

110. Stanley Cavell, "The Fact of Television," *Daedalus* 111.4 (1982): 85–95. This essay is also contained in *Video Culture: A Critical Investigation,* ed. John G. Hanhardt (Rochester, NY: Visual Studies Workshop Press, 1986), 192–218. See also

Philip Auslander, "Live Performance in a Mediatized Culture," *Essays in Theatre* 11.1 (November 1992): 33–39.

111. See Jacques-Alain Miller, "A Reading of Some Details in *Television* in Dialogue with the Audience," *Newsletter of the Freudian Field* 4, nos. 1, 2 (Spring/Fall 1990): 16–17, on the "gaze [always] coming from the TV and filling the void of the subject."

112. According to his confessions, Dahmer took some of his victims' body parts to work with him and kept them in his locker at the Ambrosia Chocolate factory (Schwartz, *The Man Who Could Not Kill Enough,* 195)—another highly symbolic gesture in the Dahmer drama. The smell of chocolate from that factory pervades a certain area of Milwaukee, including its downtown. But that scent has a different meaning now for those who remember that Jeffrey Dahmer once worked there.

5

THE POLITICS OF APOCALYPSE IN THE CINEMA OF SERIAL MURDER

PHILIP L. SIMPSON

In the 1990s mainstream American cinema of serial murder, the critique of conservative ideology implicit in earlier, lower-profile serial murder films, such as John McNaughton's *Henry: Portrait of a Serial Killer* (1990) or Michael Mann's *Manhunter* (1986), becomes subsumed by the showman's desire to craft the most visually striking murder spectacle possible. While sensational depictions of violence can radically subvert cultural ideology, the latest serial killer films typically construct their sensationalism from a conservative political stance that allows for commercial success. Thus, while the films radically appear to transgress taboo, especially in their depiction of violence, they actually serve mostly to uphold a patriarchal, law-and-order status quo derived in large measure from a repressively puritanical heritage. As part of this agenda, the cinematic narratives work very hard to depict their serial killers as monstrous beings. They are human, to be sure, but they are also unmistakably signified in terms of a demonic Other that justifies the most violent and reactionary impulses in the American character. The threat, while capable of corrupting the social fabric, arises primarily from outside the culture, rather than from within its most precious policies and ideologies.

The serial murder genre's gradual but unmistakable shift in emphasis from internal political critique to expressionistic demonizing of

119

the external Other, largely solidified by the mainstream breakthrough of Jonathan Demme's 1991 neo-Gothic spectacle, *The Silence of the Lambs,* parallels the larger 1990s cultural movement toward apocalyptic millennialism and a bleak acknowledgment that the American cult of barbarism is far too deeply ingrained in the national character for cathartic expurgation. Only widespread, generalized destruction of the whole mess will suffice. Whereas earlier violent films such as Terrence Malick's *Badlands* (1974) or Stanley Kubrick's *A Clockwork Orange* (1971) typically adopted extreme violence as the last methodological tool in the use of overthrowing an irredeemable culture, the cinema of murder of the 1990s typically depicts protagonists who have been so dehumanized by a combination of violent lived and media experience that they are incapable of accepting, or even recognizing, more constructive options.[1] Just as real-life serial killers are often profoundly conservative members of the American lower-middle class who have no vested interest in overturning an ideologically violent system that allows them a fair degree of "success" in their ghoulish endeavors,[2] the popular 1990s films that mythologize serial murderers' exploits are also unremittingly conservative in many aspects and generally dispense with social critique in favor of depictions of apocalyptic (as opposed to cathartic) levels of violence. The films most representative of this millennial tone are Oliver Stone's *Natural Born Killers* (1994), Dominic Sena's *Kalifornia* (1993), and David Fincher's *Seven* (1995). The values championed in these films are mostly those of a patriarchy that fetishizes reactionary law-and-order policies. Sociological explanations, to the extent that the films even bother with academic discipline as a legitimate force for social change, focus on individual deviancy—a demonic Other—rather than mass ideological culpability. All of this imposes severe limitations upon the contemporary filmmaker wishing to utilize the serial killer theme's profoundly subversive features in order to explode the American ideologies that contribute to the perpetuation of serial murder.

This is not to say, however, that the mainstream 1990s serial killer spectaculars are monolithically reactionary. They do not completely abandon the radical subtexts of their genre's ancestors. Nor do they revel in mindlessly graphic or cartoonish depictions of gratuitous bloodletting, as do many of Arnold Schwarzenegger's celluloid epics. All but one of the murders in *Seven,* for example, happen off stage. Even *Natural Born Killers,* the subject of congressional denunciations and legal targeting because of its supposed extreme violence,[3] contains nowhere near the number of on-screen murders of the typical PG-rated summer action flick. Rather, serial killer spectaculars invest horror in the dehumanizing and brutal techniques of the killers, which are rendered even more horrifying to the imagination by the mere suggestion of the broad outlines of the individual killer's modus operandi. This narrative focus on the killer's ritualistic technique or pattern-making accounts for the frequent textual analogies between serial murder, artistic creation, and religious sacrament.[4] Through such symbolic associations, serial murder becomes regenerative for its fictional practitioners, who seek a mythic existence that transcends the destabilizing change inherent in temporal existence and thus have no interest in true social reform, unlike many other violent "action heroes," who at least fight for their own reactionary visions of the "American way of life." In fact, the texts imply that the serial killer's success depends on American culture staying exactly the way it is, and while this *can* be presented as a scathing indictment of the culture, in most cases it is not. The texts portray ritual, repeat murder as the apolitical strategy that these primitives choose in order to transcend materiality.

The serial killer, typically portrayed in fiction as a contemporary practitioner of magical thinking, is a manifestation of a general pre-millennial turn to primitivism. Not romanticism, with its implications of idealized individual insularity as negotiated between the poles of innocence and experience, but primitivism, with its implications of anti-discursive, eternal individual communion: an absorption of the ego into a larger entity for the paradoxical purpose of self-aggrandizement (an essentially fascistic project). This brand of neo-primitivism is the ego-centric's natural response to a complex modern existence that, by com-partmentalizing knowledge into specialized and exclusive branches of expertise, threatens to overwhelm the ego.[5] Drastic measures are required to preserve the ego and restore one's sense of empowerment in the con-temporary environment. In our environment, the real-life phenomenon of serial killing, surely one of the most melodramatic expressions of the will to power, serves such a purpose for a limited minority whose mindset otherwise differs in no significant fashion from the neoconservative, latently fascistic majority. The fictional serial killers generally reflect this alliance.

But from an idealist perspective of history, one begins to tire of an unrelenting battle to shore up the ego and wishes to end the war through a divine intercession that rewards the faithful and damns the unjust. The serial killer in film longs for the deliverance of such an apocalypse in order to embrace its transcendental energies, and so attempts to will it into being through constructing a grammar of murder. His apocalyptic performance attempts to reforge, through rote performance of a murder-ous ritual whose origins lie in antiquity, a lost link between language and underlying warrant of meaning. The repetitive performance becomes being and meaning, not just a substitution for it. Through the act of murder, the performance is also quite literally the end of personal (and by metaphor, social) history. It is not really a wish for cultural suicide, though that is certainly one result, so much as a longing for meaningful (and extra-human) resolution of what seem to be insurmountable problems inextricably woven into the corrupt social fabric. America particularly resorts to eschatological thinking in times of crisis because of what Christopher Sharrett describes as a national "ideology preferring total annihilation (including self-annihilation) over radical change or even reform."[6] The apocalyptic desire permeates all American cultural modes of expression, including diverse literary genres.

It is no accident that in the horror genre in particular, we frequently find a motif which John May has labeled the "secular apocalypse."[7] The secular apocalypse borrows the Christian Doomsday pattern for works of a non-religious nature. The symbolic language of the secular apocalypse often borrows the trappings of its religious forebear, including secularized images of Satan as a wandering instigator of deceit and destruction, essentially protean in nature. Additionally, indications of general moral decline are present. Despair, not religious faith in renewal and salvation, characterizes the secular apocalypse. Destruction is the primary result, not rebirth in any redemptive sense. The threat of widespread, nihilistic devastation looms in the near-distance. May's description fits perfectly the environmental milieu of the serial killer cinema of the 1990s, in which the murderer, while human, "channels" a demonic outside force antithetical to civilized existence. Narrative construction of the murderer as a "natural born killer," rather than a logical outgrowth of a culture's flawed ideologies and practices, conforms to deeply conservative "bad seed" theories of criminality extant in the culture at large.

Thus, the level of extreme physical violence present in these narratives, combined with a metaphysical and rather fundamentalist subtext of apocalypse, tends to erase thematically any alternative, socially minded ideologies. The overt engagement with ideological criticism that shaped many 1980s serial killer narratives is subordinate to the spectacular aesthetics of apocalypse characteristic of the most recent films in the genre. Politics do play a part in the structuring of these texts, but only insofar as the serial killers attempt to divorce themselves from context and live in the eternal present of myth. Mickey Knox attempts to transcend the image pollution of his native culture in Oliver Stone's *Natural Born Killers;* (Early Grayce wants to ascend from dead-end jobs through the "doors of perception" in Dominic Sena's *Kalifornia;*

John Doe tries to achieve lasting notoriety through literally inscribing his culture's sacred texts upon the tortured bodies of those who represent the seven deadly sins in Fincher's *Seven.* These characters' murderous acts are therefore performed not as coherent political manifestos but as idiosyncratic expressions of individualism paradoxically reliant on scraps of inherited, easily graspable narratives of primal simplicity and violence. Of course, this supposedly apolitical stance is in and of itself a recognizably American political statement, a sort of politics of apocalypse wherein all class boundaries are leveled through acts of violence directed at the symbolic object of one's frustration, hatred, bigotry, and/or class envy. But such actions are destructive, not constructive—except in the most limited individual sense (for the killer).

Of course, there is the slight but intriguing possibility that subversion lurks beneath the conservative surface of recent serial killer cinema. Perhaps Early and Mickey, as extreme examples of the return of the repressed rural poor of America, do unsettle a mainstream audience's comfortable bourgeois assumptions, liberal and conservative, about the social invisibility of America's disadvantaged. Maybe John Doe gives the religious right a discomfiting look at its own methods in the larger conservative "culture war" waged against the supposed moral evils and licentiousness of contemporary existence. But any such associations seem weakly developed, even vestigial—secondary to the overall apocalyptic project. *Natural Born Killers, Kalifornia,* and *Seven* are three such apolitical political films, constituting a paradoxical brew of mockery and dialectical slipperiness typically called postmodern but, if one must apply a label to such an inchoate movement, might be more accurately called neo-primitive. As their most salient feature, however, these polemically toned texts paradoxically lack any coherent political agenda. Rather, they partake of a representational strategy that levels all political disputes into one primal scream of paranoid rage before the end of everything: the politics of apocalypse.

Oliver Stone's apocalypse-in-progress film, *Natural Born Killers,* is in many ways the weakest of the three films discussed here, not because of its violence, as some of its most vocal detractors insist, but because of what its more thoughtful critics see as its overwrought assault on the contemporary age's "image pollution."[8] However, it is difficult to doubt Stone's sincere desire to shatter audience complacency. Dispensing almost entirely with traditional Hollywood reliance on an emotionally gripping linear plot, nearly invisible editing, and engaging characters, Stone instead concentrates on giving his audience an aesthetic apocalypse wherein all genre boundaries are collapsed. He exhaustively

Apocalyptic violence and the return of evil: *Natural Born Killers* (Warner Bros., 1994

compresses multiple genre films and media formats into the film's two-hour running time: the cross-country road movie, the superhero cartoon, the monster movie, the prison-riot movie, the outlaw couple movie, the police procedural, the "reality TV" re-enactments, the tabloid prison interview, even the half-hour family sitcom complete with laugh track, applause on cue, commercials, and credits (the *I Love Mallory* sequence). Self-parodic references to other genre films (including *Scarface* and *Midnight Express,* both of which Stone scripted) fly by at a nearly incomprehensible pace. The narrative provides no clear markers for what is reality and what is hallucination for the on-screen characters,

124

especially during a mystical desert interlude when Mickey consumes hallucinogenic mushrooms and embarks on a vision quest into his own troubled past. The net result is an uneven film at best. The hyperkinetic, fetishized visuals seem a too-literal expression of Stone's surface protest against a violence-begetting media.

In fact, the final two-thirds of the film even renders the visual technique an irrelevant distraction, a red herring. Rather, Stone insists that violence is more a function of individual human evil or deviancy than cultural conditioning, and that as such there is very little we can do about it other than stamp out individual transgressors, a very American way of condoning one-on-one violence. Stone introduces his conservative concept of human evil in particularly insidious fashion; he enlists a symbolic victim of American genocidal policies into serving as spokesperson for Stone's moral vantage point. The Native American visionary whom Mickey and Mallory inexplicably encounter in the wasteland occupies a privileged moral position in Stone's revision of Quentin Tarantino's far different, less mystically inclined original screenplay, or as Cynthia Fuchs puts it, "The Indian is granted special insights into Mickey and Mallory's fiendish souls."[9] The visionary clearly "sees," without a hint of irony on Stone's part, that Mickey is an actual demon while Mallory, suffering from "sad sickness" and "lost in a world of ghosts," has just watched too much damn television and is therefore of a lesser magnitude of evil than Mickey. The Native American is also a true prophet. While dying, he tells Mickey: "Twenty years ago I saw the demon in my dreams. I was waiting for you." The narrative clearly accepts the seer's reading as the one authentic reading in a plethora of misreadings, especially since Mickey's unintentional murder of the seer in a hallucinogenic panic leads not only to the killer couple's renunciation of meaningless murder but their immediate capture.

Just as the romanticized, "primitive" Native American is outside the scope of Stone's indictment of popular media, so too, it is implied, is the brutish Mickey. These are sublime characters, one light and one dark, and their sentimentalized portraiture does not sit well in the midst of Stone's accusatory tract. The Native American is absolved of all blame in the hyper-real proceedings, and oddly, Mickey is, too, a point Stuart Klawans makes: "Mickey's evil isn't just a shadow of the media after all. His evil must be something absolute, something that escapes the media."[10] The director's cut video release restores an excised scene that only strengthens Mickey's association with the Satanic: in the desert, he is purposefully led to the Native American prophet by a mutated, three-horned goat of decidedly diabolical appearance and temperament.

So, in spite of Mickey's Tarantino-esque cribbing of tough-guy lines from pop-culture texts ("Let's make a little music, Colorado," he says just before blasting Wayne Gale), which misleads us into thinking he is as media-brainwashed as sitcom-viewer Mallory, Mickey can be most accurately read as a demon of apocalypse. The demon is not necessarily Christian (though Christian images of the Beast, the number 666, the horned devil, and so on are obviously present as a part of the continuum of the iconography of evil) so much as pre-civilization. Because he is textually coded as an Other clearly outside of human agency, he manages to relieve society of its culpability, and thus the need for self-correction, in some of the narrative goings-on. Significantly, Mallory is also excluded from Mickey's homosocial mystical interlude, capable only of standing outside the sacred hoop and berating Mickey in stereotypical nagging-wife style ("Bad, bad, bad!") when he fails his vision quest. The presence of these two extra-human and hyper-masculine characters, the Native American and the demon, renders *Natural Born Killers* at times into a reactionary, misogynistic tale at odds with its own reform-minded pretensions. The film becomes an odyssey of Mickey's personal quest to "kill the demon" within himself.

The reconstruction of a primal, pre-media identity through violence dominates the film thematically, coloring its derivative, "outlaw-couple-on-the-run" narrative arc. Mickey and Mallory find a fulfilling joint identity in murder. Their demonic courtship and marriage, complete with a blasphemous exchange of blood vows over a global vista, which Mickey calls "my world," is the metaphoric culmination of a transformation of their separate identities into one murderous hybrid.[11] Their romance has been consecrated by divine intervention: the concealing whirlwind that allows Mickey to escape prison, and the rattlesnakes that attack the pursuing guards. Their divinely sanctioned union thus unleashes a personal apocalypse upon the land, as Mallory envisions in response to Mickey's assertion that the end of the world is nigh: "I see angels, Mickey. They're comin' down to us from heaven. And I see you ridin' a big red horse. . . . And I see the future. There's no death, because you and I are angels." As Wayne Gale summarizes, they tear "up the countryside with a vengeance right out of the Bible." Spiritual identity is linked to violent sexuality.

The doubling between villain and observer in the film further desta-bilizes identity only to recreate it anew in the guise of the apocalyptic demon—a narrative strategy that again renders futile any notion of progressive reform even at the individual level. Of course, Mallory is the female mirror to Mickey, but others in the narrative also embrace his methods, destroy themselves and others, and in effect become Mickey. This is true of Jack Scagnetti, a homicide detective whose hatred for killers stems from witnessing as a child the shooting of his mother by sniper Charles Whitman. This hatred has transformed Scagnetti into a psychopathic obsessive who sees no contradiction between his loathing of criminality and the pleasure he takes not only in his vigilante style of manhunting but in the strangling of prostitutes. In a devious narrative strategy typical of the cinema of apocalyptic serial murder, Stone raises the possibility of social, environmental, and material causes for Scagnetti's murderous behavior and then rejects those explanations completely. At first, it seems that Scagnetti's childhood trauma of witnessing his mother's murder has given him a reservoir of helpless rage, which, like Mickey's agonizing memories of childhood disempowerment, expresses itself in adult over-compensation. However, Stone's repeated visual linkage of Scagnetti to demonic Mickey belies any such material explanations. Scagnetti's character is a double for the killer he pursues: some of the most obvious examples include the title of his shamelessly self-promotional book ("Scagnetti on Scagnetti"), which initiates the doppelgänger associations for the viewer; his abuse of the prostitute in a hotel room visually similar to the hotel room in which Mickey rapes and kills a female hostage; and his barely concealed sexual desire for Mallory, which parallels Mickey's.

The message conveyed by Scagnetti (and to a lesser extent, Wayne Gale, who willingly participates in the bloody prison riot that allows Mickey and Mallory to escape) is that all men are latent psychopaths and it takes but an inspired mentor to bring that latency roaring to life in the form of the apocalyptic demon.[12] Mickey Knox, in an interview with tabloid reporter Wayne Gale that sparks a riot in the prison, summarizes this attitude: "Everybody's got the demon in here, okay [pointing to his breast]. . . . It feeds on your hate. It cuts, kills, rapes. It gives you your weakness, your fear. Only the vicious survive." The demon is Mickey's metaphor for the inborn human desire to kill, but he also posits it to be an essentially innocent instrument of survival: it is the *culture* represented by Wayne Gale that twists it into an image of something evil and perverse, to be vicariously experienced by an audience that has repressed its murderous impulses but nevertheless retains the collective memory of the hunt. The hunt sanctifies Mickey's identity; Gale's voyeurism demeans himself and his audience. It is up to Mickey, as demon, to bring down Gale's house in a final media Armageddon, but pointedly not as part of any clearly articulated reform agenda. As Mickey tells Gale shortly before killing him: "Killing you is making a statement. Now I'm not one hundred percent exactly sure what it's saying." Thus, in spite of his rough-edged articulateness during the interview, Mickey is at his core a non-verbal primitive who communicates primarily through his violent actions, as any other form of authenticity is virtually impossible in the image-polluted society he at one moment gleefully inhabits (agreeing to the Super Bowl interview) and then in another moment protests (shooting Gale). Mickey as the image of the apocalyptic destroyer offers no compromises, no alternatives, and no solutions other than The Final Solution. The Information Age culture cannot be redeemed or reformed—only destroyed by its own bad seeds.

No matter how much the film superficially insists that the media environment is to blame for rampant murder, the title "natural born killers" non-ironically suggests determinism, that Mickey was elected by God or destiny to be what he is, a human embodiment of the "natural" killing instinct symbolized by the rattlesnakes that litter the film's landscape, and that he was in fact helpless or unable to choose otherwise. There is some textual evidence for precisely this view, as already noted in Mickey's relationship with the mystic Native American. Mickey himself puts a lot of stock in the concept of fate, telling Gale that he had been a killer, or bad seed, from birth: "I came from violence. It was in my blood. My dad had it. His dad had it. It was all just my fate. My fate." In response to Gale's socially minded assertion that one must learn evil and is not born to it, Mickey questions the premise that murder is evil: "It's just murder, man. All God's creatures do it. . . . the wolf don't know why he's a wolf. The deer don't know why he's a deer. God just made it that way." He also questions Gale's use of the phrase "innocent victims" by implying that these people have been preordained to die through Original Sin, and specifically by Mickey Knox's consecrated hands: "But I know a lot of people who deserve to die. . . . everybody got somethin' in their past. Some sin. Some awful, secret thing. A lot of people walkin' around out there already dead, just need to be put out of their misery. That's where I come in. Fate's messenger." The riot that follows hard on the heels of this interview, a riot that allows Mickey and Mallory to not only reunite but escape prison in the confusion, vindicates for them the belief that fate has meant them to be together and free—after, of course, symbolically destroying the forces that attempted to keep them apart. But theirs is no social protest or call for reform—only an expression of individual fulfillment.

Stone's apocalyptic film, as controversial as it may be to those who decry its nastiness and question its intentions, conforms to traditional American literary millennialism that simultaneously laments and masochistically welcomes whatever spiritual ills the author chooses to blame for the downfall of the United States.[13] As Mickey proclaims the "Whole world's comin' to an end" and Mallory fantasizes their transmutation into angels in a future without death, they confirm Stone's thesis, however obscured or fractured by intruding thematic tangents, that image pollution necessitates the apocalypse. But *lustmord* itself is a pure force for rejuvenation somehow transcendent of humanity's tendency to clutter its world with bloodless symbols. In keeping with American reactionary impulses, total destruction is favored over reform.

Dominic Sena's *Kalifornia* (1993), while on a much more modest and personal scale of apocalypse than Stone's film, also demonizes its murderous anti-hero for ultimately reactionary political purposes. For example, as one reviewer puts it, the movie's "gruesome cross-country ride argues for capital punishment."[14] *Kalifornia* superimposes what reviewer Chris Darke calls "an Olympian moral perspective on matters of Good and Evil"[15] in the form of a cliché-ridden voice-over provided at frequent intervals by its writer protagonist, Brian Kessler. Brian also emphasizes his retrospective opinion that random killers like Grayce suffer not so much from evil intent as moral imbecility—not knowing "there was a line to cross." In Brian's initial apportionment of blame, Grayce's actions remain relatively pure, if not commendable; it is society's abusive treatment of him that receives the lion's share of blame. It is this kind of supposedly hegemonic "liberal" opinion that is put to the conservative's test in the course of *Kalifornia*'s narrative. In the morally ambiguous manner so central to serial murder narratives, most ideologies are found culpable. Again, this could be a progressive stance, were it not so obvious that the only ideology *Kalifornia* is interested in is restoring evil and Original Sin to the American mythscape. What comes through most clearly is a stridently conservative insistence that moral relativism is nothing short of spiritual damnation, and *all* men and women, but especially elitist liberals with intellectual and artistic pretensions, are just asking for Armageddon.

Kalifornia's narrative arc clearly validates the early observation of one of Brian's friends that multiple murderers are simply "born evil." Early in the film, Brian insists to a skeptical cocktail-party crowd that serial killers, because of their mental illnesses, "should not be imprisoned, let alone executed." The narrative thus establishes its primary agenda: as a callow liberal, Brian must come to accept the reactionary beliefs of his friends. Ironically, Brian's intellectual curiosity as a writer is the very engine that powers his flirtation with murder (represented by his homosocial attraction to Grayce) and corresponding near-downfall. His

Evil and the neoconservative moral landscape: *Kalifornia* (Gramercy Pictures, 1993).

knowledge of murder, which he feels he needs to increase to secure a contract on a proposed book about serial killers, is frustratingly academic; he complains that "What little I knew about serial killers I'd learned in the university library, and the only thing I knew for certain was that people didn't kill each other in libraries." Then, after visiting a notorious local murder site, Brian strikes upon the idea to take his photographer-girlfriend Carrie on a nationwide, photojournalism tour of notorious murder sites and to solicit fellow riders to share expenses on this unusual cross-country roadtrip. Serendipitously, serial killer Early Grayce answers Brian's call. The stage is thus set for Brian's education in the fine art of murder.

During the long trip, Brian inevitably gravitates to Early's exaggerated masculinity, a character trajectory that suggests at least the possibility of a radical critique of the corruptive power of patriarchal violence. The narrative instead chooses to construct Early as demonically tinged Other—a common reactionary strategy. Early Grayce, as his rather

130

heavy-handed name implies, stands mostly outside the complex linguistic structures encoded into law, sociology, politics, formal education, and good home training. To the extent that it is possible for a human being to eschew language and still function in the society of others, Early does so, relying on non-verbal snorts and, when he has to, rural colloquialisms to convey his messages. He does exhibit some rudimentary knowledge of a popular culture and mythology shared with others; for example, he quotes from a Lynyrd Skynyrd song while beating Brian senseless at the film's conclusion and subscribes to the half-joking American stereotype that California is populated by "cuckooheads." He shares a rustic paranoia of cities and authority. In particular, he possesses a right wing–flavored suspicion of the government and corporate sectors, believing that covert missions to the moon are happening "all the time" and that the standard nutritional advice to "eat a good breakfast" is propaganda put forth by "the cereal people"; certainly a terrible pun in the context of a serial killer film. But, generally speaking, he lives a pre-verbal existence based largely on immediate gratification: eating, drinking, screwing, and killing. As Brian says of him: "Early lived in the moment. He did whatever he wanted whenever he wanted."

Through his unreflective primitivism, Early as murderer completely overturns Brian's assumptions about the roles child abuse and mental illness may play in the creation of a serial killer. Instead, Brian learns to enact a typically reactionary strategy wherein brutality is answered with even greater brutality. To do so, he must first admit that his intellectualism is not capable of meeting the challenge posed to it by Early. For example, when Early finally reveals himself to be a murderer, Brian attempts to diagnose him: "Who are you angry with? Your mother? Your father?" Early teases Brian by hinting that all this may stem from child abuse, leading Brian to assume that Early symbolically murders his father when he kills. However, Early refutes this pat theory when he retorts to Brian, as they argue over the prone body of a policeman that Early has wounded, "I know that's not my father, you idjit." Though Brian refuses to kill the policeman as Early urges him to do, Brian is still well along the path to renouncing his progressive beliefs, illustrated most clearly by giving up his attempts to understand Early's psyche. Finally, after Early abducts and rapes Carrie, Brian surrenders to the urge to murder. By killing Early in the film's climactic moments, the initially anti-death penalty Brian ironically endorses the very method he so criticized earlier in the narrative. He also gives up on intellectual pursuits, abandoning his book project as he and Carrie hide from the world on a California beach. He confesses his inability to make sense of murder: "I'll never know why

Early Grayce became a killer. I'll never know why any of them do. When I looked into his eyes I felt nothing." Brian learns to kill a tormentor, but he does not learn much of anything else—certainly a regressive narrative agenda.

In the tradition of reactionary Hollywood crime drama, *Kalifornia* validates Brian's solo act of vigilantism as the only proper response to the Other. The narrative clearly links its murderer to images of apocalypse. As an apocalyptic free agent, Grayce roams a suitably bleak setting that cries out for the cleansing fire. From the opening of *Kalifornia,* Sena provides constant reminders that this is a debased world winding down into entropy. The camera tracks through a rainswept, uninhabited expanse of featureless concrete roadways and shadowy overpasses, an urban dystopia where the only two people visible, a female hitchhiker and the married man who hopefully picks her up, are quickly killed by a hunk of crumbling concrete deliberately thrown onto the man's windshield by Early. Early is a demonic invader from the American Third World, where farmhouses and trailer parks and abandoned mines in rural Tennessee, Texas, and Nevada (all famous murder sites that Brian visits on his roadtrip) conceal the unquiet memories of terrible deeds. Early is thus immediately established as a secularized Satan figure from another world who brings down the apocalypse upon the heads of sinners, much like Mickey does in Stone's film.

The satanic associations are reinforced a few scenes later when Early walks into a chili parlor in search of Adele and encounters an old man mumbling to himself at the lunch counter. The man says over and over, "The antichrist would be a woman in a man's body, with seven heads and seven tails." Early leans in to hear him better, listens, and then affirms simply, "Yeah." The old man's ramblings are evocative of similar oracular pronouncements in other genre narratives (the *Omen* series, for example) where the "end" is foretold by apparently insane prophets, the difference here being that the existence of the supernatural in *Kalifornia* is in doubt. Early may believe in the occult, as implied by his enthusiastic endorsement of the old man's mantra, but the narrative's ambiguous positioning on this issue gives no one else such assurance. The old man's words provide no foundation for belief even if taken at face value; he does not say that the antichrist *is* a woman in a man's body, but *would* be if he/she existed. Also, if we as audience accept that Early is the antichrist spoken of by the old man, we must somehow reconcile the androgynous nature of the old man's antichrist with the hypermasculine Early. Such encounters, then, may be supernatural only in image; they are given bogus veracity by the trappings of the empty iconography of religion. Likewise, Early's repeated association with images of nuclear apocalypse—his climactic murder of a retired nuclear scientist living in the Nevada desert, his strapping of a nuclear-bomb casing to the hood of the convertible, his abduction of Carrie to an old nuclear test site named Dreamland—is not so much an indication that he is the antichrist but rather an antichrist-like figure and hence only an image of him, which is significantly different.[16] Early, then, as a replication of a traditional cultural image of evil is menacing but empty. He seeks to fill an internal void with the glaring light of a heavenly fire he claims to be able to see during moments of mystical epiphany.

The urge to level the material, temporal world and escape to a timeless one characterizes the apocalyptic subtext of serial killer cinema. Early, already given to a magical-thinking mindset as illustrated by his paranoid conspiracy theories, finds it quite easy to embrace a mystical philosophy that aims for a transcendent "rapture" up through what he tells Brian is a "door," Early's metaphor for the circuit or link between humanity and divinity. His impulsive behavior, including murder, is a self-medicating route toward the rapture of eternity, designed to free him of the troubling need for thought or social existence. Just as Brian, Carrie, and Adele envision California as "a place of hopes and dreams, a place to start over," Early hopes that his roadtrip to California will show him the sought-for door.[17]

That California-as-heaven is a piece of philosophical hokum is suggested by the misspelling of the film's title, so it is no real surprise that the protagonists fall tragically short of their goal. Ironically, the only one who may have gotten what he wanted out of the doomed roadtrip is Early. Even though he is shot to death by Brian and never reaches California, the manner in which he dies suggests that at the moment of death he believes he has reached his longed-for door. Paradoxically, he achieves transcendental heights at the exact moment he reaches the ebb of his humanity. At the remote desert locale where he takes Carrie to rape her, Early degenerates into the most bestial form the audience sees him in, nearly losing the power of speech beneath his thickening accent and resorting instead to snarling and slobbering. His swinging long hair hides his human features. At this narrative moment, the low point of Early's socialized humanity, Carrie stabs him with a broken shard of glass. Though he does not die right away, the loss of blood in combination with his sexual attack on Carrie weakens and disorients him to the point where his rationality is completely dispelled. He thinks he sees a "door" open up just outside the house, spilling intense white light over him. Gratefully, he walks toward the light, saying, "Door.

Where ya been?" Just as he gets close enough for the audience to see that the light is merely the reflection of sunlight from broken glass in a broken door frame lying in the yard (though whether Early knows this is uncertain), Brian appears from the halo of blinding light to bash Early in the face with a shovel. During the ensuing fight, Brian kills Early, but this death may have been a welcome one for the sufferer, as implied by the visual equation of Brian the avenging killer with the light of divinity *as it appeared to Early.* Though the audience knows that the door and the light were a chimera, Early may have died believing he achieved his goal.

Therefore, Early's murders have been primitive dress rehearsals for his own mystic transport. He privately appropriates the methodology of ritual sacrifice for essentially religious reasons and in doing so visits an apocalypse upon the American wasteland, which is given its most literal rendering in the nuclear test site where he finds personal transcendence.[18] While his sensational acts compel everyone around him, especially Brian, to read his personal agenda, he has none beyond that most American of all ideologies: the cult of personal regeneration through violence.[19] As with Mickey, Early's *lustmord* elevates him to a perceived higher plane of existence and identity.

The serial killer "John Doe" of Fincher's *Seven* is in many ways a polar opposite to Early: Whereas Early is illiterate, Doe is scholarly; Early rural, Doe urban; Early sloppy, Doe methodical; and so on. Yet both are visionaries preparing in their own spiritual ways for mystic transport, and both win their goals first through killing and then through dying. John Doe's project is inarguably successful for him, as the film's celebrated "shocking" ending makes clear. This killer's pattern, which is to punish ritually and gruesomely a given practitioner of one of the seven deadly Christian sins, is one of the most Gothic and fetishistic yet mainstream serial killer films, leading many critics to lambaste the film for its supposedly radical transgressions against cinematic propriety.[20] Yet, for all its violence and sadism, indeed *because* of it, the film's lumpen Christianity places it quite firmly in the neoconservative tradition. The killer is a Christ-like antichrist, and the film's intellectual protagonist, Detective Somerset, is a cloistered monk (never married) who must first understand the beast and its world and then confront it on the desert battlefield of Armageddon.

Doe, as a religious-minded killer, displays a fundamentalist's hatred of worldly sin and material existence, so much so that he is willing to forsake his ascetic, contemplative life and give himself over to action as God's agent of apocalypse in a ferociously cunning way that Somerset, in many ways a narrative reflection of Doe's alienation from most worldly passion, never has and that Somerset's partner, hot-headed David Mills, could never achieve. In a revealing verbal confrontation with Mills on the way to the desert, Doe justifies his murders in terms that explicitly blame the sinner: "We see a deadly sin on every street corner, in every home, and we tolerate it. We tolerate it because it's common. It's trivial. . . . Well, not anymore." Doe's lengthy diatribe reveals that he is so disillusioned with society's perceived moral decay that he is quite willing to be the vanguard of the fundamentalist backlash. He believes that the remaining faithful will emulate his actions once they are shaken from their complacency, as he tells Mills. In spite of his murder campaign, which conventional morality as represented by Mills dismisses as "insane," Doe views himself as the exemplar of the godly man living in an ungodly world. He tells Mills and Somerset that he feels no more pity for the murder victims than he does for "the thousands who died at Sodom and Gomorrah," the biblical equivalent of the nameless city Doe has targeted for his own small-scale apocalypse. When Somerset asks if Doe sees himself as an instrument of God's will, Doe replies smugly, "The Lord works in mysterious ways." As a man who has decisively changed his ways and embraced a heartfelt course of action, Doe will no longer tolerate social apathy from the likes of Somerset, who actually agrees with much of what Doe says, if not his actions. For example, in a barroom conversation with Mills, Somerset tries to explain his impending retirement: "I just don't think I can continue to live in a place that embraces and nurtures apathy as if it were a virtue. . . . [But] I sympathize completely. Apathy *is* a solution. I mean, it's easier to lose yourself in drugs than it is to cope with life. It's easier to steal what you want than to earn it. It's easier to beat a child than to raise it." Somerset implies that the path of least resistance—caving in to human weaknesses—is understandable but nevertheless contemptible, a position shared in part by John Doe.

Significantly, Somerset, as the narrative's central character, is the first to begin to understand Doe's mindset, a development which quickly establishes the two as kindred spirits and coaches the audience to accept Doe's agenda as more than an expression of mere psychopathology.[21] In a voice not entirely unsympathetic, Somerset reads aloud some of Doe's voluminous journal entries, the gist of which is that "we are not what was intended" by the Creator. While Mills consistently underestimates Doe as a lunatic, Somerset recognizes that Doe's crimes are rational, methodical, and didactic. Somerset tries his best to enlighten Mills, urging him to read Milton and Chaucer and telling him that Doe's murders "are his sermons to us." All along, Somerset comprehends more of the sermon as it unfolds than his colleagues do. He is the first to discover the word "gluttony" written in the grease behind the murdered obese man's refrigerator; from this he is able to link the seemingly isolated crime with the much higher profile murder of Eli Gould, an expensive defense lawyer found hideously murdered in his office next to the word "greed" written in blood on the carpet. A literate man who apparently spends much leisure time in the vast city library bantering with the after-hours guards, Somerset immediately realizes that someone is committing a series of murders patterned on Christianity's seven deadly sins. At another crime scene, Somerset finds a quote from Milton—"Long is the way, and hard, that out of hell leads up to light"—and perceives that the killer is referring to his own purgatorial journey. Mills, whose classical knowledge has been grudgingly acquired from hasty perusal of Cliffs Notes, quickly loses patience with Somerset's scholarly approach to crime solving but does later provide Somerset with an inspiration when Mills gripes: "Just because [the killer's] got a library card doesn't make him Yoda." In the hope of tracking down some addresses, Somerset decides to contact an FBI source who is in a position to run an illicit computer check on books that have been checked out by the city library's patrons. Rather implausibly, this extra-legal shot in the dark brings Mills and Somerset right to Doe's apartment door.[22] But this plot contrivance does serve to illustrate the major thematic point that as a frequent library visitor, as well as someone who can justify breaking the law for a higher purpose, Somerset has been paralleling the killer in his daily movements all along.

The older detective and the killer share many similarities, all of which are designed to implicate the audience in the killer's apocalyptic mindset. Both central characters are outsiders—the Other—and aware of it. The film opens with a sequence that illustrates Somerset's alienation from his peers: a fellow detective at a crime scene tells him that everyone will sure "be real glad" when he is gone. Somerset himself admits to Tracy, Mills's wife, that others find him "disagreeable." Both Somerset and Doe live in a city they find morally irredeemable. Somerset loathes his urban environment so much that he pressured a former lover, many years ago, to have an abortion rather than bring a child into the daily turmoil of such a world, an action he now deeply regrets. Doe also detests what he calls a "shitty world," and like Somerset, he is intimately involved in the destruction of an unborn child as a result.[23] Furthermore, both men fetishize the notion of time, though in different ways. Doe attempts to arrest time's progression—certainly an expression of the apocalyptic mindset—with still photography and staged corpses.

Somerset, alternatively, keeps a ticking metronome by the side of his bed to remind him of time's passage. He is also obsessively counting down the days (seven, naturally) to his retirement. But as he plunges deeper into Doe's apocalyptic mindset, Somerset breaks his metronome, asks to stay on as Mills's partner indefinitely, and begins to engage in ritualistic behavior—compulsively throwing an open switchblade into a dart board on his apartment wall.

But most significantly to the film's narrative, Somerset and Doe share a contemptuous estimation of Mills's professionalism and reformist zeal. Somerset suspects that Mills's unusual request to be transferred to urban duty reveals the younger man's egocentric desire to clean up the city and make a name for himself. Also, Somerset immediately resents his neophyte replacement's need to talk and banishes him from the first crime scene to talk door-to-door with potential witnesses. He asks his supervisor to remove Mills from the case, because Mills does not have enough experience to cope with the demands of a serial murder investigation. Somerset disdains Mills's bellicosity and tragic professional naiveté: the same two qualities Doe decides to exploit in making Mills his final victim. For Doe, fresh-from-the-country Mills is a literal godsend, enabling Doe to complete his series in unforgettable fashion.[24] Doe's climactic destruction of the Mills family literalizes Somerset's earlier antipathy toward his hyper-emotional replacement and horribly inverts Somerset's tender regard for Tracy. Doe victimizes Mills and not Somerset because Somerset does not share Mills's self-blinding desire to take personal vengeance against the urban criminal class.

Thus, unlike Mills, who yearns to be an action hero and ends up a disgraced prisoner, the passive Somerset is the only qualified adversary against the antichrist. The desert wasteland in which this combat takes place, just like the settings of *Natural Born Killers* and *Kalifornia,* is littered with derelict cars and hulking trailers. A dead dog rots by the side of the road, soon to be joined by Tracy's head and John Doe's body. All the principal players meet personal apocalypse in the desert. Mills loses his wife, unborn child, and career. Only Somerset, by virtue of his long years of solitary study, survives the battle by knowing when *not* to act. He throws his gun aside in a vain attempt to show Mills the proper course of action when faced with Doe's atrocities, but Mills characteristically ignores Somerset's wisdom and turns an already horrible situation into a complete defeat. It is perhaps valid to argue that the film's climax, as tragic as it is, nevertheless constitutes a radical subversion of neoconservative cinema, since Mills's self-destructive action completely undermines most genre treatments of the same vigilante scenario, a point made by John Wrathall: "It's hard to imagine even the most degraded audiences cheering when Mills shoots Doe . . . because *Seven* leaves us in no doubt that in doing so he has succumbed to Doe's power, and is now irredeemably damned."[25] However, the apocalyptic associations that accompany this subversive moment still suggest that a final divine judgment—salvation or damnation—is the only way out of the moral dilemmas posed by the existence of such Others as Doe, or even Mills. The desert as metaphoric hell serves as a fitting backdrop to Mills's damnation.

In the apocalyptic terms established by the narrative, the harshly brilliant, arid desert setting serves as the dramatic counterpoint to the gloomy, wet city. The parched landscape suggests that here decisive but terrible moral decisions are finally possible. Somerset faces and rejects his own misanthropy embodied in Doe; Mills gives in to wrath; Doe completes his earthly series of seven moral lessons. Of the three films under consideration here, *Seven* is the most concerned with moral dilemmas and the one most definite in its resolutions of them; it is at once the most progressive and reactionary of them all. Mills and Doe destroy one another through their mutually entangled manifestations of wrath and envy, while Somerset, distant by choice on the margins of the struggle, remains alive to somehow carry on in the post-apocalyptic world he must face on his return to the far more ambiguous moral battleground of the city. As Amy Taubin concludes, "Somerset knows he's no match for the evil that's taking over. All he can do is stand by, grave and powerless. A witness rather than an action hero, he's our point of identification."[26] All of Mills's swashbuckling and tough-guy posturing meet with defeat, including his frantic pursuit of Doe through a city maze of alleys—the film's one concession to conventional chase scenes. The frenetic, SWAT raid on what is suspected to be the killer's home nets only a colossal red herring, another tortured victim set up by the killer. Law enforcement strategies fail to catch the killer, an observation Doe successfully uses to nettle Mills during the ride to the desert. Somerset's scholarly distance remains the film's favored vantage point. As opposed to the gung-ho Mills, Somerset is dubious of the efficacy of police work. He says, "[We're] picking up the pieces. We're collecting all the evidence, taking all the pictures and the samples. Writing everything down, noting the time things happen. . . . Putting everything into neat little piles, filing it away on the off chance that it'll ever be needed in the courtroom. . . . Even the most promising clues usually only lead to others." As such an insightful witness and relatively detached observer, Somerset finds that his perceptual distance from earthly passions allows him to survive the terrible confrontation in the desert. The local apocalypse so depicted, while damning Mills, seems to restore Somerset. Mills's hell is Somerset's purgatory, and Somerset, cleansed of an earlier numbing apathy, decides to return to the city for more evidence collecting. In one progressive sense, the narrative has suggested a possible strategy for fighting the social problems of crime and dehumanizing violence; in another more reactionary sense, the narrative postulates that the demonic Other still waits on the edges of a debased world crying out for external redemption.

Quite early on, *Seven* depicts a frustratingly indeterminate, decaying world slouching toward the much-needed clarity of Armageddon in its rainy urban landscape, quite similar to the one depicted in *Kalifornia*'s opening shot, an anonymous environment where grubby proles plod on through weary routine while waiting for the end of history. The city that serves as the film's setting remains nameless, featureless, and indistinguishable from any other. Its sharp edges are blurred by rain and gloom, a strategy employed by Fincher to increase the film's claustrophobic effect.[27] The civil servants like Somerset who have to clean it all up, be they police officers or garbage men, approach their tasks with apathetic weariness. Media members slavishly convey gory images and empty official pronouncements to the voyeuristic public. Here, indeed, is a simulacrum of the Eternal City. However, as the film opens, this is a city on the verge of having its landscape transformed by the anachronistic presence of two mavericks, or Others: the identity-less serial killer from the city and the young detective from the country. Both will eventually destroy themselves, but in the process the one survivor of the murder campaign, Somerset, is vouchsafed a lesson on the nature of human destructiveness. Ironically, Somerset is restored to a semblance of faith in police work by the serial murders. Like *Kalifornia*'s Brian, he too is educated by evil and hence in some sense profits from the murders just as the killer does, but unlike Brian, Somerset decides to continue his police work for the most existential of reasons: the daily struggle in and of itself provides meaning, without reference to an extra-human authority. Somerset, alluding to another famous existentialist, provides the moral of the story as the film's last line: "Ernest Hemingway once said, 'The world is a fine place and worth fighting for.' I agree with the second part." The irony here is that Somerset has learned to rely on limited human values by witnessing just how destructive the conflict between two moral extremists, one of whom claims divine favor, can be.

The formerly apathetic Somerset's limited rejuvenation through confrontation with the worst of human nature illustrates the fundamental and very American paradox of the slippery serial murder narrative cycle: Its deep distrust of individual outsiders is at odds with its exuberant celebration of individual initiative. Because these killers are generally depicted as flawed visionaries, they powerfully invoke—even while mocking—the language of myth and American spiritual values and thus are not so much the Other as they might seem. Through their terrible actions they also seem to justify the resurrection of traditional American methods of oppressive social control deemed necessary to counteract the threat. The cinematic serial killer method, no matter how demonic its practitioner, typically draws upon the millennial heritage of the wider culture and consequently prods the central characters in the narratives, like Somerset and Brian Kessler, into deeper consideration of metaphysical issues. Almost invariably, these characters come to reactionary conclusions that the narratives do little to complicate or undermine. The survivors of the serial killer rampage are left with very little faith in collective human virtue and generally seek refuge from further victimization by withdrawing from society—Brian Kessler—or by returning to law-enforcement methods of social control—William Somerset. Yet for all of this, the reactionary narratives do convey a strange sense of thematic exhilaration, perhaps because the ideological struggles outlined within are finally coming to some kind of moral resolution, as the blinding light of the films' apocalyptic images suggests.

A cinematic apocalypse, after all, insists that individual spiritual salvation is still possible, provided a cleansing purge is initiated or enough devastation is visited upon the hapless evil-doers who populate the narrative. In David Ketterer's terminology, these kinds of texts emphasize the "positive charge" of apocalypse, wherein the narrative prophetic voice warns of destruction but simultaneously urges social reform.[28] Unlike *Natural Born Killers* or *Kalifornia,* whose self-reflexive qualities pyrokinetically collapse upon themselves very quickly and leave their surviving protagonists wondering "What was *that* all about," *Seven* definitively restores a prophetic, revelatory, and reformist voice to the 1990s cinema of serial murder.[29] John Doe is much more interested in social reform than Mickey Knox or Early Grayce is. Fincher's film is every bit as self-reflexive and media-aware as Stone's or Sena's, yet it somehow manages to turn genre conventions on their heads in a way the other two films, for all their art-house pretensions, do not. *Seven* is most likely the next stage in the evolution of serial killer cinema: a retreat from the aesthetic nihilism courted so provocatively in *Natural Born Killers* back to the traditional narrative structure and moralistic themes that are present in Stone's film but were lost upon many of its initial viewers who mistook visual panache for thematic radicalism.

Whatever direction the cinema of serial murder takes next, the main problem remains that the eschatological voice common to the more recent films is essentially ahistorical because it so fears the historical. The only actions affirmed are those which transcend the immediate physical and social context and grope, however blindly, toward the light of revelation. It is surely not so much to ask that a genre as potentially radical as the serial murder film, which has produced progressive films like *Manhunter* and *Henry: Portrait of a Serial Killer* and which will undoubtedly generate other mainstream films hoping to be the next *The Silence of the Lambs,* should now abandon its fashionable fin-de-siècle mysticism in favor of a more balanced appraisal of the here-and-now American ideologies contributing to our national cult of violence, which includes the apocalyptic mindset so central to these narratives. However, given the current political state of Hollywood cinema and the upcoming millennium, it is more likely that the next American films hoping to replicate the financial success of a film like *Seven* will continue to revel in reactionary politics and apocalypse.

Notes

1. See Michael Stein, "The New Violence, or Twenty Years of Violence in Films: An Appreciation," *Films in Review* 46 (March 1995): 40–41.

2. For further analysis of the socioeconomic aspects of serial murder, see anthropologist Elliot Leyton's groundbreaking work, *Hunting Humans: Inside the Minds of Mass Murderers* (New York: Pocket Books, 1988).

3. Then-Senate majority leader Bob Dole came out against the film, for example, as did other public figures. Author John Grisham, no stranger to fictional mayhem himself, argued that Stone could and should be held legally liable for any violent acts that could be attributed to the influence of the film. At least one such suit was filed, by a Louisiana woman wounded in a robbery by an attacker who had allegedly seen the movie many times. See Ann Oldenburg, "Suit Blames 'Killers' for Woman's Injuries," *USA Today,* July 10, 1996, 5D.

4. The serial killer, in engaging in a program of ritual sacrifices for a higher end, fits well into Western religious tradition. Repeated sacrifice is required for the personal communion between God and man because, as our modern conceptions of entropic exhaustion only echo, the energy of the Godhead requires regeneration through mediated exchange. According to Mircea Eliade, for example, the archaically common practice of the sacrifice of the firstborn served to restore a child of God, as the firstborn was considered to be, to the depleted energy stock of the divinity and thus ensured a recycling of energy. Eliade, *The Myth of the Eternal Return*

(Princeton: Princeton University Press, 1991), 109. Whether based on faith or logic, the sacrifice, as a medium of communion between man and God, remains a constant. It appears in myths and legends worldwide, such as the Egyptian myth detailing the dispersal of Osiris's fragmented corpse across the countryside. Reay Tannahill suggests that this myth of dismemberment "is a literary sublimation of the ancient . . . practice of burying the dissected parts of a human sacrifice in the fields to give flesh, blood and power to the resurrection god." Tannahill, *Flesh and Blood: A History of the Cannibal Complex* (New York: Stein and Day, 1975), 21. Thus, repeated ritual murder is ubiquitous in Western religion, as well as a standard motif in religion's more secularly structured cousins, folklore and the dramatic arts.

5. See Jurgen Habermas, "Modernity—An Incomplete Project," in *The Anti-Aesthetic: Essays on Postmodern Culture*, ed. Hal Foster (Seattle: Bay Press, 1983), 9.

6. Christopher Sharrett, "The Horror Film in Neoconservative Culture," *Journal of Popular Film & Television* 21.3 (Fall 1993): 108.

7. John May, *Toward a New Earth: Apocalypse in the American Novel* (Notre Dame: University of Notre Dame Press, 1972), 33.

8. For example, John Powers calls *Natural Born Killers* "the most sensationalistic attack ever made on sensationalism" ("Lost Innocence," *Vogue,* September 1994, 296). Nick James argues that the film's studied simulation of channel-surfing becomes just another exercise in channel-surfing. Review, *Sight and Sound* ns 5.3 (March 1995): 45. Also present is a lack of thematic unity, as Christopher Sharrett notes: "The movie's confusion makes it enervating and passionless, surprising for an Oliver Stone project, but this flows naturally from the director's failure to find a single, focused concept and a style to carry it." Sharrett, review of *Natural Born Killers, Cineaste* 21 (1995): 84. John Simon best summarizes the film's flaws for the critics: "[The film] is manifestly far too enamored of what it pretends to satirize, even if it knew how to do it." Simon, review of *Natural Born Killers, National Review,* September 26, 1994, 72.

9. Cynthia Fuchs, " 'Man-Made Weather': Media, Murder, and the Future in *Natural Born Killers,*" *Viet Nam Generation* 6.3/4 (1995): 65.

10. Stuart Klawans, review of *Natural Born Killers, The Nation,* September 19, 1994, 285.

11. Mallory does not begin this narrative as a killer; rather, it is her seduction by the demon lover Mickey that entices her first into a patricide and then into spree killing.

12. As the character of Mallory demonstrates, women are only slightly less susceptible.

13. See, for example, G. W. Kennedy's critical survey titled "Early Cataclysmic Novels," *Journal of American Culture* (Fall 1978): 584–97.

14. Cosh Colby, "A Gruesome Cross-Country Ride Argues for Capital Punishment," *Alberta Report/Western Report* 21 (March 1994): 44.

15. Chris Darke, review of *Kalifornia, Sight and Sound* ns 4.4 (April 1994): 46.

16. The name "Dreamland" is also often assigned to the infamous Area 51, located in the desert near Las Vegas. Area 51, believed by some to be the site of military testing of top-secret warplanes and/or captured extraterrestrial vehicles,

has taken on mythical importance in the American post-atomic era and is featured prominently in the fictional cosmology of popular films and television programs such as *Independence Day* (1997) and *The X-Files*. By consistently denying that the military base exists when in fact something is obviously there, the federal government only enhances Area 51's mystique for those want to believe that aliens and U.S. leaders are engaged in clandestine activities of decidedly sinister bent against the citizenry. "Dreamland," then, is a desert staging area for predatory extraterrestrials and murderous humans, as well as magical but deadly technology, in contemporary America's mythology.

17. The central characters in *Kalifornia* also bear out Michael Atkinson's thesis that the nomadic heroes of the road movie (one of the genres to which *Kalifornia* definitely belongs) will not find whatever they envision as the American dream. Atkinson elaborates: "Whatever might be found on the road, it won't resemble any universal truth, it will elude those explicitly searching for it, and it won't be easy to tie to the hood and take home." "Crossing the Frontiers," *Sight and Sound* ns 4.1 (January 1994): 17.

18. In his important work *Violence and the Sacred* (Baltimore: Johns Hopkins University Press, 1979), René Girard argues that society's collective rituals of institutionalized murder, including blood sacrifices for religious purposes, are designed for the express purpose of preventing individual murders. A mystically inclined killer like Early, then, violates the social trust by choosing his own victims but does not deviate in any other significant way from the violent metaphysics of his culture.

19. In my use of this terminology, I am obviously indebted to Richard Slotkin's indispensable work, *Regeneration through Violence: The Mythology of the American Frontier* (Middletown, CT: Wesleyan University Press, 1973).

20. For example, Janet Maslin takes *Seven* to task for being at once dull and "uncommonly nasty" ("A Sickening Catalogue of Sins, Every One of Them Deadly," *New York Times,* September 22, 1995, C18). Beverly Buehrer compares watching the film to "gawking at an accident" (review of *Seven, Magill's Survey of Cinema,* database on-line, ca. 1995). On a more subtle level of criticism, an anonymous *New York* reviewer calls the film's philosophical overtones hypocritical: "The intellectualism of *Seven* hides the true nature of the movie's hideous appeal from filmmakers and audience alike" (*New York,* November 13, 1995, 89). Kenneth Turan, commenting on the film's tension between intellectualism and extreme violence, says: "When you add a level of pretension [to the film] that indicates somebody believed this picture had profound things to say about the human condition, the results are regrettable" ("*Seven* Offers a Punishing Look at Some Deadly Sins," *Los Angeles Times,* September 22, 1995, home edition, F1).

21. Mills, in spite of his refusal to grant Doe any degree of sanity, also doubles (to a lesser extent) for Doe. Mills and Doe share a desire, however at odds with one another's practice, to "clean up" the city.

22. Though Somerset's transgression of regulations is less spectacular than Mills's brand, the fact remains that both men share a common tendency to operate outside of institutional codes of criminal justice in the belief that the end justifies the means—a standard convention in Hollywood crime drama.

23. It is typical of the film's neoconservative approach that the pro-choice

movement is subtly criticized by scenes that conflate Somerset's natural regret over a difficult decision with Doe's savage murder of a pregnant woman.

24. Although one does wonder what grand finale Doe had in mind before Mills bumbled onto Doe's stage.

25. John Wrathall, review of *Seven, Sight and Sound* ns 6.1 (January 1996): 50.

26. Amy Taubin, "The Allure of Decay," *Sight and Sound* ns 6.1 (January 1996): 23.

27. See Edward Summer, "No Bleach: The Return of Darkness," *Films in Review* 48 (January/February 1996): 66–67. Of the unceasing rain in the film, Fincher says: "I liked the idea of rain. . . . I was looking for something so that there wasn't any escape. You couldn't go, 'I'm in this horrible, cramped, dark room and I'm going to go outside' because outside isn't that much better." Fincher is quoted in Judy Sloane's "David Fincher," *Film Review* (February 1996): 35.

28. Of course, the prophetic voice provides no material recommendations to achieve this reform—only spiritual ones.

29. A voice definitely continued in the Fox network series *Millennium,* created by Chris Carter of *The X-Files* fame. *Millennium* appears to be heavily influenced by not only the fiction of Thomas Harris but also the tone of *Seven,* particularly in the series' increasing endangerment of the protagonist's family haven.

Part II

Gender Violence
and Male Madness

6

SMALL CEREMONIES: RITUAL IN *FORREST GUMP*, *NATURAL BORN KILLERS*, *SEVEN*, AND *FOLLOW ME HOME*

JANE CAPUTI

> I hold to the traditional Indian views on language, that words have
> power, that words become entities. When I write I keep in mind that it is
> a form of power and salvation that is for the planet. If it is good and
> enters the world, perhaps it will counteract the destruction that seems to
> be getting so close to us. I think of language and poems, even fiction, as
> prayers and small ceremonies.
>
> —*Linda Hogan*[1]

On June 12, 1995, *Time* magazine's cover announced a
"Special Report." Red, white, and blue letters appeared against a mourn-
ful black background: "ARE MUSIC AND MOVIES KILLING AMERICA'S
SOUL?" This report was occasioned by presidential candidate Bob Dole's
attack on what he termed the "nightmare of depravity" projected by many
violent Hollywood movies.

Time's (and Dole's) question might seem both hyperbolic and ex-
pediently distracting. We have not yet seen such pertinent questions as,
"Is Corporate Greed Killing America's Soul?" or "Are Traditions of
Genocide/Gynocide Killing America's Soul?"[2] so prominently placed for
national contemplation. Yet, *Time*'s question does spur me to consider the
relationship of popular culture to what traditionally have been considered
religious matters: myth, sainthood, sacrament, sacrifice, enshrinement,
prayer, the nature of good and evil, ritual and ceremony, and the soul.

David Denby, writing in the *New Yorker,* associates an inescapable
initiation into popular culture with an atrophy of soul:

> We all believe in "choice," but our children, to our chagrin, may no longer
> have the choice not to live in pop. For many of them, pop has become not
> just a piece of reality—a mass of diversions, either good or bad, brilliant or
> cruddy—but the very ground of reality. The danger is not mere exposure
> to occasional violent or prurient images but the acceptance of a degraded

147

environment that devalues everything—a shadow world in which our kids are breathing an awful lot of poison without knowing that there's clean air and sunshine elsewhere. They are shaped by the media as consumers before they've had a chance to develop their souls.[3]

Denby's argument is that the narratives and practices of popular culture comprise not simply fantasy or recreation but a total and toxic environment that molds participants, willingly or not, consciously or not. Whether or not one agrees with his judgment on the quality of the culture, his assessment of the environmental and habitual nature of popular culture has merit and must be taken into account when attempting to assess the impact and influence of specific features of popular culture. Still, this immersion into a totalizing environment is by no means new.

A variety of commentators have argued that the popular media comprise a modern religion. For example, George Gerbner uses language very similar to Denby's in his analysis of popular culture as a form of religion "in the sense of one's having no choice—a cosmic force or symbolic environment that one was born into, and whose assumptions one accepted without much questioning."[4] Working from this understanding, it is inadequate to think of the popular culture spectator experience as a solely conscious, rational, and individualist one whereby discrete viewers maintain distance from what they consume, understanding it as "text" that can be accepted, negotiated, or rejected at will, or as safely contained "fantasy."[5]

Linda Hogan's articulation of a world view that understands words (and, I would think, images) as forms of sacred power, with potential to cause or counteract destruction, nurture, or atrophy soul, suggests a new model for understanding the relationship between reality and popular narratives and representations. Perhaps people participate in popular culture as in a ceremony and ineluctably are transformed by it, though admittedly not always consciously, uniformly, or predictably.

Perhaps, as well, we do not just "read" the text. Rather, enmeshed in context (that cosmic symbolic environment), we "feed" the text. As a result of our participation in these "small ceremonies," certain powers or potentialities are fed, energized, and thereby *realized* (literally, made real). Concomitantly, others are banished, neglected, degraded, starved, or undone.

Any understanding of narrative as sacred necessarily involves an appreciation of the world-building powers of mythic speech. In a rational world view, myths are understood in several ways—most simplistically as fables that are false, stemming from a primitive world view. Somewhat

148

more sophisticatedly, myths are defined as narratives that, with accompanying rituals, offer a paradigm of the basic values and meanings of a society. Communications scholar James Carey characterizes "a ritual view of communication" as one that "is not directed toward the extension of messages in space but the maintenance of society in time; not the act of imparting information but the representation of shared beliefs . . . the construction and maintenance of an ordered meaningful cultural world which can serve as a control and container for human action." In this view, the archetypal communicative act is "the sacred ceremony which draws persons together in fellowship and commonality."[6]

Myth and ritual in a sacred world view share some of these meanings but go far beyond them. In cultures that understand themselves mythically, as poet and scholar Paula Gunn Allen explains, "the word *sacred,* like the words *power* and *medicine,* has a very different meaning. . . . It does not signify something of religious significance and therefore believed in with emotional fervor—'venerable, consecrated, or sacrosanct,' as the Random House dictionary has it—but something that is filled with an intangible but very real power or force, for good or bad."[7] In this paradigm, the universe is understood as "alive and . . . supernaturally ordered," that is, subject to the actions of invisible or spiritual forces. Myths are "language constructs that contain the power to transform something (or someone) from one state or condition to another . . . at base a vehicle, a means of transmitting power."[8]

To live mythically is to perceive the commonplace as saturated with meaning and to apprehend the events one lives through as participating in the ongoing creation of the universe, as part of a unfolding cosmic story. Just as myths are sacred language constructs or stories, ritual is "organized activity that strives to manipulate or direct nonmaterial energies toward some larger goal,"[9] actions organized to produce power in order to effect transformations, to influence direction, to reconceptualize and hence reconfigure reality. Like prayer, ritual is meant to tap into cosmic sources of power to effect some end.

Extending Hogan's concept of art, filmmaker Victor Masayesva theorizes that the sacred character of film is ceremonial:

> I think this whole process of film making can be compared with medicine that has power to heal or cause harm depending on how it is used. I think that's why so many people are doing it. But what they don't know how to do is finish it, cleanse and purify. We can make people crazy. There's too many people out there making people crazy without getting them back down. Film is like that. There's a lot of people making these films which mesmerize. You get drawn into them. Hollywood seduces you and people

there have the power to do it. There are very few people who can finish it off.[10]

"Medicine," Allen writes, "is a term used for the personal force through which one possesses power. Medicine is powerful in itself, but its power can be used only by certain persons, under certain conditions, and for certain purposes."[11] Masayesva obviously believes that there are many who are using the medicine of film, but using it recklessly, making people crazy or sick without being able to (or perhaps not wanting to) heal or deal with what they have wrought.

In this essay, I look at four films through this ceremonial, "medicinal" model: *Natural Born Killers* (Oliver Stone, 1994), *Forrest Gump* (Robert Zemekis, 1994), *Seven* (David Fincher, 1995), and *Follow Me Home* (Peter Bratt, 1996). I offer some possible ways of considering the relationship between reality and representation, ways based in a knowledge of the world-building, transformative, dangerous or beneficial, sickening or healing powers of story and ritual.

SEARING THE SOUL

> I use films as benchmarks, signposts. As therapy, also . . . where everything is soul-searing.
>
> —*Oliver Stone*[12]

Some of the most potent national narratives of violence revolve around the figure of the serial killer. As I argue in *The Age of Sex Crime*, serial sex killers, in both fact and fiction, are regularly proclaimed heroes—given folk nicknames; immortalized in every manner of story, song, and image; and characterized as geniuses, preternatural entities, and charismatic sexual dominators.[13] The serial killer functions as a cultural hero, one who ritually enacts and enforces male supremacy. He represents an extreme of traits associated with masculinity: aggression, individualism, violence, and eroticized domination (over the "feminine," which can be embodied in females or males). He sacrifices scapegoats, often in highly symbolic and public ways. He provides for those who identify with him a pornographic fantasy of unlimited excess and absolute power, and he serves to terrorize those who identify with the victims. Ultimately, he acquires a sacred aura, that of a being who transcends normal human existence.

Countless films and novels, both overtly and covertly, present the serial killer as sacred monster/hero. One of the most expensive and artistic of these, *Natural Born Killers,* delivers a praise song to the magnetic, philosophically articulate, preternaturally cunning, charmed, and charming serial killer. Mickey (Woody Harrelson) and Mallory (Juliette Lewis) are star-crossed lovers on the run across the resonant western landscape. Both are European-American, young, slim, and good-looking. The film opens in a diner in New Mexico. Rapidly shifting images, beginning with a clip from the quintessential family sit-com *Leave It to Beaver,* issue as if from a television. Mallory dances suggestively to music from the juke box, while Mickey orders pie and milk. The waitress asks him if he likes key lime pie. He tells her that he tried it ten years ago and did not, but that he "was a completely different person back then." Right away, we know that Mickey is a transformer, a shape-shifter, a being characterized by change. A leering man grossly propositions Mallory. She begins to beat him up. Mickey joins in with firepower and soon everyone save one witness is murdered.

Next, there is a flashback to the lovers' first meeting. It is framed as an ironic family sit-com, *I Love Mallory.* The narrative, accompanied by a horrifically incongruous laugh track, reveals Mallory's imprisonment in the nuclear family, headed by an incestuous father and attended by a complicitous mother. Grotesque denial rules: Mallory is raped by her father in a bed covered with smiley-face sheets. Mickey, the meat delivery man, shows up one day and the two fall immediately in love. Soon, he and Mallory murder her parents and initiate their adventure as serial killers traveling through the western landscape.

Mickey, like most outlaw heroes, actually serves as an enforcer of patriarchal gender; he is the only "real" man in the film, as defined by his superior ability to commit violence. Mallory, though violent under Mickey's influence, is stereotypically feminine in all other ways—whiny, childlike, and utterly submissive to her unfaithful and out-of-control man. As an incest victim, she has been broken (in) by her father and thus is ripe for the sadistic Mickey's embrace.

Although it might appear that the film condemns incest by inverting standard sit-com visions of the happy family headed by a benevolent father, that is not so. While *Natural Born Killer*'s inversion successfully exposes the incest subtext layered into all that valued family imagery, it simultaneously takes pop culture's embrace of incest to a more subtle level. The intent of father-daughter incest as a form of social control is to break the girl's self at an early age, rendering her unable to act on her own, and forcing her to remain a "Daddy's girl" in perpetual obeisance to the nuclear father and his representatives.[14] Mallory is patently unable to break away from this damage. This is evidenced by her attraction and virtual enslavement to her father's alter ego, the sadistic rapist/murderer and abusive lover, Mickey.[15] The film actually then endorses incest and its intended effects.

Right after committing patricide and matricide, Mallory and Mickey run away and get married. During the ceremony Mickey, who functions as priest as well as groom, pronounces himself the "god of his world." They commit scores of random murders (after which Mallory usually jumps into Mickey's arms and screams, "Oh Mickey I love you so much"). Significantly, they always leave a witness to spread their legend.

While wandering through New Mexico, they run out of gas, eat psychedelic mushrooms, and get sick in the desert. Mickey verbally attacks Mallory, echoing her father by calling her a "stupid bitch." They encounter an older Navajo man (Russell Means) who recognizes Mickey as a supernatural "demon"; Mallory, all too human, has, in his astute diagnosis, the "sad sickness." In the midst of dreaming about the childhood incident in which he witnessed the suicide of his violent father, Mickey shoots the Navajo man. Mallory is unnerved, "That was bad, bad, bad," she tells Mickey.

Soon, the pair are captured by a corrupt policeman (who is himself a sex-murderer) and jailed. The second half of the film takes place in prison. An unctuous TV-talk show host, Wayne Gale (Robert Downey), conducts a live interview with Mickey as part of his series on "American Maniacs" (the mass and serial murderers with the highest number of kills) to be broadcast live just after the Super Bowl. During this interview, Mickey philosophizes compellingly about the purity and honesty of murder, the spurious character of innocence, the innate nature of his violence, the existence of his inner "demon," and the culpability of the mass media in sullying the purity of murder by making it a commodity. Mickey's words further reveal him as not only the sexiest and most efficacious but now the wisest presence in the film. They also inspire a riot, allowing the pair to escape, taking Gale hostage. At the film's end they shoot him, symbolically annihilating the "media" who, according to *Natural Born Killers'* philosophy, are responsible for sensationalizing violence, making heroes of serial killers, and creating social chaos. The last shot shows Mickey, a pregnant Mallory, and two children riding around the country in an RV. On the soundtrack, Leonard Cohen prophesies that the "future is murder."

Stone, perhaps informed by feminist criticism of patriarchal violence, ably suggests the false opposition between cops and killers, family values and family horror, the legendary Western outlaw hero and the contemporary psychopath, the genocide upon which this country was founded and the contemporary fascination with serial and mass killers, conventional gods and their companion demons.[16] He neatly juxtaposes the obsessive score-keeping of football and multiple murder.

Still, what pretends to be parody is actually praise. *Natural Born Killers,* despite the incisiveness of these insights, delivers a conventional sermon about the beauty, erotic thrill, freedom, masculinity, and sacred character of American violence. Stone purports to mock fan adulation of Mickey and Mallory, yet the film itself is similarly starstruck. All of *Natural Born Killer*'s energy, beauty, and poetry is invested in the pair of killers, themselves figures of ready identification: young lovers with an intense life-long commitment. Mickey, in the grand tradition of pop multiple murderers, becomes a philosopher king with a manifest destiny.

Cara MariAnna cites Steven Schiff, who describes *Natural Born Killers* as a "breakthrough" movie for Stone. "For all his usual excesses, Stone has never been quite as excessive as this: his furies have driven him across a frontier."[17] Indeed, as MariAnna argues, the movie reads as a Western, a "violent and bloody adventure on the great frontier," a re-inscription of Manifest Destiny. The opening scene of the movie shows "Mickey and Mallory in a Challenger convertible driving through a hallu-cinogenic landscape of demons and monsters," crashing unconcernedly through a series of signs that read "Road Closed." Horses gallop beside the car. Soon, Indians will be confronted and killed. Yet, as she argues, the frontier of *Natural Born Killers* is not only the western landscape; it also is a spiritual one. With the land long since conquered, the imperial frontier has pushed onward by going inward: "In *Natural Born Killers* the doctrine of Manifest Destiny, which justified and inspired the conquest of the land and indigenous people of North America, is turned inward . . . to conquer the human spirit and soul."[18]

Religious references appear regularly throughout *Natural Born Killers.* Sometimes, the demon who animates Mickey is represented as a satanic figure. At other times, Mickey himself transposes into the demon, his face becoming fluid and distorted. Repeatedly, in a type of visual incantation, we see the demon as Mickey with blood dripping over him, bald and wearing sunglasses, standing amid flames. Much of the film takes place in a "dreamtime." Angels, cartoon figures, and violent scenes from history come in and out of view.

Mythic beasts as well as animals traditionally associated with power and sorcery in the Southwest—the coyote, snake, and bear—appear. Early in the film, Mickey describes himself as "Mr. Rabbit," a crea-ture that mythically can be understood as an apocalyptic harbinger, a consumer who devours even the seed, thwarting the possibility of regen-eration. In her oral history, Lucy Young, a member of the Lassik tribe of

Round Valley in today's Mendocino County, tells of her grandfather's words: "My grandpa say: 'White Rabbit'—he mean white people—'gonta devour our grass, our seed, our living. We won't have nothing more, this world.' "[19]

Natural Born Killers, as MariAnna has further observed, can be read as an initiation ritual.[20] After his sacrificial murders culminate in the slaying of the Navajo medicine man, Mickey has completed the initiation ceremony. His old self has died and he is to be reborn, assimilating the powers of the grandfather and transcending his former state. For a time, then, he goes "underground," that is, to solitary confinement in prison. During the interview with Gale, he testifies: "You'll never understand Wayne. You and me, we're not even the same species. I used to be you, then I evolved . . . I realized my one true calling. I'm a natural born killer."

Just prior to this speech, there has been a commercial break that points to the metamorphosis that Mickey has undergone. In the ad, a familiar one for Coca Cola at the time, computer-animated polar bears drink Coke as they watch the aurora borealis, which takes the shape of the Coke logo. In the oral traditions of several Native American groups, both the aurora borealis and the bear are sacred powers, meaning they are profoundly dangerous; if you are careless, they can mesmerize you and take your soul.[21]

An ancient Germanic tradition concerns the transformation of men into bears. A group of male warriors, known as the Berserkers (those who wore the bear shirts) magically identified themselves with the bear. Through a series of ordeals, a candidate "took to himself a wild-animal mode of being; he became a dreaded warrior in the measure in which he behaved like a beast of prey. He metamorphosed himself into superman because he succeeded in assimilating the magicoreligious force proper to the carnivora." Part of their rites included terrorizing women and exercising a "a 'right of rapine.' "[22] The young warrior transcends his humanity through a fit of aggressive and terror-striking fury, which assimilates him to the raging beast. In this way he embodies "furor . . . a sort of demonic frenzy."[23] This describes quite accurately the trajectory of Mickey's journey and transfiguration.

Embodying this furor, Mickey is able to inspire others to emulate him. As Mickey testifies on live camera to his "calling," prisoners witnessing his performance are inspired to riot. The film's narrative itself ascribes a causal connection between Mickey's words and the prisoners going berserk. In the real world, several murderers have explicitly pointed to *Natural Born Killers* as the direct inspiration for their violence.[24]

In a key ceremonial moment, Mickey describes himself as "the god of my world." Of course, the berserk Mickey is, in truth, the reigning god of *our* world—and one who demands recognition, emulation, propitiation, sacrifice, and the regular reiteration of his narrative. Stone fulfills that agenda by telling the story and, most particularly, by spinning the story from the viewpoint of the berserk.

In a brief statement that appears at the beginning of the "director's cut" version of *Natural Born Killers,* Oliver Stone reports that his film garnered both positive and negative reviews. He is most indignant that some critics actually suggested

> that the film glorified violence and was part of the problem and not the solution. . . . By saying that, you are trying to kill the messenger because it's not the filmmaker's fault that society is where it is. The filmmaker does his best to reflect society the way he sees it. And our society is culturally in a very violent and bankrupt mode.

The question remains: How is *Natural Born Killers* not a part of "the media" that creates such cultural bankruptcy? Does it simply reflect that condition, or does it work to conjure the murderous future it so saucily envisions?

Stone acknowledges an innate fury: "There was in me, I feel, a huge violence when I was born."[25] Like Mickey, he refers to his own violence as "the demon." Stone's most influential teacher at New York University's film school, Martin Scorsese, passionately declares his spiritual approach to filmmaking: "I made it [*The Last Temptation of Christ*] as a prayer, an act of worship."[26] Similarly, *Natural Born Killers* feels just like a prayer. It is not a critique nor even a reflection of the "demon." It is a paean, an outburst of worshipful and exultant praise, a ceremony not of exorcism but of invocation.

REBIRTH OF A NATION: *FORREST GUMP*

Natural Born Killers makes evil and violence, in a word, attractive. It does not simply reflect those realities but ceremonially feeds that "demon." It cannot do this job alone, however, but needs self-consciously virtuous movies that in a complementary vein promote the same message.

Nineteen ninety-four saw the release of not only *Natural Born Killers* but also its "good" twin, *Forrest Gump,* the story of a mentally impaired white man who becomes a fateful force in American history. Not surprisingly, Bob Dole highlighted *Forrest Gump* as an appropriate picture for American audiences. One critic praised the film as functioning as a ritual of "national reconciliation."[27]

Yet however different a family values celebration like *Forrest Gump* initially appears to be from a violence-fest like *Natural Born Killers,* there are uncanny similarities between the two. Both, obviously, are intended to serve as epic visions of contemporary America. Each film poses its protagonist against dramatic backdrops of the American landscape. The heroes are white men, both paired with an incest-damaged white woman. The heroes' stars rise in direct proportion to the misery and death rate of those around them. Talk of fate or destiny preoccupies each of them. While one hero represents pure innocence or good and the other represents pure demonic evil, these polarities actually function as false opposites, secret twin faces of one belief system, one practice, one god.

A retarded southern man, Forrest Gump (Tom Hanks) begins life as a physical cripple. Not only does he miraculously regain the use of his legs, but his presence also continually provides a sort of divine catalyst of destiny, inspiring and influencing such celebrated figures as Elvis, John F. Kennedy, and John Lennon. (In one of the film's many racist conceits, it is little boy Gump and not Big Mama Thornton who inspires Elvis's moves!) Gump figures in such deciding national moments as school integration, the Vietnam War, the opening of U.S. relations with China, Watergate, the home computer boom, and the AIDS epidemic. As these key moments reveal, Gump is a mythic ambassador; his job is to renew our faith in America's traditional image of itself as a primordial, creative innocent. Literary critic R. W. B. Lewis traces the development of this figure in nineteenth-century literature, designating him the "American Adam," "the authentic American . . . a figure of heroic innocence and vast potentiality, poised at the start of a new history."[28] This myth of natural innocence, adhering primarily to white men, belies the historical realities of colonization, genocide, slavery, and rapine. The Anglo-American nation grew strong through the sexual and reproductive servitude of women (as slaves, prostitutes, and wives), the displacement and destruction of Native peoples, the enslavement of Africans, and an unbalanced use, therefore abuse, of the land and resources. In *Forrest Gump* the mythic figure of the innocent American reasserts his sway, again reinscribing Manifest Destiny (most dramatically figured in his runs across the continent), and stakes his claim on the future. To be sure, Gump's lifetime is no longer the time of pure beginning. Guilt-laden events from recent history—resistance to the civil rights movement, assassinations, war—are showcased. But in the vision of *Forrest Gump,* these are anomalies, unable to touch Forrest and therefore unable to stick to the heart and soul of white America.

The hero, significantly, is named after one of his ancestors, the Confederate General Nathan Bedford Forrest, founder of the Ku Klux Klan. His mother explains that this deliberate naming is to remind him that sometimes "we all do things that don't make no sense." But, really, it is the mother's explanation that makes no sense. One names children after ancestors in homage, to invite that ancestor's memory into the present and to ensure continuation of her or his example. Gump's profound link to that ancestor is underscored when, in black-and-white flashback scenes of the Klan that are reminiscent of D. W. Griffith's epic film *The Birth of a Nation* (1915), General Forrest is played by Tom Hanks. Gump's characteristic "innocence" then functions to deny and negate the historic guilt of his namesake.

Griffith's *The Birth of a Nation,* as its epic title implies, provided a national creation myth,[29] overtly heroizing the founder of the Ku Klux Klan and dramatizing with great force the fundamental components of the commingled racism and sexism that characterizes white and male supremacist belief systems: the deification of white men as the destined force in history, the objectification of white women as emblems of racial and sexual purity, the dread of the power of women of color, the consignment of men of color to the role of buffoon or sexual predator, and the horror of miscegenation. *Forrest Gump* is essentially a kinder and gentler remake of Griffith's text. Subtly, it resuscitates that tradition, continues that story, and rebirths that "nation."

Forrest, the emblem of American innocence, never actively hurts anyone, but, significantly, most of those around him serve him in some way or another and then drop dead. His self-sacrificing mother dies of cancer. Her dying insight, offered in one of the film's many conversations about fate, is the self-effacing realization that, as she tells her son, "I was destined to be your Momma."

Jenny, his childhood friend with whom he is obsessed, is, like Mallory, an incest victim. She leaves her hometown and goes to college. She tries to become a protest singer (to get a job, she has to sing nude), participates in the anti-war movement (where she has a boyfriend who batters her), and finally becomes a sexually promiscuous drug user. She seems fated only to sexual humiliation, victimization, and failure. Gump forever pines for Jenny, despite her recurrent rejections. Finally, Jenny joins him just long enough to have one sexual encounter, which results in a pregnancy. She leaves again, only to summon Gump some years later when she is dying of AIDS. Gump marries her and regains his son—who is also named Forrest, continuing the homage to the KKK—before the fatally impure Jenny conveniently expires. Incest (as it has for Mickey)

157

ultimately has furthered Gump's agenda. Without that wounding, the dynamic and ambitious Jenny might have been able to make something of her life and would not have had to return, beaten, to Gump, a man who clearly could never satisfy her need for a vital, engaging, and equal partner.

Gump emerges virtually unscathed from Vietnam, though all those around him die or are maimed. His African-American sidekick Bubba, though as slow as Forrest, is not technically retarded. As the bell tolls or, rather, curves, Bubba is markedly slow.[30] Yet there is no mention of his being handicapped. He is black, so the film could be seen as suggesting that retardation is his natural state. Bubba is killed in Vietnam, but Gump carries on his dream of founding a shrimping business. Bubba and Jenny are sacrificial victims. Gump absorbs their energies and benefits from their disasters, growing more powerful.

The moronic god: *Forrest Gump* (Warner Bros., 1994).

Lieutenant Dan, Gump's commanding officer in Vietnam, believed himself destined to die in battle like his forebears. Badly wounded, he is saved by Gump and survives, much to his dismay, with both legs amputated. For most of the film he is a bitter, substance-abusing wreck of a man. Cynically offering to serve as Forrest's first mate on the shrimping boat, he grimly notes their initial failures, scornfully asking Forrest where his "God" is to help them. "Right then," as Gump narrates, "God showed up" in the form of a hurricane that wipes out the entire shrimping fleet except them. Again, profiting from others' disasters, Gump goes on to make a fortune. Later, Dan shows up at Gump's wedding with prosthetic legs and an Asian (war) bride in tow. No sinuous "Dragon Lady," she is frumpily dressed, with plump cheeks and a submissive manner. The war, it seems, has finally been won.

Bob Dole distinguishes *Natural Born Killers* from a good clean picture like *Forrest Gump,* but this is a spurious distinction. They are complementary morally bankrupt visions. On his mythic series of runs across the continent, Gump attracts followers who seek inspiration. One man, trying to come up with a successful t-shirt offers Gump a blank one to wipe his mud-splashed face. Like Veronica's veil (in one of the film's many allusions linking Gump to Jesus Christ), the t-shirt retains a sacred image of Gump's visage—the smiley face.

Forrest Gump is a smiley face stamped on the violence and injustice in American history. It equates goodness with static, sexless ignorance, a denial that has solidified into an absolute inability to know. Throughout his life, Forrest remains completely innocent of his own motivations or effects, despite their momentous implications. He claims that he does things for "no particular reason." Significantly, Forrest is utterly immutable, as underscored in the monotony of his voice, his dress, and his devotions. On the other hand, Mickey's core characteristics are transformation, complexly and poetically articulated evil, violence, beauty, and sexual dynamism. The impossible and stupid purity of the "good" in the Jesus-like Forrest Gump, as in the Christian tradition, allows all evil to be projected on to an "other"—a devil, demon, or Satan.[31] At the same time, the utter banality of "good" in *Gump* makes that carefully collected, elaborated, and sexualized evil in *Natural Born Killers* irresistibly attractive.

Both *Forrest Gump* and *Natural Born Killers* wage war on the soul by apotheosizing heroes/gods who steal and consume souls (as signified by the attrition rate of those around them). Gump enshrines a moronic god; *Natural Born Killers* adores a berserk one. However distinct they appear, they are philosophically and morally identical. One revels in knowing exactly what he is doing, the other in remaining blissfully unaware; yet the result is the same. Alone but particularly together, they are signs of doom. Their journey is to climb to the top over a pile of dead, sacrificial bodies. Their destiny is disaster.

PARTICIPANT/OBSERVATION

"Help Me."
—*message scrawled on the wall of a murder scene in* Seven

"Jack the Ripper," the folk name of the unknown man who killed and mutilated five prostitutes in London in 1888, serves as the paradigm for the mythic serial killer. The London murderer tried to make his crimes as public as possible, horrifically mutilating the bodies and leaving four of them outside to be found. In the words of Tom Cullen, he "signposted" his murders, using them as a form of ritual communication.[32] After his last murder, Colin Wilson writes, "Jack the Ripper left 13 Miller Court and walked out of history."[33] Leaving history behind, he entered firmly into legend. Indeed, the most common motif of the innumerable Ripper, and subsequent serial killer, narratives is the survival of the killer beyond death, his attainment of immortality through the ritual human (female) sacrifice, his becoming a supernatural entity who thrives on fear.

If the initiation in *Natural Born Killers* is one of the warrior/berserker, in *Seven,* a film once again focused upon a serial killer, the initiation more closely corresponds with that associated with shamanism. Unlike *Natural Born Killers, Seven* does not eroticize its serial killer; rather, director David Fincher and screenwriter Andrew Kevin Walker *aestheticize* murder, connecting it thematically with elite art, setting up gruesome scenes as high concept, "beaut[iful] . . . lush and lyrical" performance pieces."[34]

Seven's artist/killer performs in an unnamed city; there, he plots out, stages, and completes a series of elaborate murders, each more or less dependent upon the participation of the victim, and each set around one of the seven deadly sins: gluttony, greed, sloth, lust, pride, envy, and wrath. For example, he forces a fat man to eat himself to death (gluttony) and a lawyer to cut away a pound of flesh from his body (greed). To enact a tableau for the sin of pride, he cuts off the nose of a famous model and then glues one of her hands to a telephone and the other to a lethal dose of sleeping pills. She opts for suicide rather than life with disfigurement.

Two detectives are assigned to the case. One, Somerset (Morgan Freeman), is an older, educated, single man burdened with the pessimism that comes after a long career in homicide work. The other, Mills (Brad Pitt), is a brashly optimistic, happily married, impetuous hothead. The detectives identify their erudite killer, John Doe (Kevin Spacey), through his library card; he has been reading Milton, Dante, Chaucer, and Thomas Aquinas. They go to the address on his card and encounter him there, but he manages to escape. The apartment is a shrine to religious sacrifice; a neon-red crucifix hangs over his single bed.

Film critic Michael Medved has identified *Seven* as one of several films that feature Christian serial killers, a representation he reviles as inaccurate and biased.[35] Yet, Christianity is one of several patriarchal religions that have sanctified the misogyny that drives sexual murder. It is a faith in which women have been seen as sexually impure and responsible for the introduction of sin into the world. Such beliefs fueled the massacre of hundred of thousands of women in the early modern European witch-craze.[36]

Christianity, through its fixation upon a divine sacrificial victim, has instituted, moreover, what radical feminist philosopher Mary Daly identifies as the "scapegoat syndrome":

> While the image of sacrificial victim may inspire saintliness in a few, in the many the effect seems to be to evoke intolerance. That is, rather than being enabled to imitate the sacrifice of Jesus, they feel guilt and transfer this to "the Other," thus making the latter "imitate" Jesus in the role of scapegoat. . . . They . . . affirm themselves as "good" by blaming others.[37]

The serial killer in *Seven* follows such logic with total precision.

Finally, the cross itself, a veritable instrument of torture on which hangs a near-naked, flagellated, helpless, submissive, and virginal body, is as likely to inspire sexual sadism as it is to inspire religious devotion.

After his ordeal, Jesus ascended into heaven. Doe expects no less. After completing five of the murders, he inexplicably turns himself in. Walking into the police station covered with blood, he tells the police that there are two more bodies yet to be found and proposes a deal. He will lead the police to these bodies and sign a full confession if Detectives Somerset and Mills accompany him to a site remote from the city. There is some uneasiness. The killer might be setting them up. But they do not see how, so Mills declares, "Let's go finish it."

During their drive beyond the city limits, the killer gets to expound on his religious philosophy, some of it similar to Mickey's: "Only in a world this shitty could you say these [victims] were innocent people with a straight face. We see a deadly sin on every street corner, in every home and tolerate it because it's common, it's trivial. Not anymore.

161

Serial murder as initiation: *Seven* (New Line Cinema, 1995).

I'm setting the example and what I've done is going to be puzzled over and studied and followed forever." They arrive at a place marked by high tension electric towers. A dead dog lies in the road. Almost immediately, a van drives up. Somerset directs Mills to guard Doe and goes to query the driver. He is told that there is a package for detective Mills. When Somerset opens the package he finds Tracy Mills's severed head. Meanwhile, Doe tells Mills that he visited Tracy that morning, and he found himself irresistibly coveting Mills's happy, normal existence. That envy, he proclaims, caused him to kill Tracy. Mills, fulfilling Doe's design, becomes the embodiment of wrath, and vengefully kills Doe.

Early on, Somerset understands that these are not simple crimes, that the killer has religious intent and is "preaching." But soon it becomes clear that it is more than a sermon. The killer intends to orchestrate a personal quest, the performance of a series of works or ordeals that will make him "die to the human condition and . . . resuscitate him to a new, a transhuman existence."[38] The killer in *Seven* aspires to be initiated into a superhuman realm of existence through this dramatic and seamless series of murders.

Mircea Eliade writes that those who aspire to become or are called to be shamans often exhibit strange behavior; they are solitary, seemingly insane, cut themselves with knives, and so on.[39] Doe is a cipher; no one knows anything of his history (except that he is independently wealthy and well-educated). He lives a solitary existence in a dark, cave-like apartment. He regularly cuts off his fingerprints. During the final sequence, he tells the two detectives: "I did not choose, I was chosen" to perform what he calls his "special work." Doe comprehends what he is doing as a ritual that ensures that he will be remembered, transfigured, raised over the level of human existence, and moreover, that his initiation ritual will provide a model to be imitated.

At the site of the second murder, the killer writes in blood on the wall, "Help Me." He intends this literally, for the ritual cannot be completed without the collusion of those who pursue him, specifically Detective Mills. Doe needs Mills not only to embody the sin of wrath but to turn that fury on Doe in his embodiment of envy. By executing Doe, Mills assures completion of Doe's ceremony and the accomplishment of his transformation. Somerset understands this and warns Mills, "If you kill him, he will win." But Mills is too foolish to comprehend, too much like the killer to stop himself from mirroring and completing him.

This last scene is highly reminiscent of the final scene in Leslie Marmon Silko's novel *Ceremony*. Here, the protagonist, Tayo, while bringing to completion an involved ceremony of healing (for himself and the world), must resist an overwhelming impulse to murder an evildoer. He is able to restrain himself, but "it had been a close call. The witchery had almost ended the story according to its plan."[40] Had this occurred, it would have brought unspeakable destruction, not healing. In *Seven,* there is no resistance. The "witchery" wins; the ceremony of evil is completed.

Doe's ceremony hinges in every respect upon participation of others. The victims must participate in their own murders. Of the detectives, Mills is the obvious participant, but Somerset is also complicit. Rituals must be observed and witnessed. Somerset plays the crucial role of observing the ceremony, authenticating it, solemnizing it, and carrying the knowledge of it forever seared into his memory. He provides the film's voice-over. Like the one witness spared by Mickey and Mallory at each murder scene, he survives to tell the tale.

A reviewer on the Internet writes of his recognition that "There's a palpable sense as the story winds down that something very real is at stake. . . . The climax is likely to resonate in your head for hours, perhaps days after viewing. . . . *Seven* finds the dark heart of the soul and pokes at it 'til it bursts."[41] This palpable sense of something very real at stake is perhaps because the film not only represents or tells a story about a ceremony of soul-murder. It actually functions as such a ceremony and one that is equally dependent upon participation—in this case, that of the viewer. "Help me," pleads John Doe. Have we?

HEALING THE SOUL WOUND

> Art unfailingly reflects its creator's heart. Art that comes from a heart open to all the possible paths there might be to a healthier tomorrow cannot help but be medicine for the tribe.
>
> —*Alice Walker, on* Follow Me Home[42]

Film, like all art both popular and elite, is a form of power for creation or destruction. It has the power to stir emotion, to dramatize myth, to tell the stories that shape reality, to tap into the dream and reach deeply into the unconsciousness of viewers; it is a medium, some would even say, with the capacity to summon transformative forces, for good or evil, and to carry messages from and to nonhuman sources.[43]

Follow Me Home, directed by Peter Bratt, is a film of exceptional healing powers. It purposefully recognizes that creation is ongoing and is a collaborative project between the dreamtime and the real world. In Peter Bratt's words: "What often gets called the dreamworld and reality aren't really distinguished in many traditional cultures, so I try not to get wrapped in that very western linear way of telling a story. The spirit and the contemporary voices are present all the time. It's just that at different times, different voices get loud."[44]

The narrative concerns four artists. The two most completely drawn characters are Tudee (Jesse Borrego), the group's leader, a Chicano who is battling to keep his integrity and who wants to be an activist against oppression, and Abel (Benjamin Bratt), his misogynist, self-destructive, and preeminently vital cousin. The other two are Kaz (Calvin Levels), a well-educated African American, intent on living a serene and healthy existence, and Freddy (Steve Reevis), a Native American man who is a recovering alcoholic.

The very first scene takes us into the dreamtime, the world of spirits, origins, magic. Ancestors come in and out of view. Drumming and whispering are heard. The scene cuts to reality; an old, homeless blind man drums a conga on a city street, asking for change. The scene shifts again, and we see a mural in the process of being painted.

Called "The Ancestors," it depicts a collage of "Pre-Columbian and Post-Colombian images. Faces and bodies: plant, animal, human, Indian, African, Asian—a surreal dreamscape." This is the mural Tudee, Freddy, Abel, and Kaz are finishing. Tudee plans that they will travel east from Los Angeles to paint a mural of their ancestors on the White House, "putting our images, our colors on the walls of LA CASA BLANCA." They plan to leave that evening but still are squabbling about the feasibility of their quest. Tudee articulates the importance of the project: "It's like words are symbols, like these images we paint. And every image or word we use to describe a reality, helps to create and define that reality. It's only a matter of time before whatever it is we project becomes the reality itself. . . . Tu sabes?" Abel, frustrated with this theoretical tone, tells his cousin, "You want a 'reality projection'? Shit, I got one right here between my legs." Kaz then joins in, "Actually, you're right. The, quote-unquote, reality in which we live is very much a projection of the male organ, that is the penis. The absence of the female energy, or as you understand it, the energy of the 'bitch,' is why the world is so, excuse me, fucked up, and why some people think and speak in the misogynistic way that you do." Abel responds, "[I]t was a bitch, excuse me, Eve, who got Adam's ass kicked out in the first place." Kaz takes this opportunity to clarify, "You're saying that we live in a patriarchal theocracy that sanctifies male dominance by an authoritarian religion. And I'm saying, what about other creation myths, yours, mine, ones that don't necessarily displace the female principle?"

All this talk of creation myth, Eve, and the female principle prepares us for the introduction of the fifth central character, Evey (Alfre Woodard). Stopping for food at a roadside diner, they encounter an African-American woman, Evey, carrying a sealed package. She is clearly in a state of mourning. We later find out that she bears a funeral urn, carrying the ashes of her dead daughter, slain when she was caught in gang crossfire.

As the four travel east, Tudee repeatedly slips into the dreamtime where he has a servant/apprentice-like relationship to an older man, the "White Man," who represents historical phases of colonization and economic exploitation. Back in real time, the four again meet up with Evey, this time on the road. A white man dressed as an Indian suddenly dies and rear-ends her car. He is part of a group of cavalry enthusiasts who dress up and reenact historical battles. Three of the dead man's friends, all white men in military dress, come upon the group at the scene of the accident and immediately draw their guns. While searching his van, they discover that a valuable "antique tomahawk" is missing. Abel, who has been asleep in Freddy's van, comes out with his own gun and takes charge. They loosely tie up the white men and leave with Evey. As they drive along, Tudee once again slips into dreamland. There he meets a girl, Evey's dead daughter, although he does not realize who she is. She is singing her favorite song, "Rapper's Delight." Tudee joins in; it is his favorite song, too. They walk around a schoolyard, and the child invites Tudee to touch up the faded images on a mural and then says good-bye.

We are back in the real world. As the five drive down the road, Abel begins to flaunt his misogyny, continually taunting Evey and referring to her as the "bitch." Evey challenges him: "You know if you ever tire of calling me a bitch, you can always substitute it with nigger. For me the terms mean the same thing." Abel, reeling, nevertheless mocks her, "I bet you're one of them feminist type bitches ain't you? Like those ho's who go around trying to cut a motherfucker's balls off." Evey looks deeply into his eyes, demands and then gets his respect with these words: "I am not a ho and I am not a bitch. Like your mother who gave you life, and her mother who gave her her own; like your aunts and sisters and daughters— I am a woman. Do you understand me, A WOMAN." Abel finally greets her gaze with respect. He has heard her and learned something.

Meanwhile, the three battle re-enactors wait in their car, hoping to intercept the five travelers and regain the tomahawk. A deejay heard on the car radio offers "a big warm welcome to all of you re-enactment enthusiasts and historians who have convened in town for the sixth annual Days of Blue. These boys have come from every part of the country to re-create the battles of our nation's glorious past. And by doing so, they not only honor our proud American history, but literally, literally keep it alive." Larry, the group's leader, congratulates the deejay on his insight.

Two of the men, Larry and Farmer, while away the time with sexist and racist commentary about sex with women of color. They mock the other man, Perry, because he has studied Eastern religions and because his wife left him to be with a Japanese meditation leader. Larry and Farmer are incredulous that he sees no need to avenge this; they also joke about killing the artists when they find them. Eventually, the van does come by. The white men give chase and fire upon the van, causing Tudee to drive off the road. The five are taken to a cabin, taunted, and threatened. A key concern is the return of the tomahawk. Freddy, the only one who actually reached into the dead man's van denies ever having even seen the tomahawk. Larry and Farmer taunt and threaten the captives. Perry becomes increasingly uncomfortable as the situation gets more and more dangerous.

166

Tudee, mysteriously, begins to chant the opening verses of "Rapper's Delight," Evey, then Freddy, and then Abel and Kaz join in. The chant is clearly magical, summoning the spirits, conjuring force. More out of fear than anything else, one of the white men, Farmer, holds a gun to Tudee's head. As the five continue chanting, their voices fade, replaced by the whispering of spirit voices. Tudee slips into the dreamland. He begins to tell a story in the voice of an indigenous person of centuries ago who is looking eastward, knowing that invaders are coming to claim ownership of the Earth. He is aware that they will try to destroy him, that they will consume until there is nothing left "and there will be no more blood to let but your own." At that point, he fears, "I will become like you, and I will be unrecognizable even to myself." Now Tudee, enraged, picks up an iron bar and moves to injure lethally the "White Man." He is just about to strike when Evey's daughter appears; she points to an Indian woman emerging from a shaft of light. The woman beckons to Tudee "to follow" her. The voices of the spirits grow very loud. Suddenly we are back in real time. The five are still chanting from "Rapper's Delight" but what we hear are the spirit whispers. Larry signals Farmer to fire into Tudee's head. A shot rings out. But it is Farmer who is lying injured on the ground. Perry has clipped him in the leg. Perry then releases the captives, telling his former compatriots that what they were doing was wrong. The film closes as the five now head once again for Washington, D.C. We learn that Freddy actually has taken the tomahawk: "It never belonged to them," he avers.

Follow Me Home is a ritual of sacred reversal. Freddy's reclaiming of the tomahawk names the real crime—European-American seizure and exploitation of land, resources, iconography, and religion—and symbolically redresses that injustice. Teresa Córdova writes, "The taking of the tomahawk is an act of retrieval, an act of recovery that symbolizes the first step in reversing the damages, the hidden pain, of colonial terrorism."[45] *Follow Me Home* does not reinscribe, but rather unravels Manifest Destiny. Acting as a symbolic counter to that fatal story; its seekers journey East on a quest to honor, not desecrate, the ancestors and spirits of this land.

Follow Me Home's vision restores the female principle to her sacred centrality. Evey's presence evokes and invokes the mythic Great Black Mother. As Lucia Chiavola Birnbaum observes, "Contemporary paleontology, archeology, and genetics indicate that the mother of the human race came from Africa and she is black."[46] Her memory is enshrined worldwide in the traditions of Black Madonnas, even in countries such as Italy, France, and Poland where the people are light-skinned. Through

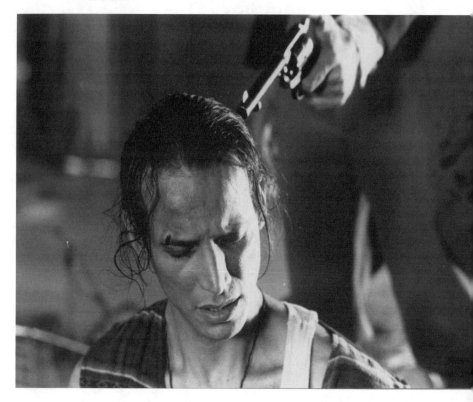

Follow Me Home: Ritually reversing Manifest Destiny (New Millennia Films, 1995).

her dignity, presence, and presentation of the original and divine Dark Mother, Evey begins to heal Abel (and, concomitantly, viewers) of misogyny.

Follow Me Home is about healing, not searing, the soul. The producers of the film, Eduardo and Bonnie Duran, offer a conceptualization of the "soul wound" in their book, *Native American Postcolonial Psychology:*

> The core of Native American awareness . . . is the fabric of soul and it is from this essence that mythology, dreams, and culture emerge. Once the core from which soul emerges is wounded then all of the emerging mythology and dreams of a people reflect the wound. The manifestations of such a wound are then embodied by the tremendous suffering that the people have undergone since the collective soul wound was inflicted half a millennium ago.[47]

168

Peter Bratt cites the influence of the Durans' conception of the soul wound on the story of *Follow Me Home:* "All of the main characters carry . . . the soul wound . . . a result of the perpetration that was committed against the Indian people of the Americas, and also the Africans, who were brought here as slaves."[48]

Reviewing the film for *La Voz de Berkeley*, Marina Estrada-Meléndez describes Chicanos' intense feelings of identification with the characters. Her words, regarding Abel, profoundly convey the trauma of the soul wound:

> We are all like Abel, in too many ways. Displaced, out of place, in torn up cities, disconnected from any form of nature, smothered with pollution, diseases, drugs, tv, a death culture, a culture that is not our own, we find ourselves caught up in and completely lost at the same time by its insanity. In turn, we are eating ourselves alive, we are going insane.[49]

This soul wound, however grievous, can be healed. The Durans offer this insight: "Since the soul wound occurred at the level of myth and dream, it follows that the therapy of transformation of the wound should also occur at the level of myth and dream."[50]

In Marshall McLuhan's sense of media as an extension of human capacities, both physical and psychic, film is an extension of the dreaming faculty.[51] Film, like dream, takes place in the dark; it speaks in the language of symbol, myth, and ritual. *Follow Me Home* pictures the dreamtime within its narrative and necessarily grounds Tudee's healing in that realm. At the same time, it opens a passageway into the dreamtime, offering the diverse viewers/participants a parallel experience of healing, blessing transformation.

This restorative medicine is explicitly for the soul. Tudee has begun to mirror the oppressor. He is becoming individualistic, greedy, deceptive, and egocentric, characteristics epitomized by his plan to sell-out his collaborators by claiming sole credit and taking all the profits for their collective art work. That self-alienation culminates in the moment in the dreamtime when he almost goes berserk and becomes a "natural born killer" murdering the "White Man." Of course, had he done so he would have fulfilled the oppressor's ceremony; his soul wound would have been a fatal one.

While virtually every distributor in the United States turned down *Follow Me Home, Seven* was number one at the box office for five weeks and was among the most profitable films of 1995.[52] Peter Bratt talks about his film being dismissed as "too unmarketable," "too inflammatory," and "too alienating to mainstream audiences." A review by one of these alienated mainstream voices appeared in a the *New York Times.* Stephen Holden deemed *Follow Me Home* to be mired in "paranoid fantasies" epitomized by the "white racist stereotypes" who appear in the movie.[53] Could the director, I wonder, have presented the reality of racism in any way that would satisfy this reviewer? Are Larry and Farmer not apt symbolic representations of such types as the two white soldiers, James Burmeister II and Malcolm Wright, who in December 1995 randomly selected and killed an African-American woman and man, Jackie Burden and Michael James, in Fayetteville, North Carolina, as part of an initiation ritual for a white racist organization? At the same time, Perry, the third man, shows an alternative. He models refusal and resistance, taking definitive action to interrupt injustice in a situation that he had helped to create, and works to heal himself (and those who identify with him) in that process.

Holden further fumes: "They have conceived the loony idea of painting a mural honoring their ancestors on the side of the White House. The notion of asking for permission to execute this artwork hasn't even crossed their minds." To me, it is this reviewer who sounds not only paranoid but a bit "loony." The White House is a completely appropriate setting for a mural honoring the Native ancestors of this land. As Alice Walker writes: "The White House . . . has been a symbol of oppression to subjugated people of color since it was constructed during the colonial period; transforming it into a colorful expression of the presence of American people of color as we approach the next century (perhaps leaving one side of it white, as an example of fair representation) is a cheerful ambition in itself."[54]

What of the artists' disinclination to seek permission? This is a curious complaint in a culture that typically glorifies taboo violation and conventionally has its heroes "boldly going where no man has gone before."[55] Have the museums and collectors who hoard Native American sacred objects and even body parts sought permission for such abominations? Do the manufacturers of the Jeep Cherokee seek authorization from or pay any royalty to the Cherokee nation? Does the Human Genome Project ask permission to patent and own the very genetic structures of the various people whose genes they collect? Has anyone ever asked the Earth for permission to mine uranium? One wonders if this reviewer, and the many he speaks for, reserve any indignation for these and the larger historical expropriations from which they stem. Manifest Destiny, after all, means never having to say "Mother may I?"

Muriel Rukeyser writes, "The universe is made of stories / not of atoms."[56] Creation is ongoing. Popular culture is a realm of collective dream and nightmare; it is a living, contemporary emanation of the oral tradition, a potential shrine for the enactment of ritual, a repository of stories, some with powers to heal, some with powers to sicken, to create and to destroy. As such, both the makers of and the participants in these stories must take responsibility for the sacred powers in which they deal, the gods they feed/worship, the sacrifices they re-present, the medicine they prescribe and/or take.

Follow Me Home is an invitation, a call to creation of a new, more just, story/world, to undertake a sacred journey of soul healing, a call to find one's way out of that totalizing toxic and insane environment that those who have been wounded "find ourselves caught up in and completely lost at the same time."[57] The dreamland Indian woman finds Tudee when he is lost, that is, when he is about to lose his soul. She spins out a thread for him to follow, and beckons him home, toward wholeness. The mainstream, widely distributed and acclaimed films *Natural Born Killers, Seven,* and *Forrest Gump* only lead us ever more deeply into the insanity—and then strand us there.

Ritual enactments, including those transmitted through the techno-logical dream of film, do indeed "keep history alive," do continually re-create and regenerate certain realities, do, potentially, bless or blight us. *Follow Me Home* asks us to examine with utmost seriousness the gods we worship, the rituals in which we participate, the words we speak, and the symbols and images we both create and reflect upon. Perhaps *Time* magazine's question is not so far off the mark. Is anything less than our souls at stake?

Notes

1. Quoted in Pam McAllister, ed., *Reweaving the Web of Life: Feminism and Non-Violence* (Philadelphia: New Society Publishers, 1982), 352.

2. For information on genocide in American history see Russell Thornton, *American Indian Holocaust and Survival: A Population History Since 1492* (Norman: University of Oklahoma Press, 1987). Gynocide or femicide is the sexually political murder of women, individually or en masse, for reasons of misogyny, sense of ownership, objectification, or enforcement of male supremacy. See Jane Caputi, *The Age of Sex Crime* (Bowling Green: Bowling Green State University Popular Press, 1987); Jill Radford and Diana E. H. Russell, *Femicide: The Politics of Woman Killing* (New York: Twayne, 1992).

3. David Denby, "Buried Alive," *New Yorker,* July 15, 1996, 47–58.

4. George Gerbner, "The Dynamics of Cultural Resistance," in *Hearth and Home: Images of Women in the Media,* ed. Gaye Tuchman, Arlene K. Daniels, and James Benet (New York: Oxford, 1978), 46–50.

5. Classically, Western liberalism elevates rationality, which is also gendered as masculine, into the supreme mode of consciousness as the best mode for organizing society and life itself. Consistently, those who argue that images or narrative have unconscious persuasive power to spur emulation, devotion, or frenzy are most often refuted by the hegemonic invocation of "the rational mind." For example, Jacob Sullivan, a senior editor at *Reason* magazine ("Victims of Everything," *New York Times,* May 23, 1997, A19), believes that whatever media influence is at hand, "A conscious mind must intervene, deciding how to interpret the message and whether to act on it." Ironically, Mr. Sullivan's opinion is based in a what can only be a religious faith in rationality.

6. James Carey, "A Cultural Approach to Communication," *Communication* 2 (1975): 1–22, esp. 6.

7. Paula Gunn Allen, *The Sacred Hoop: Recovering the Feminine in the American Indian Tradition* (Boston: Beacon Press, 1986), 72.

8. Ibid., 104.

9. Ibid., 80.

10. Quoted in Beverly Singer, "Film and Video Made by Native Americans: A Cultural Examination of Native American Participation in Film and Video Production" (Ph.D. diss., American Studies, University of New Mexico, 1996), 233.

11. Allen, *Sacred Hoop,* 72–73.

12. Stephen Schiff, "The Last Wild Man," *New Yorker,* August 8, 1994, 40–55, esp. p. 43.

13. Caputi, *Age of Sex Crime,* 53.

14. The "nuclear father" is, like the nuclear bomb, the one who actually threatens you while purportedly protecting you. See Jane Caputi, *Gossips, Gorgons, and Crones: The Fates of the Earth* (Santa Fe: Bear and Company, 1993), 99–140.

15. One scene begins with Mickey and Mallory in bed in a motel, engaging in sexual play. The camera cuts over to the floor by the bed and there is a young, conventionally beautiful blonde hostage bound, gagged, and pornographically displayed on her knees. Mickey wants to fuck and torture her before he kills her. Mallory, jealous and hurt, runs out. In the director's cut, a more graphic rape-murder scene is reinserted into the text.

16. See, for example, Andrea Dworkin, *Pornography: Men Possessing Women* (New York: Perigee, 1981), 53.

17. Schiff, "The Last Wild Man," 45–46.

18. Cara MariAnna, "Initiatory Themes in Popular Film: The Mythic Roots of a National Destiny" (Master's thesis, American Studies, University of New Mexico, 1996).

19. Lucy Young, "Out of the Past: Lucy Young's Story," in *No Rooms of their Own: Women Writers of Early California, 1849–1869,* ed. Ida Rae Egli (Heyday, 1997).

20. MariAnna, "Initiatory Themes in Popular Film."

21. Leslie Marmon Silko, *Storyteller* (New York: Arcade Publishers, 1981).

22. Mircea Eliade, *Rites and Symbols of Initiation: The Mysteries of Birth and Rebirth* (New York: Harper and Row, 1958), 81.

23. Ibid., 83, 84.

24. For example, a Utah teenager murdered his stepmother and half-sister after becoming obsessed with *Natural Born Killers*. Before doing so, he shaved his head and started to wear tinted granny glasses like those worn by the film's hero, Mickey. See "Police Seize Suspect Obsessed by a Movie," *New York Times,* Nov. 4, 1994, A9.

25. Schiff, "The Last Wild Man," 55.

26. Richard A. Blake, "Redeemed in Blood: The Sacramental Universe of Martin Scorsese," *Journal of Popular Film and Television* 24.1 (1996): 2–9.

27. Peter N. Chumo II, " 'You've Got to Put the Past Behind You Before You Can Move On': *Forrest Gump* and National Reconciliation," *Journal of Popular Film and Television* 23.1 (1995): 2–7.

28. R. W. B. Lewis, *The American Adam: Innocence, Tragedy, and Tradition in the Nineteenth Century* (Chicago: University of Chicago Press, 1965), 1.

29. For commentary on *Birth of a Nation* see Thomas Bogle, *Toms, Coons, Mulattoes, Mammies, and Blacks* (New York: Bantam, 1974); Michael Rogin, *Ronald Reagan, The Movie and Other Episodes in Political Demonology* (Berkeley: University of California Press, 1987).

30. Richard Herrnstein and Charles Murray, *The Bell Curve* (1994), is a racist polemic that argues for the biological intellectual inferiority of people of African descent.

31. After elaborating this theory in my 1995 class on American popular film and writing the first draft of this essay, I came upon a similar critique in James Hillman's *The Soul's Code: In Search of Character and Calling* (New York: Random House, 1996), 247–48. Hillman also refers readers to Elaine Pagels's *The Origin of Satan* (New York: Random House, 1995) for her relevant analysis of the development of scapegoating and projection of all evil on to the "Other" in early Christian thought.

32. Tom Cullen, *When London Walked in Terror* (Boston: Houghton Mifflin, 1965), 14.

33. Colin Wilson, *A Casebook of Murder* (London: Leslie Frewin, 1969), 139–40.

34. Amy Taubin, "The Allure of Decay," *Sight and Sound* (January 1996): 2–5, esp. 3.

35. "The Show," *Encarta on the Record* (Microsoft Corporation, 1996).

36. Caputi, *Age of Sex Crime.*

37. Mary Daly, *Beyond God the Father: Toward a Philosophy of Women's Liberation* (Boston: Beacon Press, 1973, 1985), 76.

38. Eliade, *Rites and Symbols of Initiation,* 87.

39. Ibid., 87–88.

40. Leslie Marmon Silko, *Ceremony* (New York: New American Library, 1977), 265.

41. Bryant Frazer, "Seven," 1995.

42. Alice Walker, "Follow Me Home," in *Anything We Love Can Be Saved: A Writer's Activism* (New York: Random House, 1997), 170–72, esp. 172.

43. See Cara MariAnna, "The Seven Mythic Cycles of *Thelma and Louise,*" *Trivia: A Journal of Ideas* 21 (1993): 82–99, for an extraordinary analysis of the mythic frame of *Thelma and Louise.* Other films which might be fruitful to analyze in

this way include *Daughters of the Dust* (Julie Dash, 1991); *Sugarcane Alley* (Euzhan Palcy, 1983); and *A Nightmare on Elm Street* (Wes Craven, 1984).

44. Gary Dauphin, "Homeward Bound," *Vibe* (March 1997): 119–20.

45. Teresa Córdova, "Trying to Keep Us Silenced—Again: A Review of *Follow Me Home*," *Voces Unidas* (Albuquerque: SouthWest Organizing Project, November 1996), 16.

46. Lucia Chiavola Birnbaum, *Godmothers of Color* (Boston: Northeastern University Press, 1991).

47. Eduardo Duran and Bonnie Duran, *Native American Postcolonial Psychology* (Albany: State University of New York Press, 1995), 45.

48. "About the Production," New Millennia Films, 1997.

49. Martina Estrada-Meléndez, "Reconnecting People of Color to Spirit and Ancestors through Film: A Review of *Follow Me Home*," *La Voz de Berkeley* 6.4 (April 1997): 6.

50. Duran and Duran, *Native American Postcolonial Psychology,* 45.

51. Marshall McLuhan, *Understanding Media: The Extensions of Man* (New York: New American Library, 1964).

52. Henri Norris founded a distribution company to carry *Follow Me Home: New Millennia*, 788 Riverside Drive, Suite 8E, New York, NY 10032; telephone: (212) 283-0735; fax: (212) 283-0765.

53. Stephen Holden, "Uneasy Riders with Plenty to Fear," *New York Times,* Feb. 28, 1997, C14.

54. Walker, "Follow Me Home," 171.

55. Caputi, *Gossips, Gorgons, and Crones,* 169–73.

56. Muriel Rukeyser, "The Speed of Darkness," in *The Speed of Darkness* (New York: Random House, 1968), 111.

57. Estrada-Meléndez, "Reconnecting People of Color to Spirit and Ancestors through Film."

7

RAGING BULLY:
POSTMODERN VIOLENCE AND
MASCULINITY IN *RAGING BULL*

FRANK P. TOMASULO

Throughout human history, physical violence has been a staple of the arts, as well as an all-too-common component of real-life interactions between individuals and nations. In mythology, literature, and the other arts, violence has often been used as a device to dramatize the conflict in the narrative. And in the commercial cinema, violence, along with sexuality, has always been the primary component of the *jouissance* of both filmic expression and spectacle.

In the late capitalist period of economic history and in the coterminous postmodern phase of Hollywood film production, however, screen violence has become more prominent and increasingly graphic, exaggerated to such a degree that it no longer provides the Aristotelian emotional catharsis and narrative closure that characterized previous eras in motion picture history. Indeed, the sheer spectacle—the least artistic theatrical device, according to Aristotle—of violent displays in much of the post-classical Hollywood cinema (i.e., *Bonnie and Clyde* [1967], *The Wild Bunch* [1969], *A Clockwork Orange* [1971], *Taxi Driver* [1976], *Apocalypse Now* [1979], *Natural Born Killers* [1994], *Braveheart* [1995]) has become an artistic substitute for the meaningful power of characterization and narrative in traditional tragedy.[1] The celebratory aspects of this bloody excess and choreographed mayhem constitute a veritable "iconography of death,"[2] an apocalyptic *danse macabre,* that ultimately tells us little or nothing about the personal, national, or historical causes of violence but offers instead a mere simulacrum of horror, a ritual without redemption. Pervasive violence has become endemic to the American mythos, almost to the point of being an accepted part of our national character or "genetic" makeup, often with no obvious social, historical, or psychological causation. As such, unexplained violence has become not only a dominant motif in recent American screen entertainment but a powerful mythology that constitutes its own meaning as part of a reactionary social and political agenda.

Martin Scorsese's *Raging Bull* (1980) marks a site for an interrogation of these problematic postmodern parables of violence. Released in the year of Reagan's election and hailed by many critics as the best film of the 1980s,[3] the film's representational strategies—particularly its visual portrayals of physical violence—can be studied to illuminate the postmodern predicament in Hollywood cinema. Many commentators, for instance, concluded that the movie's "succession of sordid, violent images and incidents . . . confronts us with a decentered universe" and that Scorsese was therefore "a celluloid deconstructionist."[4] More important, the film can be dissected for its unconscious appropriation of American societal symbols and its substratum of cultural mythology.

As an important exemplar of a set of contemporary violent motion pictures, *Raging Bull* can be viewed as a film whose internal contradictions are homologous to the Derridean aporias of a post–Vietnam War, post–Watergate, postmodern American psyche that seemed to embrace both feminism and Ronald Reagan, born-again Christianity and nuclear brinkmanship, tolerance for homosexuals and minorities and regressive social policies. The postmodern pastiche valorized by so many contemporary critics may be nothing more than the aesthetic counterpart and end game of these antinomies of late capitalism, the decentered and destabilized hodgepodge of cultural discourses that are part and parcel of modern multinational corporatism.[5]

The specific ways those societal contradictions get worked out in what Herbert Marcuse called "the aesthetic dimension" of the film text can be studied through an examination of *Raging Bull*'s cinematic style and its depictions of characters. Both aspects are uniquely postmodern, yet both ultimately convey mixed messages about genre, ethnicity, class, history, violence, and gender. In particular, the film's violence— enunciated on the levels of cinematic style, narrative, and character— can be seen as having revivified moribund traditional gender and class stereotypes within the context of an emerging neoconservative national discourse, in which the "angry white male" reasserted his domination through the agency or threat of physical force. At the same time, the movie's exaggerated representation of personal savagery—although enunciated by the same cinematic techniques—seems to provoke a spectatorial response in opposition to the bullying tactics of the central character. As such, *Raging Bull*'s postmodern cinematic style may be a significant exemplar of what Robin Wood called "the incoherent text."

MARTIN SCORSESE: POSTMODERN CINEMATIC STYLE

The postmodern aesthetic is often defined in terms of a Lévi-Straussian *bricolage* of intertextual citations, a pastiche of prior genres and artistic techniques. In the case of *Raging Bull,* many commentators have cited its simultaneous effacement and amalgam of genre conventions, mix of realistic and expressionistic cinematic techniques, abrupt shifts in chronology, combination of black-and-white (indeed, film noirish) and color cinematography, discordant editing strategies, and narrative conventions borrowed from both classical Hollywood movies and European art cinema. In short, the film is emblematic of what Guy Debord has called "the culture of the simulacrum."

The opening credit sequence employs many of these signifiers of postmodernity. The use of melancholic operatic music (the ethereal "Intermezzo" from Pietro Mascagni's *Cavelleria Rusticana*) over the slow-motion scenes of Jake La Motta (Robert De Niro) shadowboxing alone in a mysterious smoky ring, visually trapped by the ropes, represents the antithesis of an upbeat action movie. The black-and-white film stock suggests fight films of the 1940s, yet in 1980 the black-and-white photography connotes a stylistic departure from the color-only expectation of modern major motion pictures, thus calling attention to the film's formal properties. When the title appears, a blood-red filter foreshadows the film's violence and harkens back to an intertextual precursor, *Bonnie and Clyde* (1967), whose credits also featured blood-red coloration.[6]

Soon pandemonium breaks out in an arena and the sound of a woman screaming is prominent, another foreshadowing device signaling that La Motta's brutality will be directed not only toward his male opponents, but also toward women. The woman is on the floor of the arena, being trampled by the rioting spectators. The salvo of punches thrown in the ring coincides cleverly with the sight and heightened sound of photographers' exploding flashbulbs, a technique that calls attention to the postmodern self-reflexiveness of the film's signifying practice. The exaggerated whiplash noise of clicking camera shutters adds to the subjective feel of the ring experience, but it also conveys that the media (and, by extension, *Raging Bull* itself) is punishing the protagonist as much as his opponents. Even La Motta's inarticulate dialogue has a self-reflexive dimension; while berating his first wife, Irma, for improperly frying a steak, the fighter yells, "Don't overcook it! It defeats its own purpose." This line is an unconscious admission of his self-defeating tendencies, as well as an early omen of his eventual self-inflicted downfall.

The courtship scenes between Jake and his future wife, Vickie (Cathy Moriarty), also employ postmodern cinematic techniques. When the two first converse, the sequence is shot in alternating reverse shots with both principals visually separated and imprisoned behind the chain-link fence of the neighborhood swimming pool. Later, on their first outing together, Jake and Vickie are seen together in close-up, visually separated by a barrier image—the metal bar in the middle of his car's windshield. When they arrive at their destination, a *miniature* golf course, their dysfunctional sexual relationship is foreshadowed by the use of symbolic Freudian props. He demonstrates his prowess with a phallic golf putter (a club designed for short strokes); her cunnic golf ball gets lost (inside a miniature chapel). When the couple finally has sex (at his parents' apartment), the camera focuses on a snapshot of Jake and his brother Joey (Joe Pesci) in boxing poses. As Jake and Vickie move to the bed, their tumbling bodies momentarily block the audience's view of the picture, suggesting that male violence and sexuality are intimately related and perhaps that Vickie has temporarily eclipsed Joey in Jake's heart. The prominent crucifix over the bed and the rosary beads near the photo become, in this context, symbols of unheeded authority, similar to the mini-church that came between them on the miniature golf course. The cut from their lovemaking to La Motta's second contest with Sugar Ray Robinson links sexuality with violence.

The slow-motion effects used in the fight scenes to intensify and subjectivize the blows are also used in the non-boxing sequences. For instance, when Jake spots Vickie getting into a Cadillac convertible with the local Mafioso, sees her greeting Salvy, the local mobster, or kissing the neighborhood don at the Copacabana, the rapturous slow motion shows both his subjective entrancement by Vickie and his jealous perception that he is being dealt an emotional blow both by her Desdemona-like "unfaithfulness" and by a male rival. Similarly, the montage editing that juxtaposes sex and boxing scenes demonstrates La Motta's confused equation of the two. The second and third Robinson fights, as well as the bouts with Zivic, Kochan, Edgar, Satterfield, Bell, and Janiro all are intercut with scenes of Jake and Vickie's sex life, wedding, and home movies.

As to the political effectivity of these departures from classical norms, the film's postmodernist reflexivity, intertextuality, and rule breaking do not constitute *sui generis* a recipe for revolution. Devices are used to heighten the sensation of violence, not to destroy the codes of realism or the conventions of genre.

GENRE

The boxing genre has always been a locus for exemplifying screen violence. As Andrew Sarris said, "The violence, kinesis, and uncompromising individualism of the boxing spectacle make it the movie sport, *par excellence.*"[7] As such, "Fight movies have been more successful as dramatic entertainments than have movies on any other sport because boxing remains the most brutal sport."[8] Undoubtedly, the *agon* of classical tragedy takes dynamic diegetic and visual form in the classical fight film. Thus, physical ferocity is an axiom of the Hollywood fight movie, fundamental to the genre.

Although the boxing genre has historically been a site for conventional narrative patterns (linear plots, understandable characters, idealized and heroic protagonists, physically dramatized conflicts, heterosexual romance, strong family values, and uplifting endings), *Raging Bull* defies and discredits the generic architecture of the fight film to forge a postmodernist backlash against the classical tradition. Screenwriter Paul Schrader's decentered narrative flashes forward and backward in time, lurching from one violent locus to another without regard to strict chronology. The "hero" does not evince time-honored traits, tragic flaws, or explainable motivations; indeed, Jake La Motta is a character without "character," a subject without subjectivity.[9]

Furthermore, unlike the noble fictional prize fighters of the classical boxing movies (e.g., *Somebody Up There Likes Me* [1956]), Jake La Motta does not achieve spiritual redemption in the ring. His matches are purely physical brawls, not agonistic morality tales. La Motta's limited interiority is played out on the mat of his body, not his soul. As such, he is a post-Freudian, post-Marxist (hence postmodernist) "cluster of connotations, an ensemble of multiple effects,"[10] not a working-class hero. Thus, the apotheosis of ultimate triumph (*Body and Soul* [1947]), noble resignation (*Requiem for a Heavyweight* [1956]), or even pride in "just going the distance" (*Rocky* [1976]) found in the typical boxing film paradigms are elided in favor of an ambiguous and circular narrative and a despicable protagonist that mock the traditional conventions of the genre.

Scorsese's reputation as "the poet of violence"[11] is directly related to his stylization mayhem in and out of the ring. Indeed, the director's aestheticization of violence—the slow-motion shots of spurting blood or a collapsing nose, expressionistic soundtrack, lush musical score, and editing finesse in the fight scenes—poeticizes a proletarian sport and canonizes fighters who are inhuman at their cores.[12]

ETHNICITY AND SOCIAL CLASS: THE SCAPEGOATING OF THE OTHER

Despite the use of groundbreaking postmodern generic, narrative, and aesthetic devices, Scorsese's tropes of ethnicity (Italian Americans), class (lumpen proletarians), and gender (aggressive, domineering men and passive, domestic women) produce iconic stereotypes that perpetuate old Hollywood clichés about working-class Italian men, even though an Italian-American male from a working-class background directed the film.[13]

Ten of Scorsese's twenty-one films have dealt with Italian themes or characters, usually among the criminal class. Although the director tries to transcend clichéd stereotypes through irony and visual and aural experimentation, most spectators probably interpret *Raging Bull* relatively "straight," so to speak, as a raw, unvarnished, depiction of real Italian-American males, and not as "discursive constructions in a free play of signifiers," especially when presented as part of "Scorsese's anthropology of Italian-American males."[14] The filmmaker's acclaimed documentary-like film techniques—especially the superimposed subtitles listing specific dates and locations, the attention to detail in the period set design and props, and the close-up camera work that puts spectators in the middle of the action—certainly contribute to the Barthesian "reality effect" of the film, but his images and portrayals are "realistic" only if they square with one's preconceived notion of Italian identity. If one's image of Italian Americans is that they are ignorant, cursing, tumultuous batterers, then *Raging Bull* easily confirms that formulaic vision.

Even the cliché of the close-knit Italian family is eschewed (La Motta's parents are never seen or discussed), thus eliding depth psychology in favor of an unsentimental, behaviorist portrait of a self-centered and despicable brute in a society of like-minded males. As George Custen remarked, "Little in the way of family environment is specifically offered as an explanation for Jake La Motta's rage; it exists, pure and unmotivated, in a state of its own."[15] As such, all the audience sees is the protagonist's ethnicity. Indeed, all the audience *hears* are

Italian songs on the radio and the swelling nondiegetic Italianate music of Mascagni. In short, Scorsese's Jake La Motta is violent simply because he is Italian.[16]

All of La Motta's movie opponents are foreigners or African Americans, although in real life he fought many white Americans. Indeed, he loses his first screen match to a black boxer, Jimmy Reeves, who Joey La Motta calls a *melanzana* ("eggplant," slang for "nigger"). Interestingly, the film strongly insinuates that the decision against La Motta was an unjust one; Reeves is demolished by his opponent but saved by the bell. This early scene, set in 1941, has relevance to the 1980 release date of the film: it could embody a social allegory about and critique of America's affirmative action policies in that the less-deserving black man is awarded the victory over the more-qualified Caucasian. Later, in a rare reflective moment, Jake bemoans that he is "never gonna fight Joe Louis . . . the best there is." This ostensible admiration for the Brown Bomber is undercut immediately when La Motta insists, "I'm better than him!" Throughout the film, racial bigotry is ascribed to Italians, not to systemic causes. This scapegoating seems to imply that members of the lower class—no matter what their race—are in conflict with each other, rather than with the ruling classes in society.

Similarly, Sarris has said that "competitive sports help perpetuate the most evil excesses of the capitalistic system."[17] The cutthroat values and achievement ideologies fostered by the sport of boxing are inextricably linked to class ideology because prize fighting is supposed to be an articulation of a meritocratic system that closely mirrors the brutal ethos of laissez-faire capitalism. Like the mythic New Right ideologies promulgated in 1980, *Raging Bull* seeks to glorify an earlier epoch in which poor white ethnic males could successfully resist oppression and scrap their way out of the immigrant gutter through animal energy, skill, discipline, training, and competitiveness in the boxing ring by using their own virile entrepreneurial talents. In the film, Jake La Motta rises above his class through individual initiative, à la Horatio Alger, but he cannot rise *with* his class.

The protagonist's material circumstances change little as the film progresses, even when he attains the middleweight title. His rise from the Bronx slums to a modest house on Pelham Parkway suggests an economic distinction of little difference. Although he attends fancy cabarets regularly and occasionally wears a "monkey suit," he remains more of a "hairy ape," a working-class lout, than a sophisticated man about town. Even in these tony high-society settings, La Motta is surrounded by his compatriots from the Bronx or by well-dressed Mafioso dons. More often, his attire consists of a sleeveless undershirt and checkered boxer shorts.

This portrayal of the working-class person reveals more about the condescending perceptions of the cultural elite than it does about the working class itself. In the absence of explanations for the character's fury, viewers must rely on subtle gestural codes, elements of the mise-en-scène, costume, and other characters to adjudge the basis for his outbursts. Those postmodernist cues all point toward La Motta's lumpen proletarian roots as an explanation for his coarse temperament; as a scapegoat, his class becomes his character. In short, Scorsese's Jake La Motta is violent simply because he is working class.

JAKE LA MOTTA: THE POSTMODERN CHARACTER

Postmodern theory posits that human subjectivity is fundamentally split, a notion that challenges and rejects the classical positivist and essentialist characterization of the self as fixed, autonomous, and unitary. The latter view is seen by postmodernist thinkers as an antiquated fiction, a vestigial representational schema that elides the contemporary nature of personal identity. Whereas traditional realist codes of character symbolization assume a congruence of external action and inner life—wherein the inner life motivates outer behavior and, conversely, outer behavior is explained by inner psychological or sociological motives—the postmodern individual is constructed and perceived as decentered and destabilized, a pastiche of often contradictory traits. Moreover, postmodernism insists that personal identity is a cultural production, part of a performative discourse.

In *Raging Bull,* for instance, Jake La Motta's personality is articulated through a series of performances—rehearsing in his cabaret dressing room, on stage at his nightclub in Miami, in the boxing ring, and in his family life.[18] Indeed, the first scene of the film, set in 1964, shows the ex-champ practicing his monologue in front of a mirror before going on stage at the Barbizon Plaza. He concludes with the lines, "The thing ain't the ring, it's the play. So give me a stage where this bull here can rage; and though I can fight I'd much rather recite. That's entertainment; that's entertainment." Scorsese cuts on those last words to a shot of La Motta being struck in the face during his 1941 match against Jimmy Reeves, suggesting that La Motta's boxing career was also entertainment, albeit brutal. La Motta's first words after this bout—"Put my robe on right"—imply that he is well aware of the showmanship of the sport.

Although boxing is euphemistically called "the sweet science" and "the manly art of self-defense," La Motta is far from sweet or scientific, and his self has no defense—in both senses of the term. He has no defense mechanisms, personal resources to draw on in times of crisis, and no moral defense against charges of brutality and abuse.

The contradiction between the character's self-destructive violence and crudity and his latter-day conversion to poet (trading curses for verses, so to speak) may stem from authorial tensions between the director and screenwriter. Scorsese stated that "the thing that fascinates me is that Jake La Motta is on a higher spiritual level . . . as a fighter. He works on an almost primitive level, almost an animal level."[19] That animal level is clearly evident in his behavior (an off-screen neighbor calls him an animal at the beginning of the film, to which Jake responds, "I'll eat your dog for lunch. Your mother's an animal!" and, near the end of the film, La Motta cries out, "I am not an animal," from his cage-like jail cell) and in his predilection for wearing leopard-skin robes into the boxing ring.

But the higher spiritual level, the "priestly vocation"[20] the Catholic Scorsese sought to portray, is hinted at in the way La Motta's handlers offer him a mouthpiece as if it were a Eucharistic wafer, but it is most obvious in the end credits. The film concludes with a quotation from John 9:24–26: "Whether or not he was a sinner, I do not know; all I know is that once I was blind and now I can see." The screenwriter, Calvinist Paul Schrader, however, saw La Motta differently. Although conceding that "there's a pseudo-religious masochism" in the boxer's ritual bleeding, Schrader objected to the New Testament quote: "I think [La Motta's] the same dumb lug at the end as he is at the beginning, and I think [Scorsese] is just imposing salvation on his subject by fiat."[21] The real-life Jake La Motta seemed to concur with the idea of predestination: "I was a bum and I lived like a bum."[22]

The film concludes with a scene that mirrors the opening, a return to the cabaret dressing room. Here, Jake shadowboxes in front of a mirror, unconsciously replaying his lifelong battle against his most aggressive opponent, himself. Lacanians will no doubt make much of the fact that La Motta finally gets his monologue right while practicing in front of a mirror—that is, he comes into the world of mastery of language as he anticipates on an imaginary plane the mastery of his bodily unity. More to the point, the recitation is the taxicab scene from *On the Waterfront* (1953), in which ex-boxer Terry Malloy (Marlon Brando) confronts his brother Charlie (Rod Steiger) for betraying him (by setting him up to take a dive). Just before La Motta's successful rehearsal of his monologue,

Male sacrificial myth in postmodern cinema: *Raging Bull* (United Artists, 1980).

his "mirror stage," his entrance into the Symbolic, he had attempted to reconcile with and hug his brother Joey in a parking garage. The diegetic irony here is that it was Jake who had betrayed his sibling throughout his ring career. (Although Joey set up Jake to take a dive in the Billy Fox match, he did so to ensure a future title bout for Jake, a far cry from the circumstances in *On the Waterfront*.) The larger, postmodernist irony is that far from discovering his true identity in this final scene, La Motta "finds himself" only in the words of someone else, a fictional character named Terry Malloy. As such, his identity scene is actually a Lacanian *méconnaissance*, a misrecognition of self.

Scorsese's resolute externality offers a more detached perspective on his protagonist than that of the classical cinema. This objective observation (admittedly layered with exaggerated cinematic and sonic effects) allows the filmmaker to present his dysfunctional subject without the traditional cloying Hollywood techniques of identification and empathy. The flat, anti-dramatic presentation is documentary-like in its articulation, mirroring the character's lack of affect when being pummeled in the ring. Any emotion is conveyed by the cinematic techniques, particularly the use of recurring motifs. Specifically, the fact that La Motta is shown shadowboxing in both the first shot (the credit sequence scene of warming up in the ring) and the last (in the Barbizon Plaza dressing room) suggests that the character has not changed or been redeemed; he is still striking out against phantom opponents (paranoia) and himself (masochism). Although we do see some subjective shots of fists being thrown at the camera, we never get inside La Motta's thick skull. This postmodern problematicization of subjectivity is most apparent in La Motta's hysteria, his violent reaction to his perceived loss of male privilege. His comeuppance—his loss of wife, family, nightclub, championship belt, and freedom—signifies nothing less than the demise of traditional masculinity.

MASCULINITY

Masculinity is a term of history and culture, not biology. It is a sign of social identity linked to the nexus of patriarchy. Boxing and boxing movies are part of a worldwide culture of machismo that reproduces hegemonic forms of masculinity. But in the postmodern, postindustrial environment of advanced capitalism, brawny men may no longer be needed, yet their vestigial muscles are still part of their genetic and cultural inheritance and of the social construction of gender roles.

Pam Cook argues that although *Raging Bull* may have some odd appeal to feminists who see their worst suspicions confirmed by its explicit representation of the male social disease—violence—it "does not offer a radical critique of either masculinity or violence." On the one hand, muscular violence is validated as La Motta's resistance to a corrupt and repressive social system (battling one's way out of the slums). On the other hand, his violence—in the ring and out—is "so excessive, so self-destructive, that it has to be condemned."[23] Either way, *Raging Bull* can be seen as a postmodernist meditation on mythic masculinity. According to Cook, manliness—socially defined and constructed in real life and in boxing movies—is shown in crisis so that we can mourn the loss of male power and "celebrate the overthrow of the phallus."[24] In the postmodern absence of overt signifiers, the audience can only equate the protagonist's character with his gender. In short, Scorsese's Jake La Motta is violent simply because he is a man.

Robin Wood's analysis of boxing is predicated on an etiology of repressed homoeroticism: pugilism is a public display that demonstrates the prize fighter does not love men but hates them. The boxer needs to live a Don Juan lifestyle that proclaims, "I don't love men; I love women." He must publicly and violently assert his hypermasculinity to deny his latent homosexuality to himself and others. Wood bases much of his reading of *Raging Bull* on a remark made by Scorsese during an interview. The director allegedly admitted that the movie had "a homosexual subtext." Wood therefore contends that "*Raging Bull* is a film in which [traces of repressed homosexuality] exist close to the surface."[25] Although Wood essentially tries to explain a postmodern text that is, in essence, unexplainable, there is ample textual evidence to support his interpretation.

Early on, La Motta's first wife screams, "Fucking queer! Faggot!" as Jake and his brother Joey leave for the Copacabana. She adds, "You're not going out on business. You're going to suck each other off!" Jake frequently refers to himself or other men in effeminate or gay terms: He laments that he has "small hands," "a little girl's hands." La Motta says of one of his opponents, the handsome Tony Janiro, "I don't know whether I should fuck him or fight him," adding, "I'll open his hole like this."[26] In the ring, La Motta deliberately pulverizes Janiro's face, with a complicit smile to his wife, Vickie. As blood pours copiously out of Janiro's eyes (the ultimate fate of Oedipus), La Motta kisses his own gloved fists (later equated with his phallus). Thus, La Motta's victory "effectively destroys the threat that Janiro posed, not as attractive to Vickie, but as attractive to himself."[27] Upon winning the middleweight belt from Marcel Cerdan, Jake kisses his defeated opponent. Later, he hugs and kisses his brother—his true object of desire, according to Robin Wood. In one scene, while Jake and Joey spar in the gym, an onlooker comments that the brothers "look like two fags up there." Even La Motta's wife-beating may have a sublimated homosexual basis, as it may portray his attempt to subconsciously attack the feminine side of his own psyche. On a less violent level, the jokes he tells at his Miami club usually entail some crude form of sexist buffoonery.

In *Raging Bull,* these overt homoerotic allusions vie with more subtle examples of a Freudian subtext. In one scene, Joey La Motta starts a brawl in the Copacabana when he breaks a bottle over the head of Salvy, screaming, "I'll put your fuckin' eyes out!"—again reviving the Oedipal threat. Much later, after retiring from the ring, Jake operates a nightclub in Miami. In one of his signature acts, he constructs a tower of stacked champagne glasses that he fills from the top down and then removes one by one. This precarious glass phallus represents his public construction of a fragile male identity before an admiring female gaze. Immediately after "castrating" his glass phallus in the club, Vickie announces her divorce plans.

It goes without saying that Jake La Motta is far from the classical hero; even characters within the diegesis repeatedly critique his repugnant behavior, and most viewers are no doubt repelled by his excess. Nonetheless, his perversity makes him a postmodern anti-hero who is the guilty perpetrator of his own transgressive desires and who "is more likely to be a functional alienate himself, acting out of some private motive stemming from his alienation from society."[28] Unlike other boxing film heroes, Jake La Motta alienates virtually everyone, including the spectator, in his all-consuming macho determination to become champion. Such disgust with the protagonist violates Darryl F. Zanuck's cardinal rule for biopics, that there has to be a "rooting interest" for the viewer in the life of the famous person.[29] Postmodern biopics, however, no longer feel the need to glamorize or whitewash the lives of their subjects (e.g., *Sid and Nancy* [1986], *The Doors* [1991], *Frances* [1982], *Nixon* [1996]).

Kaja Silverman has argued that "the male subject . . . cannot avow his masochism without calling into question his identification with the masculine position. . . . What is acceptable for the female subject is pathological for the male."[30] La Motta's masochistic male pathology is particularly evident in two scenes: in the kitchen when Jake urges his brother to "hit me in the face," and in the final bout with Sugar Ray Robinson. In the former, Jake berates his brother for not punching hard enough: "Don't be a faggot." When Joey does punch him, Jake chastises him, "You throw a punch like you take it up the ass." In the latter scene, La Motta masochistically allows himself to be beaten to a pulp by Sugar Ray, scarcely retaliating (indeed, he urges Robinson to hit him more). La Motta's crucifixion-like pose—with both arms stretched out along the ring ropes—adds a religious dimension to his "suffering" and "redemption" during this bombardment. La Motta's eyes, like Oedipus's, are bloodied as Robinson delivers a devastating overhand *coup de grâce* haymaker punch that is underscored by a subjective camera, slow-motion cinematography, exaggerated sound effects, montage editing that shows blood splattering on the ringside spectators, and an artsy close-up of blood dripping from the ropes. Despite the devastating beating he takes, La Motta boasts to his opponent, "You never got me down, Ray," leading one commentator to say that "the film depicts Robinson as La Motta's only truly complete lover."[31] La Motta retires from the ring shortly thereafter, "pulling out" of a scheduled match.

The real-life Jake La Motta was not known as a particularly effective fighter; his chief claim to fame was his ability to take a beating. Thus, his boxing style involved taking pleasure in pain, an internalized form of erotogenic sadomasochism also seen later when he bangs his head repeatedly against a squalid jailhouse wall, screaming, "Why? Why?" That La Motta does not understand his unrelenting self-punishing behavior is linked to the viewer's inability to fathom the character's motives; the postmodern film does not provide him with an authentic back story or history.

History

> Any given set of real events can be emplotted in a number of ways, can bear the weight of being told as any number of different kinds of stories. Since no given set or sequence of real events is intrinsically tragic, comic, farcical, and so on, but can be constructed as such only by the imposition of the structure of a given story type on the events, it is the choice of the story type and its imposition upon the events that endow them with meaning.
>
> —*Hayden White*[32]

White's postclassical notion of "emplotment" as a form of historical storytelling defines a major contemporary approach to the study of historiography. The postmodern paradigm questions the very existence of facts, reality, and real events because history is never unmediated by discourse, and events are always stories or texts that only purport to represent historical occurrences. Traditional concepts of historical referentiality are thereby called into question by the near nihilism of the New Historicism. Indeterminacy, polysemy, and the endless play of signifiers now reign supreme. As White put it, "History is up for grabs."[33]

Clearly, the classical Hollywood biopic often used poetic license to dramatize (or elide) certain aspects of the subject's life. But Scorsese's *Raging Bull* takes so many liberties with Jake La Motta's autobiographical books that its status as authentic biography can be called into question. For instance, although the film offers no real explanation for La Motta's lifelong rage, the champion's autobiography provides a rather complex etiology, a combination of child abuse, poverty, and lack of education: "All I remember ever since I was a little kid was fighting and yelling and working and stealing and more fighting. And getting beat up by my old man. We're five kids at home and we never have a goddamned nickel. My old man never had a steady job . . . and he ain't the type to go to night school."[34]

In the movie version, these motivations were elided in favor of an unexplained symptomatic violent streak based on personal aberrance. Also eliminated from the film was La Motta's primary motivation for seeking the championship: guilt over his supposed murder of Harry Gordon, the

188

neighborhood bookie, in a robbery attempt during his teen years. This incident is recapitulated throughout the pugilist's autobiography, until La Motta wins the crown. At the victory party, the "slain" Gordon appears, alive and well, having recuperated from La Motta's attack. La Motta theorizes that his boxing career went downhill immediately after learning of his victim's miraculous "resurrection": "The moment I discovered I was not really a murderer, I also stopped being a killer in the ring."[35]

One of the most important omissions from the Scorsese film is La Motta's testimony before the Kefauver Senate Anti-Trust and Monopoly Subcommittee in 1960. Although his notorious fixed match with Billy Fox is shown, La Motta's courageous public admission that he threw the contest to please the Mob and get a shot at the middleweight crown is eliminated. This pivotal moment in La Motta's personal history, in which he risked his life by being honest, was not used in the movie. Its structuring absence leaves a void in the audience's comprehension of the character; one of the only noble deeds he ever performed is cut from the trajectory of his life, leaving him unredeemed and unpenitent. More important, this postmodern elision makes the film both *a*historical and pseudohistorical.

Another major change involved La Motta's brother, Joey. Although Joey was nominally Jake's manager for most of his ring career, many of the film's scenes are based on incidents from the real-life relationship between Jake and his childhood friend Pete Savage (identified as Rick in La Motta's 1986 sequel book). The film sequences of Jake demanding to be punched in the face by his brother, telling him he cannot fight Joe Louis, viciously beating Joey to a pulp, telephoning to reconcile, and accidentally meeting Joey on the street and hugging him all occurred in real life with the champ's best friend, not his brother. Pete/Rick was in prison during most of La Motta's boxing years and hence would not have made a good "buddy" figure. Nonetheless, despite the narrative necessity of consolidating characters, Joey La Motta actually sued United Artists, Martin Scorsese, Robert De Niro, and even his brother Jake for libel over his screen persona in *Raging Bull,* even though Pesci's performance was nominated for an Academy Award.[36]

Such discrepancies between the historical record (or, more accurately, the record according to La Motta) and the motion picture version are not unusual in biographical movies. Such films usually take great pains to establish their authenticity. In the case of *Raging Bull,* quasi-documentary black-and-white cinematography was used to approximate the style of old fight films, printed titles were used to validate actual places and dates (e.g., "Madison Square Garden, February 14, 1951"), and La

Motta himself was hired as a consultant to the production company. Robert De Niro studied boxing films, went into training, and gained more than fifty pounds to impersonate the dissolute older La Motta—a fact much trumpeted by United Artists' publicity campaign. Although these steps were taken to assure faithfulness to the real-life characters and events, the film's discourse nonetheless decontextualized and rewrote history and reprocessed it as myth.

Although La Motta's published accounts of his life may have their own inconsistencies and contradictions, subject as they are to willful distortions and memory lapses, they are also imbued from the outset with a filmic intertext: "When I think back, I feel like I'm looking at an old black-and-white movie of myself. . . . Not a good movie, either, jerky, with gaps in it, a string of poorly lit sequences, some of them with no beginning and no end. No musical score, just sometimes the sound of a police siren or a pistol shot. And almost all of it happens at night, as if I lived my whole life at night."[37]

Ultimately, it is more important to study the effect a biopic has on its audience than to ascertain how true to life it is. But, seen in historical context, the changes wrought in recent postmodernist biographical films explain much about contemporary society and moviemaking. During the classical Hollywood period, biopics "helped prepare average people to accept their place in the social structure by valorizing a common, distant, and elevated set of lives that [viewers] could hope to emulate."[38] This was far from the case in *Raging Bull*.

CONCLUSION: *RAGING BULL* AND/IN HISTORY

Prize fighters are legally licensed to express their animus against other male bodies directly and in public before an approving audience.[39] Similarly, soldiers are legally allowed to commit violence against their fellow human beings in times of war. This analogy between pugilists and warriors goes further. During wartime, nations valorize violence and aggrandize aggression; during peacetime, boxing movies provide the vicarious "grease" that keeps the rusting war machine lubricated.

In the midst of World War II, for instance, Raoul Walsh's *Gentleman Jim* (1942) saw Errol Flynn take time out from winning the war to play Jim Corbett, the suave turn-of-the-century boxing champion who used the newly instituted Marquis of Queensberry rules—the "kinder, gentler" prize fighting laws that mandated gloved fists rather than bare knuckles—to defeat the brutes and ruffians of his day. Walsh's movie was a thinly veiled fictitious retelling of America's "gentlemanly" waging of

World War II against the uncivilized "Huns" and "Japs." Gentleman Jim's sobriquet thus put a patina of elegance and refinement on male cruelty that belied the sport's (and the war's) true nature.

In the 1970s and 1980s, however, the feminist movement critiqued violent male behavior and domineering patriarchal structures. Men began to see themselves as sadistic bullies. In that context, *Raging Bull* proposed that hegemonic masculinity was necessary to victory, yet, by its ending, it also allowed that barbarous brutes could be redeemed through more "feminine" pursuits, like literary readings. The "Raging Bully" could become "Gentleman Jake." Thus, the material dislocations in the relations of production under the postindustrial regime of late capitalism and their effects on the "workers of the world"—"the sexual, intellectual, and economic disempowerment of traditional male subjects"[40]—were translated into cinematic form.

Another possibility, which also places *Raging Bull* in historical and political context, implies that mythic masculinity is shown in crisis in order to reinvigorate its macho connotations. After all, why was *this* celebrity chosen as the subject of a major motion picture at this particular historical moment? According to George Custen, "Certain careers and types of people become the prime focus of public curiosity in each generation."[41] *Raging Bull* was released in an important election year, 1980, the year of the conservative Republican victory at the polls. The film depicts the destabilization of traditional masculinity that Reagan-era politics sought to restore. Indeed, in an early scene, the "Star-Spangled Banner" is played to becalm a riot in the ring, but the anthem continues over the next shot, of tenement fire escapes ("The Bronx, 1941"). The commentary of the cut intimates that the United States is going to war (the riot) but that the violent culture of its immigrant slums needs to be channeled into patriotic efforts (the national anthem).

Because "biography is one mode of channeling latent messages of Americanism,"[42] Robert De Niro's Oscar victory suggests that U.S. society (through the Motion Picture Academy) "nominated" a legendary male figure from the past, Jake La Motta, to personify a conflicted 1980 American society.[43] In confusing eras, art and mythology have often fulfilled this sort of complicit conservative social function; the cinema in particular can contribute to the collective catharsis by which a nation can delegate a fictional character as its avatar and historical stand-in.

In this sense, dominant ideology speaks the text of *Raging Bull;* that is, American social, political, and gender myths write the master narratives of significant films, for, in order to renew social cohesion in times of Habermasian "legitimation crises," nations frequently resort to retrospective gestures, what postmodernists call *la mode rétro,* to consolidate national unity and purpose. Karl Marx elucidated this representational process long before the advent of postmodernism: "The tradition of all the dead generations weighs like a nightmare on the brain of the living. . . . They conjure up the spirits of the past to their service and borrow from them names, battle cries, and costumes in order to present the new scene of world history in time-honored disguise and borrowed language."[44]

By this logic, Jake La Motta *is* America circa 1980, an *aging* bull who scrapped to the top in his day but who grew soft—defeated abroad in Vietnam, Iran, and on world financial markets and at home by females, gays, and blacks. In that era, when advocates for women, gays, and minorities had a growing voice in American culture, U.S. foreign policy seemed unable to control uprisings and "terrorism" by people of color around the globe, and the domestic and international economies were as flabby as Robert De Niro in his last scenes. In the wings waited a superhero, the strong, manly patriarch Ronald Reagan, to rectify the national "lack." Once Reagan assumed office, male movie heroes drifted away from the feminized, "new male" cultural images (seen in *Tootsie* [1982] and *Mr. Mom* [1983]) and reverted to mythic types such as Indiana Jones, Rambo, the Terminator, and Rocky Balboa, who defeated black upstarts and a ferocious Russian in the ring.[45]

In 1980, however, the final loss of De Niro's threatening persona and muscular "hard body" as an object of contemplation, desire, and identification was a key aspect of the film's effectiveness in conveying the final impotence of hypermasculinity. In fact, despite their hetero*text*uality, most boxing movies defy feminist film theory by playing out Oedipal anxieties across the body of the male. Scorsese seems to have conceded as much when he said, "The film has very much to do with . . . sexual confusion, sexual ambiguity."[46] La Motta's unique sexual (and textual) stupefaction raises the question of what the alternatives to macho male sexuality/textuality might be. In 1980, boxing became the perfect answer: a metaphor for a mythic male nostalgia that epitomized the good old halcyon days when men were men, and women, minorities, and gays were repressed and/or brutalized.

Boxing's patterns of athletic socialization naturalize and reify men's power and privilege over women. The sport proscribes women, while promoting—as part of its training regimen—little or no contact with women. Indeed, the real-life Jake La Motta admitted to several episodes of sexual dysfunction: "There were times, sometimes months on end, when I'd be impotent. . . . What made it ironic was the nickname, 'The

Bronx Bull.' . . . Here you are the world's champ, which means you're supposed to be the symbol of complete masculinity, and you can't even get laid."[47]

In the film, La Motta pours a pitcher of ice water on his genitals to cool off his arousal during a masochistic sex scene with Vickie just prior to his third bout with Sugar Ray Robinson. Here the film fulfills a classical (almost Spartan) role by subordinating female desire for the sake of the patriarchal order (he is in training and "can't fool around"). When La Motta douses his raging penis with ice water, he screams "Ahhhh!" in perverted pleasure. During this scene, Vickie is visually associated with a statue of the Virgin Mary, but later she is regarded as a whore during La Motta's jealous rages. The cut, as in the previous sex scene, is to a bout against Robinson. Then, after losing the match, La Motta plunges his fist into a bucket of ice water. His "small, little-girl hands" are thus equated with his phallus as equivalent, albeit poorly endowed, visual emblems of virility. Indeed, throughout the film the pent-up sexual frustration of his abstinence finds orgasmic release only in his violent outbursts.

From a theoretical perspective, the many questions raised by *Raging Bull* provoke ambivalent responses. On the one hand, although Scorsese's intention (based on his interviews and the textual evidence of the film itself) seems to have been to present a didactic outcry against violence to a mass audience, the film's boxing-ring savagery is so expressionistic in its own right and the hero's apocalyptic apotheosis and eventual redemption through art so thorough that any rhetoric against violence is lost in the stylization. One feminist has argued that "*Raging Bull* cannot escape being a metanarrative of male privilege, of which battering is the enforcer, boxing the symbolic terrain, and the acting . . . a reification of the monologic culture it depicts."[48] Can we conclude, as one critic has, that "violence is meant to act as a redemptive force in [the] film, both alleviating socially induced tensions . . . as well as acting as a cohesive agent that re-integrates the aberrant individual"?[49] Viewed in this way, if Jake La Motta is redeemed in a religious sense (as director Scorsese has stated), then the film's ideology coincides neatly with that of the born-again Christians who turned out in record numbers to elect Ronald Reagan to the presidency in 1980.

On the other hand, the film's brutally realistic depiction of La Motta's domestic violence actively exposes the inherent misogyny, racism, and homophobia of boxing, boxing movies, American society, and post-modernist American cinema. The centrality of violence in *Raging Bull* can thus be interpreted by diverse viewers in contradictory ways.[50] As such, it is (at least) two polysemic films in one—what Robin Wood has

193

called an "incoherent text"—and its ambivalent message may be that contemporary American patriarchy's penchant for tough-guy violence or Robert Bly's "men's movement" search for the "wild man" inside has a mythological place on the national and international scenes but no place in the family unit. Furthermore, while the film seems to posit a critique of inappropriate masculine ideals and overt violence, it situates that critique in specific ethnic, class, and gender stereotypes. Hal Foster has made a useful distinction between a "postmodernism of resistance," which promulgates progressive values and experimental aesthetics, and a "postmodernism of reaction,"[51] which is complicit with the neoconservative social order of late capitalism. There nonetheless remains the possibility that, like any postmodern pastiche, an individual work like *Raging Bull* will contain elements of both.

Notes

1. Aristotle said that "the Spectacle, though an attraction, is the least artistic of all the parts, and has least to do with the art of poetry" and "Tragic fear and pity may be aroused by the Spectacle, but they may also be aroused by the very structure and incidents of the play—which is the better way and shows the better poet. . . . To produce this same effect [fear and pity] by means of the Spectacle is less artistic, and requires extraneous aid. Those, however, who make use of the Spectacle to put before us that which is merely monstrous and not productive of fear and pity, are wholly out of touch with Tragedy." See Aristotle, "De Poetica," in *Introduction to Aristotle,* ed. Richard McKeon (New York: Modern Library, 1947), 633, 641.

2. Catherine Russell, "The Spectacular Representation of Death," in *Crisis Cinema: The Apocalyptic Idea in Postmodern Narrative Film,* ed. Christopher Sharrett (Washington, D.C.: Maisonneuve Press, 1993), 181.

3. Polls conducted by both *Premiere* magazine and *American Film* ranked *Raging Bull* as the top movie of the decade. *Time* magazine's first issue of 1990 similarly declared the film the world's champion motion picture of the 1980s in an article titled "Best of the Decade," *Time* 135 (January 1, 1990): 101. Even more recently, the American Film Institute compiled a list of (and devoted a prime time network television special to) "The 100 Greatest American Movies." *Raging Bull* ranked 24th overall, but it was the highest-ranked film made in the 1980s, in this poll of 1,500 "prominent Americans." See "The 100 Best Movies of 100 Years," *Newsweek Extra,* Summer 1998, 17–20.

4. Steven G. Kellman, "Introduction," in *Perspectives on "Raging Bull,"* ed. Steven G. Kellman (New York: G. K. Hall, 1994), 7.

5. Just as literary critics Richard Ellmann and Charles Feidelson said that "the modern awaits definition," so the postmodern also awaits definitive definition. See Richard Ellmann and Charles Feidelson, Jr., eds., *The Modern Tradition: Backgrounds of Modern Literature* (New York: Oxford University Press, 1965), v.

Many commentators—Jean Baudrillard, Jean-François Lyotard, Guy Debord, Gilles Deleuze and Felix Guattari, Jürgen Habermas, Andreas Huyssens, Hal Foster, Fredric Jameson, Douglas Crimp, Craig Owens, Rosalind Krauss, Charles Jencks, Kenneth Frampton, Robert Venturi, Linda Hutcheon, and John Cage, among many other theorists and commentators in various artistic disciplines—have proffered definitions of postmodernity, or at least pointed out preliminary "family resemblances" among so-called postmodern artifacts. As an eclectic phenomenon, an eclectic approach is called for. This essay will therefore use, refer to, and accept many, even possibly differing, definitions of postmodernity in an effort to understand the trope of violence in *Raging Bull*. As Fredric Jameson suggested, "It is less important to justify a disparate range of theoretical references than it is to take some initial inventory of the objective gaps and disjunctions within the texts themselves." See Jameson, *Fables of Aggression: Wyndham Lewis, The Modernist as Fascist* (Berkeley: University of California Press, 1981), 6.

6. Louis Menand points out several startling similarities between *Raging Bull* and *Bonnie and Clyde* in his essay "Methods and Madnesses," in *Perspectives on "Raging Bull,"* 60–68. In particular, Menand mentions the anti-heroes' violent professions, attraction to tough-yet-glamorous women, sexual inadequacies, and closeness to their brothers; in addition, there are scenes that appear in both films: the first meetings of the hero and his heroine involve showing off an automobile, there are scenes of *fellatio interruptus* in both movies, the home movie scenes of the Scorsese duplicate the picture-taking rituals of the Barrow gang in the Arthur Penn film, and both use the technique of slow-motion violence. These postmodernist homages may be just part of cinephile Scorsese's penchant for allusionism, but the *differences* between the two films underscore the degree to which intertextuality has become the predominant motion picture style.

7. Andrew Sarris, "Why Sports Movies Don't Work," *Film Comment* 16.6 (Nov.–Dec. 1980): 53.

8. Ibid., 49–50.

9. Gail Carnicelli Hemmeter and Thomas Hemmeter call attention to this unexplainable aspect of La Motta's character in their essay "The Word Made Flesh: Language in *Raging Bull,*" *Literature/Film Quarterly* 14.2 (1986): 101–5. In particular, they aver that "[the] film is, at heart, about the inherent difficulties of articulation, about the impossibility of reducing the complexity of man's behavior to a few pat sentences of explanation" (102).

10. Constance Penley, ed., *Feminism and Film Theory* (New York: Routledge, 1988), 20.

11. Michael Bliss, *Martin Scorsese and Michael Cimino* (Metuchen, N.J.: Scarecrow Press, 1985), 28.

12. The June 28, 1997, heavyweight championship bout between Mike Tyson and Evander Holyfield adds further dimension to that assessment. Tyson was disqualified in the third round for twice biting Holyfield on the ears.

13. This point is discussed in more detail in my essay, "Italian Americans in the Hollywood Cinema: Filmmakers, Characters, Audiences," *Voices in Italian Americana* 7.1 (Spring 1996): 65–77.

14. Morris Dickstein, "Stations of the Cross: *Raging Bull* Revisited," in *Perspectives on "Raging Bull,"* 81.

15. George F. Custen, *Bio/Pics: How Hollywood Constructed Public History* (New Brunswick, N.J.: Rutgers University Press, 1992), 69.

16. In the sequel to his 1970 autobiography, on which the film was based, La Motta attributes his erratic, violent disposition to a hereditary genetic condition, intermittent Mediterranean porphyria, an ailment that is exacerbated by alcohol consumption. See Jake La Motta, *Raging Bull II* (Secaucus, N.J.: Lyle Stuart, 1986), 239.

17. Sarris, "Why Sports Movies Don't Work," 52.

18. This concept is explicated in Barbara Mortimer, "Portraits of the Postmodern Person in *Taxi Driver, Raging Bull,* and *The King of Comedy,*" *Journal of Film and Video* 49.1–2 (Spring–Summer 1997): 28–38.

19. Mary Pat Kelly, *Martin Scorsese: A Journey* (New York: Thunder's Mouth Press, 1991), 32.

20. Thomas Wiener, "Martin Scorsese Fights Back," *American Film* 6.2 (Nov. 1980): 75.

21. Kevin Jackson, ed., *Schrader on Schrader and Other Writings* (London: Faber and Faber, 1990), 57.

22. Jake La Motta, *Raging Bull: My Story* (Englewood Cliffs, N.J.: Prentice-Hall, 1970), 1.

23. Pam Cook, "Masculinity in Crisis?" *Screen* 23.3–4 (Sept.–Oct. 1982): 39.

24. Ibid., 40.

25. Robin Wood, *Hollywood from Vietnam to Reagan* (New York: Columbia University Press, 1986), 248.

26. Later in the film, Joey La Motta uses similar language to encourage Jake to rid himself of Vickie: "Why don't ya bust her hole and throw her out? She's ruining your life." La Motta's verbal confusion here about whether to "fuck" or "fight" Janiro reveals his psychosocial maladjustment throughout the film.

27. Wood, *Hollywood from Vietnam to Reagan,* 256.

28. James Combs, "Pox-Eclipse—The Dystopian Imagination," in *Crisis Cinema,* 21. Combs points to postmodern anti-heroes such as the Bruce Willis character in the *Die Hard* movies, Clint Eastwood's Dirty Harry Callahan portrayals, and Batman as exemplars of this sort of violent throwback character.

29. Custen, *Bio/Pics,* 18.

30. Kaja Silverman, "Masochism and Male Subjectivity," *Camera Obscura* 17 (May 1988): 36.

31. Bliss, *Martin Scorsese and Michael Cimino,* 128.

32. Hayden White, *The Content of the Form: Narrative Discourse and Historical Representation* (Baltimore: Johns Hopkins University Press, 1987), xi.

33. Ibid., 39.

34. La Motta, *Raging Bull: My Story,* 56–57.

35. Ibid., 178.

36. La Motta, *Raging Bull II,* 209.

37. La Motta, *Raging Bull: My Story,* 2.

38. Custen, *Bio/Pics,* 33.

39. Wood, *From Hollywood to Vietnam*, 253.

40. Christopher Sharrett, "Introduction," in *Crisis Cinema*, 7.

41. Custen, *Bio/Pics*, 7.

42. Ibid., 87.

43. This is not to say that the Motion Picture Academy somehow speaks for the American public or even reflects its conscious judgments. To the extent, though, that the film industry is in touch with the pulse of the audience and their psychological and political views, Oscars are rarely awarded based on pure acting ability or performance; they tend to be awarded on the basis of the role, that is, on the character, not the characterization. For more on this notion, see my essays, "The Politics of Ambivalence: *Apocalypse Now* as Prowar and Antiwar Film," in *From Hanoi to Hollywood: The Vietnam War in American Film*, ed. Linda Dittmar and Gene Michaud (New Brunswick, N.J.: Rutgers University Press, 1991), 147–49, and "Masculine/Feminine: The 'New Masculinity' in *Tootsie* (1982)," *Velvet Light Trap* 38 (Fall 1996): 5.

44. Karl Marx, *The Eighteenth Brumaire of Louis Bonaparte* (New York: International Publishers, 1963), 15.

45. Although somewhat reductionist, this point is emphasized in Susan Jeffords, *Hard Bodies: Hollywood Masculinity in the Reagan Era* (New Brunswick, N.J.: Rutgers University Press, 1994). For an analysis linking the Indiana Jones prototype to Reaganite policies, see my essay, "Mr. Jones Goes to Washington: Myth and Religion in *Raiders of the Lost Ark*," *Quarterly Review of Film Studies* 7.4 (Fall 1982): 331–40.

46. Mary Pat Kelly, *Martin Scorsese: The First Decade* (Pleasantville, N.Y.: Redgrave, 1980), 32.

47. La Motta, *Raging Bull: My Story*, 76–77.

48. Carol J. Adams, "Raging Batterer," in *Perspectives on "Raging Bull,"* 120.

49. Bliss, *Martin Scorsese and Michael Cimino*, 24.

50. The calculated ambivalence of such mixed ideological messages in the commercial Hollywood cinema is explored in Tomasulo, "The Politics of Ambivalence," 145–58.

51. Hal Foster, "Postmodernism: A Preface," in *The Anti-Aesthetic: Essays on Postmodern Culture*, ed. Hal Foster (Port Townsend, Wash.: Bay Press, 1983), xii.

8

I MARRIED RAMBO: SPECTACLE AND MELODRAMA IN THE HOLLYWOOD ACTION FILM

MARK GALLAGHER

The contemporary action film, the most profitable of post-modern film genres, uses various formal and narrative strategies to respond to cultural crises about masculinity and male social roles.[1] For men in contemporary capitalist society, a society that provides a social and economic structure that severely limits and codifies the bourgeois male's ability to establish his identity through physical activity, action films provide fantasies of heroic omnipotence and of escape from, or transcendence of, cultural pressures. Since these fantasies do not represent real solutions to the problems faced by members of capitalist societies, action-film narratives necessarily displace the present-day contradictions of male identity into visual space, into spectacle. While violent spectacle has been a prominent feature of the genre since its inception in the late 1960s, action films in the 1990s have increasingly constructed stories around threats to domesticity, marriage, and the nuclear family. By presenting spectacular violence as the solution to domestic and familial conflicts, the genre displays the ideological contradictions between idealized masculinity and familial responsibility under capitalism.

The action film has historically been a "male" genre, dealing with stories of male heroism, produced by male filmmakers for principally male audiences. The genre's most intriguing development in the 1990s is the incorporation of formal elements associated with the "female" genre of melodrama. This formal and aesthetic development is linked to crises in authority associated with postmodern culture: challenges to male power in both public and private spheres, the privileging of simulation over authenticity under capitalism, and the corresponding distance between fictional texts and social reality. In response to these crises, the Hollywood action film proffers conventional narratives of male mastery but modifies these narratives through reliance on other generic languages, particularly those central to comedy and melodrama. This process of genre hybridization accomplishes the ideological work of male-dominated, multinational capitalism; action films of the 1990s celebrate the ingenuity and physical prowess of individual heroes, while also depicting such heroes as champions of women, children, and capitalist ideology. At the same time, these films more often address women audiences narratively and formally. Women play more substantive and less submissive roles in many 1990s action films, and action films increasingly utilize elements of melodrama, structuring narratives around a logic of spectacle and excess that is emblematic of the classical Hollywood melodrama.

The mainstream action film reconfigures violence as visual spectacle and as vivid cinematic images designed to generate pleasurable sensations in audiences. By means of its hyperbolic genre conventions and its codified narratives, the action film displays the instability of cultural paradigms of race, gender, politics, and capitalist ideology in postmodern culture. Action films, like most Hollywood blockbusters, tend to present conservative narratives and iconography targeted toward adolescent males. While action films occasionally display progressive overtones, the surface narratives of such films appear to reinforce patriarchal structures of white male authority, privilege, and omnipotence. At the level of plot, the vast majority of action films of the 1980s and early 1990s support conservative forms of militant, heterosexual, white masculinity.[2] To advance their preferred ideological positions, though, authors of generic texts invoke the competing ideological frameworks they seek to disavow.[3] The use of postmodern representational strategies such as exaggeration, parody, irony, and self-reflexivity indicates the anxiety that accompanies the insistence on preferred readings. The significance of action films for film and cultural-studies critics lies in the ways the genre articulates prevailing ideological positions. Despite their masculine overtones, contemporary action films formally and narratively follow patterns developed in popular media geared toward women rather than men. Such a cultural positioning indicates a shift in the rhetorical strategies of popular texts. Whereas cultural discourses and texts of the 1980s promote militant masculinity as an alternative to feminine or liberal weakness, discourses of the 1990s synthesize categories of feminine domesticity and sentiment with those of masculine discipline and strength. Evidence of this shift appears in the action film at the level of visual style, setting, and in the context of violence.

Action films present violence as a component of a spectacular visual style, usually to thrill or excite rather than to shock. Action films present graphic violence and pyrotechnic spectacle as exaggerated simulations of real violence and destruction rather than as credible, discomfiting representations of these phenomena. Increasingly, critics refer to action films' "cartoon violence" to suggest that viewers—especially younger viewers—will not find that violence objectionable. The phrase connotes the perceptible distance between cinematic representation and its social referent—in this case, a distance substantial enough that a child could recognize it. With screen violence distanced from reality by elaborate special effects and fantasy narratives, action-film violence appears legible and comprehensible to viewers. In his analysis of the role of popular texts, John Fiske suggests that violence in media appears as a cultural response to perceived social pressures.[4] The visibility of real violence in news media, the unequal distribution of wealth, and the diminished utility of physical strength for bourgeois males under multinational capitalism all indicate complex social conditions disadvantageous to many members of society. In the face of these social and cultural crises, action films, like other popular texts, retain their currency because they offer conventional, definitive solutions to otherwise insurmountable problems.

James Cameron's 1994 film *True Lies* combines an action narrative involving terrorists with a romantic narrative about the action hero's marriage and family life. This combination allows the film to make extensive use of melodramatic formal elements and narrative situations. Late in the film, following the resolution of the conflict between the couple and just prior to the climactic action sequence, the romantic leads embrace passionately while a nuclear bomb detonates in the background. The mushroom cloud offers a spectacular display of phallic power and a metonym for the sexual fulfillment the pair never achieve during the film. The scene aestheticizes destructive weaponry, as the kissing couple in the foreground lends a lyrical quality to the image. The excessive visual display also punctuates a rather unspectacular moment in the romantic narrative, an intimate exchange between husband and wife. In addition, the image announces the linkage of the film's romantic and domestic elements to its action environment while simultaneously heralding the demise of the domestic sphere. When the understanding wife tells her spy husband to "go to work," ceding to him the role of provider and protector, the film sets aside its domestic plot in favor of an extended action sequence. The kiss scene places the couple at the site of action but also necessitates the woman's departure from that space. The film's linkage of active and domestic realms follows a pattern established in Hollywood melodramas, and as in melodrama, this action-film episode derives its impact from stylistic excess and from its conflation of social and personal spaces.

As *True Lies* demonstrates, the melodramatic combination of traditionally male spaces of action and female spaces of romance and domesticity makes the contemporary action film a synthesis of historically male and female genres. The explosion scene transforms a display of nuclear

Domestic virtues and violent assumptions: *True Lies* (Twentieth-Century Fox, 1994).

weaponry into a sentimental framing device, and elsewhere in the film, spectacular violence and destruction induce responses of excitement, fear, and, occasionally, anger. In complementary fashion, the film, like the genre as a whole, transforms emotional situations into episodes of public violence. Action films channel sexual and romantic conflict into physical and violent displays, producing sensation rather than emotion.[5] Meanwhile, the genre's corresponding over-representation of active, masculine space, far beyond the physical or experiential capacities of men or women in post-industrial society, suggests that the spectacle of masculinity in the contemporary action film conceals real crises of male identity. Tellingly, the action film proffers violence as the universal solution to contemporary sex role anxieties.

Melodrama, traditionally recognized as a women's genre, provides the operative mode of contemporary action cinema, which is an over-whelmingly male genre. Not only do action films venture into the narratives and themes of melodrama, but melodrama also forms an essential formal component of the action genre, particularly in the spectacle-oriented films prevalent since the early 1980s. Action films' melodramatic elements—including moral legibility of plots and characters and spectacular, excessive mise-en-scène—link the action genre structurally to the genre of melodrama, which has historically appealed predominantly to women audiences. Films like *True Lies, Terminator 2: Judgment Day* (Cameron, 1991), *The Long Kiss Goodnight* (Renny Harlin, 1996), and *Face/Off* (John Woo, 1997) build stories around threats to family and domesticity while also presenting the action genre's traditional narratives of global terrorism or other threats to the human race. Like melodrama, the action film emphasizes archetypal characters and non-psychological development of those characters, displacement of conflict through hysteria and excess, unambiguous moral oppositions, and accessibility of meaning. The action film's invocation of the domestic sphere represents a significant development in a genre that has largely set its conflicts against the backdrop of expansive public spaces such as large cities or exotic foreign settings. When the action-film milieu, traditionally a utopian space of action and individual freedom, incorporates the crises of melodrama, the films further repress such crises visually and narratively. The ideological contradictions of familial and social roles, foregrounded in the melodrama genre, erupt throughout the action film as violence. Alternately, the action film uses violence, motion, and action to stave off the resolution of ideological problems. By incorporating family matters into narratives of ritualized heroism and combat, action films sustain the illusion that viewers may attend to pressing social concerns (i.e., they may be good parents, spouses, or citizens) within the conventional terrain of a master narrative that puts a premium on individual autonomy and dominance.

The action film's structural similarity to melodrama suggests that the genre effectively repackages its anachronistic master narrative in a postmodern guise of accessible, viewer-friendly entertainment. Action films incorporate postmodern self-reflexivity and generic irony to assure viewers that they are "in on the joke," that the genre's distortions of gender, race, politics, and so forth are whimsical devices intended to gratify audiences. Allusions to star personas, action choreography that calls to mind sequences in previous films, and other self-reflexive citations imply that action films offer a metacommentary on genre rather than a reactionary depiction of social reality. The discrete disavowal of the genre's overt ideological agenda allows action films to rely continually on master-narrative tropes. Significantly, the comic tone of many contemporary action films permits a recapitulation of familiar narratives of male mastery.[6] Action films proffer male mastery as a necessary component of their generic narratives; the ability to assert control over threatening situations virtually defines the action hero. To retain this tired narrative paradigm while producing films that appeal to new generations of movie audiences, filmmakers reproduce a master narrative in popular-narrative form. This formal strategy reinforces patriarchal ideology (by assuring the reproduction of patriarchal narratives) but also renders that ideology unstable. If narratives of male mastery can be transmitted only through texts structurally similar to those constructed for women audiences, the social order underpinning such narratives may also be under siege.

Ideological contradictions, though displaced, play a decisive role in most contemporary action films. So-called buddy films compensate for the threat of homosexuality with heavy doses of homophobic humor masked as male camaraderie. Films that include spies, terrorists, mercenaries, and other international figures pit iconoclastic (though idealized) heroes against stereotypical villains in interminable battles for cultural and national identity. With remarkable consistency, action films either exclude women from their narratives or veil their protagonists' misogyny by depicting villains as even more objectionable sexual sadists. *True Lies,* which serves as the case study for this essay's arguments, makes each of these volatile elements particularly evident. Through its relatively complex treatment of a female character (though by no means equal to the male hero) and its emphasis on domestic relations and conflicts, the film highlights the function of melodrama and comedy. In action films of the 1990s, invocations of these other genres allow screen characters to negotiate between the domestic realm, which corresponds loosely to viewers' familiar real-life experiences, and the utopian space of action, a terrain of simulation, artifice, and fantasy.

HALLMARKS OF MEN IN ACTION

Action-film conventions, particularly those linked to representations of violence, derive from earlier films as well as from prevailing social norms. As in postmodern representation generally, these conventions refer to prior simulations of reality, to previous fictional narratives, as well as to a recognizable social reality.[7] Shifting social ideologies create a cultural climate in which action films remain popular and help determine what such films will or will not represent, although the principal cultural referents for action films are the stars, plots, fight sequences, stunts, and special effects (and to a lesser extent, dialogue) that appear in other films. While the action film constitutes a genre of its own, it draws from a variety of other traditional film genres. Its images of masculine authority and violence follow from earlier representations in the gangster film, the western, and the war film. The malleability of the form derives not only from the need to retain audience interest in new ways, but also from a tendency to elide or displace the genre's ideological concerns ever more spectacularly and decisively.[8] Increasingly graphic depictions of violence, for example, appeal to audiences familiar with the genre's previous plot conventions and special effects. Displays of violence also transfer violence's narrative functions into the purely visual sphere. Viewers learn to enjoy displays of violence as displays rather than as violence. Even films awash in violence need not necessarily represent conservative or nihilistic world views. Viewers may interpret action films as commentaries on violence or on cinema's propensity for violence, rather than as glorifications of social violence. Indeed, many action-film conventions refer more closely to previous cinematic representations than to corresponding developments in the material world. With this in mind, the genre's anachronistic depictions of women, non-white ethnicities, and domestic and global politics become more comprehensible, though not more excusable. The ever-increasing gap between action-film narratives and their referents in reality suggests, among other things, the estrangement that viewers feel from both normative institutions and mechanisms of social change.

Comic, stylized, or otherwise exaggerated treatments of violence in action films repress screen violence's obvious meaning: that horrific pain and suffering should repulse the viewer. Similarly, action films repress and displace other factors—paradoxes of masculinity and homoeroticism, and social and political ideology—through comedy, visual excess, and emphasis on performance or artificiality. In an essay on the ideology of popular film, Robin Wood notes the difficulty of assigning discrete boundaries to film genres. According to Wood, genres "represent different strategies for dealing with the same ideological tensions."[9] Since the action film privileges tempo and spectacle over complexity and realism, the genre allows only a limited number of available narratives and character roles. Genre limitations prevent action films from coping adequately with contemporary crises of gender, race, identity construction, political conflict, and social behavior. To contend with or stave off the threat these crises present, the genre looks outside itself, to melodrama, comedy, the western, and other genres. The action genre cannot contain all the issues that arise within it, particularly issues of male identity and gender construction. Action films' logical gaps and inconsistencies rise to the surface when their narratives diverge into spectacle and excess and when genre conventions give way to melodrama and comedy.

Perhaps because the conventions and structures of the action film appear so self-evident, their prevailing elements have not been precisely defined. On-screen action—particularly physical combat and gunplay, fast-moving bodies or vehicles, and destruction of property or landscape features—is the genre's principal feature. Location and historical setting also characterize the genre; most contemporary action films are set in the present and in North American cities. Setting distinguishes the action genre from war films, westerns, and gangster films, all of which situate their violent action in a culturally sanctioned or ritualized space (wartime, the historical past, or the underworld). Even when located in familiar and contemporary settings, action typically occurs at a distance from or as an embellishment of events that might occur in everyday reality. For example, audiences can see speeding cars on racetracks and highways, but only in action films can they regularly witness unsanctioned, destructive pursuits through city streets. Similarly, while most viewers observe real physical violence at some point in their lives, action films both locate viewers at a safe remove from conflict and choreograph action in a lyrical or spectacular style. Multiple camera positions and rapid cutting transform action from an approximate representation of reality into a rhythmic spectacle, appealing to viewers at a visual and physical level, rather than an intellectual or sentimental level. The use of extreme close-ups and computer-enhanced special effects further heightens the sensory appeal of action over its narrative or social relevance.

Contemporary action film narratives, which usually focus on a solitary hero or pair of heroes, often function simply to advance the protagonists from one dangerous predicament to another. These narratives generate suspense not by prolonging viewers' anticipation of upcoming action sequences, but by delivering a continuous flow of action as the narrative itself. *Speed* (1994), for example, extends a speeding-bus sequence over more than half the film's running time. The film pares down its story and the interactions between characters to the absolute minimum required to suture viewers into the rhythm of the action.[10] Contemporary action films increasingly reshape the familiar narrative pattern of stasis/conflict/resolution, bypassing the period of stasis almost entirely to focus on conflict that spreads across an entire film. Viewers now expect action films to commence in action, beginning with a modestly scaled conflict that introduces the lead players and provides cursory character development. The elevator sequence in *Speed,* for example, establishes the virility and resourcefulness of an L.A.P.D. officer (Keanu Reeves) and the ruthlessness and vindictiveness of his mad-bomber adversary (Dennis Hopper). Similarly, the opening sequence of *Cliffhanger* (1993), in which Sylvester Stallone leads a failed rescue operation that results in a woman's death, establishes Stallone as a flawed male whose desire to regain control over his body and physical environment motivates his confrontation with the film's villains.

The conventional action film narrative deals with a solitary hero's tests of masculine identity. The struggles usually unfold across the male body or shift onto the body's usually phallic extensions in weaponry, machinery, or larger symbols of power, authority, or physical mass, from tanks and airplanes to large buildings to mountains or entire cities. Describing 1980s Hollywood action films, Susan Jeffords suggests that displays of the male body and complementary images of masculine spaces and events construct a visibly male narrative world:

> The male body—principally the white male body—became increasingly a vehicle of display—of musculature, of beauty, of physical feats, and of a gritty toughness. External spectacle—weaponry, explosions, infernos, crashes, high-speed chases, ostentatious luxuries—offered companion evidence of both the sufficiency and the volatility of this display. That externality itself confirmed that the outer parameters of the male body were to be the focus of audience attention, desire, and politics.[11]

Jeffords suggests that 1990s films, in contrast, provide a space for more interiorized and emotive male heroes. In my view, 1990s action films more frequently narrate the exploits of psychologically and emotionally complex males but still privilege the exteriorized male body.[12] As the later analysis of *True Lies* argues, male characters and viewers continue to enjoy dominion over physical as well as emotional spaces.

The prevalence of the white male in action films highlights the genre's construction of stable, unassailable identities for its heroes. Action films routinely subject masculinity, through its metonymic representation as a male body—itself an approximation of the phallus—to rituals of combat and suffering. The triumph of masculinity occurs only when the screen male exhibits mastery over his own body. To generate conflict around the idealized space of the male body—and to discourage erotic contemplation of static or rigid bodies—action films threaten, test, and punish their heroes.[13] The films subject their heroes to ritual or conventional obstacles that, once overcome, demonstrate the fantasy omnipotence of the action hero, usually a white male. Action films tend to present white maleness as sufficient evidence of stable self-identity, in opposition to gender or racial minorities. Jeffords notes in Hollywood films "a pattern of masculinity that necessitates defining men not by content but by opposition to an other."[14] Viewers recognize a male hero not entirely through a perception of the character's positive traits, but also in opposition to villains, who often appear as characters of different races or ethnicities.[15] Action films consistently naturalize racial, ethnic, and gender difference through comic treatments. In late 1980s and 1990s action films, comedy allows the simultaneous retention and critique of conventions of masculinity.[16] Action films rely on postmodern self-reflexivity, or what Jim Collins calls "hyperconsciousness," "a hyperawareness on the part of the text itself of its cultural status, function, and history, as well as of the conditions of its circulation and reception."[17] By presuming to offer audiences a metacommentary on media culture, action films can articulate conservative ideologies that other contemporary texts and discourses have challenged.

In terms of visual style, action films consistently foreground their protagonists as the camera follows the hero's movements through space and frames him at the center of visual spectacle. In action sequences, cameras track the protagonist, whether he is pursuer or pursued, attacker or defender. Multiple camera positions during fight sequences present a variety of male selves that converge toward a singular masculine ideal. Fragmented shots of the hero's body in action and multiple-angle views of the same body signify the hero's threatened or fractured masculinity. The films represent a hero's successful combat by presenting the image of the solitary, whole male. To some extent such a presentation adheres to the narrative principles of classical cinema.[18] The centrality of the protagonist in shot compositions both activates the viewer's voyeuristic gaze and promotes identification with the screen protagonist.

Action films' visual spectacle also fetishizes the male hero, not as an object of erotic contemplation, but as a component of a full-screen spectacle.[19] Steve Neale observes that repetitive close-ups of the male body and its extensions in weaponry encourage fetishistic gazing, "by stopping the narrative in order to recognize the pleasure of display, but displacing [the display] from the male body as such and locating it more generally in the overall components of a highly ritualized scene."[20] In addition to offering their heroes as objects of voyeuristic admiration, action films diffuse the boundaries of their protagonists' bodies so that the figures transcend the physical dimensions of their representations. The male body becomes a connotative visual element in the genre's presentation of spectacular action. In turn, action film spectacle serves as a bombastic representation of masculinity, a representation that can exist only in visual abstractions. The spectacle of action (and the fantasy of masculinity it represents) finds no parallel in the domestic or personal sphere. Action films, through their overemphasis on the terrain of action, suggest the crisis of masculinity that lurks beyond the edges of spectacle-oriented narratives.

Digital effects further dilute the boundaries between the male body and the surrounding spectacle. In *True Lies,* the visual excess of the computer-enhanced battles between terrorists and airborne heroes excites viewers and replaces their desire for credibility or realism. As in other 1990s films, some of *True Lies*'s action sequences include digitally superimposed film footage of characters onto computer-generated backgrounds. Action scenes that once highlighted the virtuoso performances of stunt people now acquire their chief appeal through the visual quality of the images themselves.[21] Digital visual effects favor simulation over reality, and the human body becomes another element for manipulation in digitally enhanced scenographic space. Images of the literal body of the actor—usually male—lend scale to the simulated world and establish narrative continuity. Just as spectacle and the visual landscape define the hero, the hero's presence defines the landscape, reconfiguring it into a grandiose emblem of masculinity and control.

ACTION CINEMA AS A MELODRAMATIC MODE

The action film's emphasis on spectacle, rhythm of action, spatial properties, performance, and music links the genre to melodrama, both in its narrative structure and its formal properties. The action genre's association with masculinity and male audiences parallels the melodrama's link to female audiences and femininity. Such gender associations have resulted in critical disparagement for both genres: the contemporary action film, like nineteenth-century stage melodrama and the classical-Hollywood melodrama, is regularly pilloried for its visual and performative excesses and lack of narrative realism. Moreover, 1970s feminist critics' recuperation of the melodrama—rescuing it from its denigrated status as a vehicle for low pleasures and artificial evocations of sentiment—parallels the 1990s feminist project of revisiting traditionally male genres for representations of conflicted masculinities.[22] Feminist analyses of melodrama identify the social conflicts the genre exaggerates or displaces into personal space. Theorists of melodrama also examine the spectatorial pleasures that coincide with affective entertainment, which in melodrama is usually pathos rather than elation. Contemporary feminist analyses of "masculine" genre films have also recognized the ideological conflicts that such films generate or elide. However, these analyses often disregard or fail to account for the spectatorial pleasures associated with such texts. Action films present physical strength and dexterity as the solution to social conflicts, an attractive proposition for male viewers socialized to rely on physical force despite increasingly limited opportunities to make use of such force. For female viewers, action films provide the ironic pleasures of the eroticized, objectified male body. For both male and female viewers, action films offer uncomplicated oppositions between good and evil in a morally lucid world.

Action film violence, like the genre's other predominant elements, operates according to melodramatic codes of excess. Mary Ann Doane argues that genre conventions in American film situate violence and emotion in correspondingly "male" and "female" spheres: "In the Western and detective film aggressivity or violence is internalized as narrative content. In maternal melodrama, the violence is displaced onto affect."[23] By synthesizing traditionally male and female genres, action films shape violence into affect and reconfigure emotional displays as violent spectacles. Action films, traditionally addressed to male viewers, produce emotion through violent rather than sentimental images. Sharon Willis's reading of To Live and Die in L.A. (William Freidkin, 1985) traces the convergence of violence and affect: "By its very excessive violence, To Live and Die manages to maintain both levels of intensity; it thematizes violence and it produces bursts of affect channeled as spectator horror."[24] The relation between violence and affective intensity constitutes a prevailing convention in contemporary action cinema. Technical developments in the action cinema permit increasingly graphic displays of violence and pain. To temper the affective power of such images, action films typically surround episodes of graphic violence with comic dialogue or plot elements. Thus, the films generally offer viewers an escape valve, a means to engage with the narrative at a different level if certain images or situations become too unsettling, in other words, if viewers respond too emotionally.

Melodramatic codes also determine the action film's available content and its manner of presentation. Thomas Elsaesser notes that in melodrama, "significance lies in the structure and articulation of the action, not in any psychologically motivated correspondence with individualised experience."[25] Since the conventions of action films—shootouts, chases, international intrigue—bear little relevance to viewers' everyday realities, the films promote viewer identification based on performative and gestural codes, and on motion, rhythm, and visual excess. Genre conventions situate action film characters and narratives outside lived reality. This disjunction liberates characters and plots from "real" social and ideological encroachments while limiting the available range of narrative responses to particular situations.

Melodramatic excess engages the viewer at a visual and stylistic level. In the action genre, excess also signals the failures, limitations, or contradictions of films' stated ideologies. The classical Hollywood melodrama produces ideological contradictions through stylistic excess and narrative discontinuity, disrupting the ideological positions that films might appear to enforce.[26] In action films, pyrotechnic or violent excess substitutes for pragmatic solutions to real world problems. Combat replaces diplomacy, solitude and alienation replace personal bonds, muteness and stock phrases preclude communication, and male camaraderie stands in for dialogue between genders. Action films regularly recode male anxieties or traumas as hysterical symptoms, feminized and displaced from the active male persona.

As noted above, the audio-visual qualities of action sequences often subsume the sequences' logical narrative function. Geoffrey Nowell-Smith argues that in melodrama, "music and mise en scène do not just heighten the emotionality of an element of action: to some extent they substitute for it."[27] He links this stylistic device to the psychopathology of hysteria, in which repressed ideas or emotion reappear on the body as displaced symptoms. For Nowell-Smith, melodrama's manifestation of inexpressible ideas through visual or performative devices indicates melodrama's resistance to normative ideologies. Melodrama operates according to social norms, but it exaggerates social conventions to expose the artifice and limitations of prevailing codes of behavior. Action films, through a similar use of visual excess in place of logical resolution, may share this resistance to social repression. Visual excess transforms otherwise logical actions—logical within the framework of an action film narrative—into absurd posturing or impossible physical feats. Moreover, the notion of action film spectacle as hysterical symptom problematizes the genre's associations with masculine ideologies. The action film thus situates itself in an already feminized mass-cultural space.[28] Rather than appearing as merely another offspring of patriarchal ideology, the action film, through its mass appeal and its feminized mode of presentation, corresponds to traditionally female modes of cultural expression.

Action films' distance from realism also places the genre outside historically male—and thus esteemed—categories of cultural expression. In classical Hollywood cinema, male-dominated genres like the gangster film and the western operate according to realist conventions, particularly in their depictions of violent action.[29] Since the 1980s, though, action films have relied on increasingly cartoonish representations of action and violence and on the self-parodying personas of stars like Arnold Schwarzenegger and Stallone. The genre's development since the mid-1980s has been marked by an overt and increasing disruption of realist codes. Teenage males form a substantial portion of the action film's target audience, and the appeal to adolescent rather than adult sensibilities denotes the genre's status as a critically, but not commercially, marginalized cultural form. Appeals to teens also motivate the genre's creation of utopian or fantasy settings like outer space or the supernatural world. Similarly, action films based on video games, including *Super Mario Bros.* (Rocky Morton and Annabel Jankel, 1993), *Street Fighter* (Steven E. de Souza, 1994), and *Mortal Kombat* (Paul Anderson, 1995), provide adolescents with fantasy narratives removed from the contested familial, educational, and social spheres.

The performative, excessive masculinity that structures the action film further erodes the connection between masculinity and realism. Spectacular displays of the male body and exaggerated male behaviors extend beyond narrative requirements and beyond the limits of realist convention. For Nowell-Smith, "the 'hysterical' moment of a text can be identified as the point at which the realist representative convention breaks down."[30] This formulation suggests that the contemporary action film consists of a nearly uninterrupted series of hysterical moments. Chris Holmlund cites similar pathological symptoms in two Stallone vehicles, *Lock Up* (John Flynn, 1989) and *Tango and Cash* (Andrei Konchalovsky, 1989). The films' homophobic paranoia and their rigorous maintenance of the heroes' facade of masculinity suggests unstated challenges to

212

gender norms. As Holmlund observes, "the insistence in both films on the inviolability of masculinity has a hysterical ring to it."[31] The action hero's overstated masculinity denotes the constructedness of conventional gender paradigms. Viewers' pleasure in viewing such performative displays suggests a further contradiction between action film narratives and the genre's aesthetic excess. Though at some level action films require viewers to take male performance seriously (seriously enough to generate suspense), on another level the films allow viewers to enjoy the artifice of men masquerading as supermen.

By presenting male performance and visual spectacle as hysterical excess, action films promote negotiated viewing positions for both male and female viewers. Tania Modleski argues that conventional melodramas may appeal to men "because these films provide them with a vicarious, hysterical, experience of femininity which can be more definitively laid to rest for having been 'worked through.' "[32] Viewers of both sexes may respond similarly to action film masculinity. Though films periodically offer cinematic masculinity as an ideal toward which male viewers might strive, the excessive nature of this masculinity mediates viewer involvement with the screen image. Because of their representational distance from reality, contemporary action films do not call upon their male viewers to enact the fantasies of masculinity that appear on screen.[33] Similarly, female spectators may use experiences of hysterical masculinity to negotiate their own positions within patriarchal power structures, aided by the awareness that sufficiently exaggerated masculinity is indistinguishable from the female pathology of hysteria. Action films transform masculinity into spectacular abstractions and performative exhibitions. Such presentations may neutralize the threat that hegemonic masculinity poses for male viewers, who must live up to the masculine ideal, and female viewers, who must live in its long shadow.

True Lies and the Struggle between Activity and Domesticity

With increasing frequency, action films in the late 1980s and 1990s have dramatized domestic space and transformed it into a setting for action. This shift is linked to changes in Hollywood audiences and American society. Domestic settings may appeal to aging male viewers who, through marriage and fatherhood, may play more of a role in domestic matters than they used to and for whom domesticity highlights anxieties about masculinity. Emphasis on home and family also indicates

Hollywood's attempts to draw female viewers to action films. Moving away from the *Rambo*-era convention of the solitary male with no social or familial ties, more recent films reposition the male hero as the protector of domestic space. Conversely, threats to domestic space occur because of preoccupied or inattentive patriarchs. In this respect, *True Lies* and other films anticipated the rhetoric of groups like Promise Keepers, suggesting that the father is both the cause of and the solution to family conflict. In *True Lies,* for example, the hero's neglectful parenting leads to his daughter's kidnapping by terrorists. In rescuing her, the male hero usurps the primary care-giving role traditionally assigned to women. The apparent violation of the action film convention of the heroic loner occurs through a framework that Jeffords calls "individualism as fathering."[34] When paternal duties beckon, the male hero does not abandon his dominion over public space. Instead, the family, represented by the endangered woman or child, intrudes into the space of action. In many cases, an inadequate family structure is sufficient to generate narrative conflict. Jeffords argues that, given challenges to male power in the workplace and the U.S. political system, paternal heroes work to reclaim the world of the family as a realm of masculine authority.[35] Action film fatherhood thus offers a fantasy of autonomy, requiring no substantial behavioral change from men.

Most action films negotiate domestic and family concerns by mapping those issues cursorily onto the active, public, masculine sphere. In *True Lies,* which begins with the domestic and active spaces rigidly separated, the active sphere eventually subsumes the domestic. While the domestic world recedes from the narrative, its representatives, the hero's wife and teenage daughter, cross into the active sphere. The film enforces the separation of the familial and active spheres by presenting its few female characters as traditional melodramatic types: the dissatisfied wife, the wholesome but quietly rebellious daughter, and the greedy temptress. Meanwhile, male characters operate according to melodramatic, non-psychological principles of action, and the film repeatedly substitutes visual spectacle for emotional outbursts. Notably, the film's interplay between the active and familial realms includes some seepage between the two spaces, which occurs because of the hero's marital crisis and because of the intrusive behavior of his misogynist partner. The partner stresses the importance of events in the active sphere (regularly citing national defense and presidential authority) while zealously monitoring and constraining the hero's domestic conduct.

The action narrative of *True Lies* concerns a dashing spy, Harry Tasker (Schwarzenegger), and his battle against a group of Middle

The action hero in a hybrid genre: *True Lies.* (Twentieth-Century Fox, 1994)

Eastern terrorists. This plot is relatively conventional, but the film integrates the story of Harry's wife, Helen (Jamie Lee Curtis), who is unaware of her husband's secret identity. The film's first half comically juxtaposes Harry's spectacular exploits against his banal home life, in which he fabricates an identity as an exceptionally dull salesman. The couple's relationship is threatened when a used-car salesman (Bill Paxton) tries to seduce Helen by masquerading as a gallant secret agent. Harry mobilizes government forces to prevent her possible infidelity, and shortly thereafter, Harry's enemies kidnap him and his wife, at which point she discovers his real identity. Following the couple's hasty reconciliation, Harry flies off to rescue their kidnapped daughter and prevent a nuclear war. At the film's conclusion, the family appears briefly to exude domestic bliss—though the film foregrounds the relationship between the married couple rather than the family threesome—and Helen joins Harry as a secret agent.

Melodrama informs the narrative through comic references to domesticity during the action sequences and spectacular displacement of psychological crises. The film's opening sequence, in which Harry infiltrates a party at an enormous villa, places the action in a melodramatic context. Harry's first line of dialogue is "Honey, I'm home," a code phrase he whispers to his nearby support team through a hidden microphone. To accomplish his mission, he maneuvers through a crowded reception area and proceeds upstairs to a bedroom, where he begins stealing computer files. As in a traditional melodramatic narrative, the sequence uses the home as a site of conflict and recognizes the home's public and private boundaries. The notion that a male hero needs a team of hidden associates to guide him through social space recurs throughout the film: Harry's partner Gib (Tom Arnold) provides him with a cover story to tell his wife and daughter, and in a later sequence, Gib phones Helen to explain Harry's late working hours so the hero can pursue his foes. This later episode prevents Harry from attending the birthday party his wife and daughter have prepared for him. The film briefly shows his family's disappointment, then abandons the domestic conflict entirely by cutting away to an extended chase sequence.

The possibility of Helen's infidelity produces further opportunities for the convergence of the active and domestic spheres, centered around melodramatic representations of personal intimacy and male hysteria. In place of the heterosexual couple, the film's first third foregrounds Harry's partnership with Gib, who is a conspicuous presence in Harry's personal life. Gib appears throughout as a surrogate mate for Harry, sharing his confidences and exploits. In addition, the film thoroughly feminizes Gib's character: he rarely uses a gun or participates in action; he complains frequently about his passive, subordinate role; he chides Harry about his bravura (i.e., hyper-masculine) behavior; and at one point he dances an impromptu tango with another of Harry's male cohorts. Gib's character embodies the hysterical residue of Harry's oversufficient masculinity. Harry is largely silent when he learns of Helen's possible affair, but Gib uses the situation to comment at length about his own marital failures and his misogynist attitude toward Helen. The film presents each of these situations as comedy, relying on Schwarzenegger's comic persona to soften its displays of sexism, homophobia, male hysteria, and fears of impotence. Gib verbalizes the conflicts that Harry—locked into conventions of action hero autonomy—tries to conceal.

True Lies makes clear the contradictions between traditional melodrama, with its emphasis on conflicts in the personal sphere, and the action film's spectacular appropriation of melodrama. Traditional melodrama brings sublimated social and personal conflicts to the surface.[36] Conventions of action film heroism, however, make no allowance for family crises. Gledhill notes that "codes of action and taciturnity" structure the rhetoric of characters in the western and gangster film.[37] Such rhetorical conventions persist in the action film and leave few options for intimate communication, a problem that informs *True Lies*'s most disturbing sequence. After removing Helen from the car salesman's clutches, Harry and Gib imprison her in a windowless room and interrogate her through a voice synthesizer that transforms their voices into a bass-heavy monotone (notably, Harry and Gib's voices become indistinguishable, blending into a singularly oppressive patriarchal timbre). Only with this chilling mediating device can Harry discern his wife's feelings. Immediately following this episode, Harry adopts the guise of a shadowy voyeur who forces Helen to perform an erotic dance. Here Harry again becomes voiceless, masking his identity with tape-recorded phrases spoken in a soft French accent. This scene, the only erotic interlude between Harry and Helen, comes across as more perverse than tender. The scene exaggerates familiar cultural conventions of gender, presenting a silent, enigmatic man and a woman who displays her body for the male onlooker and the camera. Nevertheless, the film calls attention to the incompatibility of the action hero persona with the responsibilities of domestic life. At one point, Gib temporarily dispenses with his misogynist diatribes to observe that "Helen's a flesh-and-blood woman and you're never there."

True Lies demonstrates the fallacy of omnipotent masculinity but revives it by introducing female characters into the active realm. To resolve the dilemma of males' lack of control over domesticity, *True Lies* subjects Helen to action film conventions, altering her character's relationship with the domestic realm. During the interrogation scene, Helen exhibits traditional melodramatic characteristics, displaying an intense rage about her predicament that elicits the viewer's sympathy. Here the film operates in the melodramatic mode of recasting an overarching social problem onto an individual character. Helen's desire for adventure and excitement, manifest by her susceptibility to the false secret agent's advances, mirrors the concerns of women relegated to subordinate or undervalued roles in domestic society. Notably, the film—more specifically, Helen's husband—sanctions her entry into the active realm by invoking her duty to her family, not by capitulating to her plea for a more vibrant life. When Helen witnesses her husband in action at last, she states, "I married Rambo," and decides to become a suitable action hero spouse. Since the action film structure cannot accommodate conventional marital or familial relations, *True Lies* shows Helen conceding to her husband's active role and eventually stepping into this role herself.

If the melodramatic mode relies on what Peter Brooks calls "moral polarization," a Manichaean distinction between personified good and evil, *True Lies*'s action milieu presents a slightly different moral universe.[38] Elements of the film's active sphere that do not engage the domestic space are clearly coded as either good or evil. The film identifies its villains as anti-family because of the threat they pose to the hero's wife and daughter. Most of the films' characters are removed from the domestic economy; as in most action films, *True Lies* does not represent the personal lives of minor or supporting characters. Character development functions principally to delineate characters as good or evil. While the action film strongly associates principles of good and evil with specific characters, its moral oppositions do not bear the sharp relation to real social conditions that family-centered melodramas offer. In *True Lies,* the moral frameworks of the melodrama and the action film initially compete with each other but are ultimately reconciled. The film first depicts Harry as a distant father and inattentive husband, but a good spy and a staunch defender of national security. At its conclusion, when Harry rescues his kidnapped daughter and subdues the terrorists, the film conflates protection of the family and service to the nation.

By defining the hero in relation to stereotypical foreign villains, the film denotes the righteousness of the hero's cause and neutralizes the threat of the encroaching domestic sphere. Harry's inability to communicate with his wife contrasts with the multiple languages and epigrammatic wit he brings to the active sphere. Similarly, the physical power, fluidity, and kineticism he demonstrates in combat with his Middle Eastern foes compensates for his lack of control in the domestic sphere. The terrorists, particularly their leader, Saleem Abu Aziz (Art Malik, the only male villain the film actually names), appear as brutal fanatics, more visibly misogynist than the heroes and adherent to an unintelligible political cause. The film denies the villains any substantial historical or political foundations and presents them merely as unsympathetic killers. Their largely untranslated Arabic—Harry translates part of one speech for Helen, then reduces the rest to "blah, blah, blah"—also promotes the superficial clarity of the active sphere's moral world. Viewers need not look beyond the hero for an understanding of the alien culture. The film confirms Ella Shohat and Robert Stam's observations about the colonizing impulses of Western cinema. In *Unthinking Eurocentrism,* the pair argue that "the spectator, identified with the gaze of the West . . . comes to master, in a remarkably telescoped period of time, the codes of a foreign culture shown as simple, unself-conscious, and susceptible to facile apprehension."[39] Since the film does not allow viewers to grapple with the political conditions that motivate international terrorism, the villains' malevolence never need be questioned. The decorative (and unmistakably pejorative) application of Middle Eastern politics and ethnicity clarifies the film's moral dimension but obscures the real-world significance of politics and ethnic identity.

The film's climactic focus on the utopian space of action transforms both political and domestic conflict into visual spectacle. Viewers may take pleasure in computer-enhanced images of Harry piloting an Air Force jet and machine-gunning terrorists in a downtown office build-ing without troubling over the scene's consequences. By foregrounding spectacular action, the sequence displaces concerns about the dispro-portionate use of force, property destruction, and loss of life. The scene also plays on the fantasy of demolishing the corporate infrastructure, appealing to viewers disenchanted with multinational capitalism.[40] *True Lies*'s spectacular episodes produce substantial contradictions as well. The climactic battle sequence both validates the pro-social uses of mili-tary weaponry and celebrates mass destruction. Harry's appropriation of the fighter jet reinforces the action genre's masculine fantasies (through his skillful operation of the jet in downtown Miami and his familiarity with its weapons systems) and lampoons those fantasies (through his clumsy takeoff, which damages a police car, another icon of authority). Another spectacular image, the nuclear blast, celebrates reconciliation in the domestic arena but punctuates the couple's embrace with a discon-certing symbol of male aggression.

The film's combination of the fantasy space of action with the fa-miliar sphere of domesticity makes apparent the multiple contradictions between the two realms, even within the conventional territory of the action film. The narrative demands an emphasis on the realm of action, since its scenes of domestic relations are relatively static visually and narratively, despite the novelty of seeing Schwarzenegger and Curtis masquerade as an ordinary couple. To avoid an over-representation of middle-class monotony, the film refines the spectacular and performative qualities of melodrama while limiting the reach of melodrama's domestic narrative.[41] The presentation in *True Lies* of both dimensions, the dreary and the intense, points out the difficulty of negotiating between them. While the film is deeply misogynist and clearly valorizes the active sphere over the domestic, it also recognizes the masculine sphere's inability or unwillingness to accommodate domestic rituals.

Nevertheless, the domestic sphere remains here as a cherished ideal, albeit one defined through its crises and its vilification by the film's antagonists. The terrorists' threat to Harry's wife and daughter indicates the nuclear family's fragility and importance. The strongest denunciation of domesticity comes from the greedy villainess, Juno Skinner (Tia Carrere), who dubs Helen "Suzy Homemaker." Given the action film's binary logic, villains conventionally damn the virtues that the film extols. The film's conclusion shows that women need access to the active space to achieve satisfaction and, implicitly, to prevent their husbands' flirtations with foreign women. With the heroine's accession into a space previously reserved for men, the film synthesizes the traditional melodrama's moral clarity and the action film's logic of spectacle.

CONCLUSION: PROPAGATING THE ACTION FILM SPECIES

The masculine utopia of the action film is fraught with contradictions that become more apparent as the genre seeks new territory on which to graft its structures. Within postmodernity, genre narratives offer a means of compartmentalizing and ordering cultural experiences, providing accessible maps of social conflicts and ideological tensions. Action films in the 1990s resolve problems of gender in multiple ways, each of which reveals the genre's underlying repressions. One approach is to remove women entirely from the narrative, as in *The Rock* (Michael Bay, 1996). In an all-male world, gradations of masculinity are apparent, and characters are defined through their relationships to off-screen women or to more feminized male characters, whether partners or villains. Alternately, women may retain their function, conventionalized in the gangster film and the western, as decorative objects or impediments to masculine freedom.[42] Finally, action films like *True Lies* have responded to gender issues by situating women as both heroes and villains, allowing gender conflicts to erupt into narrative. In recent films with female protagonists, including *The Long Kiss Goodnight* and *G.I. Jane* (Ridley Scott, 1997), women's assumption of conventionally masculine roles appears as the central narrative conflict, not only emphasizing gender imbalances but also limiting the narrative autonomy of women characters.

Ongoing shifts in the structure of action film narratives indicate attempts to reinforce ideology, highlight tensions produced through challenges to those ideologies, and mark changes in long-standing cultural paradigms. Such shifts may represent ideological containment strategies: While *G.I. Jane,* for example, challenges the action genre's conventions of female representation, the film requires women—both as viewers and as screen subjects—to ascribe to masculine models of behavior. Action films' increasingly unstable representations of heroic masculinity in the 1990s, though, denote a growing receptivity in cultural and textual spaces to perspectives that do not correspond to dominant ideologies. Throughout contemporary action films, the inability to contain masculine representations within the physical body results in the channeling of excess masculinity into visual spectacle. If both male and female spectators recognize combat sequences, pyrotechnics, chases, and other visual spectacles as hysterical actions of unstable masculinity, the action film genre may be reclaimed progressively as a cinematic form that reveals the transparent operations of the patriarchal system. Action film narratives' artifice and exaggeration, though, can function as a tacit promise to viewers that "real," immutable masculinity exists somewhere beneath the gunplay and pyrotechnics. This putatively authentic masculinity is made evident through a network of narrative conventions, but as action film narratives adapt to incorporate the spheres of home and family, they consequently grant less conditional access to female viewers, who have historically managed those spheres.

Even when patriarchal norms dominate the narrative, visual evidence regularly contradicts the logic of action film plots. Action films repress the challenges and contradictions of visual hysteria through displays of militaristic pageantry and weaponry and through the deployment of a nostalgic rhetoric of masculine ethics. To assert patriotic or militaristic power, though, action films produce further spectacle, further hysterical disavowal of lived reality. While the action cinema continues to traffic in overwhelmingly masculine imagery, viewers may take comfort in the knowledge that the utopian or fantasy domain of action cannot successfully conceal the contradictions of masculine identity and patriarchal order.

Notes

My thanks to Kathleen Karlyn and Elaine Roth for valuable commentary on successive drafts of this essay.

1. I use "contemporary" here to distinguish the mid- to late-1990s action film from its predecessors. For the purposes of this argument, I would cite films like *Bullitt* (Peter Yates, 1968) and *Dirty Harry* (Don Siegel, 1972) as prototypes of the action film as it appears in theaters today. These films feature solitary, durable heroes in violent, urban settings. Films from the 1980s like *Rambo: First Blood Part 2* (George Cosmatos, 1985) and *Die Hard* (John McTiernan, 1988) show further generic trends, the former emphasizing ritualized male display and the latter using its protagonist's comic persona to revive a formulaic narrative. Action films of the 1990s tend to favor rapid cutting and elaborate special effects: *Terminator 2: Judgment Day* (James Cameron, 1991), *Cliffhanger* (Renny Harlin, 1993), *Speed* (Jan De Bont, 1994), and *Broken Arrow* (John Woo, 1996) offer representative examples of the form.

2. Indeed, Susan Jeffords's central argument in *Hard Bodies: Hollywood Masculinity in the Reagan Era* (New Brunswick, N.J.: Rutgers University Press, 1994) is that 1980s action films extend into cinema the ideology of the so-called Reagan revolution, suggesting that the genre is at least as reactionary as its critics contend.

3. For example, *True Lies,* to assert male mastery of firearms, includes a comic sequence demonstrating its female protagonist's inability to fire a gun properly.

4. See John Fiske, *Understanding Popular Culture* (Boston: Unwin Hyman, 1989), 134–37.

5. Rather than presenting sexual tension or emotional conflict *as* spectacle, though, action films substitute episodes of spectacular violence at moments in which different genres (e.g., the romantic comedy or sexual suspense thriller) would present sexually or emotionally charged character interactions.

6. Developing the idea of modernist narratives as "narratives of mastery," Craig Owens inquires, "What function did these narratives play other than to legitimize Western man's self-appointed mission of transforming the entire planet in his own image?" Craig Owens, "The Discourse of Others: Feminists and Post-modernism," in *The Anti-Aesthetic: Essays on Postmodern Culture,* ed. Hal Foster (Seattle: Bay Press, 1983), 65–66. In the context of this essay, Owens's statement effectively describes the U.S. action film's domination of the global entertainment market.

7. This kind of self-reflexivity is not exclusive to postmodern texts, but it may occur in any narrative that follows a previously established formula. As Thomas Schatz observes, the significance of events in a genre film "is based on the viewer's familiarity with the 'world' of the genre itself rather than on his or her own world." Thomas Schatz, *Hollywood Genres: Formulas, Filmmaking, and the Studio System* (New York: McGraw-Hill, 1981), 10.

8. For further discussion of genre hybrids in the action film, see Yvonne Tasker, *Spectacular Bodies: Gender, Genre and the Action Cinema* (New York: Routledge, 1993), chapter 3.

9. Robin Wood, "Ideology, Genre, Auteur," in *Film Theory and Criticism, 4th Edition,* ed. Gerald Mast, Marshall Cohen, and Leo Braudy (New York: Oxford University Press, 1992), 478.

10. Thomas Elsaesser's observation that "in melodrama the *rhythm* of experience often establishes itself against its value (moral, intellectual)" applies to the

action film genre as well. Elsaesser, "Tales of Sound and Fury: Observations on the Family Melodrama," in *Home Is Where the Heart Is: Studies in Melodrama and the Woman's Film,* ed. Christine Gledhill (London: BFI, 1987), 45.

11. Susan Jeffords, "Can Masculinity Be Terminated?" in *Screening the Male: Exploring Masculinities in Hollywood Cinema,* ed. Steven Cohan and Ina Rae Hark (New York: Routledge, 1993), 245.

12. Jeffords perhaps overlooks the persistence of active, and actively displayed, male bodies for the sake of her argument.

13. Conventionally, tests of the male body regenerate masculine power. After being tortured, for example, the male hero ascends to the mythic heights of physical prowess that viewers expect and proceeds to dispatch his enemies with ease. *Rambo: First Blood Part 2,* which features a self-doubting hero who reasserts his nationalism after surviving torture by Russian adversaries, offers a suggestive and oft-cited example of this convention.

14. Jeffords, "Can Masculinity Be Terminated?" 256.

15. Even films with white antagonists frequently code these villains as fallen members of the race, inferior or corrupted versions of the white ideals the heroes represent. While the tendency to set white heroes against black villains has largely subsided, other races remain convenient scapegoats or foils against which to measure the power of white masculinity and Western individualism. The Middle Easterners in *True Lies* and *Executive Decision* (Stuart Baird, 1996), for instance, despite their lack of specific nationality or political identification, appear to represent the dangers of misguided nationalism and the denial of individual autonomy.

16. For example, *Die Hard* and its sequels combine Bruce Willis's comic timing with the genre's solemn tests of masculinity. Schwarzenegger's self-deprecating persona gives free rein to his roles as phallic superman. His character in *True Lies* conceals his identity by pretending to be a computer salesman. This conceit permits the film to contrast the character's masquerade as an ordinary husband and father with the fantasy representation of his "real," heroic identity.

17. Jim Collins, "Television and Postmodernism," in *Channels of Discourse, Reassembled,* ed. Robert C. Allen (Chapel Hill: University of North Carolina Press, 1993), 335.

18. Conventions of analytical editing call for fragmented close-ups to draw attention to significant components of a larger image. In action films, though, close-ups of male heroes' limbs and muscles often emphasize these body parts' contributions to a functional male whole rather than their relevance to a particular scene (just as fragmented shots of the female body highlight the object status of that body over its narrative relevance).

19. In John Ellis's formulation, fetishism "represents the opposite tendency to that of voyeurism. . . . Fetishistic looking implies the direct acknowledgement and participation of the object viewed. . . . The fetishistic look has much to do with display and the spectacular." Ellis, *Visible Fictions* (New York: Routledge, 1982), 47, quoted in Neale. In action films, fetishistic looking involves engaging the viewer in male rituals of camaraderie, suspicion, or antagonism.

20. Steve Neale, "Masculinity as Spectacle: Reflections on Men and Mainstream Cinema," in *Screening the Male,* 17. Neale's essay discusses at length the

ways that Hollywood films attempt to minimize the erotic connotations in displays of the male body.

21. Ironically, contemporary action films' exaggerated narratives of male activity include physical feats that can no longer be staged before the camera.

22. Works like Tasker's *Spectacular Bodies,* Tania Modleski's *Feminism without Women: Culture and Criticism in a "Postfeminist" Age* (New York: Routledge, 1991), and multiple essays in *Boys: Masculinities in Contemporary Culture,* ed. Paul Smith (Boulder: Westview Press, 1996) offer representative examples of this ongoing project.

23. Mary Ann Doane, *The Desire to Desire: The Woman's Film of the 1940s* (Bloomington: Indiana University Press, 1987), 95.

24. Sharon Willis, "Disputed Territories: Masculinity and Social Space," in *Male Trouble,* ed. Constance Penley and Sharon Willis (Minneapolis: University of Minnesota Press, 1993), 274.

25. Elsaesser, "Tales of Sound and Fury," 44.

26. See Christine Gledhill, "The Melodramatic Field: An Investigation," in *Home Is Where the Heart Is,* 6.

27. Geoffrey Nowell-Smith, "Minnelli and Melodrama," in ibid., 74.

28. For an exhaustive analysis of the gendering of popular culture, see Andreas Huyssen, "Mass Culture as Woman: Modernism's Other," in *After the Great Divide: Modernism, Mass Culture, Postmodernism* (Bloomington: Indiana University Press, 1986).

29. Gledhill notes that because of the "re-masculinisation of cultural value" occurring at the end of the nineteenth century, "Realism came to be associated with (masculine) restraint and underplaying. . . . In Hollywood, realism came to be associated with the masculine sphere of action and violence" ("The Melodramatic Field," 34–35).

30. Nowell-Smith, "Minnelli and Melodrama," 74.

31. Chris Holmlund, "Masculinity as Multiple Masquerade: The 'Mature' Stallone and the Stallone Clone," in *Screening the Male,* 224.

32. Tania Modleski, "Time and Desire in the Woman's Film," in *Film Theory and Criticism, 4th Edition,* 542.

33. Of course, not all viewers regard action film conventions as ironic or artificial representations of masculinity. As Holmlund cautions, "it would be a mistake to underestimate how much and how often spectators, and performers too, see masquerade as reinforcing hegemonic power relations" (224).

34. Jeffords, "Can Masculinity Be Terminated?" 258.

35. Ibid., 258.

36. See Peter Brooks, "The Melodramatic Imagination," in *Imitations of Life: A Reader on Film and Television Melodrama,* ed. Marcia Landy (Detroit: Wayne State University Press, 1991), 52–53.

37. Gledhill, "The Melodramatic Field," 35.

38. Brooks, "The Melodramatic Imagination," 61.

39. Ella Shohat and Robert Stam, *Unthinking Eurocentrism: Multiculturalism and the Media* (New York: Routledge, 1994), 148.

40. The emphasis on the sensibility of action rather than its real significance corresponds to the principles Richard Dyer lays out in his analysis of the Hollywood musical. Dyer notes the musical's ability to offer simple solutions to the real problems of capitalist society. According to Dyer, musicals resolve the social and political crises that appear in their narratives through the lyrical, performative elements of intermittent musical numbers. The juxtaposition of narrative and non-narrative elements, and the conflict between representational and non-representational signs—among the latter Dyer includes "colour, texture, movement, rhythm, melody, camerawork"— opens up a space to explore the contradictions of these various components, both as they relate to each other and within their discrete categories. Richard Dyer, "Entertainment and Utopia," in *The Cultural Studies Reader,* ed. Simon During (New York: Routledge, 1993), 273.

41. In Dyer's schema, the utopian promise of intensity—which he defines as "excitement, drama, affectivity of living"—overcomes the real social experience of dreariness or monotony (278).

42. Refinement of genre conventions and the legacy of feminism have limited this formula, although period films like *Mulholland Falls* (Lee Tamahori, 1996) and *L.A. Confidential* (Curtis Hansen, 1997) and historical epics like *Braveheart* (Mel Gibson, 1995) use their settings to recuperate tired gender paradigms of male activity and female helplessness.

9

Mutilating Mel:
Martyrdom and Masculinity
in *Braveheart*

William Luhr

Curiously, *Braveheart* (1995) climaxes not with its hero's conquest of his enemies but with his torture, mutilation, castration, decapitation, and dismemberment. While it is not unusual for Hollywood historical epics to end with the deaths of their central characters—witness *Spartacus* (1960), *El Cid* (1961), *The Alamo* (1960), *The Robe* (1953), *Samson and Delilah* (1949), and *A Tale of Two Cities* (1935)—it is unusual for such a film to make its culminating spectacle the doomed hero's death agonies.

In *Braveheart,* which deals with the thirteenth-century Scottish revolutionary William Wallace, the scene of agony lasts eleven minutes. Condemned to death for his rebellion against British rule, Wallace (Mel Gibson) is brought on a wagon into a crowded public square with his arms lashed to a crossbar in the manner of a crucifixion. When placed on the execution platform, he repeatedly refuses to swear allegiance to Edward I, an act for which he would have been rewarded with a quick and painless death. As a result, he is hoisted into the air by his neck and painfully dangled. Then he is dropped and placed upon the rack where his limbs are pulled by ropes attached to horses. Although by this time his body seems to have been rendered functionally useless, he is tied to a cross-shaped table, eviscerated, and castrated. Still defiant, he is beheaded. But the assault on his body does not end there. A narrator tells us that it was quartered and the pieces scattered at the corners of the kingdom while his head was placed on London Bridge.

We will return to the odd way in which these scenes were shot and edited—what is shown and what is elided—but the basic question is, what is going on here? What other male action hero besides Gibson would devote so much screen time to the mutilation of his helpless body, particularly when it is not followed by his retaliatory physical triumph (as in *One-Eyed Jacks* [1961], *Yojimbo* [1961], *A Fistful of Dollars* [1964], or *Rambo, First Blood Part 2* [1985])?

Braveheart is the second film Gibson directed, and directed at considerable risk. When it more than doubled its original $30 million budget, he not only deferred his salary but invested $15 million of his own money in it. The film has a number of factors in common with the first film he directed, *The Man without a Face* (1993), in which Gibson plays an individual whose face and body are horribly disfigured. Both films not only star Gibson but also center on the graphic mutilation of his body, an intriguing fact considering his image as one of the most handsome Hollywood actors. Both films champion a conservative if not reactionary masculinity that their heroes maintain in direct opposition to the norms of the dominant culture. Their mutilations assume symbolic significance, representing the weight of social antagonism the heroes suffer as a result of their commitment. Indeed, much of Gibson's career involves an attempt at reclaiming a marginalized masculinity—highly successful in *Braveheart* considering its three profitable theatrical releases grossing over $180 million worldwide and five Academy awards, including Best Picture and Best Director for Gibson. But what kind of masculinity does Gibson want to reclaim, and how does it relate to his interest in having his heroes not only physically mutilated but also punished by society? Why does the spectacle of violence to the self figure so centrally in the film's social agenda?

RECENT SHIFTS IN REPRESENTATIONS OF MASCULINITY

These questions are significant not only within the context of Gibson's films but also in connection to what has widely been perceived as a crisis, or at the very least a shift, in media representations of masculinity. Gibson's is only one of many responses to this phenomenon. This essay will first discuss these shifting patterns of masculine representation and then return to the particulars of Gibson's response, which includes a beleaguered and sacrificial masculinity, a concern with father figures as a way of maintaining traditions of masculinity as well as a conservative social order, and a Christian perspective involving martyrdom. Such martyrdom represents violence to the body as having the potential for sanctification, allowing Gibson's heroes to be mutilated and even killed while becoming glorified at the same time.

Both of the films Gibson directed employ the sufferings of his title characters to critique the social structures that are imposed on them. The films present decadent societies that have lost contact with traditional patriarchal values. Gibson's characters sacrifice themselves in an attempt to champion a return to an older, more conservative social system. Both films intend to translate spectator horror at the violence enacted upon Gibson's characters into spectator revulsion at the social order perpetrating that violence; they also wish to provoke sympathy for a return to the conservative values Gibson's characters embody. Although in both cases Gibson's character is erased from the narrative, others successfully carry on his cause—an implicit invocation to spectators to do the same. This strategy resembles that of Eisenstein's *Battleship Potemkin* (1925), with the obvious difference being that Eisenstein employs the sufferings of the sailors and Odessa's citizens to champion a revolutionary social order to come, while Gibson champions conservative and vanishing social orders (pre-1960s patriarchal culture in *The Man without a Face* and the tribal life of Scottish clans threatened by English feudal rule in *Braveheart*).

One major difference between other contemporary representations of violence and Gibson's lies in his focus on violence directed at the self rather than at various "others." In *Braveheart,* Gibson's character does not get to mutilate and kill the leaders of his enemies as he, his wife, his father, and his grandfather before him are mutilated and killed, because the enemy leaders die of disease, implicitly punished by a higher power. This is a very different strategy from that evident in the decision leading to the alternate ending of *Fatal Attraction* (1987). The film's original ending showed Glenn Close's villain quietly committing suicide. When that version was shown to test audiences, however, they complained that she did not suffer enough. Consequently, a new ending was devised that made her a monstrous, knife-wielding threat to her married ex-lover's family, and she is, apparently, killed not once but twice. The strategy behind this ending was not only to increase spectator revulsion at the character by making her more violent, but also to increase spectator enjoyment at violence inflicted upon her by first showing her drowned and then, when she unexpectedly and menacingly rises from the water, showing her shot through the heart.[1] In fact, perhaps beginning with horror films such as *A Nightmare on Elm Street* (1984), it has become standard practice in action films today to kill the villain twice, giving the audience the pleasure of seeing the villain apparently killed only to have the wounded villain rise and be killed a second time. In *Jackal* (1997), for example, Bruce Willis's villain is apparently shot dead, and only moments later he rises as a grotesque, bloody menace and is shot dead again. At the end of *Goldeneye* (1995) Sean Bean's villain apparently falls to his death from a great height into a gigantic satellite dish. Surprisingly, the camera shows him alive at the bottom, but only long enough to have part of the dish's structure fall onto and impale him. Then it blows up, effectively allowing the audience to see him killed a third time.

These three films are among many that culminate with the spectacle of the villain's graphic obliteration. But in reversing the process—in making himself the spectacle of violent obliteration at the end of *Braveheart*—Gibson is not necessarily reversing the ideology. His social agenda is arguably as conservative as those of all three of these films, but his use of physical violence enters different spheres, spheres that can be contextualized by looking at recent patterns of masculine representation.

Two recent films, *Independence Day* (1995) and *Air Force One* (1997), contain similar premises that have previously been virtually unprecedented in American film. In each film, a contemporary although fictional U.S. president proves his merit by becoming a warrior. While it is common for films to represent sitting presidents as courageous commanders-in-chief who are resolute in the face of national or even personal danger, those presidents are seldom depicted as actually shouldering weapons and triumphantly entering into battle. In *Independence Day,* however, the president climbs into a jet fighter and battles aliens; in *Air Force One,* the president slays a brutal gang of skyjacking terrorists in hand-to-hand combat. Both films collapse traditional distinctions between the executive branch and the military and present personal skills in violence as evidence of the president's potency. Not since the era of Theodore Roosevelt has the notion of a warrior president, as opposed to commander-in-chief, been viable in popular narratives. Why, within two years and contemporaneous with *Braveheart,* has the theme of the warrior president suddenly appeared in highly visible, enormously successful films?

A glib response might cite the films as critiques of the Clinton administration, since Clinton is the first president widely known for his refusal to support the war of his generation. But the answer goes much deeper and covers a wide range of images and concerns. Part of the answer involves the representation of the president's body—the notion that it may no longer be enough to show him as a leader; audiences may

230

now want to see him in action, and action requires his potency to be manifested in his physical body.

Male bodily representation has changed in significant ways in the past two decades. It is only since the late 1970s and early 1980s that major male action stars have been known for the theatrical display of their bodies. Action stars of earlier generations, such as John Wayne, Robert Mitchum, James Cagney, Clark Gable, Clint Eastwood, and Gary Cooper, infrequently displayed their torsos in films, and they did not have or need the kind of pumped-up, body-builder look common in contemporary action films. It was not central to their images. For recent action stars, like Arnold Schwarzenegger, Willis, and Sylvester Stallone, however, such a look is central to their image. Some stars, like Harrison Ford and Keanu Reeves, have conspicuously pumped themselves up for certain roles. Furthermore, this body beautification is also often accompanied by extreme bodily punishment and even graphic mutilation, as with Stallone in virtually all the *Rocky* and *Rambo* films, or Arnold Schwarzenegger in *Terminator* (1984) or *Terminator 2: Judgment Day* (1991). Why all this focus on the physicality of male bodies, and why now?

The representation of masculinity has always been inextricably tied up with issues of power, but that power has not always been represented in bodily terms. There has long been a multitude of discourses of masculine power, involving physical strength, financial worth, social or political power, sexual potency, certain skills such as gunfighting or expertise with technology, and often these elements come into conflict with each other, indicating that masculine power is not a unified concept. Frequently, narratives are built upon conflicts between different modes of masculine power. One example would be the opposition between a rich and powerful older man and a physically stronger and more sexually potent younger one, as in Orson Welles's *The Lady from Shanghai* (1948). In *Bad Day at Black Rock* (1954), a heavy-set, middle-aged Spencer Tracy plays a one-armed character who triumphs over younger and more physically fit men through cleverness and martial arts skills. *Independence Day* and *Air Force One* are intriguing in that they collapse two traditionally separate discourses, those of political and physical power; in these films, the discourse of political power is manifest in the physical potency of the leader of the state. Such a pattern exists in many pre-twentieth-century narratives, going back at least to *The Iliad* and *The Odyssey,* in which a powerful ruler (Achilles, Agamemnon, Hector, Odysseus) is also a great warrior, but the conflation of the two has largely disappeared in modern discourse, until recently.

The increased focus on the powerful male body has appeared simultaneously with, and perhaps in compensation for, a growing cultural terror of diminishing masculine power of a specific type, a terror of a shifting social paradigm in which white male power is lost. Recent years have seen a number of "angry white male" films, such as *Falling Down* (1993), in which white males become hysterically violent and/or self-destructive due to their perceived loss of social privilege. These men are unable or unwilling to cope with social change and often take their resentments out against newly empowered groups they feel should be subservient, such as women, various racial and ethnic groups, and gays and lesbians. It is interesting that the director of *Falling Down,* Joel Schumacher, also directed two of the recent Batman movies. One widely noted aspect of these films is that Batman's outfits have changed from the pliable, body-fitting fabric used in earlier portrayals in the role into hardened, armor-like body-shaping material. One might say that it makes Batman less vulnerable to his enemies, but it could also be said that the armor indicates an anxiety about vulnerability, the very vulnerability that threatens the angry white male. Today's Batman needs a mode of protection that earlier counterparts did not require. While he still triumphs, Batman's armor and the angry white male's desperation may spring from the same cultural anxiety.

A common nexus for this shift in masculine power is the 1960s and 1970s. Various political and social events, such as the withdrawal of U.S. troops from Vietnam, the widespread resistance to that war, Watergate and Nixon's resignation, and the rise of entitlements for women, racial and ethnic groups, and gays and lesbians, were perceived by some as a multi-front assault threatening the previously dominant cultural position of white males. It was an era in which John Wayne, the preeminent American film hero of the 1940s and 1950s, became marginalized as ossified and out of date. Some considered the widespread crisis of confidence in government as a crisis in patriarchy. They felt that the government that had triumphed on two continents in World War II now lacked the manly resolve to triumph in war over a small foreign power; in addition, they felt that the men of America could no longer restrain their women and children from public protest and could not keep their own houses in order. Some, notably Robert Bly, considered it a crisis of masculinity itself. Bly's concern with initiation myths, particularly those focusing upon father/son relationships, is significant here. He feels that the United States has been in decline since the 1950s and that the reason for the decline is the growing power of women and the diminishing power of men, particularly as fathers and father figures. Boys do not get the guidance they require when they turn to mothers and sisters as role models, and they consequently enter manhood with a lack of resolve and focus. Bly considers even biological fathers less important than patriarchal male mentors in the tradition of Arthurian legends: "[F]rom all initiation stories we learn how essential it is to leave our parental expectations entirely and find a second father or 'second King.' "[2] In a chapter from *Iron John* aptly titled "The Hunger for the King in a Time with No Father," Bly focuses upon the decline of kingship and the role of the ultimate patriarch, "The Sacred King," a personage that historically provides a visible and charismatic model for all of society.

Susan Jeffords has argued that such major and successful film series of the 1970s and 1980s as the *Star Wars* trilogy, the Indiana Jones trilogy, the *Back to the Future* trilogy, and the Rambo trilogy can all be seen as reflecting this anxiety about a decline in patriarchal traditions. They are all centrally concerned with troubled father/son relationships and with the need to come to terms with a father or father figure as a way of setting history in order. Jeffords sees this focus as exhibiting a profound concern for a cultural continuity that some consider threatened by a decline in culture-sustaining masculine potency.[3] These issues are also central to both *The Man without a Face* and *Braveheart*.

Anxiety about such a decline in masculinity may have influenced the infusion of armature into popular male images during this period, as with the Batman costumes discussed above, or in the cyborg figures of recent films in which ravaged male bodies are reempowered with armor and cybernetic devices. Examples include RoboCop, Spawn, and the Six-Million Dollar Man, as well as characters that are not human at all but entirely robotic, like the Terminator. The masculinity under siege needs protection and needs to compensate for profound anxiety about its potency—about its very survival—with excessively displayed musculature or even armor itself, producing new images of hyperviolent and armored figures in popular narratives.

There has been a wide range of responses to the rethinking of masculine roles in society and culture as well as in the mass media. Some, as in *Air Force One* or the James Bond films, assert a heroic, dominant white male. Some, as in *Falling Down,* present a hysterical and desperately defeated one. Some, like *Spawn* (1997), critique white male power as evil and show a black male destroyed by evil whites but returning to life as a ravaged and armored superhero; however, the film still focuses on compensatory male power. Some, like the recent Batman films, present a deeply troubled—yet triumphant—white male. And then there is *Braveheart.*

233

A psychoanalytic approach might categorize the images of ravaged male bodies covered with protective, or even resurrecting, armature as suggesting a cultural castration anxiety. This armature, as well as the stepped-up graphic violence of recent action films, could be seen as compensating in excess for such an anxiety. Most action heroes (excepting the interesting examples of *Terminator 2: Judgment Day* and *Alien 3* [1993]) triumph by the film's end, thus reaffirming their potency. How, then, does one deal with *Braveheart,* in which the hero (along with the film's narrative) embraces and glorifies his castration and obliteration? Is there such a term as "castration desire"?

Gibson's films exhibit great concern over lost masculinities, over traditions of masculinity that he values, but sees as having been passed over by a debased culture. Perhaps the most emblematic of the films in which he has appeared as an actor is *Forever Young* (1992), in which he plays a man who is literally frozen in 1939 and thawed out in the early 1990s. His character's "old-fashioned" integrity, self-reliance, patriotism, fidelity in love, willingness to be a paternal mentor, and resourcefulness contrast directly with those qualities in contemporary men and appear infinitely more substantial. But the two films Gibson has directed are more complex in their critique of contemporary masculinity. Both deal with embattled models of masculinity undervalued by their dominant culture; both are centrally concerned not only with issues of fatherhood but also with cultural traditions that sustain their valued models of masculinity—*The Man without a Face* through education, and *Braveheart* through revolution. *The Man without a Face* explicitly situates these issues within contemporary culture.

SHIFTING PARADIGMS

In 1992, *The Advocate* announced that Gibson headed the list of that year's "Sissy" awards because he was afraid to be considered gay.[4] One might categorize *The Man without a Face,* which appeared a year later, as his response. In this film, the first he directed, he plays a man scorned by society as a pederast. Clearly, pederasty is a fundamental violation of the masculine traditions Gibson champions, and its wrongful accusation is used here to indict a debased society's attempt to marginalize traditional patterns of male bonding. Gibson's film attacks the cultural climate that would dare produce such an accusation, building much of its critique upon changing notions of masculinity.

The film's story begins on the first day of summer in 1968. A radio disc jockey segues into a song and calls it a good day to be

234

"Born a Woman," implying that it is a bad time to be a man. The film presents late 1960s culture, or counterculture, as profoundly feminized and misguided, resulting in the marginalized, and even stigmatized, masculinity represented by Gibson's character.

This masculinity values an all-male military academy as a bastion of intense but asexual male bonding and cultural continuity. The film tries to redeem that tradition, while acknowledging how unfashionable it had become and critiquing the cultural change that led to the situation. To do this, it invokes the notion of social paradigm shifts, the notion that, under certain conditions, some character types are valued unquestionably for what they present themselves to be. Later generations, however, operating within evolving social conditions, may view the same characters in an entirely different light. In Victorian England, for example, Prime Minister William Gladstone at times brought prostitutes home to his wife and they would spend the evening piously trying to talk the women out of their lives of sin. Such activity, considered admirable at the time,

The wounded hero fighting liberalism: *The Man without a Face* (Warner Bros., 1993).

235

might today be questioned as revealing perverse motives. Comparably, the sanctified behavior of some Christian saints and martyrs is, outside of certain Christian contexts, sometimes considered not admirable but pathological.

Howard Hawks called many of his films love stories between men, but he would roll his eyes in comic dismissiveness at critics who found a homosexual subtext in his films. The cultural position from which he spoke valorized close male bonding but, at the same time, held homosexual activity in contempt and saw no contradiction in doing so. But the cultural climate from his generation to the present has changed, making such a position difficult to naively maintain.

Comparably, Vito Russo in *The Celluloid Closet* characterizes the once popular character of the "sissy" as one no longer tenable in films. In the 1930s and 1940s, actors like Edward Everett Horton, Franklin Pangborn, and Eric Blore played a fussy, sissy type of male that was widely perceived as feminized but not homosexual.[5] At that time, a cultural space existed *not* to perceive such characters as gay, although today it would be difficult to present such character types as anything but gay. The earlier cultural space, the one that presumed both Hawks's "love stories between men" and the character of the "sissy" to be without homosexual implications, is the cultural environment Robert Bly sees as preceding the decline of U.S. culture. It is also the one that *The Man without a Face* champions.

The film's central issue is the construction of masculinity. It presents Gibson's character largely through the eyes of a troubled boy, Charles Norstadt, who desperately yearns for a certain type of father. Charles lives with his mother, two half-sisters, and a succession of stepfathers, and is deeply unhappy. The film opens with a dream showing him graduating from military school and triumphantly being carried on the shoulders of his classmates. In the crowd we see his mother and half-sister Megan cheering him on, but his older half-sister Gloria has her mouth taped shut. His three stepfathers are chained like enslaved prisoners of war. His voice-over tells us that it was a perfect dream except for the absence of one face in the crowd, the face of his father.

Charles does not know what happened to his father, so he has concocted a fantasy of him as a war hero who died in a test pilot accident. His goal, embodied in the dream, is to graduate from Holyfield, the military academy his father attended. At the end of the film the dream comes true. As an older Charles graduates from Holyfield, he catches a brief glimpse of the character played by Gibson, Justin McLeod, who secretly served as Charles's surrogate father and enabled him to enter the academy.

The film also contains a second dream that becomes a reality, only this one is a nightmare. In it, Charles is awakened at 3:00 A.M. by the voice of an angry and drunken McLeod who calls him a "little bastard" for revealing to friends a secret McLeod had shared with him, and asking if Charles knows the harm he has caused. This breach of confidence involves the fact that McLeod has received his disfiguring scars in an automobile accident in which a boy was killed. But when Charles goes to the window, the figure he sees is that of his natural father, not McLeod. He awakens in terror.

Although later in the film Charles confesses that he has betrayed this confidence and McLeod relieves him of his guilt by saying he is not upset, the nightmare reveals terrors that do indeed come to pass. On the night that Charles discovers his father's fate, McLeod's life is ruined, and ruined because of his relationship with Charles.

On that night Charles gleefully surprises his nasty older sister while she is having sex with her boyfriend. Hoping to hurt him, she retaliates by telling him that his father was an alcoholic who abandoned him and died by suicide in a mental asylum. Shattered, Charles runs to McLeod's house, where he spends the night. In the morning the chief of police comes looking for Charles and finds him in his underwear. This situation, combined with the facts that McLeod had been secretly tutoring him all summer, and that ten years earlier McLeod had received his scars in an automobile crash in which a male student with whom he had been accused of having an affair was killed, leads to the further stigmatization of McLeod as a pederast. Eventually, McLeod leaves the town in disgrace, legally enjoined never to communicate with Charles again.

The fulfillment of the first dream, then, comes at the cost of the fulfillment of the nightmare, and both indicate Charles's need to come to terms with his lost father. That initial dream incorporated Charles's most cherished sense of his father's heritage—graduation from Holyfield and incorporation into an honorable military tradition. The nightmare, however, involved another, darker element of his father's heritage, Charles's anxieties about and perhaps repressed memories of his father, involving drunken vindictiveness and social disgrace. These are partly displaced upon and conflated with McLeod, for whom such drunken and uncontrolled behavior is entirely out of character.

All of this reflects a social context. Even though McLeod later describes him as a star student, Charles's goals are so out of kilter with prevailing cultural norms that his mother considers him dim-witted and his half-sister cruelly calls him "Gomer Pyle." When the film begins, he fears it may be true. He has virtually no one to support him in his desire to go to a military academy until he meets McLeod. His friends tell him he will not like it, and his mother ridicules the school as "fascist and unnatural." The military academy bespeaks a masculine and pedagogical tradition woefully out of fashion in the late 1960s and yet one embodied in McLeod.

McLeod is a figure of mystery and ridicule in the town. He lives in isolation, even doing his grocery shopping after the store has closed. At first it seems as if this stems from his disfigurement; only later do we learn of the sexual scandal.

After learning that McLeod had been an instructor in a military academy, Charles begs him to tutor him for the entrance exam to Holy-field. McLeod is distant and harsh, starting the relationship with a demand for unquestioning obedience, asking Charles to dig holes on his property and then to fill them in.

McLeod's behavior contrasts with that of Charles's mother's current boyfriend, Carl, a Yale professor. Charles contemptuously calls Carl "the hairball," and Carl embodies the film's view of late 1960s counterculture: he has long hair, wears love beads, and mouths anti-establishment and anti-military discourse. He calls Charles "Chuck," and uses familiar terms of address with him like "Hey, man," pretending to erase age and class distinctions between them. McLeod, to the contrary, wears his hair cut short and is formal and authoritative in his manner, always calling Charles "Charles" or "Norstadt."

McLeod's tutoring is resolutely traditional and eschews topics of contemporary "relevance." He teaches Charles Latin, Roman history, Euclid, and Shakespeare. And he teaches it in an authoritative way, thereby embodying a pedagogical model widely attacked in the 1960s—the teacher as Law, not as friend.

McLeod's lifestyle also hearkens back to a pre-1960s mode. He is ruggedly self-sufficient and traditionally masculine. He sleeps in a single bed with a crucifix over it and surrounds himself with high culture—well-bound books, classical music, serious art. He is accompanied by a large dog, keeps and rides horses, has a boat, and drives an all-terrain vehicle. His rooms are spacious, wood-paneled, and recall a men's club or hunting lodge.

The film presents his masculinity as valuable not only by contrast with that of Carl, "the hairball," but also with that of Charles's fa-ther. Where Carl represents the trendy and feminized counterculture, Charles's father is presumably someone from McLeod's generation, but

238

who abdicated his responsibility for nurturing his son that, implicitly, a "real man" must assume. Charles's dream image of his three stepfathers in chains indicates that they, also, failed to nurture him. Such an abdication of traditional paternal roles created a cultural vacuum soon filled by the feminized counterculture.

McLeod assumes that paternal responsibility, but at great personal cost. Misunderstood by a society that has lost its direction, he is stigmatized and ostracized as a pederast. McLeod's sacrifice, however, enables Charles to succeed in military school, and at the end of the film, we see McLeod in the distance at Charles's graduation (it may be Charles's dream vision of him, but even if so, it holds the same significance). McLeod has sacrificed himself for a noble cause, and Charles's jubilant graduation testifies to the continuity of that cause in the face of daunting social antagonism. Charles has become McLeod's surrogate son and, like children in the natural order of events, carries on after the father has gone. McLeod is a man without a face due not only to his scars but also, more importantly, to his social erasure. However, the film asserts, his sacrifice enables his tradition to live on.

Braveheart ends in virtually the same way. Gibson's character sacrifices himself but his cause lives on. We learn that, years after his character's death, his revolution was successful in his name. But none of this explains why the film climaxes with such a graphic and extended dwelling upon his physical agonies.

MALE MASOCHISM AND CHRISTIAN REPRESENTATION

Braveheart and *The Man without a Face* champion a currently unfashionable, long-suffering mode of militaristic masculinity constructed upon certain Christian traditions, particularly those that valorize martyrdom and marginalize women. Two related contexts are useful. The first is masochism; the second is Christian representation, particularly in Renaissance art. These help illuminate not only the *Braveheart* scene under discussion but also the film's consideration of gender—why, for example, it deals extensively with the mutilation and display of destroyed male bodies but not female bodies, and why killings are photographed and edited in entirely different ways due to gender. An instance of this occurs with the murder of Wallace's new bride. When she is tied to a post and a British official slits her throat, the camera shows only her face; we see no disfigurement and no blood. However, soon after, Wallace has her killer held against the same post and he slits his throat in the same way, only now the camera graphically shows the slashing and the man's blood as he dies. Why the difference?

Wallace's masculinity has strong Christian associations, and his execution scene shows him twice in crucifixion poses. Speaking of the legendary status Wallace holds in Scotland, Gibson said, "People just kneel and pray when Wallace's name is mentioned. The guy was the Second Coming of Christ."[6] His reference to Christ is revealing. Although, as stated above, this film is extremely unusual among historical epics in its obsessive focus on the agonies and death of its hero, a major exception lies in the tradition of movies about the life of Christ, such as *King of Kings* (1927 and 1961) or *The Greatest Story Ever Told* (1965). (This can be extended to some films about lives of saints, like Carl Dreyer's *The Passion of Joan of Arc* [1928], although that film exists outside the Hollywood tradition.) Christianity itself exhibits a remarkable obsession with Christ's agonies and death. Unlike many of the world's major religions, Christianity focuses in extraordinary ways upon the sacrificial death of its god. This is perhaps rooted in the implications of the doctrine of the Incarnation. Christianity's most resonant symbol is the crucifix—the image of Christ enduring a torturous death.

Wallace's death scene in *Braveheart* focuses with masochistic intensity upon its hero's dying agonies. Wallace has no hope of survival; the scene is about his pain, rather than one that uses his pain as a prefatory low to be followed by a triumphant high. To amplify his suffering, Wallace earlier discards a potion secretly given him to dull pain, because he wants to keep his senses sharp. He says that if he does not experience the pain to its fullest, he will feel that King Edward I has beaten him. He prays for the strength to die well, and dying well means experiencing an orgy of pain. In effect, he wants to be a martyr.

This is not to discount the film's efforts to glorify him as triumphant in defeat, such as his refusal to pay homage to Edward I; his rejection of the pain-dulling potion; the iconic Christ associations; a coda in his disembodied voice telling us that a decade later his revolt was successful; the visible decay, death, or moral turbulence of his oppressors; the implications that he has fathered the future royal line of England; and his status as a martyr. While all of these narrativize his agonies as evidence of his moral triumph, they do so in a way that still revels in the public display of his pain. Implicitly, the worse it gets, the better it gets, and this context is profoundly Christian.

In *Male Subjectivity at the Margins,* Kaja Silverman inquires:

> What is it precisely that the male masochist displays, and what are the consequences of this self-exposure? To begin with, he acts out in an insistent

and exaggerated way the basic conditions of cultural subjectivity, conditions that are normally disavowed; he loudly proclaims that his meaning comes to him from the Other, prostrates himself before the gaze even as he solicits it, exhibits his castration for all to see, and revels in the sacrificial basis of the social contract. The male masochist magnifies the losses and divisions upon which cultural identity is based, refusing to be sutured or recompensed. In short, he radiates a negativity inimical to the social order.[7]

Wallace's castration is clearly exhibited for all to see and the scene revels in the sacrificial basis of its social contract. Silverman refers extensively to Theodor Reik's exhaustive study of masochism, *Masochism in Sex and Society,* and categorizes Reik's work as focusing mainly on what Freud called "moral" and Reik called "social" masochism,[8] associating it with exhibitionism, revolutionary fervor, and suspense.

Silverman sees Reik's concern as ultimately with what she terms Christian masochism, for which an external audience is a structural necessity, and in which the body is placed centrally on display. This form of masochism pits the figure against the society in which he or she lives, making him or her a rebel, even a revolutionary, and desires to remake the world in a new image, or a new cultural order.[9] The exemplary Christian masochist seeks to remake him or herself according to the model of the suffering Christ, the very picture of earthly devastation and loss. Insofar as such an identification implies the complete and utter negation of all phallic values, Christian masochism has radically emasculating implications.

Reik associates all masochism with exhibitionism or self-display, but acknowledges that what is rendered visible is the subject's suffering, discomfort, humiliation, and disgrace rather than its grandeur or triumph.[10]

Clearly these imperatives apply to the scene described in *Braveheart* with its intense focus on the agony, mutilation, and obliteration of the body as well as its exhibition, not only for the film's audience but also for the audience within the film. All narrative and specular structures keep Wallace at the center of attention, even for those not physically present, like Edward I or the Princess of Wales. Furthermore, he is a revolutionary, literally seeking to overthrow the established order. And throughout, his body is entirely passive, even during castration. From a masochist's perspective, Wallace achieves his greatest triumph and power through the extremity of his obliteration.

Gibson photographs the castration in a curious way. Although he has explicitly shown the previous tortures of Wallace (the dangling by the neck, the rack), Gibson radically changes the camera work when the

Martyrdom and male masochism: restoring male culture in *Braveheart* (Warner Bros., 1995).

Inquisitor moves an ugly hook downward along Wallace's chest, ripping his shirt and moving toward his groin. Where earlier Gibson had shown everything, now he shows nothing and we must infer what is happening. We see the Inquisitor doing something horrid to the body below the waist with the hook, and infer castration because the positioning is right and because earlier a dwarf in the crowd mimed hacking gestures at his groin, signaling what was to come. Then, when Wallace is decapitated, we see the axe fall below the frame; as with the slashing of Wallace's bride's throat, we do not see the bloody act. Why the sudden graphic reticence?

Traditional codes of decorum hardly apply here since the film is extraordinarily gory. Its battle scenes show all sorts of gruesome mutilations and killing, over and over again. Nor can decorous reticence about displaying the genitals apply since, prior to the Battle of Stirling, a number of Wallace's warriors stood before the British and lifted their kilts, defiantly displaying their genitals (although in extreme long shot). Then they turned around and "mooned" the enemy. So why stop short and mask such a display at Wallace's death? Would it not enhance the masochistic spectacle of his death? The answer is related to the film's refusal to display the mutilations of women, particularly the death of Wallace's bride. One might argue that at the moment of his castration, Wallace pays the ultimate price and enters the realm of the sacred. He says one more word, a defiant shout of "Freedom" to the crowd, and then we see his long-dead bride, now apparently alive and watching, in the crowd. (This parallels the sudden appearance of McLeod at the end of *The Man without a Face*.) Implicitly, moments before his decapitation Wallace has already become transfigured. His body is now irrelevant. For this same reason, we are only told about and not shown its postmortem quartering and scattering and the public display of his head.

Some Christian traditions provide help in understanding this representation. Leo Steinberg has written about the representation of Christ's genitals in Renaissance art, documenting it as a major tradition and yet one entirely ignored by four centuries of art history. Genital representation became an issue when new codes of realistic representation were embraced during the Renaissance, when artists for the first time felt challenged to depict the entire body of Christ according to realist codes. Steinberg feels that while subsequent generations felt impelled to cover or ignore the genitals in these representations, Renaissance artists, particularly influenced by the doctrine of the Incarnation, considered them entirely decorous and, in fact, important.[11]

The doctrine of the Incarnation asserts that Christ was both truly God and truly man—not a God masquerading as a man, but a man literally subject to mortality and the pressures of the flesh. Two of these pressures were pain and sexuality. Christ's sexuality was important because his purity would have little value if he were simply a castrati and not subject to sexual desire. His resistance to temptation would have exemplary value only if his temptations were real. Comparably, his agony would have little meaning if it were merely a masquerade. Furthermore, the Renaissance saw sinful sexuality, and the concomitant need for genital modesty, as the result of the fall in Eden, after which Adam and Eve covered their genitals and felt shame. But since Christ had not fallen, his genitals were not sinful, and their display as a sign of his mortality was not shameful.

At the same time, however, Christ's virginity was also important, and so most representations of his genitals tended to be in scenes of his childhood or his death—in other words, outside the realm of sexual

243

tension. One reason for this is the lack of a cult of phallic worship in Christianity; in fact, Christianity tends to consider representations of the phallus indecorous, which led to the post-Renaissance painting of loincloths on many Renaissance works. The representation of the Incarnation, then, produces contradictory tensions. When considered in relation to *Braveheart,* one might say that for Christ to become man, he had to acquire genitals, and for Wallace to become sacred, he had to lose his.

Within the post-Renaissance tradition, which avoids any representation of Christ's sexuality as proof of his mortality, there is an almost compensatory and obsessive focus on his agonies and his pain, which are also proof of his mortality. His passion, torture, and death are endlessly represented in agonizing detail.

This observation has parallels with *Braveheart,* which dwells on male pain and mutilation. While Wallace is briefly established as a heterosexual being, his sexuality is profoundly contained, and women are virtually irrelevant except as icons of male power. This is explicit even at the very beginning with the decree of Edward I that initiates the revolt that Wallace leads. The decree, called *prima nocti,* reinstates the right of nobles to sleep with brides in their domain on their wedding nights. Here, the rights of the women matter less than the issue of which man— ruling noble or husband—holds power over them. The two women with whom Wallace sleeps are models of both purity and absence. His bride is no sooner wed than killed, making her the motivation for his rage at British injustice, but also putting her conveniently out of the way as a real person. He later sleeps with and possibly impregnates the Princess of Wales, a woman whose purity is implied by the fact that her husband is gay. She thereby becomes Wallace's "woman," in exchange for his bride who was killed by the king's men. Furthermore, she is the means by which Wallace transcends his own death, since she becomes pregnant and Wallace's progeny thereby might occupy the throne of England. The princess tells this to the dying king on the eve of Wallace's execution, thereby erasing his own hope for progeny and also muting his triumph in Wallace's death. The few women visible in the film, then, really exist as implements by which men inflict pain on other men.

While women matter little and are generally ignored, used as barter, or rendered sacred, issues of paternity and father/son relations are central to the film and are manifested in bodily form, generally in terms of graphic bodily destruction. The film opens with Wallace as a boy discovering the hanged and mutilated bodies of clan leaders that Edward I had gathered, ostensibly for a parley, but actually to betray and execute. Soon after, we see Wallace's father's body graphically mutilated and learn that his father before him had been killed in the same way. These brutal deaths presage Wallace's own and all are presented as sacrificial. The evil and victorious fathers also suffer grotesque physical agonies, although their agonies are presented as neither sacrificial nor as contributing to the continuity of a noble tradition; rather, their agonies are emblems of their evil. Their paternal tradition ends with them; their sons do not follow in their footsteps. Edward I has a paralyzing stroke and cannot speak while he is dying. When the princess tells him that she is pregnant, but not by his son, he is incapable of either responding or punishing her, and can do nothing but impotently agonize over the knowledge that his line dies with him. The father of Robert the Bruce, who masterminds the final betrayal of Wallace, is shown graphically rotting away with leprosy, and his son denounces him.

Women, to the contrary, suffer no such bodily indignities. Not only do we not see the cutting of Wallace's wife's throat, but by and large, women are irrelevant, except as objects of male exchange and power or disgrace. Wallace's father is important to him, but we never see his mother, and she is only mentioned once in passing. Neither Edward I, Robert the Bruce's father, nor Robert himself have evident wives, mothers, daughters, or female companions, but their father/son relationships are central.

A brief coda closes the film. Nearly a decade after Wallace's execution, we see Robert the Bruce, who had earlier betrayed Wallace, successfully leading his army against the British, rousing them by saying, "You have bled with Wallace, now bleed with me!" His relationship with Wallace parallels that of St. Peter with Christ; although St. Peter publicly betrayed Christ, he continued Christ's teachings and became the first pope. Christian tradition also has it that St. Peter, like Christ, was crucified, but upside down so his death would not directly parallel that of his leader. Robert the Bruce's words, "bleed with me," reflect the film's masochistic ethic, since he does not say "join with me in triumph," but rather "join with me in suffering," or "let us bond in pain."

This speaks to a Christian tradition of long-suffering masculinity. In *The Man without a Face* Gibson's character lives as a celibate, sleeping in a single bed with a crucifix over it. He conforms to a way of life woefully out of fashion in the late 1960s, and he is stigmatized for it. His cherished world of male bonding is denigrated as homosexual, and he is considered a pederast, a brutally scarred one who Byronically suffers in a society that does not understand him. In *Braveheart* Wallace's alienation is comparable, only it is based on class and nation. He leads a revolt that is betrayed and crushed, and he suffers specular destruction for it, but he suffers it nobly. Where the "man without a face" shows his oppressors to be insipid, wrong-headed, or contemptible, Wallace's oppressors are literally rotting away.

In *The Man without a Face,* the pain is given a moral justification. McLeod's value is certified by the fact that the boy he mentors knows the purity of his actions and graduates triumphantly from a military school, continuing in his tutor's tradition. Comparably, in *Braveheart,* Wallace's patrimony lives on and effectively erases the patrimony of the patriarchs who destroyed him and whom we see suffering not only physical but also paternal agonies. Implicitly, Wallace's child will replace King Edward's line on the throne of England. Furthermore, Robert the Bruce explicitly rejects his own leprous father for betraying Wallace, and later leads Wallace's revolt in his name. In this film, Wallace's agonies, like Christ's crucifixion, are exquisitely justified.

This justification invites the spectator to avoid social analysis in favor of a conservative and mystical transcendence. As with Christianity, *Braveheart* presents suffering not as a necessarily evil but as a possible pathway for the righteous to inherit a better world. For Gibson, that better world lies in the past.

Notes

1. For a discussion of the different endings in *Fatal Attraction,* see Susan Faludi, *Backlash: The Undeclared War against American Women* (New York: Crown, 1991), 112–23, as well as Peter Lehman and William Luhr, *Thinking about Movies* (Fort Worth: Harcourt, Brace, Inc., 1998), chapter 1.

2. Robert Bly, *Iron John: A Book about Men* (Reading, Mass.: Addison-Wesley, 1990), ix–x.

3. Susan Jeffords, *Hard Bodies: Hollywood Masculinity in the Reagan Era* (New Brunswick, N.J.: Rutgers University Press, 1994), 86–89.

4. *The Advocate* 606 (June 30, 1992): 37–39.

5. See Vito Russo, *The Celluloid Closet: Homosexuality in the Movies* (New York: Harper and Row, 1981), 3–59.

6. Rachel Abramowitz, "Dressed to Kill," *Premiere,* May 1995, 73.

7. Kaja Silverman, *Male Subjectivity at the Margins* (New York: Routledge, 1992), 206.

8. Ibid., 195.

9. Ibid., 198.

10. See also Theodor Reik, *Masochism in Sex and Society,* trans. Margaret H. Beigel and Gertrud M. Kurth (New York: Grove Press, 1962).

11. See Leo Steinberg, "The Sexuality of Christ in Renaissance Art and in Modern Oblivion," *October* (Summer 1983), entire issue.

Part III

The Image as Policeman and the Violence of Vision

10

ALIENS, NOMADS, MAD DOGS, AND ROAD WARRIORS: TABLOID TV AND THE NEW FACE OF CRIMINAL VIOLENCE

ELAYNE RAPPING

[Punishment] does not serve, or else only serves quite secondarily, in correcting the culpable or in intimidating possible followers. . . . Its true function is to maintain social cohesion intact, while maintaining all its vitality in the common conscience.

—Emile Durkheim

Sometimes I think this whole world is one big prison yard / Some of us are prisoners, the rest of us are guards.

—Bob Dylan

"It is no longer possible to discuss crime without talking about the media, and vice versa," say the editors of an anthology on *Crime and the Media: The Postmodern Spectacle*.[1] Indeed, at a time when criminal trials have become major media events, and nightly newscasts devote "42% of their airtime to crime, violence, terrorism and disaster," the argument seems indisputable.[2] Crime is one of the major public issues of our day. As Stuart Hall demonstrated in his landmark *Policing the Crisis: Mugging, the State and Law and Order,* in a highly complex and fragmented social environment, "events and issues only become *public* in the full sense when the means exist whereby the separate worlds of professional and lay person, of controller and controlled, are brought into relation with one another and appear, for a time at least, to occupy the same space."[3] It is the mass media—especially television, which is consumed an estimated 7¾ hours per day in the average American home—that provides the means by which this public space is constructed.

To understand this space is to understand the crucial role of the crime drama—a generic staple since the earliest days of television—in maintaining social stability and the authority of the state. It is through

249

the crime drama's narratives of wrongdoing and retribution that we, as a society, internalize the shifting, often subtle and confusing rules by which we distinguish between right and wrong, what is legal and what is punishable by law, and which acts of violence are authorized—even valorized—and which are forbidden. But the role of television is even more complex than this. When major shifts in the processes and policies that drive law enforcement occur, it is invariably television—as both news and entertainment—that plays the most powerful role in "informing" the public of these shifts and helping us to adjust, culturally and psychologically, to their implications. Thus, in times of paradigmatic cultural, social, and political change, it is the media that must perform the difficult work of "redefining the cultural context within which the criminal justice system operates" and, indeed, redefining "the very concepts, of crime, justice and retribution,"[4] to fit the needs and norms of the changing social order.

The 1990s is such a time. With the Clinton administration, we have seen what can only be viewed by future historians as a radical shift in the meanings of the terms "liberal" and "conservative." A new consensus has emerged in which Democrats have joined Republicans in a middle ground far to the right of the traditional political center, and the basics of liberal, progressive policy—welfare, affirmative action, health care, and education—increasingly are falling prey to policies driven by the discourses of privatization, self-sufficiency, and race and gender "blind" notions of equality.

In no area of public policy has this rightward drift been more dramatic than in the area of criminal justice. Ironically, as social spending on education and social welfare declines, government spending on crime control rises dramatically. In 1997, prison construction and management was the single greatest growth industry in the nation. The imposition of more harsh and punitive measures (three-strike laws for simple, often nonviolent offenses; harsh mandatory sentences; the rise in legalization and enforcement of the death penalty; the trying of preadolescents and minors in adult courts; highway chain gangs; punishments involving public identification and shaming of offenders and ex-offenders; and so on) defines an increasingly repressive society in which those in power grow more and more fearful and hostile toward those they work to control.[5]

For all the hype about rising crime rates used to justify these harsher policies, the statistical truth is quite the opposite: The actual rate of violent crime has fallen dramatically in recent years. Still, new inmates are arriving in droves to fill the newly constructed prisons—some now

250

even privately run for profit—for longer and longer terms. Who are these dangerous criminals? For the most part, they are people convicted of nonviolent offenses involving drugs, prostitution, and other activities associated less with human aggression or greed than sheer survival—both psychological and material—in an increasingly harsh and hopeless world. Most of the recently incarcerated are members of minority and underclass populations. Studies show that by 1994 "one out of every three African-American men between the ages of 20 and 29 in the entire country—including suburban and rural areas—was under some form of criminal justice supervision."[6] Members of immigrant populations are also increasingly visible among the prison population. But the fastest growing of all segments of the chronically incarcerated in the 1990s is women, previously a negligible problem for law enforcement officials.[7]

It is clear that at century's end the role of law enforcement has shifted to a terrain in which social control of an increasingly large population of the disaffected, disinherited, and dysfunctional has replaced the traditional concern with punishing serious crimes against person and property. For the most part, the newly imprisoned are not armed robbers, murderers, or even—contrary to media hype—serial killers or child molesters. They are nonviolent drug users and other cultural and social outsiders and misfits, people who have fallen through the system's cracks or never been allowed to enter its gates. They pose a serious problem for the state not so much because they are viciously aggressive by nature or motive, but because they do not easily fit lawfully into the newly restrictive and intolerant version of American democracy. As Stanley Aronowitz has suggested, by the late 1990s, when the slashing of "big government" and the globalization of the economy rendered many of the state's previous functions obsolete,[8] the major role of the state became internal security and domestic repression, what he rightly describes as "criminal detention and prosecution (misnamed criminal 'justice')"[9] of an ever more broadly defined "criminal element" of the population.

It is in the context of this social transformation that the changing nature of television crime drama—what criminal violence looks like and how, why, and where it functions—must be analyzed. As we move into a new century there is, I argue, an increasing shift in the hegemonic norms by which criminal violence and law enforcement are portrayed on television, one that is very much in keeping with actual shifts in social policy. This shift is only subtly visible in the more prestigious "quality" television series targeted at the educated viewers who do most of the critical analysis of television. But it is starkly visible in a newer television genre that gets less critical attention but is increasingly popular: the

251

tabloid. This is not surprising. It is often in the "lower," less established genres that cultural innovations and shifts tend first to emerge. When one turns to these newly minted forms of crime drama, what one sees is an image of "crime" and "criminality" that is markedly different from what we are used to on prime time. It is an image, however, eerily suited to the political climate at century's end, one in which paranoia, intolerance of difference, and a laissez-faire attitude toward repressive police tactics are the order of the day.[10]

"DOWN THESE MEAN STREETS": THE CITY AS TRADITIONAL CRIME SITE

There are two ways in which crime drama fulfills the symbolic function of constructing, within the mediated public sphere, the mindset within which we come to understand and accept the values and norms of the dominant social order. The first has to do with setting. The crime drama delineates the symbolic geography within which social order must be maintained; the political imagination within which the endless rituals of social disruption and the return to harmony and peace are performed. The second is characterological. The crime drama sketches out the human (or subhuman) contours by which we distinguish deviance from normality and the outlaw from the good citizen who lives within the boundaries of the law.

In traditional crime drama, the landscape of crime has been the city, the urban centers of industrial Western society down whose "mean streets" Raymond Chandler's characters stealthily trod. According to Hall, "the city is a concrete embodiment of the achievements of industrial society," which "embodies our civilization and the degree to which we are successful in maintaining that achievement."[11] The city's fall into disorder and violence represents a grave threat to our survival and well-being. Thus, crime drama has an important social function: It is the nightly ritual through which we collectively experience the dread of the chaos that violence symbolizes and the reassurance that comes when the violent are captured.

On television, the crime genre began in the 1950s with *Dragnet,* a series about a straight-arrow cop as baffled as the audience by the iniquity he saw in the city streets. More recently the genre has been updated to fit a time when even TV audiences (perhaps especially TV audiences) are cynical and savvy enough to know that good and evil are not so easily distinguishable. In series like *Law and Order, NYPD Blue,* and *Homicide,* the ones most commonly granted the label of "quality" television, crime and criminality are no longer portrayed as wholly different from the more "normal" characteristics and actions of law-abiding citizens. On the contrary, in these sophisticated series, which are closer to Chandler and Dashiell Hammett than *Dragnet,* criminals and their actions are portrayed as more or less exaggerated versions of what is normal—even unavoidable. The characters' moral flaws and failings are represented as traits common to most people living in contemporary industrialized society. The city—still the sign of our ultimate social achievement—is a far more inherently flawed and ambiguous symbol, one that, while still worth the risk of life and limb to protect, is a rather shady, tainted arena in which cops themselves are not above cutting corners to bring about the increasingly difficult moment of reassurance and closure.

Because the dominant images of crime and violence portrayed in these series are so familiar, so "naturalized" in our common imaginations, it will be useful to briefly review and analyze some of them, in order to see how different the assumptions and conventions of the newly emerging tabloid television shows really are. I have chosen *Law and Order,* one of the longest-running of traditional crime series, for my comparison, because it provides one of the most thorough picture of the workings of the criminal justice system—from criminal act, to investigation, to trial—ever presented on network television. Set in Manhattan, *Law and Order* devotes half its hourly time slot to the investigation and arrest of a suspect and the rest to the suspect's prosecution. Typically, the cops employ a variety of psychological and forensic methods to ferret out the offender; the prosecutors use similar techniques to decide upon and negotiate a proper punishment.

In one segment, for example, a young woman is found dead of a drug overdose in an alley. The cops are led from the Lower East Side crime scene to a Central Park West apartment, to a Wall Street office, and finally to a graduate student hangout in their search for answers to why a well-dressed young woman ended up in such a downscale setting. The answer involves the greedy, unprincipled executor of her parents' estate, who had been giving the young woman and her Ivy League brother money to feed their mutual drug habits in order to keep them quiet while he skimmed from their trust funds. In another segment, a drug bust in an inner-city neighborhood seems to implicate a black Princeton scholarship student. As it turns out, this young man, an Ivy League outsider, has been coerced into buying drugs for his wealthy white classmates as a way of buying social acceptance. Another segment concerns a thirteen-year-old boy who fatally shoots a schoolmate with his father's pistol. Is it an accident, as he claims, or something more sinister? The answer emerges through careful interviews and investigations of the divorced parents, who have complex psychological and financial reasons for keeping the truth about their son's mental history hidden.

Each of these segments—no matter the age, class, race, socioeconomic background, or status of the apprehended and punished offender—is informed by a common set of assumptions about crime, criminality, and human nature. Criminals are seen to act out of a common, if complex, set of psychological, social, and economic motivations easily recognizable to viewers as "human." Greed, social acceptance, anger, revenge, the desire of a parent to control a child, and the desire of a child to please or rebel against a parent are some of the factors driving the players in these stories to their various immoral or illegal acts. Crimes are planned in advance or carefully covered up after the fact. The city, from its highest social reaches to its lowest, is portrayed as an organically unified community in which all members, regardless of race, class, or gender, share a common human nature. Everyone, even the ghetto dwellers, are reasonably intelligent, articulate, and rational (quality television is nothing if not politically correct). All criminals are conscious that their deeds are wrong but that they were driven to them through failure to control certain common, understandable desires and needs.

The cops and lawyers on these segments are not in any way different—socially, morally, or intellectually—from those they investigate and try. They too reveal common social and moral foibles and flaws. They too have skeletons in closets and peccadilloes they wish to conceal. Regular viewers have come to know all of these things, and they see how the heroes—like those they charge and try—are also part of a flawed but functional social entity, a city of diverse yet integrated individuals and institutions. The cops' and lawyers' methods of interrogation are often harsh, at times physically brutal, and their legal maneuvers and deals are often less than morally or legally satisfying. It is always clear, though, that they have a concern for the social welfare and smooth functioning of the city, for the victims, and even for the criminals themselves. While the ultimate fate of the offender is rarely portrayed, the universe in which crime is negotiated is one in which such terms as "correction" and "rehabilitation"—staples of liberal criminological discourse—are implicit.[12] These are not, after all, scenes from a police state. They are scenes from an institutional environment informed by humane, relatively liberal assumptions about human nature and its appropriate treatment. Such is the world of television crime drama, in which conventions imply that cops, prosecutors, and the myriad professional workers of tangential institutions with whom they collaborate serve a system in

254

which moral values are clear and universal. Within this world, the means to correct injustice and reform those who deviate are theoretically known, available, and relatively effective.

Interestingly enough, this is close to the landscape within which Foucault, whose writings on crime and punishment in modern times have arguably been the most influential of the twentieth century, charted his own symbolic mapping of how the assumptions, institutions, and practices of judgment and punishment have developed within liberal democracies. Television series like *Law and Order,* developed about the same time Foucault was working on this theme, are in certain ways uncannily Foucauldian in their portrayal of law enforcement and of crime itself. Foucault assumed that society, the nation-state he rarely spoke of but which is always implicit in his work, was an organic unity, a "biopolitical" whole, within which individual subjects are integral units, and thus understandable and manageable through the technologies of power/knowledge. Crime, as Foucault saw it developing in the discursive turns of modern democratic thought, was for the most part a defect, or infection, of the body politic. "This deviation, this potential danger, this illness" was how he described criminality as it had been constructed within modern discourses. Because the criminal was seen as a "pathologized subject," he was, according to Foucault, discursively transformed from a figure of essential evil, whose crimes were to be morally condemned and punished, to a subject of study for the new science of criminology to analyze and develop suitable correctional treatment for. No more did the harsh physical punishments of an earlier time, when moral terms such as "good" and "evil" defined the egregious acts that were the law's only concern, inform criminal justice. Now it was the diagnosis and treatment of "the little soul of the criminal" that were of concern. For this task, a "gentler way of punishment," in which "docile bodies" disciplined from birth to internalize the norms of society or feel guilt for failure to do so, could be easily managed within a multipartite but smoothly integrated social system.

In the quality television series mentioned above, this is very much the way criminals, even violent criminals, are portrayed. Murderers, muggers, inner-city drug dealers, and gang members are very much like us, only they have given in to their dangerous and antisocial impulses. They have acted upon the selfish desires for wealth, power, social acceptance, and even revenge—emotions we all share but manage to keep in check. "Who dunnit?" is answered with sociological, psychological, and moral analyses that make sense to us all, as "motives" in a criminal trial must make sense. The criminals are indeed "defective" units in

255

a largely functional, smoothly running society who need merely be analyzed and subjected to proper corrective procedures, which prison or juvenile detention are, it is implied, capable of providing.

AT THE BORDERS: FROM DOCILE BODIES TO ALIEN INVADERS

To turn to the tabloid television shows after watching a series like *Law and Order* is to feel more than disoriented. The conventions of setting, narrative, and characterization are radically different. Criminals are no longer "just like us," only a bit "ill" or "defective" and thus easily rehabilitated. On the contrary, they are increasingly, incorrigibly "other" and "alien." The ideas of reform, correction, and cure—terms of Foucault's "gentler way of punishment"—seem wildly anachronistic and naive in the world of tabloid crime. The creatures policed and apprehended by these cops are not capable of internalizing or abiding by the norms and values of a liberal democracy. They are far too irrational, too uncontrollable, too inscrutable for such measures to be effective. They are part of a newly constructed image of crime and criminal violence in which more harsh and repressive measures than those of the nineteenth century (which Foucault so thoroughly charted) are necessary to maintain social order, because those who threaten the social order are inhuman brutes and freaks.

There are many varieties of tabloid TV—from the "shocks, horrors, and sensations of the day" concentration of *Hard Copy* and *Inside Edition,* to the "they're still out there" tactics of *America's Most Wanted* and *Unsolved Mysteries,* to the "let's ride along with Officer Jones" mentality of *American Detective* and *Top Cops*—which have come and gone, most rather quickly, since the genre first emerged in the 1990s.[13] But all these programs share a prurient interest in the more irrational forms of criminal behavior and a low-budget, "video verite" style based on documentary interviews, tapes of actual police work, and, in some cases, dramatic reenactments of crimes. Of all of these, *COPS*—the longest running series of this genre—is the one that most dramatically reveals the contours of the newly emerging construction of criminal violence.[14] *COPS,* for example, focuses exclusively on crime, without diverging into other sensational matters, like *Hard Copy,* which includes a variety of themes. More importantly, *COPS* thoroughly jettisons the traditional paraphernalia of crime drama to present a radically new vision of the landscape and nature of crime, criminality, and law enforcement. It is a vision expressionistically marked enough to allow a striking glimpse of key assumptions and implications of current political trends.

Immediately upon tuning into this program, we know we are not in Foucault country. There are no more savvy New York cops, lawyers, and experts who work and live within a coherent, if darkened and flawed, version of the political imaginary, which it has been television's role, since the 1950s, to construct, amend, and preserve in our collective social conscience. *COPS* is set in a metaphoric border territory, "out where the buses don't run." The families and neighborhoods that set the standard for "normality" against which criminal deviance is defined, on shows like *Law and Order,* are gone. The theme of the family in danger—a staple, as George Lipsitz reminds us, not only of crime drama, but of most mainstream TV forms[15]—is largely dispensed with here, because the political imaginary within which *COPS* is set is far from any community in which traditional family life might thrive. This is a landscape of highways, strip malls, trailer parks, and convenience stores, where churches, schools, and office buildings—the institutions that make up "normal" society—have no place. While it may resemble places we have all seen and visited, it seems—despite the *echt*-verite quality of the representation—somehow more "foreign" than any American landscape we may have entered.

Each week *COPS* follows a police officer, in an area of the United States not typically seen on television, as he makes his (usually) nightly rounds, patrolling the highways and answering calls about neighborhood and domestic disturbances.[16] The program begins each week with a collage of random shots of the city's local denizens, each more strange, menacing, or simply pathetic than the last. Against a soundtrack playing an upbeat version of the reggae song "Bad Boys" ("Bad boys, bad boys, whatcha gonna do? / Whatcha gonna do when they come for you?"), we see a barrage of fast cuts of things like a drunk about to create a disturbance or wobbling on the point of collapse; a black, dreadlocked Rollerblader dressed only in a scant bikini; an armed offender of some kind being violently apprehended and cuffed as he puts up a wild but hapless struggle; a cop comforting—or even diapering—a wailing, unkempt baby as the child's parent is dragged away. All of these images are intercut with landmarks identifying the city and county featured in the episode.

There is no narrator or voice-over giving direction to the series. The cop who is featured each week—always clean-cut, articulate, and civilized in manner and speech—speaks directly to the audience, eschewing all traditional televisual apparatus by which viewers know they are in

257

The postmodern panopticon and criminal violence: *COPS* (Fox TV/MVP Video, 1997).

familiar media terrain. We are confronted directly with "real life," it is implied, with no Tom Brokaw or Hugh Downs to spin it to us. In this way, the series smoothly if disingenuously signals the viewer that it will eschew the artificial constructions by which traditional television—on series like *Law and Order,* perhaps—smooth the edges of reality and sugarcoat the horrors of what *real* cops, in the *real* world, are up against. Of course, the distortions of media convention are as salient here as anywhere on commercial television, they simply are not as familiar.

The cop begins by introducing himself in simple, down-home terms. He explains a bit about his own background, his motives in becoming a cop, the gratifications and frustrations he receives from the work, and so on. "I wanted to be a priest," says one officer, "but I began to think I could serve better in law enforcement." Another recounts his admiration for his own father, who was also a cop. Always there is a sense of altruism and service more reminiscent of Joe Friday than Sam Spade or Philip Marlowe. The cops, who always know that the camera is running, present themselves in the most positive and wholesome terms they can. They are

258

deliberately constructed, indeed self-constructed, in the image of the traditional American male hero that audiences want so much to believe in, and which police officers (in these post–Rodney King days) want so much to help them believe. Because they are so pure and angelic, the contrast between them and those they police is as dramatic as possible.

The half-hour segment takes the viewer from site to site; usually six or seven calls are covered in the twenty-two-minute period. The cop answers calls on his car radio, chases down and stops suspicious cars on the streets and highways, and apprehends suspicious individuals who happen to be walking along the unpopulated roads or highways. Intoxicated, drugged-out drivers; domestic and street brawls; out-of-control or suspicious-looking loiterers: these are the "crimes" the officers on *COPS* are most likely to attend to week after week,[17] as they drive their police cars through the rough-and-tumble streets and trailer parks they endlessly police. The structure of the series follows a serial format rather than the narrative arc of the crime drama, which includes crime, investigation, capture, and punishment. Crime itself, as we have been taught to understand it by the media, is thus radically reconstructed.[18] No more do criminals plot and scheme toward nefarious goals; act out of jealous rage, greed, or anger; hide out; and attempt to cover their tracks as in traditional narratives. Now we have a set of characters apparently driven not by reasonable, if reprehensible, desires or goals, but by brute instinct or chemical derangement; these criminals lurk, wander, and simply break down in a spiritual and physical wasteland somewhere outside society's orderly boundaries. Since the show's structure precludes any knowledge of what might have come before—of who the person is and what her or his social and psychological background might be—the impression of sheer unmotivated madness is driven home. In place of the orderly plot structure of conflict, crisis, and resolution, we have a series of endless irrational disruptions.

In such a format, the traditional construction of violence itself, as we have come to understand it through crime drama, is radically transformed. In traditional series, a motivated act of violence at the beginning of the hour drives the rest of the action, consisting of the concerted effort to find the criminal by figuring out his motives, tracking him down, and arresting him. The violence is an isolated event that stands in contrast to the rest of the action and is causally connected to the perpetrator's story, which by the end of the episode becomes a rich mesh of sociological and psychological life circumstances. The criminal in these narratives, no matter how amoral or vicious, is still a human being whose defects are theoretically understandable and correctable. For this reason, even the most vicious traditional crimes can be understood within the context of the criminal's mind, a context into which all other, lesser crimes also fit.

This traditional view of even the worst violent crimes as understandable and correctable has its origin, according to Foucault, in the criminological theories developed in the nineteenth century by which crime came to be understood in medical and psychiatric terms. It was at that time that the biological "disease model" of deviance—first applied only to the most pathologically dangerous and demented of killers—gradually came to be applied to criminals of all kinds. "There appear in the field of legal psychiatry new categories such as necrophilia around 1840, kleptomania around 1860, exhibitionism in 1876 and also legal psychiatry's annexation of behavior of pederasty and sadism" Foucault wrote in "The Dangerous Individual," so that "there now exists, at least in principle, a psychiatric and criminological continuum which permits one to pose questions in medical terms at any level of the penal scale."[19] Thus, he explained, it became possible to equate the most horrible criminal acts with the most trivial in order to put forth a systematic, psychiatric, disciplinary process of correction for all criminals. Of course, the main point was to pathologize all crime so as to subject it to disciplinary treatment. After all, few criminals were likely to commit the most serious or repugnant crimes. Yet all offenders were understood in the same terms, and this meant that the most violent offenders were lumped together with exhibitionists and kleptomaniacs as suffering from some medically treatable form of deviance. Their violent actions could therefore be studied and even synthesized into some kind of profile, which criminologists could then use to predict future acts and devise treatment.

This Foucauldian construction still applies, I would argue, even to the most demonized of criminals—serial killers and child molesters, perhaps—as seen on traditional crime dramas and in serious news media. There is no doubt that this kind of demonized imagery, so common on television today, is itself a contributing factor in the rise of the repressive policies mentioned above and in the political trend I am analyzing. As Ray Surette argues in his discussion "Predator Criminals as Media Icons," "the crimes that dominate the public consciousness and policy debates" are not common crimes but the rarest ones, because "the modern mass media have raised the specter of the predator criminal from a minor character to a common, ever-present image."[20] Surette rightly concludes that such imagery does indeed support arguments for policies that stress punitive measures for criminals rather than attacking root causes of crime itself. But Surette himself includes among those punitive approaches "intensive individual rehabilitative or educational efforts" of the kind that still adhere to an assumption that criminals are theoretically correctable and conducive to reform.[21]

On *COPS*, however, because of the way violence is represented, even this vestigial assumption of liberal policy seems no longer to apply. The offenders on *COPS*, though certainly inherently violent or prone to violence, are rarely predators. They do not molest children or go on killing sprees. They do not threaten our homes or roam city streets looking to mug, rob, or rape "our women." In fact, on the most obvious level, they are far less threatening than the criminals seen on other crime series, or on the nightly news for that matter. Their acts are not generally directed toward anyone or anything. They do not usually even do much serious damage, except maybe to themselves. Their worst violent acts are not generally of the sensational, explosive variety that is most anxiety-provoking to the public. Rather, their crimes seem to embody a constant proneness to random, sporadic violence, which is represented as a permanent condition of human—or rather subhuman—nature. They are simply inherently violent in ways that make no sense at all. We learn no clues, no "story" of any kind onto which we can hang a diagnosis. Because of these representational techniques, treatment or rehabilitation—the solutions to the threats posed by even the most demonized criminals, as Surette suggests—are not options.

Indeed, even when the cops do attempt to get to the bottom of things, they rarely get a coherent story from anyone involved. Sometimes this is because the witnesses and victims are incoherent, either because of drugs or because they speak a language other than English. More often it is because they tell incoherent narratives or contradict each other. Since we see each person only in this isolated moment of his or her irrational, out-of-control, and potentially dangerous behavior, we can never know if there is more to the story than meets the "truthful" eye of the trusted video lens. Indeed, so powerful is the appeal of the "reality" of the documentary style that the missing context—social, emotional, and narrative—seems irrelevant or is never even considered.[22]

BEYOND THE CITY: THE POSTMODERN IMAGINARY OF TABLOID TV

The implications of *COPS*'s construction of criminal violence must surely strike fear in the hearts of viewers. These inscrutable creatures, uncontrollable and beyond the ken of traditional criminological "expertise," are somewhere near us, for we see actual road signs identifying actual American locations. Because of this implied proximity to "normal" society, they are likely, it is ominously implied, to seep through our borders and spread their chaos to our own vulnerable communities if left unchecked. But who are these creatures, and where is the landscape they inhabit, which seems to be so near and also a world away? On traditional crime dramas, the landscape is the city and the criminal is someone who lives within the city's boundaries. In recent times there have been two dominant images of the dangerous criminal, both native to the city streets. The most common has been the inner-city black male. Indeed, it has been an unfortunate trend in crime drama, as well as news reporting, to demonize the African-American, inner-city male as the emblem of what most crime looks like in America.[23] If series like *Law and Order* have cleaned up their portrayals of this figure in the interest of political correctness, there are certainly other genres, the local news in particular, which have taken the opposite tack, presenting ever more brutalized images of young black males—"superpredators" is the popular term devised by Princeton criminologist John Diulio—to fit the increasingly conservative discourses on crime and punishment.[24] But this criminal, while fenced off into a separate area of the city, still inhabits and is free to move within the city's borders.

The other dominant image, more recent and more menacing perhaps, is the one Surette describes, the predator criminal who commits the most gruesome of violent acts. He, too, is a creature of the urban centers, although a particularly fearful one because he is less easily identifiable on sight. Often dwelling quietly and unobtrusively on our own streets and working in our own office buildings, he may seem the epitome of "normality" until his urge for blood sets him off on a crime spree. Again, other genres are filled with tales of this character who, like Foucault's "dangerous individual," suddenly "snaps" and reveals, beneath his deceptively mild surface, a mania-driven bloodlust.[25] Here, then, is another city dweller, a person we may pass in the streets or sit next to on the subway.

When we enter the world of *COPS,* however, we are somewhere else, somewhere far from the urban streets where the crime we are used to occurs. We may be familiar with the kinds of places pictured here— bars, strip malls, low-rent apartment complexes, convenience stores— but somehow they do not look or feel quite the same now. The way things seem to happen, with no before or after, no why or wherefore; the limited nature of the kinds of things that happen; and the absence of cues or information about who these people are and how they happened to be where we find them makes this constructed universe a place we cannot imagine actually finding ourselves in. It is a world of nothing but brawls, bars, hookers, mental breakdowns, and outbursts. It is difficult to comprehend any of it in any human or social terms.[26]

Of course the footage is real. These are real people who live in real areas of a real America. In fact, if we want to attempt a sociological profile of the most common people and neighborhoods encountered, we can fairly safely do so. These are the kinds of people who are habitually in trouble with the police, and these places are where such people tend to live and hang out. The real segment of the population from which this select group of "police regulars" is drawn—caricatured and distorted as the representation of them may be—is that group of people who are permanently down on their luck for a variety of reasons: momentarily or chronically dysfunctional, inveterate "outsiders" and misfits who do not conform to social norms, and those weak of character and prone to the worst kind of judgment. When encountered, most are under the influence of drugs or alcohol. Many are petty criminals: hookers, gamblers, and con artists so incompetent that they are always apprehended. Others are immigrants who do not speak English well and have not found a way to integrate themselves into "normal" American life. Still others are homeless, because of drug or alcohol problems or because they are mentally ill. Indeed, mental illness is a very common problem that the cops deal with each week. But since the concept of homelessness has no place in the universe of *COPS,* these individuals are simply part of the population who are endlessly and violently out of control and in trouble with the law.

Thus, *COPS* gives the impression that there is a world "out there" in "those neighborhoods" in some other part of town where human life as we know it simply ceases to exist. And this world—symbolically and expressionistically contrived out of an infinite amount of videotape—is filled with people who are indeed aliens, freaks of nature, subhuman primitive beasts whose words make no sense and whose actions are bizarre. This is a particularly *postmodern* universe, for it is a world unmoored from the very bases of civilized life and order, in which a potpourri of cultural, ethnic, racial, and sexual "types" are thrown together in a multicultural hodgepodge of generic otherness. Cut loose from community and cultural cohesion, they are set adrift along a metaphoric border territory at the very fringes of "normal" life, where all hope of a better future—and the liberal rhetoric which fuels it—disappears.

Within this quintessentially postmodern cultural mix, three types stand out in particular: the drug abuser, the sexual deviant, and the immigrant. The rhetoric of the political right is thick with jeremiads about the dangers of sexual promiscuity and deviance, of drug abuse and other forms of chemical indulgence, and of the economic and sociological threat posed by the hordes of immigrants who are flooding our borders, contaminating our heritage and traditions, and sapping our social services. It is these very people we see on *COPS,* at their most degraded and chaotic, representing multiculturalism in all its demonized symbolism. White characters are as degraded and deranged as black; women are as aggressively violent as men; and many other ethnic characters, mostly immigrants from Middle Eastern and Latin nations, mix and match with the others indiscriminately. Their households are not stable or permanent and do not follow any socially "normal" pattern of domestic life. They may contain interracial couples and families, racially and sexually mixed boarders of various ages, immigrant groups for whom English is still a foreign language and whose clothing and furnishings clearly mark them as "foreign," drug and alcohol abusers, flagrantly identifiable gays and transvestites, and so on. Often neighbors and even house members seem not to know each other. It is implied that virtually every arrangement is temporary and expedient.

To examine specific encounters in more detail is to get a clear sense of the qualitative differences etched between those who police and those who are policed and of how clearly the latter are represented as being inherently different and inferior—and especially violent—in ways that no therapy or rehabilitation could possibly affect. When called to a domestic disturbance or forced to subdue a driver on the highway, the police invariably—as far as we are allowed to see—find a person so horribly out of control that the police must respond with brute force. In these cases, the tape rolls for longer periods of time than in other cases, often focussing starkly and steadily on a person going more and more out of control, in ways that are painful to watch. Often, the person will be wildly, violently rebellious and hysterical. Unkempt, often barely clothed, and surrounded by filth and chaos, he or she is allowed to gyrate and gesticulate as the cops show saint-like restraint and patience. This stark visual contrast between the hysteria of the offenders and the patience of the cops is among the most vivid ways in which tabloid criminals are marked as subhuman and different from "normal" Americans like the police.

In one case, a man stopped for erratic driving refuses to give up his knife and surrender. He keeps shuffling down the middle of the highway, clearly in a state of derangement. The cops—five or six of them—simply follow him at a distance, calling repeatedly, "Hey Buddy, just drop the knife and we can help you." After several excruciating moments, the police are forced to subdue him, and in the process he is shot and seriously disabled. As the man jerks and shakes while being cuffed and taken into custody, the cops congratulate themselves on a job well done. "You really showed restraint, man," they say to the shooter. Indeed, under the watchful eye of the video camera, he certainly had exercised restraint in a way that could only make Rodney King wish he lived in this border territory instead of the one in which he was beaten.[27] Though we learn a lot about the virtues of the police in this segment, for all its excessive length we know no more about the man apprehended at the end than at the start. He was simply one more mad dog road warrior, unfit to drive, surely, and unfit to live in civilized society, so bizarrely incomprehensible were his actions.

This implication of irrationality and even bestiality is particularly offensive when people of color are involved. In a typical incident, it seems a Middle Eastern couple—he in turban, she in long dress and sandals—are having a physical fight. The woman is incoherent, flailing on the ground, wailing, and pointing to her bleeding leg. The man paced outside the house, incoherently mumbling as though in a trance. Neighbors are asked to explain, but no coherent story emerges. The issue, which would have surely been articulated on *Law and Order,* was domestic violence. But the shocking, humiliating visual imagery, along with the incoherent, irrational physical and verbal behavior of the couple, shifts the emphasis to something very different: the repellent, embarrassing irrationality, hysteria, and violence of "foreigners." In this way, *COPS* works to dehumanize and barbarize a range of cultural and sexual difference so emphatically that only the police are left to represent "real" human nature, a calm, superior conquering army assigned to patrol the settlements in which a primitive, subhuman, barbaric tribe dwell.

Calmly patrol they do, unflappable in the face of the most freakish events and characters. On one segment, a black prostitute is apprehended as she staggers into the road, having narrowly escaped from a violent john who has slashed her face with a knife. As it turns out, she is a transvestite with whom the cop is familiar. Out of control, incoherent, and under the influence of drugs, she attempts to flirt with the cop as he works to subdue her and get her to a hospital. From there, the cop goes on to a house call in which a drug-crazed young man wildly waves a gun and staggers about as the woman who has made the call—whom the man refers to as "my wife-type," although she seems at least twenty years older than he— cringes in terror. The couple is interracial, as are another couple on the scene, who look on in an apparent stupor. A girl of about three, filthy and unkempt, sobs nearby. All four adults, high and in possession of drugs and paraphernalia, are eventually arrested when backup comes to assist the cop. The child is lovingly calmed, cleaned up, taken into custody, and assured that she would be taken care of as she clings desperately to the heroic cop. What ultimately happens to the child and the others is not shown.

If, as I have suggested, one of the two central roles of crime drama is to delineate the contours of deviance, to sketch a portrait of the "outlaw," the individual against which what is "normal" and "legal" is measured, then it is important to note the dramatic ways in which the tabloid television shows reconfigure that image. Since the 1970s, when British cultural studies theorists such as Hall and Dick Hebdige began to study subcultures and deviance as cultural constructs, the links between cultural studies and criminology have become clearer. As criminologist Jeff Ferrell has put it, "many social groups and events traditionally conceptualized as 'criminal' are in fact," in modern times, "defined in their everyday operations" less by criminal actions than by the "subcultural meaning and style" of their appearance and social behavior.[28] Foucault, too, understood this when he developed his theories of how "delinquency" is a socially constructed concept whose disciplinary purpose is to mark the boundaries between those who cross the line of acceptable behavior and those who stay within it, thus making it possible to articulate publicly what those lines might be and to justify the disciplinary means necessary to control deviance.[29]

On the tabloid shows, however, criminals are no longer constructed in terms of simple "deviance" from accepted norms of a recognizable coherent community. The people observed on *COPS* are better described in terms of "anti-style" than any common style. There is nothing holding any of them together culturally or behaviorally except the very absence of any particular style or ritual that would bind them to a true community— even a criminal community. They are not so much "deviant" from "normal" behavior as simply "others," "aliens," hovering at our borders, held back only by the thin blue line of the police, who are presented as the true salvation of American civilization.

NEW PARADIGMS FOR NEW TIMES: THE CRIMINAL AS DOMESTIC TERRORIST

What is the policy implication of the situations encountered on *COPS*? Clearly, there is no sense that preventive or corrective measures should be taken. As we have seen, the editing techniques preclude all sense that social contexts or conditions, much less racial or economic inequality, play a role here. Rather, the conditions in which these people live—filth, squalor, chaos—are seen as of their own making, a result of their own degraded natures. Even drug treatment programs seem irrelevant here, since again and again we see junkies stopped who are well known to the cops, who have been in and out of rehab, and who simply grin sheepishly when caught and arrested yet again. The same is true of the violence, which is also seen as a choice of lifestyle or, more accurately, a condition of nature. Women in domestic disturbance incidents, for example, are usually presented as regulars who, as the cops shake their heads and exchange looks, seem incapable of learning their lesson and leaving their violent partners. More often than not, the women themselves are accused by the partner or witnesses of being the aggressors. There is no "expert" testimony to give context and meaning to the plight of battered women and the forces that keep them in place. Prostitutes are also seen as perverse by nature, determined to continue in their wayward paths and exhibiting only the most weary annoyance when stopped by the cops.

What is most striking about the image of the outsiders and misfits pictured on *COPS* is that they are seen as criminals at all. They are clearly people with a variety of economic, social, psychological, and cultural problems, whose violent acts are far less threatening to the public than to themselves. The criminalization of "quality of life" issues is not new in American society. Drug addiction and prostitution have long been criminalized in lieu of addressing the broad social and economic factors that cause such behaviors and attempting to correct them. But *COPS* extends the implications of this trend to a far broader range of people and behaviors, dragging off virtually everyone encountered who cannot be readily subdued. People of other cultures and languages, the homeless, the mentally imbalanced—anyone who is momentarily out of control for any reason will find him or herself apprehended and hauled off to jail by these cops. More often than not, the means by which this is accomplished is both brutal and devoid of all reference to civil or human rights. Rarely are Miranda rights read to anyone on *COPS,* at least on screen. Even more rarely does anyone ask for a lawyer. This, we are led to believe, is appropriate, for these people are uncontrollably irrational beings who cannot comprehend the rules by which we live.[30]

If concepts like deviance, delinquency, reform, and rehabilitation no longer seem adequate to describe the world of crime and punishment that is being constructed on tabloid television, what discourse, what rhetoric might be more appropriate? I would suggest that the criminal—or criminalized Other—just described bears a striking resemblance to another relatively new media icon meant to strike terror in the hearts of law-abiding citizens: the terrorist. Like the terrorist, the tabloid criminal is an alien, an outsider who poses a threat to social order because he does not conform to the psychological and moral norms by which we, in Western society, have learned to live peacefully together. Terrorists are irrational, inscrutable, and inherently violent. They threaten to infiltrate our porous borders, bringing with them fear, chaos, and disorder. They cannot be "reformed" or "rehabilitated" according to traditional correctional methods, because they neither recognize, nor respect, the codes to which such measures apply.

There is a literature of terrorism—both political and cultural—in which just such qualities are described in an effort to convince us that new, harsher methods of repression are needed to combat this new breed of anti-social being. Terrorists are marked, in the media, by dramatic signs of difference, physical and psychological. These signs are so repellent and horrifying that they easily justify the use of measures previously unthinkable in the enforcement of "normal" criminal law, because terrorists are not "normal" criminals; they are alien, inhuman monsters.

Mad dogs and road warriors: *North Hollywood Shoot-out* (Fox TV/MVP Video, 1997).

In a fascinating study of the rhetorical image of the international terrorist, legal scholar Ileana Porras uses just such terminology to describe the terrorist as a cultural image. "Terrorism," she writes, "has come to be the thing against which liberal democracies define themselves; . . . the repository of everything that cannot be allowed to fit inside the self-image of democracy; . . . the terrorist has become the 'other' that threatens . . . the annihilation of the democratic 'self' and an external force which democracies therefore must strenuously defend against."[31]

"In the expert literature on terrorism," she writes, "the terrorist is transformed from an ordinary deviant into a frightening foreign/barbaric/beast," a "border violator" who does not recognize laws or family ties; and who must be subdued and repressed by "extra-normal means." The political and legal implications of this cultural construction are clear to Porras: "The rhetorical transformation of terrorists into frightening alien outlaws," she writes, "suggests a justification for repression by the state and an excuse for . . . authoritarian regimes." "In fact," she continues, "repressive measures short of military dictatorship are virtually recommended by the literature on terrorism . . . because the failure to use all possible means to combat terrorism is to put society at risk of falling into chaos."[32]

I would suggest this description is very close to the image of the border criminal depicted on shows like *COPS*. Out of control, primitive and subhuman, incapable of reason, unable to abide the law, unable to maintain family ties, he or she is a creature to be repressed, to be kept out of our borders by the harshest possible measures. To allow him or her in is to invite the very chaos Porras suggests the terrorist represents. The actual acts committed by the tabloid criminals are, of course, not nearly dangerous enough to be compared with acts of terrorism. But the idea of inherent "otherness"—a term that marks the immigrant, the sexual deviant, and the drug addict—and the grotesquely expressionistic conventions by which the tabloids represent these people makes the comparison in kind, if not deed, emotionally resonant. The border dwellers on *COPS* are the dregs of society. But rather than presenting any cultural, political, or social context that might explain their subjects' deplorable conditions, these shows choose to represent these outsiders as alien, depraved, and inferior, suggesting that only the most repressive policies are appropriate for them. It may seem to viewers of the series that this kind of treatment is more than justified for such subhuman, irrational creatures. But policies enacted to control designated, demonized scapegoats—as these aliens, addicts, and misfits of various kinds have become—can all too easily be used against everyone, especially in a postmodern world in which the designation of "other" has, in one way or another, come to be a floating signifier which may be attached, at any time, to any of us.

Notes

1. David Kidd-Hewitt and Richard Osborne, *Crime and the Media: The Postmodern Spectacle* (London: Pluto Press, 1995).

2. Martha T. Moore, "Let's Go to the Bloody Videotape," *USA Today,* May 12, 1997, 3A.

3. Stuart Hall et al., *Policing the Crisis: Mugging, the State and Law and Order* (London: Macmillan, 1978), 145.

4. Richard Osborne, "Crime and the Media: From Media Studies to Postmodernism," in *Crime and the Media: The Postmodern Spectacle,* ed. David Kidd-Hewitt and Richard Osborne (London: Pluto Press, 1995), 42.

5. For a through survey of the state of crime and crime control in the late 1990s see Steven Donziger, ed., *The Real War on Crime: The Report of the National Criminal Justice Commission* (New York: HarperPerennial, 1996). Donziger documents the actual incarceration rates of various age, race, and gender groups as well as the actual figures on crime rates, which are not easily found in a credible form. He also documents the penalties and even many of the atrocities committed against defendants and prisoners, the legal initiatives pending or passed that will alter criminal trial procedures, and the arrest and prison procedures that place prosecutors and police officers at an advantage over the defendants. During the writing of this essay, a number of new bills, exacerbating this ominous trend, were being discussed as well. A federal bill to try thirteen-year-olds as adults and induce states, through the offer of large block grants, to follow suit in cases of violent crime and "serious" drug offense is only one of many such trend-setting ideas looked upon more and more favorably by Democrats and Republicans alike.

6. Ibid., 102, 288.

7. Ibid., 146.

8. See Jean-Marie Guehenno, *The End of the Nation-State* (Minneapolis: University of Minnesota Press, 1995) for an interesting overview of decline of the nation-state, its causes and implications.

9. Stanley Aronowitz, *The Death and Rebirth of American Radicalism* (New York: Routledge, 1997), 138.

10. I am not suggesting that the traditional paradigm of crime and punishment is on the way out. New paradigms have a way of overlapping and coexisting with the new as social change occurs in all areas of social life, although there is no doubt that traditional crime dramas have been increasingly influenced by the move to the Right. I am only suggesting that the tabloids do indeed represent a dramatic example of a rather pure version of a new paradigm of crime and punishment that is at the cutting edge of an ideological and cultural shift seen more mildly and subtly elsewhere.

11. Hall, *Policing the Crisis,* 136.

12. No crime series charts the dangerous after-story in which the fate and future of the convicted offender is portrayed. Even the punishment phase of criminal trials is omitted on series like *Law and Order*. It is enough for audiences to know that the problem has been taken care of. Such is the trust TV genres would have us place in the correctional system, which is virtually absent, even on newscasts, from mainstream television.

13. See Anna Williams, "Domesticity and the Aetiology of Crime," *Camera Obscura* 31 (January–May 1993): 97–121 for an interesting discussion of another form of tabloid, *America's Most Wanted,* which documents and re-enacts unsolved crimes and asks viewers to help catch the criminals. Williams reads the construction of predator crime against families in *America's Most Wanted* as still fitting within the Foucauldian model of "illness" and supposed "treatment" and "rehabilitation." But I would argue that the show's criminals are more fully understood in the terms I am suggesting, as creatures of enormous, marked difference. Foucault, after all, died before the advent of tabloid television, and he never assumed his analysis would necessarily apply to current times. It was meant only to be suggestive of trends, as indeed it has been. *America's Most Wanted* does employ generic conventions that are closer to traditional crime drama than does *COPS,* because, as Williams notes, much of the crime on the show is by predator criminals stalking decent families. See note 25 for more on this.

14. As I write, a new series has just aired on the Fox network that is far more disturbing than *COPS. Video Justice: Crimes Caught on Tape.* For a full hour, the series plays videotapes of actual crimes—some acquired from vandalized stores, some from private citizens, and some from police surveillance tapes. As the tapes—generally lurid and often horrifying in their vivid detailed footage of shoot-outs, acts of physical destruction, and brutal beatings—roll, the narrator provides rhetorically excessive commentary: "These creatures, cold-hearted and steely, have not an ounce of human fellow feeling, as you can see as they wildly attack their prey." Since this series has aired only a few times, I am not including it in this essay. If it survives, however, it will push the thesis of this essay to an even more alarming extreme.

15. George Lipsitz, "The Greatest Story Ever Sold: Marketing and the O. J. Simpson Trial," in *Birth of a Nation'hood: Gaze, Script and Spectacle in the O. J. Simpson Case,* ed. Toni Morrison (New York: Pantheon, 1997), 15.

16. I am using the masculine pronoun to refer the cops in this series because most of the cops who serve as hosts on this series are white and male. Minority and female cops do appear at times, sometimes as central figures but more often as back-up. It is significant that the standard police officer on this series, as is the case in the police forces who participate in the series, is a white male.

17. Since the series moves from place to place and presents an endless series of police encounters, there are exceptions to these generalizations. Sometimes cities are visited—Boston, or Chicago, or Pittsburgh—in which urban settings figure at least to some extent. Sometimes an actual violent crime, a robbery or murder, may actually occur. The producers certainly welcome such sensationalism when they can get it. But for the most part what occurs on these routine shifts is much more mundane. Footage is selected for the most drama possible, and this usually involves drunks, drug addicts, prostitutes, bar fights, and domestic disturbances of one kind or another.

18. For an interesting book-length study of the structure and signifying practices of traditional crime drama in the United States and Britain, see Richard Sparks, *Television and the Drama of Crime: Moral Tales and the Place of Crime in Public Life* (Buckingham and Philadelphia: Open University Press, 1992).

19. Michel Foucault, "The Dangerous Individual," *Politics, Philosophy, Culture: Interviews and Other Writings of Michel Foucault*, ed. Lawrence Kritzman (London: Routledge, 1988), 42. For an analysis of Foucault's development of this thesis and its applicability to tabloid series like *America's Most Wanted,* see Williams, "Domesticity and the Aetiology of Crime."

20. Ray Surette, "Predator Criminals as Media Icons," in Gregg Barak, *Media, Process, and the Social Construction of Crime* (New York: Garland, 1994), 131–32.

21. Ibid.

22. The relationship between documentary and "reality," and the ways in which the documentary form—in its "highest" and "lowest" generic manifestations—is both a fictional text and yet different from other fictional texts in that "it addresses the world in which we live rather than worlds in which we imagine living" is explored fully in Bill Nichols, *Representing Reality* (Bloomington: Indiana University Press, 1991).

23. Herman Gray has thoroughly analyzed the way in which race and criminality have been constructed and deployed in mass media. The most full treatment is in *Watching Race: Television and the Struggle for Blackness* (Minneapolis: University of Minnesota Press, 1995).

24. See Gray, *Watching Race,* for a more thorough discussion of the changing nature of racial representation during the Reagan years and the ways in which demographic imperatives affected this representation in terms of difference and assimilation.

25. Actually several other tabloids—*America's Most Wanted* and *Hard Copy,* for example—employ this stereotype quite often. In fact, I would argue that this form of tabloid violence, in which vicious predators suddenly and incomprehensibly turn on neighbors or even family members in the most repellent and horrifying of criminal acts, represents a kind of middle ground between traditional crime drama and the more radical version represented by *COPS.* In these cases, the "family in danger" theme is maintained as is the focus on specific, usually planned and motivated, acts and the police search for the offender. The difference—and the reason they figure as tabloids—is primarily stylistic. Documentary footage and re-enactments are employed to give the same expressionistically aberrant image of crime and criminality, and the saintly behavior of the cops contrasts sharply with the representation of criminals and even victims, whose environments (due to the "low rent" production values) have the same seedy, unsavory quality as on *COPS.* These tabloids seem to be set somewhere between the landscape of traditional urban crime drama and the border territory visualized on *COPS.*

26. A student of mine spent some time on "drive-alongs" with his local police officers and did a comparison of what he experienced and what is shown on *COPS.* The differences in quality and quantity of encounters with deranged individuals, as well as the behavior of the cops themselves (whom the student had known since childhood and who trusted him), were notable and perhaps predictable.

27. It is worth noting here that in cases, often videotaped by private citizens, in which cops in cars or on bikes are charged with beating and killing usually black suspects, the public is increasingly given evidence of police behavior which is wild, uncivilized, out of control, and vicious. It is not surprising, then, that these ideologically "corrective" tabloids should be appearing at just this moment, in which the tables are turned and the cops are seen as icons of kindness and peacefulness, while those they arrest or subdue are the ones who seem vicious, out of control, and hostile.

28. Jeff Ferrell, "Culture, Crime and Criminology," in Ferrell and Clinton Sanders, *Cultural Criminology* (Boston: Northeastern University Press, 1995), 7–8.

29. Foucault, *Discipline and Punish,* 254–56.

30. In *Policing the Risk Society* (Toronto: Toronto University Press, 1997), a detailed study of the work of police officers in contemporary society, Richard Ericson and Kevin Haggerty demonstrate this very point—a point *COPS* illustrates eloquently. "It is extremely rare for a police officer to encounter a serious crime in progress," they say. It is "traffic and liquor violations" that make up most routine patrol work, and on house calls "what officers typically find . . . is not serious crime but a kaleidoscope of trouble that requires them to provide some combination of counsel, assistance, expertise, coercion, referral, and persuasion." Indeed, "direct involvement in crime work takes up as little as 3% of their working time" (19–20). "This emphasis entails a lessening of crime control in favor of surveillance," they argue, and creates a system in which "due process protection for suspects is eroded in favor of 'system rights' to the kind of knowledge useful to surveillance" (18). While the authors argue that this kind of system is less "repressive" than simply managerial, the distinction—especially as acted out on shows like *COPS*—seems merely semantic. Repression of serious crime merely gives way to a far greater, more all-encompassing form of "repression" of a far greater range of personas and behaviors.

The authors mention the mass media's "dramatization of crime"—"*the* staple cultural product of their industry"—as important in creating the idea in the public mind, and even in the mind of the police themselves, that crime work is what cops *really* do. Thus, the implication goes, the media obscure the true surveillance nature of most police work today. Certainly in most crime drama this is true. But what is so intriguing about *COPS* is how it works to subtly redefine the very idea of crime to now include these essentially managerial functions. And by extension, it seeks to redefine the definition of "criminal" to include those who need to be controlled.

31. Ileana Porras, "On Terrorism: Reflections on Violence and the Outlaw," in Dan Danielson and Karen Engle, *After Identity: A Reader in Culture and Law* (New York: Routledge, 1995), 295.

32. Ibid., 305–9.

11

Touching Scenes and Finishing Touches: Blindness in the Slasher Film

Susan Crutchfield

> To ponder mimesis is to become sooner or later caught, like the police and the modern State with their fingerprinting devices, in sticky webs of copy *and* contact, image *and* bodily involvement of the perceiver in the image, a complexity we too easily elide as non-mysterious with our facile use of terms such as identification, representation, expression, and so forth—terms which simultaneously depend upon and erase all that is powerful and obscure in the network of associations conjured by the notion of the mimetic.
>
> —*Michael Taussig, "Physiognomic Aspects of Visual Worlds"*[1]

> The frequency, in horror, of images of victim-eyes under attack—punctured, burned, gouged out, and blinded by light, by everything from hypodermic needles and hot coffee to "blipverts"—underlines the interest of horror in hurtable vision, vision on the defense.
>
> —*Carol Clover,* Men, Women, and Chain Saws[2]

The slasher film is overtly concerned with mimesis as Taussig describes it, that is, with the relationship of contact to copies, and specifically the violent relationship of tactility to photographic and filmic copies of objects and experiences. Thus Taussig's fingerprint is an extremely fitting trope for more reasons than its connotations of criminality. The two films I will discuss in detail here use the blind touch to highlight the bankruptcy of the mere visual copy, both in its attempt to impress the viewer, and in its attempt to represent experience. The first is British director Michael Powell's slasher film prototype, *Peeping Tom,* which was released in 1960, the same year that Alfred Hitchcock's *Psycho* was released in the United States. The second film is Jocelyn Moorhouse's *Proof,* a 1992 Australian dramatic film that draws upon scenarios and themes of the slasher genre (copies them) in order to critique them, or rather, to expose the fractures in their underlying ideologies of vision. *Peeping Tom* and *Proof* examine the violence inherent to photography and film, a fitting metaphor for the slasher film's more palpable, explicit violence. Moreover, through their representations of blindness, these films reveal the slasher genre's investment in a distinction between the perceptual modes of sight and touch (and between their counterparts in the mimetic analog, copy and contact), as well as the slasher's presumption of an audience well schooled in the recognition of that difference. As I will show, blind characters in slasher films make this distinction clear at the same time that they suffer for it; their touch is scapegoated as violent, taboo, unrepresentable, grotesque, or simply "different." While slasher films are indeed preoccupied with "hurtable vision," they also work surreptitiously and violently to protect against any potential damage to the hegemony of vision over tactility, copy over contact.

In postmodernity, Walter Benjamin's recognition of the resurgence of mimesis in modernity gives way to Jean Baudrillard's announcement of the triumph of simulation.[3] If mimesis involves both copy and contact, as Taussig suggests, then its postmodern counterpart involves copies in contact with copies—in other words, a proliferation of the sign that seems never to touch down to an "original" or "authentic" object of representation. The visual realm has come to represent this proliferation of immaterial signs most forcefully for postmodernity: the advertising image in particular, but more broadly those mass reproduced images that are the products of photographic and film (and now digital) technology. This is Jean-Louis Comolli's "frenzy of the visible"; it is Guy Debord's "society of the spectacle," in which "modern conditions of production prevail, [and] all of life presents itself as an immense accumulation of *spectacles*. Everything that was directly lived has moved away into a representation."[4] Any mediating form of direct contact has been overcome by self-replacing copies, even fabrications, of once-direct experience. Benjamin's "aura"—that which bespeaks the authentic, material presence, and historical weight of an object—has been ushered out of the cultural cineplex.

It is curious, then, to find that a crisis of simulation is so much at the heart of the unapologetically postmodern genre of the slasher film, whose narratives depict a vision both "hurtable" and "on the defense" due to a physical violence that gives rise to an overwhelming sense of the possibilities of literal contact.[5] As Clover points out, watching horror is often about watching a representation of watching, in other words, about copying a copy. More precisely, however, watching horror means seeing that viewing activity undermined, as the killer/monster takes advantage of vision's embodied vulnerability in his physical attack. Thus, horror's representations of vision and the visual are profoundly mimetic in Taussig's sense of the word: visual copy and visual contact converge in a violent gesture of physical involvement. Slasher narratives include an impressive repertoire of assaults upon the eye, combining a material definition of vision with a strategy of visual entertainment that, as Clover's remarks indicate, repeatedly reminds spectators not only of their status as viewers, but also of the vulnerability of the organ of the eye that confers that status. Reflecting its viewers within its narratives, the slasher genre links the mutability of the fleshy (victim's) body to the malleability of embodied (spectatorial) vision.

The embodied, abject, and defensive vision of the slasher film is, ironically, part and product of the genre's attempts to maintain for vision a privileged, powerful status within culture. By embodying vision, the slasher film allows its viewers to see vision and thereby legitimize vision's products and effects.[6] Vision made visible is vision self-legitimated. This bid for legitimacy and power is contextualized within postmodern discourses and media practices that challenge the mastery of vision and visual spectacles. In this context, the slasher film's visual obsessions and excesses—its repeated imaging of "victim eyes under attack"—reveal a frenzied attempt to stave off the traces and effects of the postmodern crisis of visual culture. But the power of cultural doubts about vision is revealed in the forcefulness of the films' protests against them. Thus, the slasher film can be said to play out the crisis of the specular at the heart of postmodern culture; these films take up questions about the sustainability and verifiability of the visual "truths" captured by the genre's medium.

Given current critical and theoretical work on the "denigration of vision" in postmodern culture, the worries about visual epistemologies and ontologies that slasher films play out would seem well founded. Indeed, Martin Jay's study of the increasingly critical construction of vision and visuality within contemporary theory, *Downcast Eyes: The Denigration of Vision in Twentieth-Century French Thought,* traces the waning power of this sense within cultural epistemologies and politics.[7] Perhaps ironically, vision's denigration within postmodern theoretical paradigms of knowledge and social experience have erupted at a time when visual artifacts and stimuli are ubiquitous in popular culture. But even popular culture seems to privilege a vision filled with—or expressive of—uncertainty, one that disallows a masterful vantage point. Consider recent pop-cultural fads, such as the "blur" font, the out of focus advertising photograph, and the destabilized and uncentered camera of television programs such as *NYPD Blue*. Each symptomatically corroborates the notion that vision in postmodernity is not considered a transcendental, clarity- and knowledge-producing sense.

Similarly, in the slasher genre, the cultural implications of its narrative's visual duress are corroborated on the formal level, where the slasher film's reflexivity—its citation and inclusion of other horror films, its formulaic and repetitive narrative structure, its obsession with spectacle for spectacle's sake (to the exclusion of realism and the detriment of plot)—reveals the genre's predication upon a lack of authenticity or effectiveness of visual forms and experiences. The recent blockbuster slasher *Scream* (Wes Craven, 1997) exemplifies the insularity of the genre's pastiche in its reliance upon the viewer's sense of mastery of the form in order to entertain. Rather than referring out, the genre refers in, and rewards its viewers for doing so. *Scream* goes a step further to reward its characters for their knowledge of slasher conventions. In the opening scene, Drew Barrymore receives a threatening phone call while home alone one night, and she must answer the menacing caller's slasher trivia question correctly or be slashed herself. The slasher film's scenarios and images repeat themselves in a seemingly endless circuit of visual exchange and self-legitimation. This "crisis" plays and replays itself within the structures of the slasher text (both across the genre and within the individual generic narratives, as I will show), in a manner similar to Fredric Jameson's prescription for a postmodernist "metatext," which

> reshuffles the fragments of preexistent texts, the building blocks of older cultural and social production, in some new and heightened bricolage: metabooks which cannibalize other books, metatexts which collate bits of other texts.[8]

"Cannibalize" is a cogent term for the ways that slasher films' reflexivity operates, capturing how material bodies (especially the eyes) are violently subsumed, in the postmodern text, to a logic of visual exchange, repetition, and representation. Indeed, in *Peeping Tom* and *Proof* this endless simulational exchange of image for image is represented within the narratives as horrifying in itself. Only in appreciating the relevance and presence of contact within the representational practices that mediate human experience—moreover, in recognizing that copy must be balanced with contact—is there an end to the horror these films depict.

However, in moving from the smooth surfaces of simulation to the slasher's "sticky web of contact *and* copy," there is a price to pay. The embodied vision of the slasher film, which allows for the "bodily involvement of the perceiver in the image," comprises a bodily duress. Eyes are gouged and torsos are gored. And this is why Taussig's fingerprint is so appropriate: the physically contingent nature of the slasher's mimetic vision is both represented by and gives rise to a frightening, abject tactility. As Clover observes, the slasher's weapons of choice are "extensions of the body": "[k]nives, hammers, axes, ice picks, hypodermic needles, red hot pokers, [and] pitchforks," all of which "suggest that closeness and tactility are . . . at issue."[9] While touch may be the "issue" between the slasher and his victims, the tactile nature of the relationship between spectator and film seems less evident. Relying upon tactile fictions for its violent effects of mimetic contact, the slasher film puts into question the visual nature of its "spectacle," as well as its organization of visual crisis as visual pleasure.

Alfred Hitchcock provocatively outlines the potential for images of tactile violence to cause a sensational rupture of the film medium in his anecdote concerning the famous shower scene in *Psycho*. In the margins of the shooting script for this slashing scene, Hitchcock writes: "The slashing. An impression of a knife slashing, as if tearing at the very screen, ripping the film."[10] This slash, an icon of material violence, represents the violence of film and vision as well as a violence against film and vision. The corollary effect of Hitchcock's margin-note image—indeed of the shower scene itself—is a physical shock in the spectator, and this is what Hitchcock is getting at in his description. Paradoxically, however, the fantasized image of a knife ripping the film imaginatively deconstructs its own mode of address by destroying the film screen. The distance between the film's spectators and its represented subjects is imaginatively collapsed through a violent, tactile address. Touch, tactility, and material destruction are the discourses of realism and film effect here, not vision. Furthermore, physiological vision falls prey to this effect: *Psycho*'s shower scene appropriately ends with a shot of Marion Crane's dead, sightless eye. Both embodied vision and the visual medium of film are vulnerable to this "finishing touch."[11]

Placed in the broader context of theoretical discussions of film as a representational mode of copy and/or contact, it becomes clear that the slasher's "finishing touch" moves beyond hurting the vision of the film's characters to "hurt" (put into crisis) the film medium itself, as well as "hurt" the cultural privileging of vision and visual texts. Several film and perception theorists have constructed a similar relationship between visual and tactile epistemologies, representations, and effects in the context of the film medium. In particular, three film theorists illuminate the embodied orchestration of touch and vision in slasher narratives.[12] Walter Benjamin, Steven Shaviro, and Mary Ann Doane have explored the physical effects of the cinematic image on the spectator, and the myths surrounding that relationship, through metaphors of tactility. In each case, cinema's material, tactile mode of address is construed in terms of violence.

In his essay "The Work of Art in the Age of Mechanical Reproduction," Benjamin claims a "physical shock effect" for film, "the distracting element of which is . . . primarily tactile."[13] The agitation thus produced is related to film editing, which marks a discontinuity of realistic effects. Film's rapid progression of images—each frame a different image, as well as the juxtaposition of different objects and scenes via editing—collapses the distance between subject and object that is necessary for reflection. In a sense, viewers lose their freedom in the face of film and are forced to follow its unfolding images without the time or space in which to contemplate them and put them into perspective.[14] Tactile perception, Benjamin explains, is achieved "not so much by attention as by habit"; this habituation corresponds to film reception, which is "reception in a state of distraction," and which "requires no attention." Articulating Benjamin's relevance for the slasher genre, Baudrillard remarks in *Simulations* that "Benjamin compares the work of the cameraman to that of the surgeon: tactility and manipulation."[15] The slasher narrative is concerned with manually opening up the body to view; analogously, Benjamin's film pierces the flesh of reality. Form and content are propitiously linked, as in Hitchcock's shower scene, of which the suspense-artist explained: "Naturally, the knife never touched the body; it was all done in the montage."[16]

Steven Shaviro expands upon Benjamin's themes in his study of the abject bodies of pornographic and horror films, *The Cinematic Body.* Shaviro celebrates the subversive effects of film's ability to agitate the spectator physically through its "tactile image."[17] He argues against semiotic and psychoanalytic film theories that repress cinema's palpable materiality in their stress upon film's representational qualities and in their attendant preoccupation with the image's "lack." Instead, Shaviro claims a violent materiality of cinematic effect. The cinematic body is one pushed to its corporeal limits by "tactile" phenomena. In using tactile discourses to describe what is "excessive" and "ambivalent" about cinematic effects, Shaviro's work outlines the tactile as challenging not only to traditional, pre-industrial notions of vision as the controlling, omniscient sense, but also to the postmodern conceptualization of simulated spectacle as unassailable due to its immaterial ubiquity. Notably, discourses of vision must be replaced by those of tactility in order to convey this idea. The outcome of this search for language adequate to the physiological effects of the image upon the spectator is symbolically indicative of the threat that the sense of touch poses to vision in the slasher film.

Mary Ann Doane approaches this issue symptomatically in her work on early cinema's anxious disavowal of the perceived ability of the image to physically "hurt" the spectator.[18] An omniscient camera point of view and the obsessive over-embodiment of the female form within film spectacle (Doane's specific example is a Busby Berkeley musical, *Gold Diggers of 1935*) sutured early film's ideal male spectators into the subject position of a disembodied eye. Doane argues that this counteracted, by effectively repressing, anxieties related to the negative effects of modern industrial technology upon the male body and mind. To have an embodied (camera) eye would be to inhabit a vulnerable or disempowered subject position. Here we begin to see the revolutionary possibilities of recognizing vision as always already embodied and therefore "hurtable."

A myth of early spectatorship that Doane recounts evokes the vulnerability of the film medium and the eyeball to a tactile mode of perception.[19] At one of the first public film showings in France, a female spectator refused to believe in the illusion of the film image. To test her hypothesis, she poked her fingers at the screen, convinced that there must be "holes in the screen for the eyes of the girl standing behind it."[20] According to Doane, this spectator felt "there must be a real body there somewhere." But there is not—at least not in the sense that this particular viewer expected. This parable of spectatorship constructs touch as a sense that ambiguously reveals the film image's immaterial, illusory nature at the same time that it reveals the fallibility of the human organs of vision. Tellingly, had this early French film spectator found what she reached for with her fingers, she would perhaps have poked the girl behind the screen in the eye.

Through their revelation of the precariously embodied nature of vision within the ephemeral productions of visual media, such stories and theories of touch outline the potential for a haptic critique of the cultural privileging of vision. The conceptualization of film and photographic images as mere visual simulations is precisely that which Shaviro's tactile discourses seek to revise. However, visual simulation remains a preoccupation within slasher films, if only for how its imagistic mode can be juxtaposed against an embodied, "hurtable vision" that is represented as such through the orchestration of a violent touch.

Taken to its extreme, horror's "hurtable vision" becomes a lack of vision: blindness. Blind characters—present in *Peeping Tom* and *Proof,* as well as in *Wait Until Dark* (Terence Young, 1967), *See No Evil* (Richard Fleischer, 1971), *Manhunter* (Michael Mann, 1986), *Afraid of the Dark* (Mark Peploe, 1992), *Jennifer 8* (Bruce Robinson, 1992), and *Blink* (Michael Apted, 1993), among other slasher films—provide physical evidence of film's attempts to appropriate a tactile language or sensation for visual modes. Lacking the reflective visual sense, the blind are overwhelmingly embodied. In this, they play a paradoxical role. While their blindness intervenes in the visual structure of horror, they heighten the slasher's established formula of visual suspense and voyeurism through pitting a morally "good" but completely vulnerable underdog against a morally "bad" voyeuristic predator. As underdogs, their narrative function is akin to that of the melodrama's innocent blind victim, deployed to play on the spectators' emotions. A similar effect is achieved in the slasher genre by capitalizing on cultural discourses encouraging sympathy and concern for the vulnerable disabled.

Contributing to a heightened abjection of the blind victim is the fact that tactile perception, unlike vision, is reciprocal; each tactile experience involves both an active and a passive perceptive function. When a blind character—or anyone—touches something in order to perceive it, he or she is also touched back by the object. In the bulk of slasher films, the receptive function of touch predominates. Blind characters are deployed for their capacity to be shocked masochistically by an unexpected touch. John Hull, who became blind in adulthood, relates in his autobiography that this potential for shock is a fact of life for blind people. There is nothing to mediate between sounds and physical contact when one is blind. Therefore, such contact "becomes all the more startling. A handshake or an embrace becomes a shock because the body comes out of nowhere into sudden reality."[21] Slasher films exploit the vulnerabilities of sightlessness. In normally private spaces, the blind can be easily surprised by a would-be killer or a Peeping Tom. Confronted by an attacker, they can find it nearly impossible and certainly dangerous to attempt escape. Face-to-face with a killer, the blind nevertheless have little or no means of later identifying the attacker on their own.

As much as the slasher genre—along with theorists Benjamin, Shaviro, and Doane—may wish to appropriate a material effect for film's visual modes, slasher film narratives continue to rely upon the spectator's understanding of a difference between looking and touching. Slasher films characteristically pit a psycho-sexually dysfunctional male slasher against a series of sexually active female victims. The slasher stalks his victims, watching them from a safe distance before moving in to kill them. This cycle of stalking and killing ends when the character confronts a would-be victim who manages to turn the tables on him. Clover has coined the term "Final Girl" to designate this recurring victim-hero figure. Androgynous and uninterested in sex, in comparison to her (dead) stereotypically feminine and sexually active counterparts, the Final Girl manages to end the slasher's murderous cycle by killing him, maiming him, or fending him off until she is rescued. The most provocative Final Girl figures take on some of the slasher's characteristics in order to survive. For example, Laurie (Jamie Lee Curtis) in John Carpenter's *Halloween* (1978), finally manages to escape the film's slasher by, among other things, gouging him in the eye with a wire coat hanger. Laurie's act allegorizes the issues of vision and touch at the heart of the genre. The Final Girl appropriates the slasher's violent tactility and uses it against his eye in order to fight back. The climactic scene between slasher and near-victim represents a struggle between tactile and visual modes as much as it represents a struggle between differently gendered subjects.

The tactile violence of the slasher character foregrounds the materiality of the physical body as well as that body's vulnerability to any number of pointed objects. Slashers do not take cover when they kill. Instead of looking through the sights of a gun, they look for the sight of their victim's fear. Typically, the slasher punishes his female victim for her sexual activity (or for her sexuality pure and simple) ironically and fetishistically, with a tool that makes the murder amount to a physically violent approximation of the sex act. Brian De Palma's *Body Double* (1984) uses explicitly phallic imagery in its choreography of a murder scene in which the killer straddles and impales a prone woman with a giant power-drill. In *Psycho,* the weapon is a large kitchen knife. Tobe Hooper's *The Texas Chain Saw Massacre* and *The Texas Chain Saw Massacre, Part 2* (1974 and 1986 respectively) are true to their titles, and *Peeping Tom* portrays murder by bayonet. The tactile proximity of slasher and victim is fashioned as a so-called climax. Touch is more erotic, terrifying, and disgusting than are the visual stalking and voyeurism which begin the slasher character's view-then-kill strategy of menace. Physically distanced voyeurism escalates to a climax of physically proximate, material violence. True to simulacral form, looking alone has no material density. Relying upon its spectators' visceral understanding of a physical and emotional difference between looking and touching, the slasher genre's dramatic shift from distanced, voyeuristic watching to bloody hand-to-hand combat is a crucial component of its particular pleasure. Moreover, the maintenance of this distinction is what lends the slasher genre its iconoclastic force. This distinction is necessary to an understanding of the political differences between the simulacral (which represses tactility) and the mimetic (which involves a play between the tactile contact and visual copy).

Furthermore, the usual discrepancy of power between the slasher and victim is even more unbalanced when the victim is blind. This inequality invests the climactic shift of power from slasher to Final Girl with even more perverse appeal, for, as a matter of course, the blind character is less a subject than an object of visual perception. Still, no matter how embedded it may be in the slasher genre's obsession with abjection, the blind character's objectified shockability exists in tandem with her capacity for tactile subjectivity. The blind touch poses a powerful alternative to the visual simulation that saturates and defines the representational and ideological predicament of postmodernity. In *Peeping Tom* and *Proof,* the blind characters themselves are mysterious embodiments of a mimetic "contact" with truth, a contact that has been lost to the demands of simulation, and that might be regained through a masochistic reconceptualization of vision in all it shortcomings. These blind characters do not represent a *meta*physical trope of blindness as insight, but rather a trope of the "aura," of the materiality of "truth," of the "bodily involvement of the perceiver of the image," and of human relationships unmediated by the shifting proliferation of the commodi- fied image.

An insightful and disturbing slasher prototype, *Peeping Tom* ex- plores the scopophilia and violence inherent in cinematic representation and spectatorship, revealing in the process the slasher genre's broader relevance for the study of postmodern film. Set in early 1960s London, *Peeping Tom* self-reflexively explores the common goals and effects of popular narrative film, pornographic photography, and the explicitly violent slasher film. The film's title character, Mark Lewis (Carl Boehm), is a homicidal Peeping Tom with a day job as a focus puller for a film studio. He moonlights as a pornographic photographer. In his time off, Mark makes real-time films of his own murders, which he commits specifically for the sake of filming them. The particular structure of Mark's murders and his films of them is analogous to that of the slasher genre. His object is to capture a look of utmost terror on the faces of his victims; he achieves this by holding up to them a distorting mirror as they are being stabbed in the throat by a knife attached to one of the tripod legs of his camera. He then completes his project by watching his films, compounding his sadistic filming with a masochistic viewing experience.

The source of Mark's pathological behavior is revealed through old home movies he screens for his wide-eyed downstairs neighbor, Helen

(Anna Massey). Among the family scenes Helen sees is a selection showing Mark as a little boy, sleeping peacefully in bed. A puzzling light flickers over his face, and then he is frightened awake by a lizard thrown onto his bed from off screen. The light, he explains, was reflected from a mirror which his father, a psychologist researching fear, held up to Mark as he filmed his experiments upon his little boy. In an effort to reverse the trauma of these childhood experiments by taking up the powerful position of filmmaker, Mark desires to have the fearful gaze of his childhood reproduced perfectly in his filmed victims. This he attempts to achieve with his own version of his father's mirror—a distorting, concave mirror.[22] Mark's filming strikes to the heart of what is mimetic about film and photography, as Taussig paraphrases Benjamin:

> To get hold of something by means of its likeness. Here is what is crucial in the resurgence of the mimetic faculty, namely the two-layered notion of mimesis that is involved—on the one hand a copying or imitation and, on the other, a palpable, sensuous, connection between the very body of the perceiver and the perceived.[23]

However, Mark's project—to divest himself of the psychological trauma of his childhood by recreating that contact perfectly through mimesis— is an impossible one. Something always fails him, so that in the end the only way to ensure his success is to take the position of the victim himself. Finally, he does just that, staging his own death before a barrage of auto-triggered camera-flashes. But this changes the rules of his game, exchanging realism for mimesis' cathartic, delicate balance of contact and copy; it is more an admission of failure than it is a sublime achievement through self-sacrifice.

The thrill of the slasher genre lies in not only, in Shaviro's words, "an irrecuperable excess, produced when violated bodies are pushed to their limits";[24] this thrill is clearly elaborated in Mark's suicide as well as in the masochism inherent in his knowledge that he will never be spectator to the perfection of his craft (his film of his own death). The genre also titillates by pushing the film *medium* to its ontological limits. Mark is unable to capture the image he wants due to technical problems (lighting), and the final tragedy for Mark is that the film medium does not permit one to be its viewer and object of view simultaneously (unlike a tactile medium). Furthermore, the immaterial film medium is an inappropriate and impotent substitute for Mark's real "lack"—a loving father.

Peeping Tom embodies these crises of body and medium in a blind character whose lack of vision and compensatory touch unhinge Mark's "cinema." Mrs. Stephens (Maxine Audley), Helen's blind mother, enters into this unfolding narrative of a failed visual project as if to seal Mark's doom.[25] In a pivotal scene, she surprises Mark in his viewing room and interrogates him about the nature of his silent films. "Something tells me all this viewing is not right," she remarks, in the role of a stereotypical blind prophet or "seer."[26] "Take me to your cinema," she commands him, and he complies by leading her toward the screen on which the film of his latest murder is being projected. In an intriguing shot, Mark stands between Mrs. Stephens and the screen so that the image of his victim is projected onto his back. Mrs. Stephens then reaches out her hand toward the image in a gesture of perception. "What am I seeing, Mark?" she asks, but she receives no answer because Mark's full attention is directed at his film. However, the lights fade too soon in the "home movie"; Mark has failed again to capture the image he wants. Frustrated, he tries to turn his camera and tripod-leg on Mrs. Stephens. Trapped in front of and framed by Mark's film screen, Mrs. Stephens is a vulnerable object for Mark's sadistic cinematic "gaze." Her blindness stops him short of killing her, however. She cannot see into the distorting mirror and thus cannot produce the look of abject horror Mark craves. Her blindness alone is enough to save her from Mark's cinematic apparatus, passively disabling the exchange of looks central to his—and the slasher genre's—cinema of horrors. This scene is a parable for how a blind character undermines the entire itinerary of visual pleasure in the slasher film. Both Mark's sadistic filming gaze and his masochistic viewing pleasure are thwarted by the interruption posed by this blind woman.

A panoply of visual forms and conventions are made problematic by the active intervention of the blind character in narratives like that of *Peeping Tom:* the voyeurism represented within filmic narratives and inherent in the film-viewing situation; the formal organization of visual excess and withholding that effects suspense; the epistemology and ontology of film representation; and the general institution of spectatorship. Representations of blindness traditionally serve to deconstruct visual paradigms of knowledge, power, and identity, which sighted people might take for granted. However, Mrs. Stephens does more than just deconstruct Mark's cinema. Residing in the film as more than a symbol of visual "lack," Mrs. Stephens launches an intervention that carries more consequence than would a mere passive inability to see; rather, her compensating touch actively counters Mark's potential violence. This cause-and-effect structure is made clear at the end of the viewing room sequence. There is a moment in this scene when Mrs. Stephens is extremely vulnerable, objectified by Mark and unable to perceive or intuit his actions. She lifts up her hands to shield herself. But Mark puts

The violence of vision: Mark and Helen in *Peeping Tom* (Anglo-Amalgamated, 1959).

the sheath back on his knife and returns Mrs. Stephens's prosthetic cane. In this scene, matched shot compositions and shot/reverse shot editing directly compare the sharp metal tip of this cane with Mark's knife blade, establishing the similarity of these "weapons" while suggesting that Mark's "finishing touch" has met its real match in Mrs. Stephens's active tactile mode of perception. Almost inadvertently, she takes on some of the slasher's qualities—like Laurie in *Halloween*—revealing the potential of her tactile ability to produce subjectivity through its own violent quality.

Reminiscent of Doane's early French film spectator and of Hitchcock's *Psycho* anecdote, Mrs. Stephens reaches her hand toward the horrible images on Mark's screen, and commands him to "take me to your cinema," as she commands that cinema's demise. Choreography makes tactile and visual ideologies distinct after this viewing room scene, when Mrs. Stephens takes what amounts to a "finger photograph" of Mark's

287

face. After her visit, Mrs. Stephens has Mark help her down the stairs. Demanding of Mark what it is that troubles him, she reaches out to his face with both hands. "Taking my picture?" Mark asks. He then explains that his father was the last person to take his photograph. Here, Mark's father's and his own violently obsessive film photography are placed in direct contrast with Mrs. Stephens's motherly blind touch. Her touch is idealized as a therapeutic, socially nurturing substitute for Mark's brand of photography; this tactile mode approaches the sensuous humanness of mimetic contact in a way that Mark's father's photography did not. Suggesting the recuperative powers of tactility outside of its construction as violent within Mark's bankrupt, visual simulations, the blind touch comprises a mimetic involvement.

It follows, then, that Mrs. Stephens personifies the genre's treatment of the blind touch not only as interruptive of visual discourses per se, but also as a palliative alternative to the slasher's finishing touch. *Peeping Tom* makes a formal connection between Mark's visual compulsions—his Peeping Tom status, his jobs as focus puller and pornographic photographer, as well as the filming that captures his illicit views—and his violent tactile behavior. The architecture of his killing and filming apparatus suggests that the tactile violence he effects is an outgrowth of the structure and visual goals of his cinematic project. The tripod leg of his camera, which literally and figuratively supports his cinema, conceals his knife. This knife's purpose is to help Mark obtain the cinematic image he desires. Once this connection between obsessive vision and destructive touching is made, Mrs. Stephens's touch serves to critique not only Mark's touch, but also, and more important, the visual obsessions that his touch serves. This envisionment of a blind tactility stands between Mark and his realization of the perfect slasher film, interrupting and critiquing the genre's fluid progression from visual objectification to a violent touch, a progression that is represented in Mark's filming and that is crucial to the slasher's generic formula as I have outlined it.

A story is evolving in this sequence of scenes: the visionlessness at the end of *Psycho*'s spectacularly tactile shower scene, the tactile assurance of fallible vision at the center of the French spectator anecdote, and the alternative blind touch of Mrs. Stephens. Each suggests that tactility encodes a threat to components of visual culture—be it the eyeball, the film screen, the cinematic apparatus, or the broader concerns of visual knowledge, subjectivity, and pleasure. The simultaneity of blindness and touching in these scenes reveals an anxiety about the relationship of touch to vision and visual media. Sighted culture's anxieties about the physiological and cultural contingency of hurtable vision are displaced onto, as well as protected by, a violent tactility. Scapegoating the blind touch in this way both reveals and contributes to a sense of terror at the privileging of touch over vision. Tactile powers are pathologized (in the finishing touch) and denigrated (in blind touching scenes) in the interest of securing visuality's pride of perceptual place.

Moorhouse's film *Proof* makes a clear case for film's scapegoating of the blind touch. The film offers an avant-garde critique of the economy of violence and vision in conventional slasher films, and of the established role of touch within that system. The violence of certain sighted characters toward the blind touch is represented explicitly as symptomatic of an insecure visual hegemony. Within *Proof*'s dramatically realistic social and psychological context, viewers are given clear examples of the pressures upon visuality that are suppressed through the scapegoating of touch. Moreover, the film draws upon slasher film conventions (and sets a pivotal scene at a drive-in slasher movie), incorporating that genre's construction of voyeurism and touch to decry the current dearth of critical models incorporating modes of contact into their interpretational frameworks, and, more importantly, to condemn the violent reluctance of postmodern spectators to recognize the mimetic residue available for interpretation within the film image.

Proof's protagonist, Martin (Hugo Weaving), is a congenitally blind man who obsessively photographs objects in an effort to ascertain the truth about them. His obsession is related to a troubled relationship with his mother, who died when Martin was young. Martin thinks his mother lied to him about her impending death. He is also convinced that his mother intentionally misdescribed to him the view outside her bedroom window when he was young, and that she did this to punish him for being blind. We see his childhood interactions with his mother in flashbacks that are reminiscent of the childhood films of Mark in *Peeping Tom.*[27] For both of these men, visual recording in the present is a means of working through their past traumatic experiences of disempowerment in the face of visual media and culture. Indeed, Martin is as much a counterpart to Mark's slasher figure as he is a counterpart to Mrs. Stephens's blind interloper. Martin has a photograph of his childhood backyard, and is searching for a trustworthy person to describe this photograph to him. Through such a description, he hopes to catch his mother in a lie.

Martin would seem to overturn the power dynamics of powerful onlooker and oppressed object in his photography. He engages in a kind of "stalking by photography," the overarching goal of which is to catch his mother in a lie—in other words, to put her in the position of object

289

and himself in the position of power. Attempting to displace onto his mother the feelings of castration he suffers because of his blindness, Martin sadistically interrogates his mother through his photographs, in particular the photograph he once took of the garden outside the window of his childhood home.[28] In *Proof,* power is linked to vision, rather than sexuality, first and foremost. In a flashback, Martin's exasperated mother asks him, "Why would I lie to you?" The young Martin replies, "Because you can." His mother has the power of vision, and he does not. These are the terms of his castration anxiety. But by appropriating the camera, Martin appropriates a position of power vis-à-vis a visual medium and thereby places himself in a position to interrogate his mother and make her confess her "guilt"—namely, that she lied to him as a child. Every time Martin takes a photograph, this larger context of power and powerlessness in relation to vision comes into play.

Martin's maid, Celia (Genevieve Picot), reverses the traditional gender roles in the relationship between gazing subject and gazed-upon object by also engaging in sadistic voyeurism. In the first shot of her in the film, she gazes at Martin as he, unaware of her presence, begins to undress after returning home in the rain. Later, Celia offers to describe Martin's photographs to him, but he refuses her and instead picks a local sous-chef, Andy (Russell Crowe), to be his "translator." Celia becomes jealous of the trust Martin places in Andy, whom she has not met. When she discovers among Martin's photographs a series of images of a man—snapshots of, for example, a blurry, open hand that takes up the whole frame; of the side of a man's face; and so on—she decides to do some truth seeking of her own. On a large table, she pieces the images together to form a cubist-style collage representing Andy. Celia disregards the nonindexical qualities of these images in order to arrive at a conception in her mind's eye of the reality behind them.

There is something sinister in her act. Not only is she looking at Martin's photographs when he has told her not to, but her tactile manipulation and use of the photographs run counter to their purpose. To sighted eyes, the images are more expressionistic than realistic; they represent Martin's emotionally close, non-visual relationship with Andy. In a sense, their origins in a blind man's camera lend them a true mimetic quality, imaging forth the copy that traces the contact between Martin and Andy. Celia's appropriation of the images into ideologies of sighted power and visual "realism" is diametrically opposed to Martin's photographic intentions (perhaps ironically, since Martin's interest in photography is in its visual realism). Furthermore, the motivation behind her interpretation is vindictive. Once she knows who Andy is, she begins a strategy of seduction designed to steal Andy away from Martin. Oddly, this scene represents another tactile intervention into the realm of visual, photographic representation: collage. The photographs portray Celia's first victim, a fragmented body which she can manually manipulate to her own ends. Hers, like that of *Peeping Tom*'s Mark, is a violent "touch," serving the ends of a misguided visual project.

Later we discover that Celia has been stalking Martin with her own camera. Her obsessive photographing of Martin might follow the logic that having a photo of something means you own a piece of it. More in keeping with the sadomasochistic dynamics of power in their interdependent relationship, however, Celia enjoys the power over Martin that accrues in her visual objectification and manipulation of his image. As Martin tells her, he always feels as though someone is watching him, and Celia takes advantage of that inequality between them.

Proof offers a slasher scenario in which the prevailing division of power resides in the realm of sight ability rather than of gender. Martin is the Final Girl, a figure whose gender ambiguity is here moved into the realm of vision ambiguity. The degree of power that vision gives to Celia is represented when her obsessive photographing of Martin culminates in what is interpretable as a date rape scene. This scene in Celia's apartment conveys the violent, sexual nature of Celia's touch. Until now, her thwarted desire to touch Martin has been displaced onto her surreptitious photography, which covers the walls and end tables of her living room. The spectators can see these photos, and because of this fact they are aligned, albeit uncomfortably, with Celia. Sitting on Celia's couch, Martin is surrounded by these images, and the distinction between the visual reproduction of his body and his real, physically vulnerable body is made clear. Following an escalation from vision to touch characteristic of the slasher's behavior, Celia's stalking progresses from photography to touch in the sequence that follows.

Celia has already transgressed social propriety with her inappropriate touch. Earlier in the film, Celia has a new blouse, and she purposefully moves Martin's hand onto her breast, asking, "Have you ever felt silk? It's softer than skin." Martin rebuffs her in that scene. He is not in control of the situation in her apartment, however, having been bribed into this "date" by Celia's threat to display publicly a photograph of him using the toilet. This time, she asks Martin if he has ever touched a woman. Broaching the distance between her body and his once again, she unbuttons her shirt and brushes her bare breast against his mouth. She then unzips his pants and begins to stimulate him manually. In a jarring sequence of shots that visually expresses the violence of this scene, the camera cranes back and upward to a high-angle long-shot of the two on the couch. It then moves forward and cuts to a medium-shot. The camera then continues to move forward to a tightly framed close-up of Celia over Martin's body on the couch. The camera movement follows a path similar to that used in scenes of the slasher's finishing touch: distanced voyeurism collapses into a proximate shot of tactile violence. This formal visual approximation of physical contact marks Celia's figurative castration of Martin, who manages to stumble out of her apartment and onto the sidewalk below. He is physically vulnerable: caneless (another symbol of castration), and precariously close to the traffic in the street. Recommencing their cycle of sadomasochism, Celia collects him in her car and takes him home.

This sequence plays out in the realm of sexuality, including Celia's abuse of her visual powers, an abuse apparent in her variety of sadistic behaviors, which range from placing objects in Martin's path, to taking advantage of his blindness to photograph him, to restraining his pet dog unobserved. The battle for power between Martin and his mother in the past is reproduced in the present through this sadomasochistic relationship with Celia. Celia's tactile violence and Martin's repression of his own touch are contextualized by a flashback of Martin's childhood. This romantic, golden-lit scene early in *Proof* establishes a utopian blind touch much like that of Mrs. Stephens. It also, however, dramatizes explicitly the cultural denigration of touch according to sighted norms, and it suggests one reason why Martin eschews a tactile epistemology for a visual one later in life. Shot in close-up, Martin's right hand moves along the bedroom wall, down his mother's bedstead, onto her pillow, then down her body, feeling her hair, ear, eyelids, nose, lips, chin, throat, chest, and breasts. His mother (Heather Mitchell) seems to derive some sleepy pleasure from his touch. However, just when the viewers are left to imagine Martin's hand moving towards his mother's stomach, she startles out of her sleep and chastises him: "What are you doing? Martin, I have told you before you can't touch people whenever you want. Fingers, they aren't the same as eyes. It's rude."[29] For Martin's mother, his touching is "rude"—in this instance—because it seems sexual to her. She fails to recognize a blind standard of touch. Inappropriate according to sighted standards of behavior and interpretation, her son's touch straddles unacceptably the boundary between compensatory perception and incest. Meanwhile, Martin's childish touch reifies the conflation of copy and contact inherent to mimesis, making it strange by translating it into a tactile, rather than a visual, discourse.

This strangeness, and the transgression of behavior standards that it comprises, is the very substance of horror. Stephen Prince describes the formula for horror as a "play upon boundary conditions and the ordering and violation of distinctions that give form to the social environment."[30] Prince's model is derived from sociological concepts of taboo such as those explored in Mary Douglas's study *Purity and Danger*.[31] The taboo object or experience generates fear because it is indescribable or unrecognizable; it defies categorization according to culturally established and accepted definitions of things or events:

> Malevolent and anti-social powers . . . emerge from the ill-defined, contradictory lines of the social structure where networks of authority and allegiance are unclear, and the categories which arouse the greatest fear, interest, and sense of mystery are the ambiguous ones. These are the categories which become taboo because they play on the distinction between form and formlessness.[32]

Proof reveals how touch taps into the simultaneously titillating and horrifying qualities of the transgressive taboo. Uncategorizable within traditional discourses of film representation, the blind touch, and the mimetic contact it entails, threatens to subvert dominant visual ideologies of simulation, including postmodern cinematic paradigms of perception, knowledge, and power.[33]

Titillatingly entertaining as such subversion may be for the slasher film audience, it is often met with reactionary violence both on and off screen. The self-reflexivity of a scene in which Andy and Martin attend a slasher film at a drive-in theater makes clear the correspondence between slasher films' representations of a violent, vision-challenging touch and the scapegoating of the blind. As they sit in the car, Martin explains to Andy that "if you analyze your feelings, you really want the killer to get the girl." It would certainly seem that way, because each time the slasher strikes on screen, the motorists gleefully honk their car horns and flash their lights in participatory response. When Andy leaves the car to go to the concession stand, Martin takes the opportunity to feel out his surroundings. As in the flashback to his mother's bedroom, here the camera follows Martin's hands in close-up as he meticulously touches the contents and dimensions of the car interior. He begins with the car seat, then moves his fingers across the dash-board, encountering a plastic dinosaur figurine and a King Kong doll hanging from the rear-view mirror. When he begins to feel around in a compartment on the side of the driver's door, the film cuts to a shot of the driver in the car next door, a young male "tough." He is obviously confused by what he sees.

A reverse-angle shot provides his point of view, and reveals Martin, who is wearing his dark glasses and who seems to stare out menacingly at his neighbors. The ominous soundtrack of the drive-in movie provides apt accompaniment to this image, and it invites a comparison between screen and parking lot, which the rest of the carefully constructed scene elaborates.

When Martin pulls out from the door compartment a long strip of packaged condoms, the oddness of his image is compounded. Unaware of his audience, Martin holds up the condoms and runs his fingers over the package. Next door, the driver and his companions—another young man and a young girl—become outraged. They get out of their car and violently confront Martin, jumping on top of the car and writing "pervert" and "faggot" on the car in lipstick. Martin yells for Andy and honks the car horn for help, but everyone else in the lot happens to be honking his horn at the same time in appreciation of the latest conquest of the slasher on screen. Eventually, Martin and Andy manage to speed away.

Here again, Martin's touch is misread sexually. This time however, Martin's own visual fetishes are recreated in the thugs' behavior. They label his image "faggot" and "pervert" in the same way that he labels his photographs according to Andy's abbreviated descriptions. His own conviction that an image can be easily and categorically interpreted is turned against him in the thugs' similar hermeneutic behavior. Here, however, the objects of interpretation are embodied, making explicit the physical stakes of Martin's photography as well as the points of subjective "contact" inherent to the interpretation of any representational image.

Characters and events in the slasher film on the drive-in screen find real, material counterparts in the drive-in lot. Confronted by the thugs while a teenage girl is strangled and knifed on screen, Martin quickly changes from a would-be slasher counterpart to a would-be slasher victim, just as he does with Celia. Unable to maintain a spectator's, nor a photographer's, position of distance and control, he becomes the object of the thugs' gaze and then of their physical violence in a "view-then-kill" structure of rising action. Martin's ignorance (or denial) of his bodily involvement in the image is quickly and violently addressed as he becomes the "girl." This "girl," or blind man, could be any of us—just as, in Doane's formulation, Busby Berkeley's endless rows of girls' legs carry the fleshy weight of the male spectator's denial of self-embodiment.

The toughs' violence, like Martin's mother's earlier reprimand, is a consequence of their difficulty in understanding and interpreting the complexities of Martin's "touching scene" in the car (as well as of their homophobia). According to the thugs' analysis, Martin is clearly making homosexual advances when he holds up the condoms. This they perceive as a physical threat, and they respond to it in kind. Metaphorically then, the threat represented by the blind touch and the violence it elicits in response are the products of sighted culture's difficulty with grasping the many possible meanings of the image of Martin's touch. The blind touch is translated according to sighted standards that misperceive touch as only either violent or sexual. Furthermore, their misreading represents their reluctance to legitimate the mimetic play of copy and contact. *Proof*'s metafilmic critique of the slasher genre reveals that the touching scenes of the blind cannot avoid being maligned by social standards that interpret touching as a threat to visual ideals and norms. It further reveals how the tactile violence of the genre testifies to an ambivalence about the potentially subversive role of touch in the postmodern society of the spectacle. At the center of this violence lies a repressed truth: just as Martin discovers the truth in his own hands.

Both *Proof* and *Peeping Tom* construct an ideology of the blind touch, a tactile ideal that would collapse the violently dehumanizing distance between the subject and object of visual perception. *Proof*'s final scene depicts Andy touching the hands of Martin's mother as she is represented in an old photograph. Martin then releases the plaguing photograph of his youth to Andy, in a gesture that would exorcise the horror of visual simulation from his life. However, both films also treat the social barriers erected in front of this mode of perception and the people who practice it. Even while Mrs. Stephens's touch seems the socially acceptable counterpart to Mark's destructive cycle of filming and stabbing, Mrs. Stephens herself is depicted as a drunken social outcast. She is isolated and relegated to the margins of society. She is freakish in her deviation from sighted norms, a figure of fascination not unlike her Peeping Tom counterpart, as the following example suggests. During an evening conversation with her daughter, Mrs. Stephens suddenly announces that Mark is at their window. Eerily, she is correct. When her daughter asks how she knew this, Mrs. Stephens answers, "The back of my neck told me . . . the part that I talk out of." This remark betrays Mrs. Stephens's insight into how visual culture projects her blindness back onto her material body as freakishness, or, to use a less glamorous term, as "disability." This imagined figure for the transgression of visible body standards is a grotesque analog to Mrs. Stephens's invisible but shunned cultural difference. The "all-seeing" mouth on the back of the blind woman's neck, which "tells" her what she cannot see, embodies something horrifying for the sighted cinema audience: the denigration of the privileged visual sense that is literally "displaced" by the blind character's powerful, knowledgeable touch. Martin's obsession with photography is equally as "disfiguring." The barriers placed in front of Martin's touch are portrayed to be largely his own, but only in as much as he claims the values of an oppressive visual culture of simulation.

It has not been my intention to state categorically that touch and vision are diametrically opposed modes of perception, nor that they are at complete ideological odds with one another. On the contrary, the slasher genre's effectiveness seems to hinge upon their interplay—made possible only through an understanding of their points of separation. Blind characters distill that distinction for the audience, making explicit the genre's juxtaposition of tactile and visual experiences. These blind characters' "touching scenes" depict a tactile mode of perception outside of the violent "finishing touch" of the slasher. Even more threatening to visuality than the slasher's weapon, touching scenes of the blind analogically reveal the potential critique of visual simulation that resides within the slasher's finishing touch. However, slasher narratives' systematic violence against this tactile mode starkly reveals the genre's investment in simulational visual forms of experience, knowledge, and power, despite the fact that showdowns between the blind touch and the slasher's finishing touch betray the limits of those forms. So, while slasher films revel in the sadomasochistic pleasures of "hurtable vision," the genre's denigration of touch symptomatically points toward a more systemic cultural condition, namely, the continuing repression within visual culture of the revolutionary possibilities of the mimetic play of copy *and* contact.

Notes

1. Michael Taussig, "Physiognomic Aspects of Visual Worlds," *Visualizing Theory: Selected Essays From V.A.R. 1990–1994,* ed. Lucien Taylor (New York: Routledge, 1994), 207.

2. Carol J. Clover, *Men, Women, and Chain Saws: Gender in the Modern Horror Film* (Princeton: Princeton University Press, 1992), 205.

3. See in particular Walter Benjamin's brief essay "On the Mimetic Faculty" (1934), reprinted in *Reflections: Essays, Aphorisms, Autobiographical Writings,* trans. Edmund Jephcott (New York: Schocken Books, 1986), and Jean Baudrillard's *Simulations,* trans. Paul Foss, Paul Patton, and Philip Beitchman (New York: Semiotext[e], 1983).

4. Jean-Louis Comolli, "Machines of the Visible," *The Cinematic Image,* ed. Teresa de Lauretis and Stephen Heath (New York: St. Martin's Press, 1980); Guy Debord, *Society of the Spectacle* (Detroit: Black and Red, 1983).

5. Note that in this essay I am not concerned with the distinctions between the "low-horror" slasher form and its "middle-" or sometimes "high-brow" counterpart, the mystery or psychothriller. Much could be made of how these particular formulas differently exploit the visual field, including their varying investments in realistic visual effects and different deployments of suspense and cathartic visual climaxes. However, the crucial similarities between each horror genre subset, and among the specific films I will explore here, are what interest me: the villain is a human being (not a monster); there is a series of murders rather than a singular killing; the blind character is a potential victim but does not die—is, essentially, a Final Girl (see Carol Clover); and the threatened violence is of a tactile nature, as I will explore.

6. I am indebted for this concept to Vivian Sobchack, who writes, in the phenomenological tradition of Maurice Merleau-Ponty, that "it is the flesh through which vision is accomplished. . . . This flesh is of the world as well as in it, sharing in the world's materiality and thickness. It is a flesh that occupies space and is occupied by it as time—a flesh that is finite and thus experiences finitude, that is durable and thus experiences duration, that is malleable and thus experiences form and change and motion. This is *vision embodied*—a material activity that not only sees but can be seen, that makes vision itself visible." See Sobchack, *The Address of the Eye: A Phenomenology of Film Experience* (Princeton: Princeton University Press, 1992), 93.

7. Martin Jay, *Downcast Eyes: The Denigration of Vision in Twentieth-Century French Thought* (Berkeley: University of California Press, 1994).

8. Fredric Jameson, "Reading without Interpretation: Postmodernism and the Video-Text," in *The Linguistics of Writing: Arguments between Language and Literature,* ed. Derek Attridge, Alan Durant, Nigel Fabb, and Colin McCabe (Manchester: Manchester University Press, 1987), 222.

9. Clover, *Men, Women and Chain Saws,* 31–32.

10. Hitchcock as quoted in ibid., 199.

11. These violations of vision converge around a scene that also violates traditional plot structures of Hollywood narrative film of the period. *Psycho* is unconventional in killing off its protagonist early in the narrative.

12. These works fit into a larger field of study on perception and subjectivity in Western thought, which spans a variety of disciplines and philosophical movements, and which I do not have space to examine here. Other thinkers who have theorized a relationship between tactile and visual modes of perception include Maurice Merleau-Ponty, Emmanuel Levinas, Jean Baudrillard, and Jacques Derrida.

13. Walter Benjamin, "The Work of Art in the Age of Mechanical Reproduction," *Illuminations,* ed. Hannah Arendt, trans. Harry Zohn (New York: Schocken Books, 1969), 217–51. See especially Benjamin's discussion of film spectator response and of the receptive mode of distraction on pages 238–41.

14. Later in the essay, a distinction between tactile and visual modes is stressed in Benjamin's discussion of the two ways in which humans interact with architecture: "by use and by perception—or rather, by touch and sight." Benjamin, *Illuminations,* 240.

15. Baudrillard, *Simulations,* 119.

16. Alfred Hitchcock in an interview with François Truffaut, in Truffaut, *Hitchcock,* rev. ed. (New York: Simon and Schuster, 1985), 277.

17. Steven Shaviro, "Film Theory and Visual Fascination," *The Cinematic Body* (Minneapolis: University of Minnesota Press, 1993), 1–65.

18. Mary Ann Doane, "Technology's Body: Cinematic Vision in Modernity," *differences: A Journal of Feminist Cultural Studies* 5.2 (1993): 1–21.

19. Ibid., 1.

20. Ibid.

21. John M. Hull, *Touching the Rock: An Experience of Blindness* (New York: Pantheon, 1990), 56.

22. Something similar occurs in *Manhunter,* in which the killer uses a mirror shard to kill his victims. The reflective shard satisfies the killer's desire to see the supplication of his victims reflected up at him as they die. Other more recent films have reprised the essence of Mark's cinema, namely, that the most fearful sight is the image of one's own murder. See, for example, *The City of Lost Children* (Jean-Pierre Jeunet and Marc Caro, 1995) and *Strange Days* (Kathryn Bigelow, 1995).

23. Taussig, "Physiognomic Aspects of Visual Worlds," 206.

24. Shaviro, "Film Theory and Visual Fascination," 61.

25. In this, Mrs. Stephens is reminiscent of the blind street vendor in Fritz Lang's *M* (1931). This character aids in capturing the film's psychopathic child murderer (Peter Lorre) by identifying his characteristic whistle.

26. For more on film's "blind seer" trope, see Martin Norden, *The Cinema of Isolation: A History of Physical Disability in the Movies* (New Brunswick, N.J.: Rutgers University Press, 1994).

27. There are similarly constructed childhood scenes in Martin's flashbacks and Mark's films; for example, Mark approaching his mother on her deathbed, and Martin knocking on his mother's coffin; and Mark being frightened by the lizard in his bed, and Martin being chastised by his mother in her bed.

28. Martin's relationship with his mother falls almost precisely into the patriarchal structure of sadistic voyeurism mapped out by Laura Mulvey. The image of the female causes castration anxiety, a threat the man can defuse by "investigating the woman, demystifying her mystery." The pleasure of attaining the woman's confession "lies in ascertaining guilt (immediately associated with castration), asserting control and subjugating the guilty person through punishment or forgiveness." Mulvey's scenario revolves around the power discrepancy between the active looker and the passive object of the gaze. Martin has felt a victim of this discrepancy of power throughout his childhood. Laura Mulvey, "Visual Pleasure in Narrative Cinema," *Visual and Other Pleasures* (Bloomington: Indiana University Press, 1989), 21–22.

29. Martin's mother's chastising comment is reminiscent of a line from Michelangelo Antonioni's film *Blowup* (1966). The film's plot revolves around a photographer stumbling ignorantly upon a murder in progress. The photographer takes photographs of this scene: an older man and a young woman retreating into a secluded section of a park for what seems to be a romantic tryst. Aware of his need to be unobtrusive, the photographer mindlessly shoots a series of photographs. Meanwhile, another man hidden in the thick trees surrounding the park shoots and

kills the older man. His action is invisible to the photographer. The woman, who has calculatingly lured her "lover" to his death, sees the photographer at work and runs to stop him and retrieve the incriminating film. She pleads with him, appealing to his sense of propriety: "What are you doing? You can't just photograph people like that." She might have continued, along the lines of Martin's mother, by claiming that photographs are not the same as looking (a lesson which Martin would do well to heed). Even on the developed photographs the murder is invisible to the photographer's ignorant eye. However, after he becomes suspicious, blow-up techniques finally allow the photographer to "see" the shadow of a man with a gun as well as the shadow of the corpse. More than these similar remarks suggests Moorhouse's citation of *Blowup*. The public park in which Martin takes his photographs is similar to that in which *Blowup*'s photographer finds and photographs his "lovers." Each film carries the messages that photographs contain more than meets the naked eye, and that the truth is not always visible.

30. Stephen Prince, "Dread, Taboo, and The Thing: Toward a Social Theory of the Horror Film," *Wide Angle* 10.3 (1988): 28.

31. Mary Douglas, *Purity and Danger: An Analysis of the Concepts of Pollution and Taboo* (New York: Routledge, 1984).

32. Prince, "Dread, Taboo, and The Thing," 23.

33. Joseph Grigely's response to a photography and mixed media installation by French artist Sophie Calle, titled "The Blind," discusses in detail the problems involved in categorizing the blind touch. See Joseph Grigely, "Postcards to Sophie Calle from Joseph Grigely," *Parkett* 36 (1993): 89.

12

THE TECHNOLOGY OF HOMICIDE: CONSTRUCTIONS OF EVIDENCE AND TRUTH IN THE AMERICAN MURDER FILM

KEN MORRISON

INTRODUCTION

In the last several decades Hollywood cinema has displayed a range of images that transgress important social boundaries between the natural body and the cinematic body, between cinematic death and the idea of death suggested in reality. Matter-of-fact presentations of mutilated bodies, severed limbs, exploding heads, scenes of annihilation and graphic wounding are of such frequency as to promote the universal fear of violent death or death by annihilation.[1] My argument in this essay is twofold. First, I put forward the proposal that there has been a shift in attitudes toward the body in Hollywood cinema and that this shift is evident in patterns of destruction, wound style, and homicide technique. Second, by comparing homicide techniques in Hollywood films about murder, I will show how bodily zones and wound style have changed from the closed, concealed, and even invisible wounds of films such as *Psycho* to a mortality pose associated with cadaverous death, a contemporary configuration in which the living body and the dead body are presented simultaneously. My purpose in this discussion is to isolate the shifts in boundaries and conventions of the last three decades and to raise the level of debate from a focus on violence and its influences to a focus on Western attitudes toward the body. Because the body is a field of institutional action and a framework of social and political practices, it gives us important clues about social ideas and cultural attitudes related to boundaries and boundary crossings. Here, I ask two questions: Do the somatic techniques and practices used in American murder films constitute a "turning point in the history of the body in the West";[2] and, alternatively, what kind of trajectory do we envisage for the representation of violence in postmodern media?

After a brief discussion to establish historical linkage between the body, the technology of homicide, and the rise of murder writing as a genre, I have chosen two Hollywood murder films for analysis and review: Alfred Hitchcock's *Psycho* (1960) and Oliver Stone's *JFK* (1991).

THE BODY AND SOCIAL LOCATION

All societies assume rights over and display attitudes toward the body at different stages during the life cycle. This attention is especially evident in various social practices of bodily mutilation that take place within the confines of social institutions which serve violent purposes. In Eastern societies, for instance, the binding of women's feet reproduced relations of domination and sexuality in the family; in Western medieval society the self-inflicted wounding of the body in the form of stigmata served the purpose of religious expiation; and among societies of the South Philippines, institutions of head-hunting and head severing served as a defense against grief, rage, and mourning.[3] In modern Western societies, the first systematically organized regimes leveled at the body coincided with the emergence of industrial capitalism and Protestant puritanical doctrines. Habits of work, regulation of desire, expression of the abhorrence of excess and the renunciation of the material pleasures of the body in the form of self-denial are among the technologies of the mortification of the body still evident in practices such as excessive work, self-control, dieting, and fitness.

THE TECHNOLOGY OF HOMICIDE

I use the term "technology of homicide" as a way of designating the actions, moral principles, scientific measures, police practices, means of explanation, and the strategies for arriving at the truth that are set in motion after a murder has been committed. Different societies have vastly different technologies of homicide. For example, among the Azande of Zaire, homicide is believed to be caused by witchcraft rather than individual acts of violence. The procedure the Azande use to reveal the truth behind a homicide is called the poison oracle, a method by which poison is administered to small domestic fowl. From the fowl's response, the Azande believe they receive true answers to the questions they place before the oracle.[4] As it applies to Western societies, however, the technology of homicide refers to the entire framework employed to determine the "truth" about what happened. This may include propositions about where the truth lies, the belief in the procedures, the investigation of the crime scene, gathering of evidence, interdictions by law, the production of a chain of evidence, and so on. All these elements make up the technology of homicide so far as they are procedures for the production of truth.[5]

THE ORIGIN OF THE MODERN MURDER PROBLEM

The modern murder problem has its origins in early nineteenth-century society with the emergence of the industrial city, the appearance of capitalism, and the transition to town economies. With these economies came the concentration of populations, the intensification of the struggle for existence and the need for police functions on a large scale. As societies in the West began to respond to the crime problem, they put into practice an entire machinery for placing the criminal within a system of law, science, and punishment. In 1887 Raffaele Garofalo, one of the founders of modern criminology, commenting on the nine thousand murders recorded in Europe that year, stated, "Who is the enemy who has devastated this land? It is a mysterious enemy unknown to history, his name is the criminal."[6] In these comments, Garofalo draws our attention to two important developments with respect to the modern murder problem. The first is that the criminal as a lone murderer is a historically new concept and a product of certain social and historical arrangements. In early societies, murder was carried out within the confines of social institutions that put obligations on individuals to engage in acts of warfare, revenge, head-hunting, etc. In this sense, "murderous institutions" prescribed acts whose rules lie beyond individual volition.

A second thing that can be noted about Garofalo's comment is that by the middle of the nineteenth century there developed specialized techniques and literatures of criminality, including news reporting, detective fiction, medical accounts, and scientific investigations that acted to promote the idea that the criminal was a subject of intense interest and investigation. By the end of the century, the "criminal" was separated from society by the forces of medicine, psychiatry, and law, and this process continued right through to the twentieth century. As this process intensified, an image was built up of the criminal as the enemy of society, and as a result, this led to the conception of the criminal as a threat to the well-being of society and to the universal fear of crime. Only when the criminal was conceived of as a monstrous figure motivated by uncontrollable impulses and separated from the values of society was it

303

necessary to develop a technique of detection, law, and punishment that intensifies discipline and subjection.

DISCIPLINARY TECHNOLOGY

In direct relation to the individualization of the criminal is what Foucault speaks of as the age of disciplinary technology. According to Foucault, discipline was a technique that arose at the end of the eighteenth century and was perfected by the nineteenth century.[7] It appears in the form of control over the body and refers to the precise techniques whereby institutions concern themselves with bringing the body under control in response to the routines of the factory, the school, the prison, and the workhouse. In his work, Foucault goes on to point out that as disciplinary technology acts upon the body it divides it into zones that are subject to controls in the form of rules and interdictions that attach themselves to various social institutions. From this perspective, the development of the modern classroom, for instance, could only have emerged as a space for teaching when controls were leveled at specific zones of the body—arms, legs, and head—so as to ensure that direction and attention is confined to the space where the lesson takes place. The aim of disciplinary technology is thus conformity and obedience, and this technology becomes a central dynamic in society because it is a precondition to economic production and wealth. Disciplinary technology is not static but spreads throughout the wider society and is evident in the practices of commerce, schooling, medicine, and military life.

After these developments came the application of disciplinary technology to the deviant and to human behavior in general. This laid down a whole grid of expectations and requirements for human behavior that exerted itself at the level of speech, sexuality, and public conduct and served to demarcate the normal from the pathological. As the criminal was conceived of as either "dangerous" or "monstrous" and separated from the values of the wider society, it was necessary to develop and perfect a technique to intensify subjection. At this point, says Foucault, "the human body entered the age of the machinery of power which explored the body, broke it down and rearranged it."[8] It was at this stage that the practices of torture and confession perfected themselves in the political and religious realms of society. Both torture and confession, according to Foucault, are "technologies of truth" in the sense that when applied to the body, truth will be produced. Religion and later psychiatry perfected confession, individualizing it to accommodate the work of truth, internal cleansing, and self-liberation.

THE DEVELOPMENT OF MURDER WRITING
AS A GENRE

By the twentieth century, those societies that had to confront crime on a large scale put into practice an entire machinery for placing the criminal within the social coordinates of law, medicine, and psychiatry. By the end of the nineteenth century, a specialized technology of murder had arisen and was celebrated in forensic science, fingerprinting, weapons cataloguing, crime scene evidence, and wound and weapons experts. As a result, murder was raised to the level of a literary form as is evident in the works of De Quincey's writing on murder and Edgar Allan Poe's "Murders in the Rue Morgue," which consolidated the narrative elements of the murder genre by 1841.[9]

Generally, four broad elements preceded the development of murder as a new literary genre. The first was the development of a new mapping of urban space after the breakdown of rural economies and disposition of experience into the private pursuits of individuals. The second was the rise of the new police functions of surveillance and public order that arose in relation to the new topography of the city.[10] The third was the need for a closer surveillance of urban spaces, which came as a result of the individualization of the criminal and the concept of the city as a corrupting and dangerous environment. The fourth was the scientific treatment of the violent act. This development brought together criminal justice with scientific procedure and led to the opening up of police techniques to the investigative methods of science, an activity designed to obtain access to the telling world of clues found at crime scenes. Techniques such as fingerprinting, blood analysis, determining bullet trajectories, weapons analysis, and wound analysis eventually brought the spheres of criminal justice and scientific method together. This led to a science of criminal man, a science destined to become a diagnostic and explanatory tool.

As a consequence, a whole system of narration emerged, informed by an age of the criminal sciences, that was to shape the ethic of the investigative search for truth behind homicide. From this developed a whole language of murder: the language of the murdered body, the nature of the wounds, the type of weapon, the details of the crime scene, and the presence of the police. The work of detection within literary space was designed to show how murder was to be handled, how it would be investigated, and how it would be accounted for. At the center of this system of narration is the detective, whose abilities surpass those of the criminal. The presence of the investigator is predicated on the idea that the

305

truth is hidden from view and that the investigative gaze alone will reveal this truth. This genre makes a hero of the detective and coincides with the appearance of law in murder literature. The aim of detective fiction is to bring the murderer to justice by unraveling or disclosing the truth.

PSYCHO: DETECTIVE FRAMING AND THE
TECHNIQUES OF LAW AND PSYCHIATRY

Alfred Hitchcock's 1960 classic, *Psycho,* provides narrative elements that capture the structure of Hollywood murder up to the 1960s. *Psycho* employs three dominant techniques in its structuring of the murder framework: detection is used as a system of producing truths; law is a normalizing agent; and psychiatry is sovereign over law in explaining murderous acts.

Psycho is the story of the murder of Marion Crane, a real estate agent who works for a company in Phoenix. Marion, played by Janet Leigh, steals a sum of money, leaves town, and drives to California, where she arrives at the Bates Motel. There she meets Norman Bates (Anthony Perkins), a troubled man with a psychiatric history, and is taken to a room where she unpacks and prepares for a shower. As Marion steps into the shower, a blurred image comes into view through the shower curtain, raises a large knife, pulls back the curtain and violently stabs her. The rapid editing of the scene, the cuts between victim and attacker, between knife and flesh, are repeated until her body sinks to the floor. After meticulously cleaning up the scene, Bates drags Marion's body to her car, puts her effects in the trunk and disposes of the car in a nearby swamp.

Shortly after the murder an insurance investigator, Arbogast (Martin Balsam), arrives on the scene to search for Marion. Arbogast sets out for the Bates Motel where he subjects Norman to a battery of questions: "Do you remember a Marion Crane who may have stopped here on Friday?" "No," says Norman. "I don't recall such a person." "Can I look at your books?" asks Arbogast. "I happen to have a sample of her handwriting." By comparing Marion's handwriting with the false entry she placed in the register (Marie Samuels), Arbogast reveals an investigative truth: Marion can be traced to the Bates Motel where she checked in Friday and stayed the night. This sets the stage for the second murder, which takes place as Arbogast, seeking to talk to Norman's mother, enters the house situated near the motel. As Arbogast arrives at the top of the stairs, Bates, dressed as his mother, emerges from a room off the hall and violently stabs Arbogast, who falls awkwardly backward down the staircase.

The concluding scene in *Psycho* opens in the courthouse, in full institutional presence of psychiatry and law. "Well," says the sheriff, "if anyone gets any answers it will be the psychiatrists." This Hollywood stylization of a pending motive and diagnosis serves to structure the way we arrive at the truth and come to understand the murderous acts in the film. Here, law and psychiatry frame our comprehension of murderous acts by structuring what we have been shown in the film about Norman Bates. In the course of the film's narrative, he has murdered two people: Marion and Arbogast. He is a psychotic murderer in that he talks in his mother's voice and dresses like her when he kills. He lives on the top floor of the family home, in a bedroom that has been preserved as it was when he was a child. In a jealous rage, he murdered his mother and hid her decomposing body in the basement. His weapon, a large kitchen knife with a fourteen-inch blade, is held downward in a menacing fashion when he murders. As for his mother, she was a clinging, demanding woman with whom he formed a pathological bond. When she took a lover, she threw Norman over, and in a furious rage he murdered them both. In unlawfully taking away her body he reconstitutes her and thus restores the relationship to the way it was prior to the murder, at least in his mind. This is why everything in the house is preserved exactly the way it was; his room, her room, the fruit cellar, etc. As a result of this pathological bond, the mother forms a dominant part of his personality and acts through Norman. At times, he exhibits both personalities, talking to himself in his mother's voice; and at other times, his mother's persona takes over completely.

With this knowledge of Norman in hand, the narration sets in motion a system of psychiatric evaluation that explains murderous behavior by placing it within an intelligible framework of acts, motives, and impulses. "Norman murders," says the psychiatrist, not because he is a monstrous individual but because "his mother half takes over." "I got the whole story," says the psychiatrist, "but not from Norman Bates, from his mother." "Norman Bates no longer exists, he only half existed and now the other half has taken over probably for all time." "Did he kill my sister?" asks Lila. "Yes and no," says the psychiatrist. "When Norman met your sister, this set off the jealous mother, and the mother killed Marion."

Psychiatry became a part of criminal law in the nineteenth century as a technique for explaining dangerous individuals and murderous acts. In *Psycho,* the grid of criminal justice and psychiatry are put into play by the Hollywood system, and this grid is used both as a moral brace and as a technology for producing the truth of the official explanation.

The destruction and restoration of the normal world: the shower murder in *Psycho* (Universal, 1960).

Here we see how psychiatry, one of the sciences for explaining and curing the illness of crime and homicide, is the technique that provides an interpretation of the criminally monstrous by placing a senseless act onto the plane of intelligible motive. The psychiatric revelation, like the moment of the confession of sin, tends to confer the conditions of truth, and thus both share the same grammar of production.

OLIVER STONE'S *JFK*

A different murder narrative is explored in Stone's depiction of the Kennedy assassination. Stone's purpose in making the film was to examine the plausibility of conspiracy in the assassination of John F. Kennedy. Largely a depiction of Jim Garrison's failed efforts to bring charges against those whom he believed were involved in a conspiracy, *JFK* is a three-hour investigation of Kennedy's murder. For its violent scenes, Stone's film draws heavily on the Zapruder footage, a twenty-two-second account of the president's motorcade that records the impact of Lee

Harvey Oswald's gunfire on Kennedy's body. First aired in 1975 on ABC's *Good Night America,* the Zapruder film publicly shocked millions of Americans for its graphic depiction of the fatal head wound sustained by Kennedy, and it has become central to all reconstructions of the case in two important ways. First, it provides the definitive cinematic record of the assassination, eventually dubbed the "time clock" of the Kennedy murder; and second, it brought to the American public the visual details of Kennedy's head wound, showing his brain and skull violently exploded outward onto the rear of the limousine. In a central courtroom scene in *JFK,* Garrison (Kevin Costner) argues the case for conspiracy by using the Zapruder footage as incontrovertible evidence that Kennedy was shot from the front, implying a second shooter and therefore a conspiracy. The scene is highly technical in nature, and many factual assertions relying on bullet trajectories, army ballistic experts, and physical evidence are used to put forward various truths about what happened. During the trial scene, frames 223, 224, and 313 of the Zapruder film are used, first to demonstrate when the first shots hit Kennedy, and second, to demonstrate the direction of the fatal head shot. At stake in the Zapruder film are judgments about body positions, gunshots, wounds, timing, shooters, Governor Connally's reaction, and the position of Kennedy's body subsequent to the shooting. Each of these aspects are read forward and backward, repeated and replayed, started and stopped, and placed in retrospective and prospective positions to draw conclusions leading to either conspiracy or to lone-shooter theories.

Earlier I stated that the technology of homicide includes propositions about where the truth lies, the belief in the procedures, the moral maxims, the scientific measures, and the means of gathering evidence to get at the "truth" about what happened in a murder. In *JFK* the prevailing technology of homicide is scientific in that all the powers of science including physics, forensics, geometry, ballistics, medicine, optical enhancement, audio analysis, and computer reconstruction are drawn upon in an effort to reveal the truth in the Kennedy murder and to provide a definitive explanation of what happened.

In Stone's *JFK,* the Zapruder film is broken down into a frame-by-frame analysis, accompanied by optical enhancements of the frames recording the impact of the wounds. Wounds in turn are broken down into trajectory paths, which are tracked and analyzed to verify the origin and direction of the shot.[11] The bullet (the so-called magic bullet) has its own special history and markings (C.E. 399) and is the subject of intense investigative analysis invoking the assertions of the natural sciences such as physics and geometry.

Near the end of the courtroom scene, Stone draws on frames 313 and 314 of the Zapruder footage and methodically presents them in slow motion with visual enhancement, showing the head shot and Kennedy's body moving violently "back and to the left." This presents conclusive evidence of a shot from the front, demonstrating a "second shooter" and, by definition, a conspiracy. Stone systematically pursues a line of truth that uses the Zapruder film as an evidential basis to claim that a "team of shooters" killed Kennedy in a military coup motivated by Kennedy's readiness to end the war in Vietnam, a decision that threatened the prevailing powers of the U.S. military. Yet, in a recent work by Gerald Posner, opposite conclusions are drawn.[12] Using the identical frames of the Zapruder footage, bullet trajectories, ballistic analysis, and medical evidence, Posner presents different facts and different truths while still claiming rigorous scientific analysis.[13]

Psycho and *JFK:* Shifts in the Technique of Homicide

Earlier I stated that the technology of homicide involved strategies for arriving at the truth that are set in motion after a homicide has been committed. These strategies are largely technical and moral in nature, and their main aim is to provide narrative closure, meaning, and ultimately the truth about what happened. In *Psycho* these strategies are put to work by the techniques of investigation, law, and psychiatry, which function as a test for truth and as an explanatory account of Marion's murder. These techniques provide both narrative closure and explanatory truth when Norman Bates is brought to justice and his motives and acts are examined and explained in psychiatric terms. But what about the techniques of murder portrayed in these two films? Both the shower scene and the Kennedy head shot are among the most graphically disturbing filmic images. What shifts in the techniques of homicide can be observed in these two scenes?

The Shower Scene

As a murder technique, the shower scene in *Psycho* is one of the most shocking in film history. Marion is violently stabbed to death while the soundtrack magnifies the repeated gestures of the stabbing and the editing, famous for its technical ingenuity, amplifies the shocking nature of the murder. But, what is important to notice here is that the violence in the scene is not overt. This is so for several reasons. First, the shower scene is technically a "woundless murder" in that the knife is never shown touching the body, but only moving away from it, an action that is clearly part of the editing technique rather than a movement initiated by a murderer. Although the shower scene is itself shocking, from a contemporary perspective the shocking quality of the scene exists not in its actual violence to the body, but rather in the power the scene exerts over the ability to transgress what is normal in relation to the world and the body. This means that the shower scene in *Psycho* is not a body-annihilating murder as much as it is a violent intrusion into the normal. In fact, the transgression of normalcy is a recurring theme in Hitchcock's work, and this, it seems to me, is what Hitchcock finds so enormously appealing about the murder genre. In the shower scene, Hitchcock's camera is exercising its powers over the normal—for what can be more mundane than a shower?—in which we are defenseless against reality. The shower scene, in fact, exercises its optical powers not only in its spectacular editing but also in its violent rupturing of the normal. This is also true in regard to Hitchcock's tendency to use the law in a kind of mocking play against the normal, which is evident in *Psycho* in at least three central scenes. Finally, to the extent that the shower scene is not about violent wounding, Hitchcock in reality is staging the murder of Marion as a critique of the normal and that which normalizes, just as he stages a critique of police powers by exaggerating their capacity to normalize.[14] To the extent that Hitchcock's work can be seen as a series of studies in the power of the filmic over the normal and the violent rupturing of the normal, his lens is always at home in the murder genre.

THE ZAPRUDER-STONE HEAD WOUND

Frames 313 and 314 of the Zapruder film represent one of the most violent images in the history of film. Encompassing only a fraction of a second, the color image of Kennedy's head wound and the detail of the aftermath became a new visual image that immediately surpassed the previous boundaries and taboos with respect to what had been publicly visualized in homicide technique. While it is true that all murders involve violent acts, frames 313, 314, and 315 of the Zapruder film introduce a new filmic image of death by fusing together the appearance of the wound with a cadaverous aftermath. In cinematic techniques up to the time of the Zapruder film, wounds were fatal, brutal, visible, hidden, or merely assumed. Wounds were typically sustained during an act of violence or during a murder attempt and were something from which the victim recovered or did not. Wounds in the old cinematic code were transition points used for the entry and exit of characters or to elicit identification with the protagonist. Taboos about wounds in film existed in respect to visualizing the actual impact and the explosive aftermath, and even then these were generally well away from the zones of the body associated with the image-generating features such as the face or head. The Zapruder film of the Kennedy head wound, however, introduced a new somatic dimension in the technology of bodies, wounds, and homicide. The magnitude of the wound coupled with the convulsive body movements and configuration of Kennedy's dead body played out for the camera the transformation from life to death, so that Kennedy is at once both a living body and a cadaverous body.

The Zapruder film gave to Stone and thereby to Hollywood an image of cadaverous death in which the spectator witnesses the transition from the living to the dead in two frames. In Stone's *JFK,* the Kennedy head shot is lifted out of the Zapruder film and exploited by techniques of close-up, replay, and optical enhancements. Moreover, it is strategically held until the end of the courtroom scene to maximize its impact in an entertainment medium. In this way, frames 313 and 314 are placed within a Hollywood homicide technique. In all cultures, including our own, there are taboos restricting the filming of death, the purpose of which is to mark off by proprietary regulation the private from the public, the sacred from the profane. Stone's examination of the Zapruder footage brought into public view the details of the head wound, marking a turning point in somatic conventions in which the head shot became a filmic terrain to explore and subject to American homicide technique.[15]

In his anthropological work, Marcel Mauss argues that certain body configurations can be linked to specific cultures, and he used the term "body technique" to describe the relationship between social conventions and body styles. Mauss initially defines body technique as "the ways in which from society to society individuals know how to use their bodies," and goes on to point out that we are "apprenticed in these techniques which are products of training and education." In putting forward the concept of body technique, Mauss shows how the body is connected to various cultural practices and demonstrates the way variations in body activity (eating, walking, marching, fighting, etc.) are products of cultural conventions. Mauss first arrived at this idea while he was in the United States and drew on a cinematic image to make his point:

> A kind of revelation came to me in the hospital. I was ill in New York. I wondered where previously I had seen girls walking as my nurses walked.

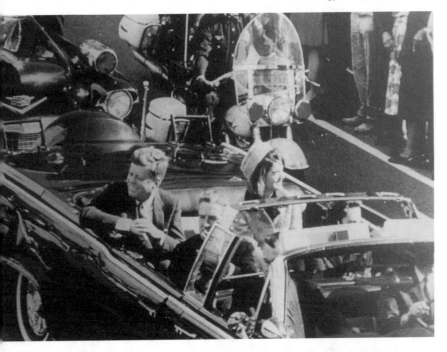

The first postmodern murder: the Kennedy assassination's explosion of reality.

I had the time to think about it. At last, I realized that it was at the cinema. Returning to France, I noticed how common this gait was, especially in Paris; the girls were French and they too were walking in this way. In fact, American walking fashions had begun to arrive over here, thanks to the cinema. This was an idea I could generalize: The position of the arms and hands while walking form a social idiosyncrasy, they are not simply a product of some purely individual almost completely physical, arrangements and mechanisms. For example, I think I can also recognize a girl who has been raised in a convent. In general she will walk with her fists closed.[16]

As Mauss states, the position of the arms and hands forms a social idiosyncrasy which together comprise American walking fashions. The Zapruder-Stone head wound likewise forms a filmic idiosyncrasy that represents American dying fashions.

To this point, I have traced two broad periods in the technology of homicide and have pointed to a shift in the conventions for framing the murderous act: In Hitchcock's *Psycho,* murder is framed as the disruption of the normal as portrayed in the shower scene and explained by psychiatry and law, whereas Stone's *JFK* frames homicide with the graphic head wound and explains it through science and conspiracy.

While these examples constitute only two moments in film history, I ask whether there is anything like a trajectory of violence in the film medium in the context of a postmodern world. In order to answer the question, I want to conceptualize violence as having two distinct and separate paths: violence in the real world and violence in the film world. In the real world violence circulates—it goes around—from offender to victim, and from police to the administration of justice. The social goal is to eradicate violence from circulation, so in this respect, it is reviled in the real world.

By contrast, in the film world violence constantly circulates and is extended in its scope with every sort of technical virtuosity and inventiveness. What takes place in film is the valorization of the violent act whereby a value is conferred upon it outside of the "real" and outside of human relationships. In this respect, it not only circulates in perpetual motion with no hope of dropping out, but it also takes on a value in which its goal is completely the reverse of the goal in the real world, so much so that it is technically celebrated and perfected. An example of violence taking on a value within a representational medium can be drawn from a recent interview with Quentin Tarantino. When asked about a technical point in the direction of *Reservoir Dogs* (1992), during which Michael Madsen tortures a victim while dancing to "Stuck in the Middle with You," he responded by saying that the scene was "boring until we hit on the idea of the music! . . . It was just perfect. We knew we had it."[17] Tarantino's comment shows that inside the film medium violence participates in the same political economy as money in the real world in that both create value outside the real and outside human relationships. Just as in the abstract world of the market where money creates value outside of itself, so violence creates value for itself once inserted into the film world. In this strange place where violence takes on value, we find a continuity between the modern and postmodern. In the postmodern there are no grand narratives or totalities, therefore the narratives become incoherent and resolve themselves into difference, otherness, and a simulacrum of their former selves. However, what makes some films coherent in a postmodern world is their modernist circuit of violence in which (like money in the market) it finds a value outside of itself, thus securing an assured path of valorization outside the real.

Notes

1. For further discussion of this issue see Pete Boss, "Vile Bodies and Bad Medicine," *Screen* 27 (1986): 14–24; and Barbara Creed, "Horror and the Monstrous-Feminine: An Imaginary Abjection," *Screen* 27 (1986): 45–70.

2. Caroline Walker Bynum, "The Female Body and Religious Practice in the Later Middle Ages," in *Fragments for a History of the Human Body Part One,* ed. Michel Feher (New York: Zone, 1989), 162.

3. For a discussion of the social practices related to body mutilation and their cultural justifications, see Frances E. Mascia-Lees and Patricia Sharpe, eds., *Tattoo, Torture, Mutilation, and Adornment: The Denaturalization of the Body in Culture and Text* (Albany: State University of New York, 1992); Paul Bohannan, ed. *African Homicide and Suicide* (New York: Atheneum, 1967); Renato Rosaldo, "Grief and a Headhunter's Rage," in *Culture and Truth: Remaking of Social Analysis* (Boston: Beacon Press, 1989).

4. For discussion of Azande truth production, see E. E. Evans-Pritchard, *Witchcraft Oracles and Magic among the Azande* (Oxford: Clarendon Press, 1976), 120–64.

5. In the cinema, as in literature, various technologies of homicide respect genre boundaries in which implements, moralities, philosophic propositions, and tests for truth operate in a mutually exclusive manner. For example, the vampire genre provides a technology of homicide that contrasts sharply with detective fiction. Here the dangerous individual is the vampire, who is beyond control of the law and whose action is the strange fusion of desire and corrupted will. Murder takes place by blood infusion and by blood exchange and the weapons of mutilation emanate from various body zones and environments, including items such as teeth, stakes, and crucifix. In addition, the wound is in the form of discrete punctures to the body in the region of the neck and carry with them the stigma of a creature who is of another world. The murderous act is thus beyond psychiatry and law and can only be thwarted by religious interdiction. This preference for stakes, teeth, crucifix, blood exchange, and wound morphology constitutes a technology grafted to a homicide form and operates to exclude the preferred techniques evident in detective fiction. In the vampire genre, religion is the test for truth over psychiatry, law, or reconstructive investigation.

6. Raffaele Garofalo, *Criminology* (Boston: Little Brown, 1914) [1891], xii; Michel Foucault, "About the Concept of the 'Dangerous Individual' in 19th Century Legal Psychiatry," *International Journal of Law and Psychiatry* 1 (1978): 12.

7. Michel Foucault, *Discipline and Punish: The Birth of the Prison* (New York: Vintage Books, 1979).

8. Ibid., 61.

9. Joel Black, *The Aesthetics of Murder: A Study in Romantic Literature and Contemporary Culture* (Baltimore: Johns Hopkins University Press), 1–29.

10. Foucault, "The 'Dangerous Individual'," 6–7.

11. The reconstructive work that has gone on around Zapruder and continues to this day has inspired many Hollywood murder themes. In *Blow Out* (1981), for

instance, directed by Brian de Palma, the story involves an audio tape of a political murder in which the technician, played by John Travolta, attempts to match video fragments to an audio tape of a suspected murder. What is interesting is that in the central scenes, the moment of truth is provided when Travolta is able to precisely calibrate sounds on an audio tape to video frames to prove, definitively, that a murder was committed. The Zapruder film has no audio portion, and much scientific analysis has focused on the attempt to match the only sound recording of the assassination, which was obtained by a police motorcycle unit near the scene.

12. Gerald Posner, *Case Closed: Lee Harvey Oswald and the Assassination of JFK* (New York: Random House, 1993) claims to present the final and conclusive proof that "Lee Harvey Oswald, driven by his own twisted and impenetrable furies, was the only assassin at Dealey Plaza on November 22, 1963" (472).

13. In yet another work, *The Killing of a President* (New York: Viking Studio Books, 1993), Robert Groden, working diligently on the Zapruder footage, has produced claims at variance with Posner. Groden, using techniques of optical enhancement, claims that six—not three—shots were fired and that the head wound at frame 313 was a shot from the front, implying proof of a conspiracy. While the techniques and methods are the same, the truths are vastly divergent and contradictory.

14. This theme is evident in Hitchcock's *Shadow of a Doubt* (1943), where Uncle Charlie (Joseph Cotten) is a sort of mass murderer of his day and who engages in a serious critique of the normal and of those who live within the confines of the normal.

15. In *Pulp Fiction* (1994), Quentin Tarantino takes the head shot to another level in the car scene where the explosive moment is treated as a comedic event.

16. Marcel Mauss, *Sociology and Psychology: Essays* (London: Routledge and Kegan Paul, 1979), 100.

17. "Hollywood Minute," CNN, December 12, 1997.

Part IV

Otherness, Aliens, and Trauma on the Transnational Scene

13

THE TRAUMA IS OUT THERE: HISTORICAL DISJUNCTIONS AND THE POSTTRAUMATIC NARRATIVE AS PROCESS IN *THE X-FILES*

ILSA J. BICK

Not all people exist in the same Now.

—*Ernst Bloch, 1977*[1]

Harold Blum writes that trauma, "by its very definition, is of an overwhelming nature . . . [impacting] on the present personality, and [influencing] further development."[2] Whether intrapsychic or societal, trauma stands apart, to one side, separate, inviolate, pervasive. Trauma defines itself, defines the past, defines the future, defines the Now, and the logic is circular. There are triggers to trauma: isolated fragments, whether of sight, smell, or touch, representative of the whole. An event is reduced to a symbol: the woman whose feeling of rage at her husband triggers the dissociation she experienced during a rape; the child for whom all blue eyes stand for the eyes of her murdered playmate. Because trauma is a violence to the psyche, the traumatic event, irreverent to temporal demands, is wrenched from a stream of psychic causality to become an eternal, irreconcilable referent. To the afflicted, a flashback is a rupture into consciousness, the lid of a memory lifted and its contents violently disgorged in excruciating detail while the individual gazes on, immobilized and helplessly transfixed by the spectacle. Not infrequently, the victim dissociates by pulling herself out of mind, out of body, out of her own historical context. Distanced, she becomes a spectator to the specular flow of her personal history—perversely, much like a moviegoer who watches images flicker on a screen in an endless loop. It is the essence of what is "para"-normal.

Just as there are personal traumas, there are wider ruptures and chasms in history. Of the many historical traumas of the twentieth

319

century, one might convincingly point to the Holocaust—the capital "H" ensures that there can be no other—as the traumatic fulcrum upon which history has pivoted. Writing about Steven Spielberg's *Schindler's List* (1993), Thomas Elsaesser notes "the paradoxical nature of an event such as the Holocaust that defies representation and yet demands it with equal finality,"[3] much in the way that a flashback or a recurring traumatic nightmare shatters the stream of consciousness or sleep. Nazism is a deep, wide gash in the terrain of history, an ideological precipice. Dissociated from history, the traumas of Nazism and of the Holocaust are spectacular in their kitschy melodrama and evocation of "ravishing images,"[4] symbols standing for the whole, where the symbols themselves become more important than the history and events to which they refer. There is no easy shorthand for, say, Vietnam as there is for Nazism, no symbol quite like the swastika. George Bush can, with relative impunity, liken Saddam Hussein to Hitler, and, implicated in the same disdain for history and the over-valuation of symbols, we all know what he really means. Their arms raised in a "Heil Hitler" salute, *Star Trek: The Next Generation*'s Borg can goosestep their way through the *Enterprise D,* and we know what that means.[5] The general trauma of Nazism, and of the Holocaust in particular, stubbornly resists being placed "in a context," in the same way that one doubts that Auschwitz "can stand for anything at all other than itself in its stark, ungraspable singularity."[6] Nazism represents a traumatic, historical disjunction refusing reparation that is ahistorical; its symbols—swastikas, gas chambers, ovens, cattle cars, corpses—stand for the whole yet trigger a string of associations: the beginning of history, the end of history, the limit of representation, the very definition of trauma.

This peculiarly twentieth-century trauma and the repression of history flowing from it are represented in the emblematic postmodern television hit, *The X-Files.*

Personal and social a-historicity and the traumatic meet in *The X-Files.* The series is paradigmatic of the disruptions and disjunctions of personal and social histories, the composition of what I term a "posttraumatic narrative," and the incorporation of larger, unassimilated historical traumas. It is invested, literally, in that which is dissociated, that which is alongside the "normal" flow of life, that which is "para"-normal. Devoted to investigations into the unexplained, the series centers on the obsessive quest of F.B.I. Special Agent Fox Mulder (David Duchovny) to reconcile, incorporate, and psychically metabolize a single trauma—his sister's disappearance. This trauma is articulated into an overtly paranoid construction as he and fellow Special Agent Dr. Dana Scully (Gillian

Anderson) uncover government conspiracies and retroactive denials of these conspiracies. This one, highly personal event, of which Mulder possesses only fragmentary memories, is the nexus about which he organizes the world and is the rupture in his history to which the series ritualistically returns.

Placed within a cultural context, this posttraumatic narrative is also reflective of the continuing dissolution of a particular type of American mythology—a belief in regenerative violence—just as series creator Chris Carter has come to typify *The X-Files*'s trajectory as mythic.[7] Perhaps *The X-Files* is the postmodern, posttraumatic doppelgänger of the western, and Mulder its heroic protagonist, just as *The Searchers'* (1956) Ethan Edwards scoured the West for Debbie, or, in a more perverse, overtly sexualized, and atomized urban landscape, Travis Bickle rescued Iris in *Taxi Driver* (1976). Unlike either of these narrative predecessors, however, *The X-Files* pessimistically concludes that violence infiltrates the boundaries of and overwhelms the law in spaces these narratives viewed sacred: the family. In fact, the law and order signified in the characters of Mulder and Scully is itself implicated in a crisis of patriarchal authority, as government officials take their orders from a (male) government operating outside of (male) government. *The X-Files* recognizes the futility and the failure of redemptive violence—and perhaps of revolution—as a means to effect radical change, but the series articulates no solution. Instead, *The X-Files* returns to loss, whether this loss is something just out of reach or briefly glimpsed (and therefore doubted as "reality"). These are losses of information, memory, belief, faith, and trust. These are losses of love. These losses are transmuted to a need to understand the trauma "out there" as a prelude to coming to grips with the trauma "in here." For Mulder, these losses and traumas are signified as crises of belief, gaps in memory, and fabrications in (personal) history overlaid with a preponderance of loaded, culturally predetermined symbols of which the Holocaust stands preeminent.

This analysis will center upon a psychoanalytic investigation of *The X-Files* in terms of the developmental level of its structure and then address the eruption of the posttraumatic narrative from within this developmental structure. Psychoanalysis is an investigation into intrapsychic development. Consonant with my previous writings, my focus will be on the ways in which intrapsychic processes are mirrored in the evolving narrative—the explicit project of psychoanalytic endeavors.[8] Much of *The X-Files* is structured around adolescent concerns, yet specific to all plot development is the continuing articulation and re-working of unconscious agendas informing intrapsychic life. What this analysis will demonstrate is that the agendas with which *The X-Files* is concerned are not startlingly new or different; they are ancient and primitive intrapsychic concerns, circulating finally around fearful, archaic images of women.

Yet the way *The X-Files* expresses its concerns is colored by the cognitive and developmental capabilities specific to an "age"—both real and cultural. Mulder and Scully are not "real people," but their narrative is a journey forward into the unknown of the past. Because the narrative details trauma, it co-opts characteristics emblematic of popularized notions of trauma and the experience of the "para"-normal—all features that function in the "breaks," discrediting previously established, constructed histories. Ultimately, this results in a "break"-down of the narrative, requiring of the audience leaps of faith, acceptance of codified symbols masquerading as true knowledge (the audience "in the know" of a mountain of facts and pseudo-histories that amount to nothing), or a weary dismissal of any attempt to make sense of it all.

Just as these breaks in the narrative flow of *The X-Files* reflect the trauma to which Mulder continually returns and which he remains unable to metabolize, so the series has chosen the Holocaust as the historical referent from which this trauma—and we—may take a cue. Never truly explored in the series in a broader, more objectified historical context, the Holocaust, with a capital "H," becomes the vehicle through which the series takes off, spinning out its own version of the Conspiracy, with a capital "C." Because the Holocaust triggers readily accessible, communal associations and a perverse type of knowledge based upon easy generalization into discrete symbols, *The X-Files* is then free to co-opt these symbols and embellish them with just enough fiction disguised as fact to articulate a parallel, "para"-normal history of its very own.[9]

> I don't want him to know how much this is bothering me. I don't want him to feel like he has to protect me. . . . I know the world is full of predators, just as it's always been.
>
> —*Dana Scully, "Irresistible" (1/13/95)*

All narratives speak to psychological development. Because of its preoccupation with radical change in a prevailing system of authority, combined with themes of self-actualization and emancipation, *The X-Files* is an "adolescent" narrative. The concerns of the adolescent period explicitly address challenges to authority, separations from families of origin, and individual autonomy.[10] In contradistinction to latency-age narratives, the adolescent narrative does not focus on the maintenance of sameness but on radical alterations within the self mirrored in the environment (compare, for example, a film like *Logan's Run* [1976] to *The Wizard of Oz* [1939]).[11] These are the explicit premises of many horror and science fiction narratives, where the known universe is transposed to an alien setting: precisely the feelings of many an alienated adolescent. Central to adolescent narratives is ambivalence over the preservation of pre-existing norms. This ambivalence fuels a variety of typically adolescent behaviors, from the excessive to the ascetic, designed to counter the press of archaic fantasy.[12] An upsurge in the concerns of previous developmental epochs is also experienced, with their myriad and twisting paths negotiating sexuality, potency, and fears of developmental regression.

In its overt refusal and exploration of the failure of generic norms circulating in dominant American mythology, *The X-Files* can be regarded as an attempt at a "subversive" narrative, an adolescent production aimed at exposing and negating prevailing authoritarian structures by juxtaposing them against a new, radical, and "alienated" view. "Traditional" gender roles and expectations are reversed. *The X-Files* situates logos and established law—and ultimately, a type of truth—within the feminine and posits a female protagonist, forensic pathologist Scully, who is the intellectual and visceral equal of the series' male protagonist. Intuition, gestalt, and emotion reside almost solely within Mulder, whose ambivalent, antithetical credos—"I want to believe" and "Trust no one"—negate one another, for there cannot be belief where there is not also trust in the agents of that belief.

The X-Files reveals its adolescent ambivalence from the start, undercutting its female protagonist in ways both subtle and large. For example, by aligning Scully with prevailing authority structures even while cementing her opposition to this same authority in her alliance with Mulder, *The X-Files* guarantees that part of its project will ultimately be a refutation of the authority Scully embodies—a symptom and synonym of an ambivalent (male) adolescent view of established norms and, as we shall see, of women. For all Scully's presentation of scientific fact, Mulder ultimately resorts to that which can neither be proven nor disproved, engaging in a debate admitting of no possibility that his world view can be challenged or changed. His is fuzzy logic; in rebellion against Aristotelian binaries, Mulder admits to neither 0 nor 1 but something para (to one side of, beside, dissociated from) normal. Mulder's refutations come from a compendium of data lacking objectification but presented as legitimate. The scientific enterprise based upon falsification is itself negated because what Mulder presents as para-scientific evidence cannot participate in the same semiotic code. There can be no reproducible experiments and, therefore, no opportunities for falsification.

Consonant with an adolescent redefinition of a world view, Scully's character has undergone a subtle shift as the seasons have progressed and "the Conspiracy" becomes more articulated (and increasingly obfuscated). In contradistinction to her previous attempts to disprove Mulder by finding alternative explanations, Scully now more frequently explains away contradictory elements or employs her science to work on his behalf (her science in ironic lockstep with the ex-Nazi scientists working with the Conspirators). She has, in her words, "heard the truth. Now what I want are the answers" ("Paper Clip" [9/29/95]). Tellingly, this shift occurs after Scully has lost her own sister, as if, in some covert way, *The X-Files* has moved to lending Mulder the voice of Scully's authority, to re-make her in Mulder's image.

As an adolescent narrative, *The X-Files*'s structure circulates around the negation of generic norms while simultaneously reaching back—in history, in intrapsychic time—in an attempt to move forward. Mulder is a victim of trauma, an adult survivor of the dissolution of family (his parents' divorce and his sister's disappearance). He is an alien, isolated and distanced from his culture just as he incorporates cultural simulacra as tools for his interrogation of and quest for the elusive woman (the woman literally in his dreams, nightmares, and flashbacks). In his separate wasteland, Mulder is a hollow, "para"-noid man, telling his story in a curious, detached monotone void of inflection and passion. Mulder's is a world existing alongside the norm; scopophilic in the extreme, a watcher watching the watchers, Mulder delights in the pornographic and is a ravenous devotee of television. Consonant with his developmental fixations—his need to fill in historical gaps—Mulder is continually looking out to gaze backward (watching old movies). Or, by affixing a taped "X" to his window to summon first Deep Throat, then Mr. X, Mulder causes the world "out there" to materialize into his own claustrophobic, self-referential matrix. Furthermore, because Mulder's is a journey back in intrapsychic time, he not only resides at FBI headquarters below ground (his basement cubicle is reached only after negotiating a labyrinthine sequence of corridors), but also Mulder's proximity to the repressed is emphasized by the fact that he is continually depicted as falling asleep in front of his television. Many times, he awakens from sleep to find his nightmares realized, as in "Paper Hearts" (12/15/96), implying that Mulder's dreams are amalgams not only of his own psyche but of what the pastiche of media history constructs. Like flashbacks, these dreams and visitations—eruptions of archaic,

unconscious material or traumatic events into the conscious world—
form the basis for his waking reality.

Before anyone draws any conclusions, remember we're in the Arctic.
—Mulder undressing in front of two other men, "Ice" (11/05/93)

Christopher Sharrett points out that Travis Bickle, in an inversion upon
the western motif of *The Searchers,* engages in a mythic quest, making a
dramatic last stand for Iris, in a way that Mulder, in his (heretofore) unresolved search for his lost sister, is denied. An atomized Bickle reaches
an endpoint, although not necessarily a resolution nor rehabilitation, and
the film suggests that the family is a (very ambiguous) salvation which
Bickle, like Ethan Edwards, is denied.

Such resolution forever eludes Mulder. In part, this lack is dictated
by the fact that *The X-Files* is a weekly television series. But central
to Travis Bickle's nebulous apotheosis is release through a cathartic
paroxysm of violence; he gets "some*where*" because "some*thing*" gets
out.[13] In step with his society, Bickle is a pastiche, assimilating the
icons of masculine quest genres—the cowboy personas of men of action
from James Bond to Dirty Harry—and acquiring the accouterments of
violence to conquer violence.[14] While Mulder "investigates," there is
no sense of resolution, no attitude of closure. True, Mulder and Scully
may track down their man/woman/alien/beast, but, as often as not, the
truth "out there" eludes them, just as rationality breaks down in the
face of that which exists next to normality. Furthermore, the violence
of *The X-Files* frequently occurs off screen—a concession to television
standards and practices—but there is no sense that these unseen eruptions
of violence comprise a formula for redemption or regeneration. Generic
constructions assume that violence and the capacity for (masculine)
action reside in the expression of something signified as potent—the
gun, the scalpel. In *The X-Files,* not only does Scully have better aim,
but she is as likely to be brandishing a gun as Mulder, and the only one
of the two who wields a scalpel. Mulder may have a gun, but he rarely
uses it with any effect. The gun symbolizes the potential for action, but
this potential frequently results in stalemates, as various characters point
guns at one another in literal stand-offs, or as guns "ejaculate" uselessly
(a number of times male characters shoot away from or *around* people
in frustration, as in the episodes "Zero Sum" [4/27/97] and "Demons"
[5/11/97]). There are only two episodes where Mulder actually settles a
score, but such action leads to more loss, not affirmation or closure. In
"Young at Heart" (2/11/94), Mulder guns down John Barnett, a killer he
had previously been unable to shoot (his inaction having led to the death

of a fellow agent, and an episode from Mulder's past which, in an ironic inversion of the spectator's position, *Scully* watches on video). Far from being cathartic, Barnett's demise is simultaneously the supreme irony and the hidden agenda of the series: whatever information he possessed regarding a process that would reverse aging—that which would halt forward movement—dies with him. In "Paper Hearts," Mulder shoots Roche and saves one little girl while leaving unresolved the identity of another murdered twenty years before who might have been Mulder's lost sister. Despite the fact that Mulder always drives the car, he frequently ends up—and goes—nowhere, and his potency is, like the size of his penis, insubstantial.

The X-Files's world has been termed "paranoid," largely because of its emphasis on hidden cabals and government conspiracies and its invariant association with secrets, the unseen, and (a literal) darkness illuminated only briefly by the beam of a flashlight. Key to any paranoid construction is the creation of a "personal myth,"[15] a defensive constellation manufactured as autobiographical and constituted from unconscious fantasies and screen memories. In the creation of his own myth, Travis Bickle writes page after page of rambling, inchoate musings, delivered in a voice-over that directs his narrative. Bickle's internal commentary functions as a primitive form of self-mediation, and, as Sharrett demonstrates, Bickle's address to the mirror—"You talkin' to me?"—closes the circuit between self and object, "the moment where the film reveals Travis, the postmodern subject as image repository."[16]

The X-Files employs the same strategy yet masterfully undercuts the narrative as a masculine construction. Mulder recites a litany of "facts" and pseudoscience in a faux rationalism designed to bolster his theories. Far from subversive, Mulder's articles and work are popular cultural productions, quoted as appearing in magazines like *Omni* under the pseudonym M. F. Luder, an anagram for F. Mulder. He both participates in and colludes with a dominant culture. Indeed, the act of writing anything subversive in *The X-Files*—and therefore, critiques of the legitimate sphere of scientific inquiry and observable proof—belongs almost entirely to Scully. Her "captain's log" of explanatory voice-overs serves as an historical record, the voice of commentary and continuity, and, by association, omniscient authority, just as this voice serves as a repository for the subversive—her assertions that cases remain unsolved or unexplained, opening the door to the paranormal.[17] Only occasionally is Mulder given the final voice-over ("Fearful Symmetry" [3/24/95] and "The Calusari" [4/14/95] are two rare examples). In an inversion of Western mythologies, a Navajo elder, Albert Hosteen, delivers the voice-over at the beginning of "The Blessing Way" (11/22/95). A digital tape of crucial information, previously encoded by the military in Navajo, is destroyed by Assistant Director Walter Skinner (Mitch Pileggi), but not before Hosteen has memorized the contents in Navajo and related it by word of mouth to twenty other men in his tribe.

Tellingly, once the X-Files unit is shut down by Skinner at the close of the first season, Mulder and Scully are effectively separated in time and space until "Firewalker" (11/18/94). With Scully's disappearance from the narrative for the episodes "The Host" (9/23/94), "Blood" (9/30/94), "Sleepless" (10/07/94), "Duane Barry" (10/14/94), "Ascension" (10/21/94), and "3" (11/04/94),[18] there is no attempt to provide the series with a bracketing voice-over narration until the second episode marking Scully's reappearance when her concluding voice-over is restored ("Red Museum" [12/09/94]).

In an interesting reversal of masculine logos, *The X-Files* suggests that expressions of potency and omniscience reside within the feminine and that the feminine mediates the world at large, as demonstrated by Scully being the one who testifies before her superiors, in court, and before Congress.[19] She becomes, to a certain degree, Mulder's voice and stand-in, as well as his mediating other, the link to the world around him, as the two constantly trade phone calls (sometimes as many as seven times in the same episode), and Mulder talks incessantly to her (into a tape recorder) in "Little Green Men" (9/16/94). Put another way, Scully inhabits both the Imaginary and the Symbolic, just as she is the voice of prophesy ("Demons" [5/11/97]).

The X-Files's truth is "out there," but it is a truth outside the masculine and inside the feminine. Gradually, Scully's opposition to Mulder's constructions has been negated, consonant not only with the development of something "inside" her (her cancer) but in concert with further elaborations of the *unconscious* determinants of Mulder's core trauma. The closer Mulder comes to an answer, the more Scully's objections ring hollow; the more Mulder scrutinizes, the more frequently Scully becomes the object of his—and other men's—scrutiny. As this occurs, Scully is re-situated into stereotypical positions, first by undergoing an adolescent rebellion of her own, and then by gradually coming under the sway of Mulder's dominant world view. In the episode "Never Again" (2/02/97), and for the first time in the series, Scully voices her dissatisfaction with her subordination to Mulder's plans. She aggressively challenges Mulder concerning her relative importance in his world view; she complains that she does not have a desk and initially refuses to follow Mulder's directives. She confesses to another man, Ed Jerse, that she always seeks out authoritarian structures, and then (it is implied) she impulsively sleeps with him.[20] Echoing Scully's split from Mulder, Jerse is furious over the terms of his divorce settlement and plagued by a hallucination of a belittling woman (emanating from a tattoo) who repeatedly calls him a loser. Jerse almost kills Scully, a surprisingly stereotypical development overtly critical of Scully's sexuality. Paradoxically, the omniscient voice of the woman prompts man to action as it also impels him toward self-destruction.

Scully's position is further undermined in "Small Potatoes" (4/20/97), an episode chronicling the "tale" of Eddie Van Blundht, who can morph into the form of anyone he chooses (and who is also possessed of a vestigial tail).[21] Having responded defensively to Scully's earlier assertion that only through coercion would a woman sleep with him, Eddie goes to Scully's apartment as Mulder, plies her with wine, and encourages her confidences in a style reminiscent of (feminine) confessional discourse.[22] Just as he bends to kiss her, Eddie is exposed by the real Mulder, who, brandishing a gun he does not fire, bursts into the apartment and "rescues" Scully. Like "Never Again," Scully's actions are in stark contradistinction to most of what has gone before; each episode has Scully's inhibitions removed by a drug. A telling fact is the episode following "Never Again," "Memento Mori" (2/09/97), which has Scully discovering her cancer. This is both a narcissistic assault and a move that posits Scully in need of salvation *and investigation* (not only by Mulder, who in the same episode exposes the fraud behind Scully's medical science, but also by Skinner, who in "Zero Sum" is curiously impotent while, paradoxically, the camera pays almost loving homage to his penis in a protracted low-angle shot of his jockey-shorted crotch and muscular torso). Despite the fact that, at first glance, Scully appears to de-legitimize Mulder's beliefs in the fourth season finale (tellingly titled "Gethsemane" [5/18/97]), the episode makes clear that Scully is merely explaining yet another facet of the Conspiracy (she now believes that she was given cancer as part of a plot to convince Mulder of the veracity of his own theories, thereby indirectly affirming Mulder's importance in the narrative). Through her illness (and the seeming failure of her science), Scully's voice of authority and opposition has been silenced and replaced by one concerned with interrogations consonant with Mulder's.

> Agent Mulder undertook this treatment hoping to lay claim to his past—that by retrieving memories lost to him, he can fully understand the path he's on. But if that knowledge remains elusive, if only by knowing where he's been can he hope to understand where he's going, then I fear Agent Mulder may

lose his course, and the truths he's seeking from his childhood will continue to evade him, driving him more dangerously forward in impossible pursuit.

—*Scully, "Demons"*

As I have stated earlier, *The X-Files*'s form is a construction within which the concerns driving adolescent development are articulated. The most superficial of these concerns are centered on challenges to and articulations of prevailing authoritarian structures. Scully's gradual transformation in the series from investigator to that which needs to be investigated, atomized, dissected, and exposed signals that *The X-Files*, consonant with other (male) adolescent aims, is also involved in an incisive interrogation of the female body just as the posttraumatic narrative in this series centers around this "probing" and breaking down of barriers. As with all trauma, development continues, but its eternal referent will be the trauma that defines how the world is viewed both before and after, as if the "now" will always be inhabited by the "then." This includes the world of unconscious fantasy. Given the ways in which unconscious phenomenon, the paranormal, and the continual and repetitious return of the repressed are presented in this series, it is fitting that *The X-Files* is truly framed as a posttraumatic narrative, structured around flashbacks, dreams, nightmares, and loss.[23] *The X-Files* seeks to resolve a core trauma that leads to frequent ruptures and breakthroughs of traumatic material into the narrative proper while the series incorporates and co-opts larger historical traumas into its narrative framework.

At the core of *The X-Files* is a reality with which most of us are familiar: the secrets and crises emanating from within the family. It is not an accident that these concerns can only come to light in a narrative form structured around adolescence, an epoch that demands an interrogation of the family as a prerequisite to further growth. Cast as a story about a search for his missing sister but one that extends beyond the bounds of the individual to engulf the social, Mulder's narrative posits a central, catastrophic betrayal leading to a consuming, ritualistic obsession—a search for his metaphorical white whale.[24] As the series has progressed, the narrative's "memory" of Samantha's disappearance has altered considerably.[25] Mulder's first recollection is that Samantha was taken while he lay paralyzed and helpless in his bed. ("The X-Files: Pilot" [9/10/93]. This is reiterated in the episode "Conduit" [10/01/93], where Scully listens to a tape of Mulder's regression therapy at the episode's conclusion.[26])

Not until "Little Green Men," however, is the event shown (though Mulder glimpses a vision of Samantha in "Miracle Man" [3/18/94]). In this memory (signaled by a lap dissolve), we see the twelve-year-old Mulder with his eight-year-old sister Samantha playing a game of *Stratego* (a board game overtly concerned with take-overs, spies, and enemy infiltrations). The date is November 27, 1973, and the Mulders's television is tuned to a discussion of the Rosemary Woods tape of Nixon's crucial Watergate conversation and its mysterious eighteen-minute gap.[27] Samantha complains that she wants to watch a movie, and Mulder counters by stating that their parents left him in charge and that he wants to watch *The Magician* at 9 P.M.[28] Samantha impulsively switches the channel (to a western!), then screams at Mulder when he switches it back. He rises to tower above her, but at that moment the house is shaken with strong vibrations; red and yellow lights flicker through the drawn blinds; picture frames fall from the mantle, and first the television, then the power goes out. Samantha calls Mulder's name, and at that instant the doorknob turns. Terrified, Mulder runs to a bookshelf, grapples in a cigar box for what is presumably his father's revolver (a six-shooter), but drops it and then can only stare transfixed as his sister's body first levitates (in a curiously crucifixion-style position—the only abductee so photographed) and then sails out the window, her nightgown billowing and her form bathed in orange-yellow light.[29]

This memory contains the key elements that are elaborated in the larger world of *The X-Files,* just as it incorporates real world events into its structure. For example, echoing the gap on the Woods tape, there are many references to gaps and losses of time in multiple episodes: from the pilot episode, where Scully and Mulder lose nine minutes during what is supposed to be an alien visitation; to "Deep Throat" (9/17/93), where Mulder loses a whole day; to "One Breath" (11/11/94), where Scully loses three weeks; to the ironically titled "Tempus Fugit" (3/16/97) and its companion episode "Max" (3/23/97), where time is slowed, figures are shown in freeze-frame, and nine minutes are lost. Watergate itself figures into the text several times, with the appearance of Deep Throat (Jerry Hardin), scenes in the Watergate Hotel, and innumerable references to tapes, eavesdropping, and blank or missing tapes (e.g., "Little Green Men," "The Blessing Way," "Piper Maru" [2/09/96], "Apocrypha" [2/16/96], "Musings of a Cigarette-Smoking Man" [11/17/96], to name just a few). Moments of revelation and loss are punctuated by blinding, bright lights ("The X-Files: Pilot," "Conduit," "Little Green Men," "Fallen Angel" [11/19/93], "Tempus Fugit," "Max," and a host of others). As demonstrated above, guns are brandished but are never used or cannot be fired, just as the young Mulder cannot fire his father's weapon; the *Stratego* game is continually "replayed" in the larger scheme of a narrative implicating foreign governments, double identities, spies, and forays into the unknown. Samantha's abduction is repeated in Scully's abduction arc ("Duane Barry," "Ascension," and "One Breath"). In fact, in "The Field Where I Died" (11/03/96)—the only episode to depict a woman suffering from multiple personality disorder as sequelae of abuse—this doubling is made explicit. Under regression hypnosis, Mulder asserts that the son he lost in a past life is Samantha, whose place in this life is inhabited by Scully.[30]

Much as posttraumatic play is transmitted from child to child,[31] loss and trauma flood out to engulf Scully in her father's death in "Beyond the Sea" (1/07/94), her former boyfriend's death in "Lazarus" (2/04/93), and her sister's murder in "Paper Clip" (9/29/95). Loss doubles back to Mulder in Deep Throat's murder in "The Erlenmeyer Flask" (5/13/94— arguably the first installment in the conspiracy mythology), the Samantha imposter(s)' re-appearance and death in "Colony" and "End Game," Bill Mulder's (Peter Donat) murder in "Anasazi" (5/19/95), Mr. X's murder in "Herrenvolk" (10/04/96), and Mulder's mother's (Rebecca Toolan) stroke in "Talitha Cumi" and "Herrenvolk." Loss even extends to Skinner as his marriage dissolves in "Avatar" (4/26/96).[32]

Aliens are the best movie villains since Nazis.
—*David Devlin, speaking of* Independence Day[33]

Certainly this trauma, whatever its origin and true nature, is both organizing and catastrophic. As Mulder asserts in the series' pilot, Samantha's disappearance "tore our family apart." Perhaps it is not accidental that Mulder, who wants so desperately to believe in something, comes from a family whose parents have divorced, while Scully, a woman with faith in the linearity of science and logic, comes from an intact family.

Central to an understanding of adolescence is the observation that the adolescent passage to adulthood can only be successfully negotiated with the re-experiencing and resolution of repressed conflicts. These conflicts include an acceptance and placement of family within an historical framework. To paraphrase Anna Freud, a family has to be there to be left. What I suggest is that it is the rupture of the family itself—and all that this rupture implies—that is the core trauma beneath *The X-Files*'s surface, the event that disrupts history and derails development, which is symbolized by the rural and primitive settings of many of its stories. This disruption, set in fairly stereotypical ways around Oedipal exclusion, reverberates in an absolute failure of patriarchal authority entangled within a web of desire camouflaged as curiosity.

In the classical sense, the Oedipal scenario postulates the son's desire for the mother—to "investigate" the unseen, unrepresented, unspoken secrets of the female body. (Tellingly, Mulder's mother is never given a name and is known simply as "the mother"; she is, as with so many other traumatic stand-ins in the series, reduced to a symbol.) The father exists as barrier to and arbiter of this desire, denying access while prompting identification with his law. That *The X-Files* situates the site of ambivalence within the family and literally focuses this ambivalence within the woman's body would indicate that there is a gap—a space—resistant to reconstitution. With the death of Mulder's father, Bill, the catastrophic, unresolved, and un(der)represented nature of these traumas—of the dissolution of the family, the removal of patriarchal limitations, and the closer proximity to the mother of both pre-Oedipal and Oedipal fantasy—is mirrored in the narrative's incorporation of larger traumas that follow in the wake of Bill Mulder's murder.

Fittingly, these are constituted around the Holocaust and Nazism, perhaps the most unrepresented, unassimilated traumas of this century.

Scully and Mulder face the trauma: *The X-Files* (Twentieth-Century Fox TV, 1997).

Beginning with the episode "Anasazi," continuing through "Paper Clip," and reaching its zenith in "Demons," there are clear intimations that the trauma Mulder believes he remembers is not exactly the trauma with which he is obsessed. The truth, like memory, varies according to new information and context, just as the opening credit's tag line—"The Truth Is Out There"—does not have a fixed meaning, but shifts depending upon context to "Deny Everything" ("Ascension"), "Trust No One" ("The Erlenmeyer Flask"), the Navajo translation of "The Truth Is Out There" ("Anasazi"), "Apology Is Policy" ("731," [12/01/95]), and "Believe the Lie" ("Gethsemane").

"Anasazi" begins a story arc implicating Bill Mulder in a shameful episode of real American history, Operation Paper Clip,[34] and then incorporates the elements of this secret operation into subsequent story lines as the axis around which the conspiracy arc of *The X-Files* is drawn. Fittingly, Duchovny has stated that he believes Mulder is Jewish, and in "The Field Where I Died," Mulder accesses a past life in which he is a Jewish woman who loses her son to the Gestapo (seen by Mulder as a double for the Cigarette-Smoking Man) in a Polish ghetto. In "Kaddish" (2/16/97), the only episode to deal explicitly with Jewish concerns and mysticism per se, a neo-Nazi accuses Mulder of looking "like one of them."[35] Furthermore, not only is Bill Mulder implicated in an underground operation to bring Nazi scientists into the United States to further his own project (in "real" history, to exploit their knowledge as part of the government's agenda in furthering the cold war), but he also works alongside Nazi scientists such as the fictitious Victor Klemper, a character modeled after Hubertus Strughold. Strughold was a Nazi physician whose experiments at Dachau made him the darling of American space medicine;[36] the fictitious Klemper is touted as giving the United States government crucial expertise in its race to space against the Soviets. By extension, Bill Mulder's project—the creation of an alien-human hybrid—is directly linked to knowledge shared with Klemper. In these same episodes, piles of alien corpses, marked by strange "tattoos" (smallpox vaccination scars) are found heaped in cattle cars. Mulder concludes that the victims had been gassed ("Anasazi"). Mulder is nearly incinerated in this same cattle car by the Cigarette-Smoking Man, and in "Paper Clip," we discover that, in a style reminiscent of *Sophie's Choice,* Mulder's mother was asked to choose between her two children, sending one of them away with the Cigarette-Smoking Man to ensure Bill Mulder's continued silence.[37] In "731," Scully discovers a concentration camp filled with hybrids who have been executed and buried in mass graves. Again, in keeping with a filling-in of the traumatic gaps of real history, "731" and its companion episode "Nisei" (12/01/95) reference work in biological warfare perpetrated by the Japanese Imperial Army during World War II, using as test subjects prisoners of war and captured civilians.[38]

The equation *The X-Files* posits is a paranoiac's perversion of Aristotelian logic:

> The Holocaust happened; Mengele existed; experiments were performed on concentration camp inmates.
> Strughold was a real man, Operation Paper Clip was a fact, ex-Nazis furthered the American Space Program.
> From outer space come aliens.
> The Nazis wanted to take over the world.
> Ex-Nazis still want to take over the world.
> Aliens want to take over the world.
> There are "others" who want to take over the world.
> Ex-Nazis must be working with aliens.
> "Others" must be working with Ex-Nazis.
> Aliens must be working with the "others."
> *Ergo,* the Conspiracy exists.

Thus, the crisis of patriarchy and established law posited in *The X-Files* lies in betrayal and trauma juxtaposed against larger, historical crises perpetrated by social and authoritarian structures. Conspiracies exclude the inquisitive from the "truth," but could it be that the "conspiracy" from which Mulder is excluded is, in fact, a reference to and repetition of an Oedipal scenario, where a child is excluded from the secrets existing between husband and wife? Do the secrets with which *The X-Files* is concerned circulate around the mysteries of the female body? Are these archaic fantasies concerning the gap within a woman—the fact of her womb—the ultimate mysteries *The X-Files* wishes to fathom?

> You've kept things from me. You've kept secrets from me.
> > —*Mulder to his mother, "Demons"*

> Protect the mother.
> > —*Mr. X, "Herrenvolk"*

The X-Files implies that Mulder's mother has had an affair with the Cigarette-Smoking Man ("Talitha Cumi" and "Herrenvolk"). The Cigarette-Smoking Man may even be Mulder's father, a matter suggested by the photograph of the one-year-old Mulder and his mother that the Cigarette-Smoking Man carries ("Musings") and from questions Mulder asks ("Demons"). It requires only a small leap of intuition to understand that the conspiracy mythology centers on Mulder's investigations into the realms of birth, death, procreation, and origins, while excising the father as an impediment (through the consistent elision of official law, and the manifest story line of conspiracies that threaten to topple sanctioned, Oedipal authority). Fascinating indeed is *The X-Files*'s official homepage misremembering its own series, claiming that in "Demons," Mulder has a flashback to a young Cigarette-Smoking Man, who pulls Mulder's mother close to kiss her. In fact, this is not the case. While it is true that there is a flashback to a scene between Mulder's mother and the Cigarette-Smoking Man (substituting Scully's face for his mother's), they are not kissing—rather, the Cigarette-Smoking Man has hold of the woman's hair and roughly jerks her head back while she stares at him, terrified. It is Samantha whom the young Cigarette-Smoking Man pulls to him (putting her head against his chest), not Mulder's mother. Furthermore, in this same sequence, Mulder's parents argue furiously: His mother strikes out at his father; she cries out continually in horror, "My baby!" and is seen repeatedly closing a door; a young Cigarette-Smoking Man calls the young Mulder "a little spy"; and a younger Bill Mulder closes the door in his son's face three times over. Fox's exclusion from the scene, both in actuality (as much as can be trusted in the flashback) and fantasy (there are hidden conspiracies and powerful cabals—interestingly imaged in the series as a cadre of shadowy powerful men) intimates that it is the secrets and traumas of the family and, in particular, of the woman as the purveyor of life and death that the series seeks to uncover.

Narratives concerning investigations of outer space and aliens serve as vehicles with which to explore the terrain of the female body, and, quoting E. P. Bernabeu, to "[deny] the female as mother and [confer] on the male the exclusive processes of direct reproduction."[39] The same could be said of *The X-Files*. The project begun by Mulder's father and headed now exclusively by men involves the manufacture of new life forms—alien-human hybrids. What was formerly within the purview of the female—the power over life and death—is continually being usurped by men wishing to have the same power or hungering after the mother's secrets. In "Talitha Cumi," only Mulder's mother knows where "something very old . . . something very important" (an alien stiletto) is hidden. There are multiple references in both the Conspiracy arc and paranormal narratives to fetuses ("The Erlenmeyer Flask," "Colony"), clones ("Eve" [12/10/93], "Colony," "End Game," "Tunguska" [11/24/96], and "Herrenvolk"), and alien-human DNA hybrids ("731," "One Breath," and "Red Museum"). Strange implants are discovered in bodily cavities more frequently in women than men ("The X-Files: Pilot," "Duane Barry," "Ascension" [which includes a bizarre vision Mulder has of Scully on an exam table, a laparoscope protruding from her swollen belly]; "The Blessing Way," "Paper Clip," and "Nisei"). In an inversion upon male fears about pregnancy, beings invade and control men, from aliens ("Piper Maru" and "Apocrypha"), to spirits ("Lazarus," "Grotesque" [2/02/96], and "Teso Dos Bichos" [3/08/96], the latter brought on from the exhumation of the remains of a female shaman), to new life-forms ("The Host" and "Firewalker"). Echoing archaic fantasies regarding impregnation and penetration, there are multiple references and flash-backs to drills boring into bodies (male and female), including "Duane Barry," "Ascension," and "Demons." The one episode that involves a pregnant woman, "Aubrey" [1/06/95], posits that the pregnancy itself is transformative, the "catalyst" for the evocation of murderous, male character traits embedded in genetic memory—and, not surprisingly, the fetus is a boy.

All these episodes have in common what I pointed out regarding Scully: It is woman who is alien; the body of the woman is synonymous with and has been substituted for the alien, and the parasitic fetus is her little alien. In abducting and probing woman, the male can claim, usurp, and negate her functions. For example, "Nisei" begins with a brief glimpse of an alien being worked over by a group of doctors, then segues to Mulder and Scully watching a video of an alien autopsy.[40] Yet this is only the cover for the episode, as it moves instead to focus on Scully's discovery of a circle of women, who are all abductees and have been "taken" multiple times over. Scully has a flashback to her abduction as she views this same video later in the episode, where she sees her body substituted for the alien's being dissected upon the examining table. These "taken" women all succumb to cancer, and we discover that Scully's cancer is seeded, implanted, deposited into her by men intent upon discovering her secrets. Like the aliens who are caricatured fetal monstrosities with their smooth bodies and bulbous, oversized heads, Scully's cancer is a grotesquery of a fetus gone awry.

> I wish I could say we're going in circles, but I feel like we're going in an endless line—two steps forward and three steps back—while my own life is standing still.
>
> —*Scully, "Never Again"*

> There's no sense to make! You make the sense yourself.
>
> —*Chris Carter* [41]

There are few solid conclusions one can draw from this, save to reference that what is most unrepresentable and traumatic for *The X-Files* are the same archaic fantasies about women found in a preponderance of horror

336

and science fiction narratives. Yet, making sense, making meaning—these are the projects of a postmodern age, statements as much about the audience's plight as Mulder's. *Facts* abound in *The X-Files,* but they no more serve as *explanation* than do dates in history or troop movements on a battlefield (or game pieces in *Stratego*). Organized around unrepresentable trauma, *The X-Files* takes its cue from such iconography. The series amasses a plethora of images, flashbacks, and memories admitting of no coherence and no direction save its own circular logic.

The X-Files may be a reaction to or product of epistemological breaks in history and narrative typical of a postmodern culture reliant upon fabricated images and a discourse manipulated by the media. The show's popularity may be indicative of the need for a restoration of historical continuity from multiple and unresolved, un(der)represented traumas. To that end, this narrative transposes intrapsychic concerns and unconscious/hidden agendas to the real world, incorporating within its paranoid, self-referential matrix a mirroring host of unmetabolized social (and international) traumas, codified into easy acronyms, visual shorthand, and psychic condensations. (That blinding white light was not the flash from an atom bomb; it was the arrival of the aliens.) These larger traumas are re-enacted upon the much smaller, intrapsychic stage as ruptures, betrayal, and secrets within the embattled post-nuclear family.

Steven Best and Douglas Kellner paraphrase Baudrillard's "fatal strategy" as that which "pursues a course of action or trajectory to its extreme, attempting to surpass its limits, to go beyond its boundaries . . . and in going beyond all hitherto conceivable limits produce something new and different."[42] It is a synonym for adolescence. Structured around this developmental epoch, *The X-Files* gives the illusion of movement in its attempted negation of established belief systems, but it is not about renewal, illumination, education, or creation of an alternative "real" history. Chameleon-like, this traumatic, "as if" narrative draws upon the now and exploits, in a peculiarly postmodern way, breaks and gaps in knowledge, fact, science, culture, society, and history to construct its own virtual history and transposes these gaps to the literal gap and space within woman. Stripped of real history, this series cannot do what a closely allied series, *The Twilight Zone,* always did—investigate moralities—because there are no moral or historical frameworks the series interrogates. Similarly, Sharrett maintains that *Taxi Driver* cannot provide dramatic closure because its "general alienation is profound, pervasive, and resistant to any interpretation or cure."[43] Yet that film still saw the family as restorative in a way that *The X-Files,* delving into and dissecting the horrors and secrets of the nuclear family in a postnuclear age, does not. Mulder and Scully may exhibit the trappings of complexity, but theirs are histories made up as the series goes along, structured more around absence than substance, vortices circulating around loss. These are empty people bound together by circumstance in a chaotic, empty world blighted by horrors, crimes, and atrocities inadequately assimilated and from which we are encouraged to look away in search of fantastic yet perversely more acceptable explanations that absolve us from any true knowledge, understanding, or avowal of our history and our culpability for that history. Looking to the alien, the extra/outside/beyond-terrestrial, *The X-Files* returns, paradoxically, to what is alien within us, to the unknowable space within woman, and to the (constructed) and ultimately null, empty, enviously impotent male subject. The truth *The X-Files* seeks, articulated as simulacra "out there" in a discourse of primitive fantasy, is fleeting, lost, ungraspable, unseen, ultimately unrepresentable—the signature narrative for a posttraumatic, postmodern age.

POSTSCRIPT

Since the original writing of this paper, the fifth season of *The X-Files* has aired and the film *The X-Files: Fight the Future* (Rob Bowman, 1998) has been released. Not surprisingly, the series continues its interrogation of woman's space, positing the search for and ultimate loss of Scully's daughter in the season's first two episodes. The film expands on this archaic material, explicating little but continuing with primitive impregnation fantasies and birth imagery. The primary themes again center upon historical disjunctions, traumatic loss, and woman as alien. Once more, the Conspiracy is explicitly linked to the Holocaust and World War II, as Strughold now reappears as dislocated fiction wrested from fact, the leader of the operation in Tunis (who will, presumably, replace the Well-Manicured Man, the erstwhile British ally who helps Mulder and is killed). In the film, Scully is again impregnated and abducted, though this time her disease is not a cancer but a fetus (the alien viral pathogen that has mutated into a biologic, independent entity). Coming closer to the archaic mother of fantasy, Mulder literally enters a womb as he descends through a labyrinthine tube to arrive in the belly of a huge Mother Ship, reminiscent of the alien ship in *Alien* (Ridley Scott, 1979). He discovers alien embryos gestating within the body cavities of humans.[44] Aliens are briefly glimpsed; evidence, except for the Africanized honey bee, disappears; and tellingly, when Mulder urges Scully to look as the Mother

Ship blasts free from beneath the Antarctic, she loses consciousness. All that is left—for us and for Mulder—is a huge, gaping hole in a featureless, frozen waste. *The X-Files: Fight the Future* is regressive and circular; the subtitle is apt.

Notes

I am indebted to Christopher Sharrett for the time and insights he gave, without complaint and always with compassion, in our countless hours of discussion.

1. Ernst Bloch, "Nonsynchronism and Dialectics," *New German Critique* 11 (1977): 22.

2. Harold P. Blum, "The Concept of the Reconstruction of Trauma," in *The Reconstruction of Trauma: Its Significance in Clinical Work*, ed. Arnold Rothstein (Madison, Conn.: International Universities Press, 1986), 12–13.

3. Thomas Elsaesser, "Subject Positions, Speaking Positions: From *Holocaust, Our Hitler,* and *Heimat* to *Shoah* and *Schindler's List*," in *The Persistence of History: Cinema, Television, and the Modern Event*, ed. Vivian Sobchack (London: Routledge, 1996), 147.

4. Saul Friedlander, *Reflections of Nazism: An Essay on Kitsch and Death* (Bloomington: Indiana University Press, 1993), 21.

5. Cf. Judith Witwer, "The Best of Both Worlds: On *Star Trek*'s Borg," in *Prosthetic Territories: Politics and Hypertechnologies*, ed. Gabriel Brahm, Jr., and Mark Driscoll (Boulder: Westview Press, 1995), 250–79.

6. Elsaesser, "Subject Positions," 147.

7. See Jane Goldman, *The X-Files: Book of the Unexplained, Volume Two* (New York: Harper Collins, 1997), 213.

8. Cf. Ilsa J. Bick, "Boys in Space: *Star Trek,* Latency and The NeverEnding Story," in *Enterprise Zones: Critical Positions on Star Trek*, ed. Taylor Harrison, Sarah Projansky, Kent A. Uno, and Elyce Rae Helford (Boulder: Westview Press, 1996), 189–210.

9. A general familiarity with *The X-Files* story "arcs" is assumed. At the time this paper was originally written, the fifth season had not aired, and the movie had not yet been released; therefore, this analysis will concern itself only with seasons 1–4. Furthermore, this series is so dense that to claim that this analysis can be all-inclusive is doomed from the start. This work will not discuss, explain, or defend trauma and posttraumatic phenomenon in terms other than those used by clinicians. The controversy regarding "recovered" memories and "false" memories will not be explored. A rudimentary knowledge of psychoanalytic principles and theory is assumed. The interested reader is referred to work by Lenore Terr for more in-depth study: "Chowchilla Revisited," *American Journal of Psychiatry* 140 (1983): 1543–50; "Time and Trauma," *The Psychoanalytic Study of the Child* 39 (1984): 633–66; "Childhood Traumas: An Outline and Overview," *American Journal of Psychiatry* 148 (1991): 10–20; and "True Memories of Childhood Trauma: Flaws, Absences, and Returns," in *The Recovery Memory/False Memory Debate*, ed. Kathy Pazdek

and William P. Banks (Washington, D.C.: Academic Press, 1996), 69–80. All air dates are taken from the official *The X-Files* homepage (www.TheX-Files.com).

10. See Peter Blos, *On Adolescence: A Psychoanalytic Interpretation* (New York: Free Press, 1962) and *The Adolescent Passage: Developmental Issues* (New York: International Universities Press, 1979).

11. Cf. Perry Nodelman, "Out There in Children's Science Fiction: Forward into the Past," *Science-Fiction Studies* 12 (1985): 285–96.

12. See Anna Freud, *The Ego and the Mechanisms of Defense, Vol. II* (New York: International Universities Press, 1966), 137–72.

13. Sharrett examines the collapse of the subject's self-mediating functions with "authentic experience," just as the film paradoxically struggles to reaffirm the purgative and regenerative powers of violence. Sharrett underscores that within the trauma and violence of the urban setting, Travis Bickle emerges as a figure emblematic of a "postmodern culture of simulation . . . a collage of media images divorced from history." See Sharrett, "American Apocalyse: Scorsese's *Taxi Driver,*" in *Crisis Cinema: The Apocalyptic Idea in Postmodern Narrative Film* (Washington, DC: Maisonneuve Press, 1993), 231.

14. Ibid., 230.

15. Ernst Kris, "The Personal Myth: A Problem in Psychoanalytic Technique," *Journal of the American Psychoanalytic Association* 4 (1956): 653–81.

16. Sharrett, "American Apocalypse," 230.

17. Cf. Sara Kozloff, *Invisible Storytellers: Voice-over Narration in American Fiction Film* (Berkeley: University of California Press, 1988).

18. Gillian Anderson's pregnancy precluded her appearing in one episode following "Duane Barry," and while she figures in three episodes leading up to "Duane Barry," she is central only in "Little Green Men" (9/16/94). Thereafter, she is invariably photographed from the chest up, usually feeding information to Mulder via her cellular phone, or, as in "Duane Barry," calling him from the phone in her apartment.

19. In "Little Green Men," for example, Cigarette-Smoking Man (William B. Davis) and Skinner rely upon Scully to find Mulder, not the other way around. This episode contains the first and, to my viewing, the only instance where Mulder avows his absolute trust in Scully, though she herself is not present (he talks into a tape recorder). It is also one of the rare episodes where Mulder delivers the opening voice-over. Ironically, Scully, the woman Mulder trusts, gains access to Mulder's computer files by correctly guessing his password: TRUSTNO1.

20. It is assumed, however, that Scully's exposure to an ergot hallucinogen might be responsible for her lapse—a reference, perhaps, to adolescent experimentation. Interesting, too, is the fact that Mulder is disbelieving that Scully could possibly have a date, and her temporary separation from him is signified in the fact that she withholds her voice—she hangs up on him.

21. It is tempting to see a parallel between Scully's reaction and popular cultural conceits regarding feminine investments in and infatuations with images (daytime television, soap operas, game shows).

22. Cf. Mimi White, *Tele-Advising: Therapeutic Discourse in American Television* (Chapel Hill: University of North Carolina Press, 1992).

23. Freud (1914, 1920) viewed repetition as a form of memory, and the compulsion to repeat and enact these memories as a form of mastery, where the repeated action substituted for recall of unassimilated (though forgotten) memories. In the case of the repetition compulsion, the ego's resources are brought to bear in a creative re-negotiation of the (forgotten) memory with the environment as it exists in the here and now—to re-cast the now in the intrapsychic agenda of what was left unfinished in the past. See Sigmund Freud (1914) "Remembering, Repeating and Working-through," in *The Standard Edition of the Complete Psychological Works of Sigmund Freud,* ed. James Strachey (London: Hogarth Press and the Institute of Psycho-Analysis, 1953–74), 12:486–519, and "Beyond the Pleasure Principle," *SE* 18 (1920): 7–64.

The phenomenon of repetition is not, however, only a symptom of pathology and is manifest in a variety of different contexts, not all of which are driven by trauma, such as in repetitive attempts to avoid the new, to engage in pleasurable activity (and though one could argue that there is a certain pleasure in masochism, the clinical phenomenon of repetitive attempts at seeking pleasure have a different flavor and cast), or to complete something left incomplete. For example, children play in a compulsive, repetitious way until they "get it right." See Hans Loewald, "Some Considerations on Repetition and Repetition Compulsion," *International Journal of Psychoanalysis* 52 (1971): 59–65.

24. Interestingly, it is Scully who references Melville explicitly, not only in her father's choice of her nickname ("Starbuck"), but also in his profession as a naval captain, who is always shown in her dreams and memories in full dress whites, and in the name Scully chooses for her dog, Queequag, who is eaten by a giant alligator in "Quagmire" (5/03/96).

25. Chris Carter explains this by indicating that since "Mulder's memories are derived from regression therapy, those images are understandably vague, explaining why he would recall the incident differently at a later time." See Brian Lowry, *The Truth Is Out There: The Official Guide to the X Files* (New York: Harper Prism, 1995), 163.

26. Asked under hypnosis if he believes when a man's voice tells him that his sister will be all right, Mulder states, "I want to believe."

27. Mulder's memory of the abduction is prompted by a sign in the Watergate Hotel parking garage.

28. The premise of *The Magician,* a real show, involves a protagonist who solved mysteries with sleight of hand. Though I have been unable to locate a copy of this show, I remember an interview in which Bill Bixby expressed his enthusiasm about playing a character who did not use a gun.

29. In one of its many nods at prevailing cultural depictions of alien visitations, this sequence contains elements common to Spielberg's films. Not only does the little boy in "Conduit" receive his impressions from the television (cf. *Poltergeist,* 1982), but the aliens' arrival mimics *Close Encounters of the Third Kind* (1977), the types of ships the aliens use seem eerily similar to the Mother Ship of the same film (and another Spielberg-related vehicle, *Seaquest DSV,* paid homage to Spielberg's vision by using the same type of ship), and the aliens invariably look like the aliens Spielberg posits in *Close Encounters* (ditto for *DSV*). There is even an explicit link in "Ice" to *Star Trek II: The Wrath of Khan* (Meyer, 1982) as the alien worm is inserted in

a dog's ear. *The X-Files* continually draws upon the real and the fabricated, from historical events, to films, to individuals active in *The X-Files* fandom.

30. Mulder goes on to state that a sergeant killed in battle—and thus the person who directs and commands him—is also Scully.

31. Lenore Terr observes that "what is experienced in popular culture as the paranormal has its roots in contagious, posttraumatic phenomenon. . . . Because we can easily fantasize overwhelming helplessness, whether or not we have ever experienced an out-and-out trauma, we can easily empathize with the traumatized person. We transmit his games without pausing much to consider." See Lenore Terr, "Remembered Images and Trauma: A Psychology of the Supernatural," *The Psychoanalytic Study of the Child* 40 (1985): 529.

32. The avatar of the episode's title refers to a recurring vision/nightmare of an old woman, dressed in red, from which Skinner, a former Marine, has suffered since his own near-death experience in Vietnam. The succubus, figured as an apparition who kills other women out of jealousy, is here depicted as Skinner's stand-in, acting out of his rage at his wife, while Skinner himself seeks psychiatric treatment for a sleep disorder. For a former Marine, Skinner is a picture of impotence, being manipulated by Cigarette-Smoking Man and in "Pusher" (2/23/96), being sprayed with mace and kicked multiple times over by a woman (who is, albeit, controlled by a man).

33. Sharon Waxman, "Aliens Take Over U.S. Theaters," *The Washington Post,* July 9, 1996, A2.

34. The episode's title references a covert JIOA (Joint Intelligence Objectives Agency) operation through which over 1,600 Nazi scientists, such as Wernher Von Braun, Arthur Rudolph, and their dependents, were spirited out of Germany, their pasts expunged, and their talents put to the service of the United States in its cold war with the Soviet Union. The operation was named for the immigration form "paper clipped" to the dossier of each scientist. See Christopher Simpson, *Blowback: America's Recruitment of Nazis and Its Effects on the Cold War* (New York: Weidenfeld and Nicolson, 1988); and Linda Hunt, *Secret Agenda: The United States Government, Nazi Scientists, and Project Paperclip: 1945 to 1990* (New York: St. Martin's Press, 1991).

35. Isaac Luria, the murdered Chassid who is subsequently resurrected as the golem, is clearly named after the real Luria, who was a sixteenth-century Kabbalist. See J. Abelson, *Jewish Mysticism* (New York: Hermon Press, 1969), and Perle Epstein, *Kabbalah: The Way of the Jewish Mystic* (New York: Doubleday, 1978).

36. Hunt, *Secret Agenda,* 85–86, 88–89, 232–33, 259.

37. Mulder's mother then contradicts herself, stating, "It was your father's choice, and I hated him for it. Even in his grave, I hate him still."

38. See Peter Williams and David Wallace, *Unit 731: Japan's Secret Biological Warfare in World War II* (New York: Free Press, 1989). The reader is also referred to Goldman, *Book of the Unexplained,* for short summaries of the history of Paper Clip and Unit 731.

39. Bick, "Boys in Space," 196–98.

40. This is the same "alien autopsy" footage in *Alien Autopsy: Fact or Fiction?* (Tom McGough, 1995) released roughly contemporaneously with the episode.

41. Brian Lowry, *The Truth Is Out There: The Official Guide to The X-Files* (New York: Harper Prism, 1995), 20.

42. Stephen Best and Douglas Kellner, *Postmodern Theory: Critical Interrogations* (New York: Guilford Press, Inc., 1991), 131.

43. Sharrett, "American Apocalypse," 234.

44. Cf. Ilsa J. Bick, "*Alien* Within, *Aliens* Without: The Primal Scene and the Return to the Repressed," *American Imago* 45 (1988): 337–58.

14

ALIEN/NATION: INVASIONS, ABDUCTIONS, AND THE POLITICS OF IDENTITY

LIANNE MCLARTY

A certain sign of the absorption of extraterrestrial phenomena into North American popular culture is its appropriation by the system of commodity exchange. Lately, aliens sell: anything from candy bars (Reese's Pieces and, predictably, Mars chocolate bars) to Maytag washing machines, long-distance telephone companies, and cough syrup. Extraterrestrials populate many recent television series (*The X-Files, Dark Skies,* and *Earth: Final Conflict*) as well as tabloid news shows and special event programming such as *Alien Autopsy.* The abduction of humans by aliens and government conspiracies and cover-ups form a large part of the New Age and Paranormal sections in book stores. The summers of 1996 and 1997 saw the release of *The Arrival, Independence Day* (which broke box office records), *Contact, Men in Black,* and *Mars Attacks!,* respectively. That the last of these takes alien invasion scenarios to the point of parody signals the assimilation of aliens into popular culture. Extraterrestrials look out at me from the t-shirts and paraphernalia of my students. "They" are among us.[1]

Of course, they have been here before, typically in the science fiction films of the 1950s and at the service of a cold war ideology that depended on a clearly delineated enemy in order to validate itself. Invasive aliens, blindly bent on the reproduction of their kind, provided a convenient (if thinly veiled) metaphor for a Communist threat to American democracy. As Robin Wood points out with respect to the horror film, the fear generated around an absolutely evil Other is a particularly poignant means through which ideological beliefs are encouraged, managed, and maintained.[2] Like some horror films, stories about alien abductions and invasions can work to establish clear boundaries between "us" and "them" and contribute to and validate paranoia about the Other's imminent attack; in doing so, these stories endorse the necessity of violent defense at all costs. Absolutely different from "humanity" and responsible for sheer irrational savagery, the alien Other both ignites and justifies the violence enacted upon it. Social conflicts are displaced onto it and "resolved" in the "lawful" employment of force.[3]

In his discussion of scapegoating as the means through which socially sanctioned collective acts of violence are both generated and excused, René Girard argues that in myth "we can expect the violence of the group to be condoned and justified. The violence will be presented as a legitimate defense against a fearsome monster, as the just punishment of a guilty criminal."[4] Built into the concept of the scapegoat is both the community's rationale for violence (the scapegoat is a "monster") and its validation (social cohesion results from the annihilation or banishment of the scapegoat). Violence is not the responsibility of the group but of the Other for "bringing about some evil that must be avenged."[5] Myths set up an immutable opposition between a Norm (the community) and an Other that is both different from and threatening to the Norm, and the resulting conflict between the two works to endorse the values and identity positions consistent with the community. Central to this validation is the violence the group enacts on the Other. It is through the psychological violence of banishment or the physical violence of annihilation of the Other that the community constitutes itself by defining and defending its borders. Violence is embedded in the ideological enterprise of enforcing social cohesion.[6]

Similarly, Richard Slotkin locates violence, and the construction of an Other to bear its burden, at the center of American mythology. While Girard's analysis treats the scapegoat as a universal phenomenon, Slotkin demonstrates its role in securing the economic imperatives of industrialization and validating the violence the execution of these imperatives demands. In his historical discussion of the myth and ideology of expansion and industrial "progress," he argues that an "American mythology of violence . . . continually invokes the prospect of genocidal warfare and apocalyptic, world-destroying massacres."[7] What is particular to this American context is the "regenerative" potential of violence provided by the combination of the history of the "Wars of Dispossession" and the Christian "myth of redemptive blood sacrifice."[8] Slotkin argues that after 1700 the writing of history into myth was the "fable of a race war," marked by a Native/white opposition in which colonial culture conflicts with Native Americans but "emerge[s] as spiritually regenerate heroes of Christian civilization."[9] Depending on the "belief that certain races are pre-disposed to cruel and atrocious violence," the "ideology of the savage war" provides the mythology with both its regenerative function and a rationale for the violence enacted on, and excused by, a monstrous Other. It "enriches the symbolic meaning of specific acts of war, transforming them into episodes of character building, moral vindication, and regeneration," justifying, in advance, extreme acts of "extermination," while putting "the moral responsibility for that outcome on the enemy, which is to say, on its predicted victims."[10] The Other bears the burden of blame for the violence central in celebrating and maintaining hegemonic positions of power.

Slotkin's analysis of the centrality of violence in American mythology and Girard's discussion of the psycho-social function of the scapegoat provide a useful framework for considering the recent fascination with beings who are so Other as to be literally "out-of-this-world" and, in some cases, whose unmitigated acts of aggression demand violent retaliation in the extreme. This construction of a monstrous Other against and upon whom dominant ideology is affirmed through the violent annihilation of its difference also calls to mind Wood's characterization of the reactionary horror film in which patriarchal capitalism is endorsed in its confrontation with and destruction of the monster who embodies all that the dominant order represses and seeks to disavow.[11] Indeed, there is an ideological correspondence between contemporary alien invasion films and the reactionary horror film, inasmuch as they provide an opportunity to displace anxieties about this social world onto an absolute Other. The construction of an extraterrestrial threat, equipped with advanced technologies, is a particularly effective means through which the contours of dominant power can not only be defined but also aggressively reinforced, all the while posing as the victim of a superhuman force.

As part of the current cultural "possession" by the paranormal, stories about aliens can function to deflect attention from the politics of this social world to the Other-worldly, displacing the oppression structured within patriarchal capitalism onto alien difference. (What is the current fascination with the New Age in general—crystals and channeling are of the same order as divine and/or dreadful alien beings—if not an avoidance of the alienation structured within this age?) Yet, the ideological similarities among recent alien invasion films, science fiction films of the 1950s, the framework of the Other as scapegoat, and the reactionary horror film are complicated by shifts in the construction of the Other that occurred in the post-*Psycho* (1960), post-*Exorcist* (1973) horror film.[12] Unlike the reactionary horror film described by Wood, which is said to clearly demarcate "them" from "us," contemporary postmodern horror is distinguished by its tendency to collapse those very boundaries.[13] It is the difference between a monstrous threat that exists "out there," embodied in the Other, and the suggestion that the monster is located "here," in "us." Films that portray aliens imitating or replacing humans can provide rich soil for cultivating a horror of the commonplace in which the monstrous is systemic, the scapegoat dismantled in the collapse of the distinction between "us" and "them," and acts of violence owned.[14] The tendency in postmodern horror to situate the threat in the practices of this world troubles a categorical reading of alien invasion films as the ideological means through which social cohesion is constituted in acts of aggression both inspired, and suffered, by the Other. Having one tentacle (as it were) in reactionary mythology, and one clinging, however tentatively, to contemporary horror's collapse of the boundaries separating "us" from "them," these films provide an opportunity to explore the ways in which alien Otherness, and the violence central to its construction and extermination, is figured at a time when "them" *might* be "us." The question, of course, is "who are we?"

Because they construct alien species capable of imitating, replacing, or invading humans, films about alien invasions underscore the central role questions of identity (its vulnerability, and its need of violent defense) play in scapegoating. Identity in these films is often inscribed on the body, specifically in the encounter between human and alien biologies. Alien invasion films are distinguished from the paranormal and supernatural by their fascination with the body. Opposed to the psychic's mental powers and the disembodied specter of the ghost, the alien has a physical manifestation, whether it is as a human (having imitated, invaded, or duplicated the body), or as a separate creature (humanoid or not). (In terms of UFO cultural phenomena, this focus on alien identity as biological difference marks a general shift in focus from the comparatively distant saucer sightings prominent after World War II to the current "close encounter" accounts of physical abductions, alien/human hybrids, and autopsies.) It is in the encounter between alien and human physiology that some identities are violently reinforced and "Others" annihilated. Some of these films hinge their horror and justification for violence on absolute alien biological difference, and in doing so, collapse social divisions among people into the universal category of "human." Given the ease with which the frontier is translated into the last frontier of outer space in American mythology, Slotkin's observation that ethnic, religious, and class divisions among whites are erased through their common racial ground in opposition to Native Americans is applicable here. This common ground is less common than the ground of a biological essentialism that served to validate white hegemony by invoking a notion of natural right instead of a European notion of aristocratic right. That identity and its inherent privileges or disadvantages are seen to be based in biology is evident in the use of the term "half-breed" to describe and deride those renegades who, in their confrontation with the Other, became too familiar.[15] Fear is not only generated by "different bodies" and the identities these bodies are seen to insist upon but, specifically, by their intermingling. Horror results when borders are crossed; violence is validated as a means of defending biological as well as geographical territory. A similar fear of miscegenation informs the politics of identity in recent stories about abductions and alien/human hybrids.

While moments of an oppositional critical stance can be found in the refusal of some of these films to ground monstrous biology in an alien Other, most of the recent examples cited here forge a rather firm divide between human and alien identity. These films recall the myth of the frontier, which displaces "internal social [class] conflicts . . . outward onto racial war on the borders."[16] Similarly, conservative alien invasion films project social anxieties about class, race, and sexual difference onto an alien Other beyond the borders. Humanity is universalized as "white" and patriarchal, and its victimized relation to racial and sexual alien Others is articulated by invoking class disenfranchisement. Whereas Slotkin argues that the racial symbolism that structures the myth of expansion masks the economic inequalities of the metropolis (erasing class disparity), recent alien invasion films exploit issues of social class. Class, as social and economic disenfranchisement, not only provides an alibi for the exercise of violence by dominant power (the Other is oppressive), but it also casts that power as victimized. Like Girard's scapegoat myths in which the victim is made responsible for the violence it endures, these films write marginalized racial and sexual identities into positions of superhuman power and simultaneously pose dominant power as a form of powerlessness.[17] That working-class (or in some ways disenfranchised) characters are used to represent humanity under siege is evidence of commodity culture's skill at incorporating some contradictions while annihilating "Others."

ALIEN/NATION: "THEM" IS "US"

They Live (1989) provides a poignant point of departure and comparison to more recent alien invasion films precisely because it embeds the monstrous in the familiar social organization demanded by consumer capitalism. Here, alien Otherness is not a matter of physiological difference. These aliens are more than mimics; they actually look human to the naked eye, but even with the special sunglasses needed to detect them, they resemble sub-epidermal human anatomy. Importantly, they facilitate their invasion from within mainstream media by broadcasting a television signal that annihilates consciousness, rendering humans "asleep, selfish, and sedated." In the interests of free enterprise, they promote an ideology of consumption and conformity. When the protagonist, Nada, wears the sunglasses and sees beyond the "veil of reification" the aliens have induced, he realizes that an advertisement for a tropical vacation is really a promotion of the heterosexual family: Without the glasses the billboard portrays a sexualized white woman reclining on a beach; with the glasses we see the directive "marry and reproduce." Promoting consumption as a way of life, the aliens seduce with the promise of an expensive car and a big house. Refusing, by reversing the logic of scapegoating, this film suggests the source of violence is here, in capitalism, and in the cultural and repressive state apparatuses that support it—the aliens control law enforcement as well as the media. The separation between aliens and humans is a matter of social-economic privilege, not biological differences. As one alien describes the rationale for their invasion, "it's business": Monsters wear suits.

Unlike the frontier myth, *They Live* does not employ class as a means of erasing capitalist relations by displacing conflicts about economic disenfranchisement and disparity onto a visible Other. Significantly, the first character whom Nada confirms is human is an African-American newspaper vendor, and, as if to underscore this point, he makes a subsequent alien/human distinction between a white, upper-class woman in a fur coat (alien) and an Asian woman (human). Although Nada's alien baiting is largely directed at the appearance of the women (he says to the Asian woman, "you're O.K., but this one, [referring to the alien in fur] real fuckin' ugly") and a complicit female betrays him, it is class privilege that is characterized as the site of social violence, not sexual or racial difference. Complicit humans get promoted.

Similarly, this dread of sameness informs films such as *The Invasion of the Body Snatchers* (1979), *Invaders from Mars* (1986), and the more recent *Body Snatchers* (1993); alien biology depends on the replacement of specific humans suggesting an affinity between "us" and "them."[18] In *The Invasion of the Body Snatchers,* for example, the pod people maintain the minds and memories of their human hosts; "everything," we are told, "remains intact." *Body Snatchers* makes this point obvious: If the human is revived during the process of transformation, the duplicate graphically decays. Not only do these aliens sustain themselves through our biology, they are systemic. In *Invaders from Mars* they work within the family, the educational system, and communication networks (one of them works for the phone company); and in *Body Snatchers* the alien threat is attached to the military industrial complex (aliens launch their infiltration from an army base that stores toxic waste). The pods spread randomly in *The Invasion of the Body Snatchers* and thrive in "devastated ground, like the war-torn cities of Europe," suggesting an association between the practices of earth and alien survival.

The Hidden (1990) and *The Hidden 2* (1994) suggest a similar dependency. Here, the takeover defines the relationship between alien and human, and although it is a separate, invasive creature, this alien is strengthened by its close encounter with our biology: It can only be destroyed when it leaves its human host. While those humans possessed by aliens act uncharacteristically violent, these films imply that their excessive violence is simply an exaggeration of worldly social relations: aliens consume excessively, take what they want, and like Ferraris. The text at the beginning of the sequel reads: "The alien's pattern of behaviour is consistent with that on other planets: indulgence in drugs, sex, and violence." Earth is a "perfect host" for this alien species. Although the two versions of *The Hidden* suggest that "human" is alien, the "alien/nation" structured within earthly relations gives way to a fascination with alien biological difference, not only in opposition to human, but *among* alien species as well. Significantly, the gentle, nice extraterrestrial is pure consciousness, has no physical body, and manifests as pure light, while the violent, monstrous alien is pure body, carnal, and self-indulgent with respect to the flesh.[19] What is threatening about alien Otherness is being too much in the body. Violence, both literal and figurative, is seen as a failure of surplus repression, a failure to conform to social conventions. Acts of violence are problematized to the extent that they are enacted outside of the law and as an indulgence in the body. The equation of violence and drugs with sex in the opening text fuses the body with horror (violence) and deviance (drugs). It is the body, and not the system of social conventions with which it is indulged, that is the source of the threat; unlike *They Live,* violence here is more a matter of the flesh than the ideological imperatives of consumer capitalism.

The Thing (1982) exploits this fascination with alien biology through what were, at the time of release, stunning visual effects that focused on the body as a graphic site of violent transformation and mutant manifestations.[20] While this film takes as its premise the imitation of humans through violent invasion and hinges its narrative on the inability to tell "us" from "them," the mutation process, which violently transforms human into monstrous alien Other, is central to the visual demarcation of difference. Importantly, difference is inscribed on the

351

biological boundary between alien Otherness and "humanity." Given that some contemporary films about violent invasions focus on the body as a site of monstrous difference and link that difference to marginalized identities, it is perhaps prophetic that this film ends with two men, one African American, the other white, each suspecting the other of being the Other. In more recent films, it seems that alien biology comes to depend on racial and sexual difference.

ALIEN DIFFERENCE: THE POLITICS OF IDENTITY

Species (1995) figures the alien as a beautiful young woman, whose human incarnation frequently transforms—especially during sex—into monstrous biological difference. What specifically makes this alien threatening is her instinctual drive to physically reproduce; as one character comments, "her biological clock must be in hyper drive." It is interesting that her first incarnation is as a prepubescent girl. While she rapidly matures, she maintains a certain naiveté: she is unaware of various social conventions and television is new to her. Although this initially provides her with an aura of vulnerability (which the film warns is a sham as she is ruthless and will kill anyone who blocks her compulsion to breed), it also helps code her as pre- or nonsocial—she is described as "a psychopath with no moral sense, no social structure."[21] Like the aliens of *The Hidden* and its sequel, this extraterrestrial exists for the body, but, more specifically, she exists to have sex (indulge the flesh) and propagate (reproduce it). This alignment between alien and feminine is underscored by the professional specialty of the female protagonist; she is an expert in "exobiology," the study of alien physiology.[22] Similar to some contemporary horror films analyzed by Barbara Creed, *Species* hinges its abject on the feminine, particularly on a horror of reproduction.[23] Yet, it also associates that "monstrous feminine" with a racial Other: It is the African-American "empath" (enlisted to explain her motives to the government agency hunting her) who is psychically connected to alien difference. He feels what the alien feels and acts as a translator of her moves and motives for the government. Significantly, he is the first to encounter the Other, the most emotionally affected by her violence, and in the film's conclusion, his body actually forms a link between human and alien (the alien has hold of his leg while the other humans pull him to safety by his arms). Here, the Otherness culled from the feminine is made intelligible through the emotive, inexplicable, and instinctual qualities of the African-American character; alien biology depends on the intersection of two marginalized identities.

The Arrival (1996) and *Independence Day* (1996) share this concern with alien biology as the site of monstrous difference, but they rely less on gender than racial difference for marking the boundaries between alien and human. Both films offer a clear demarcation between the bodies of "us" and "them": *Independence Day* constructs aliens as big bugs, and although in *The Arrival* aliens are able to look like us, they are also marked by their radical biological difference. Even when they appear human, they assume physical alien characteristics: they bend their knees backward, transport themselves by loping, and are able to jump to extreme heights. Their human form is a mask, not an identity they absorb or incorporate; they imitate the generic human form, not specific individual identities, thus remaining biologically distinct. Human identity is not so much invaded as used as a disguise. This is underscored when the aliens make the mistake of imitating the same human form twice. Significantly, this mix-up threatens to collapse racial and ethnic boundaries; one identical alien is white, the other Mexican (the latter played by Ron Silver in "brown face").

The centrality of biological difference to the meanings of these aliens is suggested by their terraforming the earth to suit their physical needs. They increase greenhouse gases in order to speed up global warming so they can colonize the planet (aliens like it hot). Unlike the aliens in *They Live,* who "fit right in" and speak the language of consumer capitalism, these represent an inversion of the system; they manufacture gases not goods. That is, the potentially apocalyptic violence done to environmental systems by social systems is disconnected from material, economic relations and aligned with the demands of alien biological difference.[24] But this film does more than simply abstract material relations into space and onto fantastic biologies; it also imagines the so-called third world as the earthly incarnation of the threat of alien Otherness and the source of the very real environmental damage to which it alludes. The aliens set up their terraforming plants, primarily in Mexico but also in other developing countries, where we are told, "regulations aren't as strict" (presumably, they are very strict in the first world). Alien biology demands a dry, hot climate; videotape of an African draught provides visuals for the ideal alien environment.

The relationship between the white protagonist, Zane, and his African-American prepubescent (and, as it turns out, alien) sidekick, Kiki, is central in coding the boundaries between alien and human biology as racial difference. Even though he is disguised as human, Kiki is marked by alien difference from his introduction: Zane first meets him when Kiki is trapped in a tree, hanging upside down, invoking the inversion of social relations the aliens promote. Interestingly, it is Kiki who speculates about the physical, biological differences between aliens and humans. He ponders: "I wonder what they'll look like?" Conversely, Zane wonders what contribution the aliens will make to knowledge. The alien biology that fascinates Kiki is visually layered onto him; as he delivers this line he looks directly at the camera, which films him from a bird's-eye view. Humans rarely return the gaze in mainstream films. This construction of a threatening Other around racial symbolism is particularly clear in the film's conclusion. Zane, aligned with his girlfriend and standing on a ruined satellite dish, lectures Kiki: "Why couldn't you just come and ask for our help? . . . You go back and tell them that others will know. . . . It's not going to be easy anymore." Having listened silently from below, Kiki then re-joints his knees to their alien form and lopes off into the desert, back to the aliens and presumably the "third world." Significantly, Zane delivers his speech (on behalf of "humanity") from atop a symbol of Western communication networks (the white satellite dish), while Kiki wears earth tones, remains close to the desert, and is visually consumed by it as he lopes off.

Like *The Arrival, Independence Day* fuses radical alien Otherness with racial difference; the film does not even invoke the possibility that aliens can look human. Significantly, it is the African American, Steve, who is the only person on earth qualified to operate the captured alien ship; his affinity with and delight in alien technology is underscored by his reaction when he gets to fly it. After he "gets a feel" for its operation, he gleefully exclaims "I have to get me one of these," and "I've been waiting my whole life for this." In the latter example, he means that he has been waiting his whole life to fly the space shuttle, but his comfort in the alien ship is contrasted to Jeff Goldblum's character, David, who is not biologically suited to alien transport: he gets motion sickness.[25] Importantly, the first physical encounter with alien biology relies on constructions of race.[26] It is Steve who makes the first "close encounter" with an alien and brings it to the military base, and his colloquial description of the captured and unconscious alien ("heavy ass," "big, bad attitude," tentacles that look like "dreadlocks") underscores the racial dimension of the alien's Otherness. The visuals compliment this construction of alien Otherness as Steve uses his parachute to drag the alien across the desert; alien and African American are fused, linked by the parachute. Indeed, the cords of the parachute Steve drags behind him provide him with his own set of tentacles (or dreadlocks, as the case may be).[27]

In contrast to this, humanity is constructed as white. This is partly achieved by the tendency to foreground race as a matter of difference

Postmodern sci-fi and radical Otherness: *Independence Day* (Twentieth-Century Fox, 1996).

from whiteness. Whiteness is universalized; the specific comes to represent the whole.[28] In *Independence Day* this association between human and white is made from the outset in the shot of the U.S. flag on the moon and the monument inscribed: "Here men from the planet earth first set foot upon the moon. We came in peace for all mankind." Whiteness is simultaneously disavowed (nowhere)—its specificity unacknowledged—and universalized (everywhere)—made to stand in for all "mankind"; coming in "peace," its colonizing efforts appear benign. Like *The Arrival, Independence Day* constructs whiteness and patriarchy as the disempowered counterpoint to the invasive violence of alien sexual and racial difference and, in part, invokes social and economic disenfranchisement as a means to do so.[29] Significantly, the character victimized by alien abduction—the most extreme position of powerlessness—is Russell, the crop duster who lives with his family in a trailer; it is he who sacrifices himself for the good of all. Similarly, in *The Arrival,* Zane has given up career advancement and a decent paycheck to pursue his dream of making contact with aliens. His girlfriend confirms the sincerity of her feelings by assuring him, "I got tired of guys with good futures." And, in *Independence Day,* David has given up a promising career in science and works as a "cable guy."[30]

These films invoke class disparity as a context within which to articulate the oppressive nature of alien difference. They displace the conflict and subordination structured within capitalism onto the identities

355

of Others who are themselves marginalized by that which they are made to represent. Like the scapegoat myths described by Girard, these films reverse the relations of power between victim and persecutor. The experience of social and economic disenfranchisement provides the symbolism through which the vulnerability of humanity/whiteness is constructed. Not only are class conflict and disenfranchisement abstracted into space and displaced onto alien difference, they are incorporated by their perpetrator as an alibi. Invoking social-economic disenfranchisement is a convenient way to construct (white, male) humanity as not only disempowered but also violently victimized precisely because of the (monstrous) identities of Others. In this respect, it is interesting that Kiki's identity is doubly articulated in the repeated syllables of his name, and that his first act when entering Zane's loft is to write his name in the frost on the window glass. These films not only express a horror at the assertion of different identities, they also suggest the need for a fierce defense of boundaries delineating difference.

That difference, and the violence it demands, is made intelligible through marginalized Others suggests the ability of commodity culture to incorporate challenges to patriarchy and white supremacy (such as feminism and postcolonialism) by turning the tables: in an Orwellian move, power becomes powerlessness, hegemony is vulnerability. It is through violence, seen to be an inevitable action of the scapegoat and necessary as a means of defense against the Other, that identities are constructed in the delineation of biological borders. Given that these films express horror at boundary crossing and construct those boundaries around the politics of identity, it is not surprising that a recurring feature of alien biology is the tentacle. What is monstrous about alien anatomy is its ability to penetrate physical boundaries and to unsettle the identities those borders are seen to imply. Order is restored in these films when the boundaries between human and alien are reestablished, when a "common" humanity is united, when hegemony affirms itself. Recent alien invasion films construct identity as a matter of biological essentialism, promoting a kind of purity which depends not only on the violent defense of boundaries, but on the obliteration of differences altogether.

Notes

1. At the time of this writing, aliens abound; the parody *Men in Black* (1997) was marketed for Christmas sales, *Starship Trooper's* (1997) video release is imminent, *Sphere* was released in 1998, and the summer of 1998 saw the release of *Species 2* and *The X-Files* movie.

2. Robin Wood, "An Introduction to the American Horror Film," in *The American Nightmare*, ed. Robin Wood and Richard Lippe (Toronto: Festival of Festivals, 1979).

3. While the focus of this paper is the violent invasion of earth and/or human bodies by sinister aliens, other films in this subgenre offer a benign alien Other and hope for humanity in its nurturing contact with other life forms (such as *Contact*). This dual portrayal of aliens, and the ambiguity it creates around the Other, is a structuring feature of the currently running television series, *Earth: Final Conflict*. Vivian Sobchack argues that the construction of an alien Other who is innocent and childlike and yet capable of inspiring awe is a means through which patriarchy reaffirms its authority (at a time of crisis) while masking its power. She finds in the non-threatening alien "a single figure that is both powerful and lovable: the innocent extraterrestrial who is at once childlike, paternal, and patriarchally empowered." See Sobchack, "Bringing It All Back Home: Family Economy and Generic Exchange," in *The Dread of Difference: Gender and the Horror Film*, ed. Barry K. Grant (Austin: University of Texas Press, 1996), 156.

4. René Girard, "Generative Scapegoating," in *Violent Origins: Ritual Killing and Cultural Formation*, ed. Robert G. Hamerton-Kelly (Stanford: Stanford University Press, 1987), 79.

5. Ibid.

6. Following Girard, Christopher Sharrett points out that, like the scapegoat, the Other in horror films functions ideologically to encourage social cohesion. See Sharrett, "The Horror Film in Neoconservative Culture," in *The Dread of Difference*.

7. Richard Slotkin, *The Fatal Environment: The Myth of the Frontier in the Age of Industrialization, 1800–1890* (New York: Atheneum, 1985), 61.

8. Ibid., 62.

9. Ibid., 53, 62.

10. Ibid., 61.

11. Wood, "An Introduction to the American Horror Film."

12. While recent films such as *Independence Day* and *Starship Troopers* are clearly reminiscent of an extraterrestrial threat of the cold war era, this analogy is also troubled by the renewed alliance between the United States and Russia.

13. Andrew Tudor, *Monsters and Mad Scientists: A Cultural History of the Horror Film* (Oxford: Basil Blackwell Ltd, 1989).

14. This owning of the Other does not necessarily imply a progressive critique of dominant ideology. Recalling Marcuse, Christopher Sharrett has shown how revealing the "bankruptcy" of patriarchal capitalism in apocalyptic visions is evidence of "a cooptation of the horror film's radicalism." Neoconservative horror films (such as *Near Dark* [1987] and *The Silence of the Lambs* [1991]) recognize the Other "only as a preface to its total destruction or incorporation into dominant ideology." See Sharrett, "The Horror Film in Neoconservative Culture," 254, 257.

15. Slotkin, *The Fatal Environment*, 73.

16. Ibid., 51.

17. Girard argues that in scapegoat myths "the roles are reversed. The victimizers see themselves as victims of their own victim, and they see their victim as supremely active, eminently capable of destroying them. The scapegoat always

357

appears to be a more powerful agent, a more powerful cause than he really is." See Girard, "Generative Scapegoating," 91.

18. The physical encounter between humans and aliens takes a variety of forms: replacement (aliens stand in for specific human subjects); takeover (a separate creature invades the human body); and duplication (the generic human type is imitated).

19. The bodies of benign or ambivalent aliens (such as in *E.T.* [1982] and the dead alien of *Alien Autopsy*), although humanoid, often bear no sign of sexual difference. Indeed, the benevolent aliens of *Contact* are more consciousness than body. Yet, in this film the disembodied alien is more a disguise for than a dismantling of patriarchal power; significantly, alien consciousness makes contact with the female protagonist by appearing as her dead father.

20. For a discussion of how these excessive, mind-boggling special effects constitute a postmodern disruption of illusionism by calling attention to themselves, see Philip Brophy, "Horrality—the Textuality of Contemporary Horror Films," *Screen* 27.1 (1986): 2–13.

21. *Starship Troopers* also adopts this absolute alien Otherness, locating monstrous difference in the body, and its survival, rather than social structure. In this film, the aliens are literally big (spiderlike) bugs who, like the alien in *Species,* are motivated solely by their instinct to propagate. Recalling the scapegoat described by Girard, they are compelled toward violence because of who they are—it is simply a matter of their survival, and, while they cannot be faulted, their annihilation is demanded by their very nature.

22. It is worth pointing out that the trailers for *Sphere* introduce the female protagonist as a biochemist, hired to study alien biology.

23. Barbara Creed, "Horror and the Monstrous-Feminine: An Imaginary Abjection," *Screen* 27.1 (1987): 44–70.

24. *Independence Day* also invokes the destruction of the environment as a consequence of the alien invasion; aliens are described as "locusts," moving from planet to planet consuming natural resources.

25. Given the unabashed stereotyping of Jewish characters in *Independence Day,* it should be noted that, like the African American "empath" in *Species,* David acts as a translator between alien and human: He is able to decode the aliens' signal and warn of the imminent attack.

26. It is interesting that the aliens first enter the earth's atmosphere over Iraq— an eyeline match between Muslim women in veils and the alien arrival forges a further link among "Others."

27. This "dreadlocked" alien recalls the monstrous and excessively violent (he kills for sport) alien of *Predator* (1987) and its sequel. Race and gender associations provide the Predator with his alien Otherness; he is metaphorically aligned with both Jamaican drug dealers, and female biology by virtue of his nickname, "Pussy-face."

28. Richard Dyer, *White* (London: Routledge, 1997).

29. While aliens in *Independence Day* and *The Arrival* are made intelligible through racial and ethnic symbolism, they also indirectly facilitate the regeneration of patriarchy. In the former, the heterosexual, patriarchal family is reconstituted after having been threatened, for example, by a First Lady who strays from her proper

place in the "white" house, and David's wife's political career. Patriarchal authority is reasserted in David's reconciling with his wife as well as his father's religion, in Steve's marriage to a single parent, and in the president's assuming the role of both parents because of the death of his wife. In the latter film, Zane's girlfriend comes to have faith in him, standing by his side as he fights for "humanity."

30. Such invocations of class also inform the "fact-based" *A Fire in the Sky* (1993), in which the abductee is, significantly, a childlike logger. Even when the white male abductee is economically privileged, such as the writer in *Communion* (1989), he is constructed as disempowered, childlike, and disconnected from violent aggression (he is the sensitive artist type).

15

CATEGORY 3: SEX AND VIOLENCE IN POSTMODERN HONG KONG

JULIAN STRINGER

The victim is tall, dark, and handsome, and he has been lured to the mansion with the promise of exciting sex games. She wears a pink swimsuit with black gloves; he follows her into the outside pool for some nocturnal fun. Once there, she proceeds to rip his clothes off using a knife attached to a wire, manipulating the lethal weapon as easily as a child would a yo-yo. With the camera positioned at water level and facing them both, we see him embrace her from behind. After she playfully swims away from his reach a mysterious point-of-view shot taken from the other side of the pool sets up his expectant approach. Suddenly, a second woman, dressed in a black swimsuit with pink gloves, rears up and lashes out at him with a knife. He tries to get away but is lassoed back. In three shocking jump cuts the second playmate slashes repeatedly into his neck. The mansion towers in the background, like a beast of prey. With the camera, still at water level, facing both women, the killer embraces her co-conspirator from behind. No longer tall or handsome, the victim's pulpy remains sink below the frame, his blood staining dark red the water that laps around the entwined bodies of the two lesbians.

This is exploitation cinema, Hong Kong–style. The scene is from *Naked Killer,* directed in 1992 by Clarence Fok, and starring media celebrity Carrie Ng as Princess, the most beautiful and deadly of the film's four female assassins. Princess enjoys danger, power over her male employees, and absolute wealth. She castrates a number of her victims, usually to the accompaniment of Mozart on the CD player. Like Princess, *Naked Killer* is sexy, preposterous, riveting, and potentially harmful. It is a Category 3 film.

In 1989, the Hong Kong film industry introduced Category 3 as a new ratings system for "adult only" films, those forbidden to viewers under the age of eighteen. Pitched somewhere between North America's "R" (Restricted) and "X" (X-Rated) classifications, the hundreds of titles subsequently released under this umbrella label feature unusually strong depictions of sex and violence. With their mix of murder and mutilation, large breasts and lesbianism, genre-bending and rule-breaking, titles like *Naked Killer* have performed well at the domestic box office, won guarded critical approval, and attracted cult attention from overseas video audiences.[1] Constituting both a genre of filmmaking in its own right and a stylistic hybrid, Category 3 films aspire to a clever marketability. As the repressed underside of more respectable cultural forms, it repeatedly draws for its inspiration upon such established genres as the thriller (*Beauty Investigator,* Lee Jua Nan, 1992), the ghost film (*Ghostly Love,* Wu Kwo Rem, 1990), the prison film (*Erotic Journey,* Lau Kwok Hung, 1993), the crime story (*Malevolent Mate,* Lin Chin Fun, 1993), and futuristic sci-fi (*Robotrix,* Luk Kim Ming, 1991) as well as on classical Chinese literature and philosophy (*The Golden Lotus*—'*Love and Desire,*' Li Han Hsiang, 1990; *Sex and Zen,* Michael Mak, 1992).

It is a truism of capitalist culture that film industries in decline often turn to sex and violence. Category 3 films are no exception. Generated out of the need for profit, they resemble other last-ditch attempts to stay afloat; *The Romance of the Vampires* (Wong Jing, 1994), for example, is no different from a British sexploitation title of the early 1970s like *Lust for a Vampire* (Jimmy Sangster, 1971). Yet exploitation cinema has seldom been more popular than in 1990s Hong Kong. Against the U.S. film industry's widespread penetration into the domestic market, despite a sharp drop in attendance figures, and even with insiders claiming that the exploitation bubble has finally burst, the city has generally stayed loyal to its filmmaking talent.[2] Production company response has ensured that, as one American observer puts it, "the level of sex and gore in the Hong Kong cinema is peerless."[3]

Featuring many of the anxieties that characterize postmodernism in the Chinese context, Category 3 films consequently disregard any sense of cultural value. Shocking subjects are combined into new commercial hooks, the better to squeeze the last dregs out of an uncertain economic situation. In the countdown to mainland China's resumption of sovereign control over Hong Kong on July 1, 1997, Category 3 films testified to a severe loss of confidence in the city's political stability. In these films, serial killers are pursued at night by corrupt and incompetent cops, families break up or are broken up, the media is ineffectual, triads control all the businesses, and prostitutes hang out on every street corner. Such representations of eroticism and cruelty can be read as the death dance of a wicked, economically decadent city.

Clearly, then, Hong Kong is not afraid to produce commercial pornography and violence. It is now fairly common for directors to get their start on adult films, and the genre has its own charismatic stars, both male (Simon Yam, Anthony Wong, Mark Cheng), and female (Chingamy Yau, Pauline Chen, Yung Hung), many of whom rose through the ranks from beauty pageants and talent shows to exploitation work. And just as the process of star construction contributes to the legitimation of fairly explicit material, the success of a number of recognizable names mimics the capitalist ethos of social mobility that permeates the whole settlement. Category 3 films elevated themselves to a position of cultural respectability at the very moment the Hong Kong film industry consolidated its international reputation. Soft porn star Veronica Yip made the transition from Category 3 films to more demanding art house roles with her performance in Stanley Kwan's *Red Rose White Rose* (1994), while Anthony Wong picked up a 1993 Hong Kong Film Academy Best Actor Award for his portrayal of a brutal mass murderer in *Untold Story* (Danny Lee, 1993).

Despite such recognition, the obvious argument to make about Category 3 films is that they mark a clear regression in the quality of Hong Kong cinema. With these films' misogyny, homophobia, repulsed fascination with the naked and open body, and equation of crime with the working classes, they demand to be read alongside horror and pornography's more reactionary wings. However, three other considerations are worth bearing in mind. First, the exceptionalism of Category 3 films should not be argued too strongly. In some respects, titles like *Naked Killer* and *Sex and Zen* are representative of the Hong Kong film industry as a whole in that their concern with genre-bending is shared by more mainstream popular narratives. Second, while I shall be emphasizing the negative aspects of the genre, I do not want to deny the perverse pleasures offered to anyone who wishes to read Category 3 films as "against the grain." Third, it is also necessary to point out that although this is by no means a unique genre, Category 3 films do at least make their own kind of historical sense.

In being indicative of social trends sidestepped by more "respectable" Hong Kong films, the genre serves a distinct political function. It is "adult" enough to deal with taboo subject matter and popular enough to provide an airing for repressed social issues. Such sexual and violent content can be read as a unique survival strategy on the part of one section of its target audience. However, Category 3 films tend to encourage this identification in a limiting way, refusing to suggest means by which present social conditions can be overcome. Ironically, as Hong Kong adjusts to rule from the classless ideologues of Chinese communism, the city's most graphic films are everywhere bearing witness to and

363

Sex and death in postmodern Hong Kong: poster for *Naked Killer* (Wong Jing Productions, 1992).

exploiting the class resentments of its detritus—that is to say, of those who have resolutely failed to work its economic miracle.

The following reading of the Category 3 genre is based on a limited viewing of select titles. However, watching only a score of films is enough to get some idea of the genre's key themes, which include an emphasis on sexuality, class violence, social mobility, the flattening of time, and the imagining of a dystopian postmodern aesthetic.

The pre-1997 Hong Kong film industry is often characterized by extreme pessimism and an alarmist mentality geared toward the making of as many titles and as much profit as possible before the July 1, 1997, expiration date. As such, Category 3 films present a dystopian rather than a utopian vision, thus reversing entertainment's usual ideological tendencies.[4] If the uncertain future of late capitalism in Hong Kong gives

364

You cheapy-cheapy! I taught you how to make love.

Porno, horror, and genre-bending: *Sex and Zen* (Golden Harvest Productions, 1991).

rise to an intense, urgent mass cultural conversation about what Communist rule will bring, it also illustrates the vagaries of late capitalism as a period phenomenon. Category 3 portrayals of sex and violence in postmodern Hong Kong are an aesthetic response to an economic logic that, because it has an end, must have had some sort of beginning.

While the debate about where a sense of localized Hong Kong identity might have come from and where it could be going has been significantly energized by recent social changes, one ending of sorts is provided by the media images of murder in and around Tiananmen Square, Beijing, on the night of June 3–4, 1989. A significant representation of violence for all Chinese and non-Chinese people, the brutal crushing of unarmed protesters by the state government on the mainland has been of particular concern to those Hong Kong residents who fed money to the democracy movement up to the moment of its suppression and who subsequently helped many student leaders escape to the West. Reading the actions of the People's Liberation Army as a warning of what might happen to them a few years down the road, many in Hong Kong viewed the Tiananmen Square massacre as proof positive of the forthcoming apocalypse.

During the 1990s, the events in Beijing became the subject matter of numerous Hong Kong films, but such codification happened in different ways, on the basis of differing generic and authorial concerns. The traffic flows in three directions. First (and even though it may not be recognized or named as such by domestic critics), the Hong Kong "art cinema" has gained international attention partly on the basis of its clever manipulation of political material; so while veteran director Ann Hui has not been able to raise money for her projected film on the student movement, fellow New Wave director Allen Fong immediately came up with an important protest against its inhumane termination, *Dancing Bull* (1991). Second, the extremely popular Hong Kong action cinema codified the Tiananmen Square massacre through images of blood and mayhem—it is impossible not to read political comment into the scenes of carnage in such titles as *A Bullet in the Head* (John Woo, 1990) and *A Better Tomorrow 3* (a.k.a. *Love and Death in Saigon,* Tsui Hark, 1989). Tony Rayns points out that villains in the gangster movies of 1990 were even given the name "Li Peng."[5]

However, there is an interesting cultural instability at work by the time we get to the third cinematic representation of codified political violence in contemporary Hong Kong, Category 3. While it is certainly true that more or less every significant film produced in recent years in the art and popular action genres has concerned itself in one way or another with the "China factor," films forbidden to those under eighteen tend not to do this; neither do they allegorize the Tiananmen Square massacre in any clear manner. Yet Category 3 came into existence as a privileged site for the representation of graphic violence a mere few months after the political suppression in Beijing. Why, then, does the genre exclude such subject matter? How can this "structuring absence" be explained?

Any attempt to answer these questions necessitates the foregrounding of an issue that has been studiously repressed in discussion of modern Hong Kong cinema, namely class. For class determines the shape and concerns of the Category 3 film phenomenon to such an extent that it forces yet another dilemma into the open. If exploitation genres, or postmodernism itself, objectify sexual and violent material as a means to camouflage economic forces, can the commodification of such cultural objects ever avoid the acting out of class anxieties? As with popular cinemas in other capitalist societies, individual Hong Kong titles mask class issues by displacing them onto narratives of individualized subjectivity.[6] Instead of representing political class violence as an external threat—

something that has recently happened *over there,* in the home country—it is internalized *here,* as a characteristic of the city's own bordered space.

Category 3 films are a lower-class phenomenon. Films bearing this classification are exhibited in the theaters of the working-class, projected for spectators who cannot easily afford entry to the latest Hollywood blockbusters playing in the more expensive first-run venues. Subject matter is taken from everyday working life; lead characters are people the (usually male) audience members are meant to identify with. However, in pushing the boundaries of respectability by focusing on controversial material, the performers, production personnel, and audiences associated with Category 3 filmmaking have to maintain a delicate balancing act. While legitimating exploitation material, their formulas for success cannot be *too* politically controversial. To put it bluntly, many of the people who work on the films, and certainly those who view them, are the ones least able to act on any possible desire to migrate from Hong Kong, or at least to be financially "safe" after 1997. At the same time as the genre is careful not to include material that could cause political problems later on, it also speaks in a direct way to the people who will be most affected by reunification. The core Category 3 audience does not share the same pleasures as the art-house demographic because its future is more limited in possibility.

It is significant that one of the most successful of the genre's recent sub-strands is the true-life crime drama. Represented by *Doctor Lam* (Danny Lee, 1992), *Untold Story* (Danny Lee, 1993), and *Run and Kill* (Billy Tang, 1993), this type of narrative embodies violent fantasies of working-class personal destruction along the lines of American models like *Henry: Portrait of a Serial Killer* (John McNaughton, 1990). But this commercial lineage cannot obscure the fact that the influence for such stories comes from elsewhere. As the most graphic representation of true-crime in recent Hong Kong history has been that carried out by the rulers of the People's Republic of China itself, the public display of violence committed by an official state security force in Beijing has here turned itself into private tales of domesticated maniacs in Hong Kong.

Run and Kill provides a particularly vivid example of how the true-life Category 3 murder film works.[7] Its protagonist, Fatty, is a mild-mannered owner of a gas station who comes home one day to find his wife having sex in the shower with another man. Instead of getting angry, he tells the two of them to go into the bedroom (so that the neighbors will not see them) and trudges off dejectedly into the street. After getting drunk in a bar called "Bar 1997," he inadvertently orders his wife's execution. Returning meekly to the apartment in the morning, his subconscious desires erupt in murderous fury as two assassins from a local Vietnamese gang knock him to the ground, slash his wife's lover to ribbons in the bath, and assault her. After resisting rape, she is brutally kicked in the stomach before, sickeningly, her throat is slit. Later, in a darkened cinema, Fatty meets some members of the gang he obstinately refuses to pay for these murders. The film showing on the screen is a soft-porn flick, and the first image we see is of a man and woman having sex while standing up—his back to the camera, her face in front of us—in a parody of the illicit scene Fatty witnessed between his wife and her lover in the shower. The theater itself then becomes the arena for violence as rival gangs fight each other with lead pipes and sharp knives. Between these two parallel scenes, the class preoccupations of Category 3 murder films are brought to the fore.

Because the narrative is restricted almost wholly to Fatty's point of view, the central male character acts as the audience's ego-ideal. Chosen, perhaps, by the same Hong Kong casting directors who have given roles to some of the most attractive leading men of all time (e.g., Tony Leung, Leslie Cheung, Chow Yun-Fat), Fatty is played by an alternative masculine type, the unprepossessing, puffing, sweaty Kent Cheng. The protagonist is an average worker on an average wage, living in a cramped apartment with a small family. He belongs to that pool of Hong Kong laborers who cannot afford luxuries or the security promised by greater social mobility. Like the many cages and confined spaces that constrict and symbolize his life, Fatty is thrown around by forces he cannot control—in a worst-case scenario, his own home is even invaded by murderers. For entertainment, Fatty finds his way into a soft-porn (read: Category 3) cinema, although he is not safe there either.

Fatty's adversaries are presented as of a similar social class, which is to say that in *Run and Kill* the legitimate businessman and the occupants of the city's *demi-monde* inhabit the same space. Vietnamese refugees have often been demonized as a criminal underclass within Hong Kong's migrant society. Fleeing from the Communist victory in their country's civil war, this diasporic population constitutes a tangible reminder to Hong Kong citizens of their own potential fate. In *Run and Kill*, the Viet Gang functions both as a signifier for the activities of the mainland Chinese government and as a convenient scapegoat to blame for the causes of the settlement's own social problems.

At the same time, other class signifiers are at work. Fatty first enters the orbit of violence when he stumbles across "Bar 1997," which is run and frequented by blonde-haired Europeans. No doubt these extras are meant to suggest their real-life counterparts, namely the many expatriates who have traveled in recent years from Britain to Hong Kong in search of temporary work. Usually, they have found it, but at the expense of lower-class indigenous laborers. In taking economic opportunities away from Chinese people at the very moment when economic independence is at a premium, the presence of white people in this location suggests the potpourri of ethnicities that helps to both constitute and restrict the city's sense of its own Chinese identity.

In narratives of individualized subjectivity, the family usually provides a haven from the pressures of these kinds of social contacts. In *Run and Kill,* however, there is no chance of such a cozy retreat. As the entire narrative hinges on the moment when a character who has never learned how to deal with his anger finally explodes, his intimates have to bear the burden of provocation. Fatty's wife is murdered; his eyes see the horrendous torture and gore, and his mother is thrown out of the window of a high-rise apartment. Yet it is only when the film's nominal psycho, Ching Fong (Simon Yam), incinerates his daughter in front of him that he finally cracks, avenging himself on his tormentor with much ingenuity and relish. This release of class rage occurs, however, after Fatty's support network of family members has been obliterated, symbolically moved off someplace else. Recalling the revenge scenarios of *Death Wish* (Michael Winner, 1974) or *Falling Down* (Joel Schumacher, 1993), class resentments are thereby displaced onto a single protagonist. As Fatty's family has been evacuated from the sinking detritus of Hong Kong's postcolonial society, he is left to rub shoulders with the criminal underclass in a Category 3 cinema.

Another true-crime title, *Untold Story,* starts out with a similar suggestion of claustrophobia and violence. An independent camera movement begins an overhead 360-degree pan, swinging around a block of tenement buildings. The following shot establishes one further manifestation of Hong Kong cinema's recent obsession with the arbitrary fates dealt out by gambling. A cook, Wong Chi Hang (Anthony Wong), is accused of cheating at cards by his boss. The boss demands that he pay his debts back, and a struggle ensues. Captured utilizing the remarkable stop-motion filmmaking technique pioneered in early Wong Kar-Wai titles, such as the gangster drama *As Tears Go By* (1988) and the youth melodrama *Days of Being Wild* (1991), the fight ends with Wong beating and then burning his opponent alive. As the credits roll, we see how he assumes a new identity and moves on to Macao.

At a later date, after Wong tries to secure legal possession of another man's restaurant, the police become suspicious. The protagonist commits two more grisly murders (filling, in the process, the pork buns he serves to his customers with the remains of his victims), before being apprehended.

369

It is here that the narrative really takes off, first by offering scenes of such extreme police torture that a degree of sympathy is generated for the "Bunman," and then through a strategically placed flashback that reveals, in gruesome detail, how Wong hacked an entire family to pieces. As with *Run and Kill, Untold Story* reserves its most exploitative moments for the graphic murder of defenseless children, and it suggests that those who live on the outer margins of Hong Kong's neon postmodern utopia are the ones doomed to suffer.

The film's class preoccupations are given away by its minutely observed details. The restaurant in Macao is sparse and under-frequented, its most distinguishing feature is an oversized Coke bottle that stands outside advertising the entrance as if in mockery of the lack of economic success within. Wong disposes of his victims' remains by wrapping them in black garbage bags and throwing them out as trash (he is eventually caught after he foolishly places bones in a Union Jack shopping bag he dumps into the bay). While the murderer's subsequent confession is set in motion by his being beaten by the police and some prison inmates, only the latter actually urinate on him.

These details may testify to the depressed nature of Wong's social milieu—ample evidence for an "against the grain" reading of the film is certainly provided by its critique of police complicity—but the film's flashback structure does not explain anything about why he is so violent. In most crime stories, the revelation of how the protagonist committed his or her deeds provides the resolution of all narrative enigmas: the audience will be given access to what went on, and why. *Untold Story* refuses to fulfill these expository demands, partly because, as a Category 3 exploitation title, it is more interested in presenting shocking images than in fleshing out the intricacies of character, and partly because the genre itself does not encourage any indulgence of motivational psychology. Wong does not tell us anything about why he kills, but the clues are everywhere—in his desperate attempts to make money, his gambling, his invasion of another's privacy, his resentment of a man who has both money and his own family still with him. Because these situations are familiar to the film's target audience, no further explanation is necessary.

By focusing on such violent true stories within a working-class environment, *Run and Kill* and *Untold Story* do not provide their audiences with any means out of the spiral of poverty and vice; one breeds the other, as cause and effect. Yet just as the multiethnic images of the former film suggest a postcolonial social space, the Hong Kong and Macao locations of the latter necessarily bring to the surface a politicized use of geography.

The two colonies are ostensibly used as a means to contrast corrupt police forces, as the Macao detectives are willing to put Wong in prison (with the probability of his parole after fifteen years) rather than have him face the death penalty in Hong Kong because it represents a significant coup for their department. This use of two specific regions serves to connect the dynamics of class with those of native place identity. It is important to remember that one of the issues at stake in the 1989 political crisis of Tiananmen Square was that of political hegemony. Against the logic decreeing that twentieth-century China has marched triumphantly forward thanks to its organization as a centralized nation-state, the student demonstrations in Beijing led many Hong Kong citizens to optimistically rediscover their own sense of localized "Chinese-ness." (This political lesson is of crucial importance to the future of Chinese societies, and even though it was beaten down in 1989, that does not mean it will not surface again later.)

Once the breakup of centralized political hegemony has been imagined, the need for an absolute regime of state power is thrown into relief. Prasenjit Duara has pointed out that the possibility of establishing provincial, federated regional identities provides an alternative to centralized Chinese nationhood. At certain historical moments—the early Republican period, contemporary Hong Kong—local political aspirations emerge, challenge official state decrees, and are contested.[8] Yet with the recent breakup of a similarly large imperial dynasty, the former Soviet Union, one might wonder what could happen on the mainland if these reformist provincial currents take root again, as they did briefly in postmodern Hong Kong.

Category 3 films recognize that this cannot happen at the moment—they are too pessimistic and dystopian—yet they might be seen to work with the issue inadvertently, through the negative connotations of a regional Chinese identity. Communist rule has ostensibly brought a large segment of Hong Kong's population into the international solidarity of the global working class, but it may also turn the dreary locales of *Run and Kill*'s Kowloon backstreets (and *Untold Story*'s isolated Macao?) into stigmatized native places. In other words, class oppression can be based on conditions of ethnic similarity just as much as on the perception of cultural difference.[9] Once people from a specific region are codified by the ideologues of the center as a minority, a subnational identity is forced on the oppressed. In conjunction with other class resentments, the unspoken fear behind ultra-violent Category 3 films is that Hong Kong may become one such devalued region within the purview of a centralized Chinese nation.

371

If post-1990 true-life murder films represent the displaced political nightmares of those lower-class regional audiences who cannot afford to leave the city or achieve economic independence, the impossibility of harboring fantasies of social mobility is generated by other kinds of narratives as well. Fredric Jameson has argued that the cultural logic of late capitalism encourages a form of nostalgia through the stylization of retrospective modes of expression.[10] As Hong Kong denizens do not possess the means to transform their physical space, they are also unable to hold back time. Not surprisingly, then, nostalgia for the past is everywhere in Category 3 films; in the quoting and parodying of numerous genres and in the attraction of lost traditions. Yet this past cannot be mastered, and it will return with a vengeance after 1997, which means that unlike comparable texts from other "national cinemas," Hong Kong exploitation titles dramatize the curious flattening out of the elastic potential of postmodern narrative time.

Time is a major preoccupation of contemporary Hong Kong cinema. Instead of featuring goal-oriented protagonists who force a change with each linear narrative progression, many titles organize themselves around the relationship between past, present, and future, or else they focus on the simple drip-drip-drip of minutes into hours, hours into days. In *Wicked City* (Mak Tai Kit, 1992) a vicious clock chases after people in a literal illustration of the adage "time flies"; Stanley Kwan's *Center Stage* (1991) is, in part, a study of the parallels between two great cities in historical time, 1930s Shanghai and 1990s Hong Kong; *Iceman Cometh* (Clarence Fok, 1989) stretches across different centuries as its hero battles to destroy an ancient time wheel; and even as relaxed and un-alarmist a film as *Chungking Express* (Wong Kar-Wai, 1994) features the intermittent, cruelly indifferent ticking away of the seconds and a young man obsessed with expiration dates.

According to Ackbar Abbas, many of these examples of New Hong Kong Cinema propose a double temporal framework,[11] an awareness of the contingency of time's movement. However, this movement can also be read in class terms, because the freedom to imagine temporal simultaneity presupposes the freedom to visualize another time, another place. In other words, films that utilize a double temporal framework are concerned to explore space, to indulge the intricacies of social mobility. The nostalgic power of this fantasy cannot be denied, nor can its practicality—the bringing together of the romantic couple at the end of *Chungking Express* occurs on the words: "Where do you want to go?" "Doesn't matter. Wherever you want to go."

372

Category 3 films are noticeably less likely than other films to imagine a double temporal framework, which is another way of saying that they cannot imagine another time, another place. Because the films are aimed at audiences who cannot achieve the social mobility that will lead them away from their current situation, there is no escaping time, and there is none of the ease of movement that characterizes the art house and popular genre films mentioned above. The result is that while the creative exploration of different temporal frameworks has allowed many Hong Kong films to move across historical and aesthetic borders, the postmodern retro-style of the city's "adult only" genre produces the feeling of complete stasis. This lack of dynamism is perhaps most apparent at the science fiction and fantasy ends of the genre spectrum.

Robotrix is for all intents and purposes an excellent example of Hong Kong genre mixing. Pitching three Category 3 sex queens (Amy Yip, Aoyama Chikako, and Hui Hiu Tan) against the kind of indestructible male cyborg spawned in Hollywood productions like *The Terminator* (James Cameron, 1984) and *RoboCop* (Paul Verhoeven, 1987), it works at a level of self-conscious revisionism: while the villain is Japanese (a common enough trope in Hong Kong films), the heroes are female. As it is primarily a light sex farce, however, the film is generically unstable. On one hand, its scientific discourse provides more evidence in support of positive readings of the cyborg's utopian possibilities. On the other, it provides women with the resources to fight and defeat men, but does not envisage any fundamental change in the organization of patriarchal relations. Optimists believe that the fusion of human with machine provides a space for the productive emergence of new gender definitions, but in *Robotrix* this possibility has been compromised. Here, Hong Kong's gendered future has been reduced to a technological dead end.

Like all cyborg narratives, the film is concerned with the maintenance and crossing of borders, and it might be expected to propose that a better tomorrow is possible via the blurring of existing boundaries. Yet while this theoretical paradigm welcomes the cybernetic restructuring of prevailing concepts, *Robotrix* is unable to imagine the kind of temporal mobility that would confirm such a project's subversive intent. In a neat gender spin on *Robocop,* the film starts out with the shooting of a policewoman and her subsequent transformation into a robot. After the operation, the cyborg returns to her post, which just happens to be one rank above that of her male lover (despite the three female stars, the gaze here is always male, and the male protagonist is once again depicted, through this central professional/personal relationship, as a class casualty.)

The set pieces in *Robotrix* mostly comprise explosions, crashes, and martial arts fights, and they work to indicate how the human body itself provides the locus for the cyborg's identity. As Hong Kong film crews are generally denied the inflated budgets granted to Hollywood productions, it might be emphasized here that the body is the only social object working-class Chinese people can be said to have some degree of control over. (It is certainly no accident that so many Hong Kong action films belong within "body genres" such as kung-fu, horror, and porn.) More than that, *Robotrix* is entirely free of the kind of imaginative time travel that characterizes *The Terminator;* it proposes no double temporal framework, and it sets up no dialectical tensions. In other words, no boundaries are broken, no utopian relationships are imagined, and no alternative histories are explored. For all its futuristic trappings, the film offers a technological dystopia where time travel is impossible and where existing boundaries are reasserted through the maintenance of a social space that blocks all temporal and social mobility. This denial of fantasy's temporal and erotic possibilities is also a feature of many "adult only" films of the supernatural.

It should be stated that viewing a number of Category 3 ghost films and then tracing the ripples of influence back through other aspects of the city's film industry is enough to extinguish once and for all the notion that Hong Kong cinema cannot deal with the sexual. Titles like *Erotic Ghost Story* (Lam Ngai Kai, 1990) and *Ghostly Love* (Wu Kwo Rem, 1990) carry cards of introduction from two bloodlines—the mainstream ghost story and the classic erotic tale. And the very fact that exploitation films take sexual material from these two influences is enough to indicate the submerged concerns of such "respectable" genres.

While the Hong Kong ghost comedy-drama was popular throughout the 1980s—*The Spooky Bunch* (Ann Hui, 1980), *Encounters of the Spooky Kind* (Samo Hung, 1982), *Mr Vampire* (Ricky Lau, 1985)—it really took off with Ching Siu Tung's *A Chinese Ghost Story* in 1987. The film both made a star out of beautiful leading lady Joey Wang and trapped her within a string of ghost-with-a-heart-of-gold roles. One of Wang's more notable subsequent performances is as the eponymous protagonist of the derivative, but politically challenging, *Reincarnation of Golden Lotus* (Clara Law, 1989). Mixing elements of the Hong Kong ghost film with the plot of the famous sixteenth-century novel *Chin P'ing Mei*, this non-Category 3 film utilizes an interesting triple temporal framework as it juxtaposes the adventures of Golden Lotus in the Ming Dynasty with her reincarnation on the mainland during the time of the Chinese Cultural Revolution, and then again in contemporary Hong Kong. The film extends Joey Wang's star image by making political capital out of her sexual vulnerability; at one point, Lotus is tied up by her mysterious male lover in an image of bondage that picks up on a reference to the practice of foot-binding in the original novel and turns it into an allegory about Hong Kong's possible future subservience to Chinese rule.

Chin P'ing Mei also provides inspiration for one of the earliest of all Category 3 sex films, *Golden Lotus—'Love and Desire,'* and the adult-only genre has capitalized on the erotic potential of *A Chinese Ghost Story* by quoting its iconography and casting a range of young starlets who physically resemble Joey Wang. Again, however, *Ghostly Love, Erotic Ghost Story,* and their offspring do not pick up on the spatial and temporal explorations of *The Reincarnation of Golden Lotus.* Because they tend not to ground their action within any recognizable past, they avoid all sense of historical specificity and political analogy. Category 3 films of the supernatural even refuse to assert the kind of tame social comment verbalized in *A Chinese Ghost Story,* wherein one character laments how "because of the chaotic situation, the people in town have all left. Except for the stray ghosts."

While non-Category 3 ghost films imply that Hong Kong is a lost city inhabited by phantoms, adult-only titles use the sexual allure embodied in the figure of the succubus to provide instant titillation in the here and now. Admittedly, because sexploitation pictures exist to give their audiences erotic stimulation rather than political comment, it makes sense that they are willing to lose all hold on historical reality. In this genre, settings are either in the "classical" style of some vaguely ancient period, or else they just consist of a plain, indistinct backdrop. And while such ghost films are caught up in one of the inevitable paradoxes of heterosexually oriented soft porn (they concentrate on female sexual pleasure but only so as to arouse an implied male audience), more violent Category 3 sex films utilize the metaphors of illicit sexuality that permeate all of these titles but place them at the center of voyeuristic interest.

As a serial-killer narrative, *Doctor Lam* crosses *Untold Story's* concern for bodily mutilation with *Robotrix's* dissection and remolding of the female anatomy. When viewing this film, we come to the end point of Hong Kong's postmodern dystopia. In being so relentlessly obsessed with prostitution and death, the film illustrates better than any other the reactionary heart at the center of social despair in this particular strand of postmodern Hong Kong cinema.

One of the more stylishly directed of all Category 3 offerings, *Doctor Lam* is another true-crime murder mystery. A taxi driver, Lam (Simon Yam), murders women in his apartment and takes photos of their decomposing bodies. He is turned in to the police after a worker in the photography shop where he develops his pictures gets suspicious. Within this simple tale, all the familiar class markers of Category 3 political paranoia are present. The protagonist and his family have to share a cramped apartment; Lam's job takes him on night work to the prostitute areas and sex cinemas of Kowloon; and the police are overworked and undermotivated.

At one point, a team of police investigators watches a videotape they have seized from Lam's home; it features the murderer cutting the breast off one of his dead victims, and it is presented as a joke. Such fear and revulsion toward the female body call for an expository critical framework, but as with *Untold Story,* there is no attempt to psychonanalyze or understand the villain's actions through the confessional flashback structure the film unravels. However, a pair of murder scenes give the game away. In the first, Lam rails against the prostitutes he kills, hinting he is on a "divine mission" to destroy these representatives of "evil." In the second, he tries to make friends with a virginal teenager but ends up strangling her after she tries to run away. (The film's climax occurs when the same police officers watch another home video; this time, Lam's face leers into the camera as he fucks this young victim's lifeless corpse.)

It is at moments like this that the violence perpetuated in Category 3 suffers most from the genre's lack of context, its inability to historicize or to provide some check on Hong Kong cinema's dystopian fantasies. Because any and all excess is allowed, *Doctor Lam* discourages critical engagement. In her paper on the trial of Peter Sutcliffe, the so-called Yorkshire Ripper who murdered thirteen women in the North of England in the 1970s, Wendy Hollway reports that the implications of Sutcliffe's claim that the prostitutes he murdered "deserved" to die went unchallenged in the gender discourses circulated by the legal authorities. Refusing to recognize the connections between the Ripper's extreme hatred for women and the ideologies of "normal" aggressive male sexuality, lawyers and psychiatrists argued over whether he was "bad" or simply "mad." Yet as Hollway explains, such debate fails to answer the question of *why,* in Sutcliffe's words, "I just wanted to kill a woman," why he felt the need for such sexual revenge.[12] In *Doctor Lam,* a similarly misogynist dichotomy is set up between "bad" prostitutes and "nice" virginal girls.

Just as Sutcliffe's first murder occurred after a prostitute had accused him of being "fucking useless" when he was slow to get an erection, Lam starts to kill once a prostitute ridicules him for his sexual inexperience.

If, as I have been arguing, Category 3 films encourage a masculine identification between protagonist and audience, the fact that Lam's behavior is taken to be that of a madman, rather than the logical culmination of male sexual hatred for women, is particularly disturbing. The nude photographs he takes of his female victims are initially enjoyed as sexy photos by the male police investigators; once it is revealed that they are depictions of real-life murders, however, the connection between Category 3 spectatorship and the representation of pornographic violence is confirmed. In *Doctor Lam*, sexual revenge against women is depicted for working-class male audiences in the most graphic manner imaginable. In light of 1997, this can only be read as a compensatory mechanism served up to offset the anxieties of political impotence.

I have suggested that in contemporary Hong Kong the existence of a flourishing market for exploitation films testifies to the reactionary turn of adult-only postmodern cinema in the Chinese context. At the very moment when art house and popular genre films work to assert a local identity and sense of sub-national possibility, Category 3 titles blunt all hope for the future—prostitution and murder are the order of the day. If that were all there were to say about the genre, one might be willing to herald its demise under a new regime of political censorship. Yet there may be a lot more to say. The relation of Category 3 films to other media representations of sex and violence requires further research. What role do the Western, particularly the U.S., film industries play in the Hong Kong cinematic imagination? What role do Chinese traditions play? How does the circulation of Category 3 films in overseas Asian and Western markets figure within the global traffic in exploitation cinema? More than that, are these films open to other kinds of readings? Can they afford a different kind of efficacy? My comments in this chapter are not based on any empirical research into the local reception of Hong Kong movies, and I am certainly willing to accept the necessity of different decodings other than my own. Also, as video copies of titles like *Run and Kill, Untold Story, Robotrix, Ghostly Love,* and *Doctor Lam* are now cult objects of desire in the West, it is worth asking whether this further example of subcultural reception shows any signs of providing the kind of political critique seemingly missing from the domestic context. Given the sexually offensive nature of many Western Hong Kong film fanzines, for example,

377

it would be extremely useful to have some work on the cross-cultural reception of Category 3 films by filmgoers and home video audiences.[13]

It is telling, finally, that *Naked Killer* is the first Category 3 title to be given a theatrical screening in New York. Clarence Fok's film features a wealthy female protagonist, a beautiful assassin called Princess, and opulent locations. Jettisoning the cramped apartment of *Doctor Lam, Untold Story*'s tacky restaurant, and the cheesy special effects of *Robotrix,* the film is attractive to look at, full of sexual intrigue, and all about rich people. Violence takes place in a swimming pool near a huge mansion. The ostensible model for *Naked Killer*'s feminism is Catherine Tramell, Sharon Stone's multi-millionaire murderess from *Basic Instinct* (Paul Verhoeven, 1992), and even if the flaunting of wealth and power is what makes both films successful with their respective target audiences, it is also what separates *Naked Killer* from its generic siblings. For lurking outside the frame of less glamorous examples of Category 3 filmmaking is an altogether more significant threat.

Notes

1. *Naked Killer* was given a short commercial release at Cinema Village, New York, in 1995 and reviewed in *Village Voice* by Richard Gehr (*Village Voice,* March 21, 1995, 58). B. Ruby Rich briefly discussed the film alongside other lesbian-killer narratives from around the world in "Lethal Lesbians," *Village Voice,* April 25, 1996, 60.

2. See Gary Silverman, "Business Decision," *Far Eastern Economic Review,* December 14, 1995, 32, which reports on Category 3 star Julie Riva's decision to stop making films and switch to the production of dance music instead.

3. Fredric Dannen, "Hong Kong Babylon," *The New Yorker,* August 7, 1995, 32.

4. See Richard Dyer, "Entertainment and Utopia," in *Genre: The Musical,* ed. Rick Altman (London: Routledge and Kegan Paul, 1981), 176–80.

5. Tony Rayns, "Hard Boiled," *Sight and Sound* 2.4 (August 1992): 20–23.

6. For a canonical elucidation of how this process works in classical Hollywood cinema, see Charles Eckert, "The Anatomy of a Proletarian Film: Warner's *Marked Woman,*" in *Movies and Methods II,* ed. Bill Nichols (Berkeley: University of California Press, 1985), 407–29.

7. I would like to thank Tony Williams for providing me with access to several Category 3 titles on videocassette.

8. Prasenjit Duara, "Provincial Narratives of the Nation: Centralism and Federalism in Republican China," in *Cultural Nationalism in East Asia: Representation and Identity,* ed. Harumi Befu (Berkeley: University of California Press, Institute of East Asian Studies, 1993), 9–35.

9. For an historical illustration of this point, see Emily Honig, *Creating Chinese Ethnicity: Subei People in Shanghai, 1850–1980* (New Haven: Yale University Press, 1992).

10. Fredric Jameson, "Postmodernism and Consumer Society," in *The Anti-Aesthetic: Essays on Postmodern Culture,* ed. Hal Foster (Seattle: Bay Press, 1983), 111–25.

11. Ackbar Abbas, "The New Hong Kong Cinema and the *Deja Disparu,*" *Discourse* 16.3 (Spring 1994): 75.

12. Wendy Hollway, " 'I Just Wanted To Kill a Woman.' Why? The Ripper and Male Sexuality," in *Sweeping Statements: Writings from the Women's Liberation Movement, 1981–83,* ed. Hannah Kanter, Sarah Lefanu, Shaila Shah, and Carole Spedding (London: The Women's Press, 1984), 14–23.

13. See my "Problems with the Treatment of Hong Kong Cinema as Camp," *Asian Cinema* 8.2 (Winter 1996/1997): 44–65.

16

KNOCKED AROUND IN NEW ZEALAND: POSTCOLONIALISM GOES TO THE MOVIES

JANE SMITH

In *The Piano* (1993) a husband chops off his wife's pinky finger with an ax. In *Once Were Warriors* (1995) a husband drives his fist into his wife's face. In *Heavenly Creatures* (1996) a daughter and her friend bludgeon a mother to death. In *Broken English* (1996) a father hurls his pregnant daughter into her bedroom, then nails shut the door and windows so she may never leave.

Why are New Zealand movies so keen on representing a woman suffering spectacular physical abuse at the hands of a family member, usually a man? True, not all recent New Zealand films depict women writhing in domestic agony. It is also important to remember there is probably no such thing as a purely New Zealand film, not when the movies that make it off the islands are launched by foreign money. *The Piano,* for example, though directed by Wellington-born Jane Campion, was produced by an Australian, financed by a French construction tycoon, and distributed by Miramax, which was owned at the time by the American Weinstein brothers. The truth is that New Zealand's burgeoning film industry garners massive foreign investments.[1]

Still, films originating in New Zealand that have found favor beyond its shores do exhibit a generic sameness—domestic drama with a certain edginess about history.[2] Consider the documentary *War Stories Our Mothers Never Told Us* (1995), in which New Zealand women, fifty years later, remember World War II with rancor, recounting hasty marriages, lost babies, and dead boyfriends. Lee Tamahori's *Once Were Warriors* presents the fictional Heke family, who are reminded every day of a glorious Maori past by a squalid urban present. In *Broken English* a transplanted Croatian family watches the nightly news half fearing, half hoping to glimpse a familiar face.

How is the representation of domestic violence in such films related to their unease with New Zealand's social history? Looking at three New

Zealand films popular both at home and abroad—*The Piano* (1993), *Once Were Warriors* (1995), and *Broken English* (1996)—this essay argues that images of violent gender conflict in New Zealand cinema have a complex, ultimately reactionary function. New Zealand's cinematic gender violence both uncovers and re-covers hidden histories of race and class conflict, a necessary move for a country intent on propelling itself onto the stage of global capitalism.

That scenes of men savaging women should take root in New Zealand cinema is understandable, given the young country's colonial history. Nations make sense of their social structures differently. In Britain, complicated social relations are understood under the rubric of class; in the United States, race serves a similar function. New Zealand, argue sociologists Bev James and Kay Saville-Smith in *Gender, Culture and Power*, expresses its social structures through gender relations. The British who settled in Aotearoa[3] (the country's Maori name) during the late eighteenth and nineteenth centuries created "a culture in which the most intimate as well as structural expressions of social life are gender divided" in "response to the exigencies of colonial life."[4]

British settlers came to Aotearoa because the new land offered what the Old World could not—the opportunity to wrest land from its previous inhabitants, milk its resources, and accrue capital. This capitalist mode of agricultural production required someone to perform substantial domestic labors—wives. British immigration agencies advised would-be migrants that "an extra week spent in looking for a wife would be more advantageous than buying a patent plough or a thoroughbred horse."[5] British settlers thus engaged in two distinct forms of colonization. Land could be obtained through the subjugation of the Maori race; land could be maintained through exploitation of women of their own race.

Jane Campion's 1993 film *The Piano* attempts to tell the truth about the genesis of New Zealand's gendered culture through a fictional narrative, set in the mid-nineteenth century, about an arranged marriage between a young Scottish woman named Ada McGrath and an upwardly mobile white settler named Stewart. The first scenes imply that nineteenth-century women persuaded to emigrate to New Zealand were more likely coerced into establishing homes Down Under. Ada's wealthy father, whose grim presence is felt though never seen, regards his daughter as a troublesome commodity with an illegitimate child and crazy refusal to speak. Her soon-to-be husband Stewart needs a wealthy wife so he can buy more Maori land. The men arrange a mutually beneficial exchange that sends Ada packing for an antipodean Bluebeard's castle.

That white married women were held in only slightly more regard than livestock is evidenced in New Zealand's colonial laws.[6] Until the 1884 Married Women's Property Act, settlers' wives had almost no right to own, control, or dispose of property, even that which they owned before marriage. And while an 1867 divorce law gave men the right to sever ties with adulterous wives, wives could divorce husbands only when there was proof of adultery and violence.

By the late nineteenth century, white New Zealand society had settled into fairly polarized models of masculinity and femininity. Men were encouraged by the state and in popular discourse to become what sociologists James and Saville-Smith call the "Family Man," a provider whose leisure time was often spent in the company of other men, while women were enlisted in the "Cult of Domesticity," responsible for all domestic labor within the household.[7]

The Piano imagines the price exacted by a gendered culture as a bloody one. After Ada arrives on the shores of New Zealand, Stewart trades Ada's prized Broadwood piano to friend George Baines in exchange for Maori land. Ada, who refuses to forgive Stewart for the transaction ("It is *mine*," she writes at him), bargains with Baines to buy it back with sexual favors. When Stewart learns of the bargain between his wife and friend, he nails Ada inside the house, sealing the windows and doors with planks to prevent her escape. Later Stewart attempts to rape Ada, and finally, learning of her affair with Baines, chops off her pinky finger.

As is true for any movie set in the past, *The Piano* is as much a treatise about the present, about contemporary feminism in New Zealand, as it is a story about a fictional nineteenth-century woman's suffering at the hands of her husband. During the late 1970s and 1980s, New Zealand saw the rise of what feminist Camille Guy calls a "radical feminist hegemony,"[8] a social movement that informed a cause celebre that raised much the same questions among New Zealand citizens as Jane Campion's film. In February 1984, six young women hauled Auckland University lecturer and playwright Mervyn Thompson from his car, chained him to a tree, and spray painted the word "rapist" on his car. The women, who never identified themselves, issued a statement claiming that Thompson had abused his position at the university by raping several female students. Because the women refused to speak to law enforcement officials, Thompson's actual guilt or innocence was never determined. The playwright's image in popular media, however, was confirmed: Mervyn Thompson became a symbol of transgressive masculinity, an abuser of women, a de facto rapist.

If *The Piano* sought to redress past wrongs against women by exposing the hidden history and consequences of colonial subjugation of women, it is also true that the film suppresses the history of another oppression, the colonization of the Maori, New Zealand's indigenous people. In other words, there is more to *The Piano* than the age-old story of the battle between the sexes.

Gradually, the narrative aligns Ada with the Maori. A white man's law allows the confiscation of her property. She falls in love with Baines, a European "gone native." When the film prefigures Stewart's violent act in a community theatrical, only male Maoris in the audience are disturbed by the gruesomely rendered Bluebeard story, in which the discarded wives' heads bob on a bloody sheet and the actor playing Bluebeard seems to sever the head of his current wife from her body.

The Piano may look like a postcolonial narrative, but it quietly practices an insidious colonialism all its own. A white woman absorbs the Maori plight, and the "best" Maori happens to be Baines, a tattooed European. Meanwhile *The Piano* represents "real" Maoris en masse as easygoing, effeminate, and ineffectual, much as did nineteenth-century British colonizers. Despite the Anglo-Maori wars of the nineteenth-century, the settlers insisted in popular discourse upon the nurturing, almost feminine nature of the Maori. In one such story, a fierce Maori chief was said to have such a kind regard for his enemy that he leaped over a barricade to bring water to the thirsty colonizer.

At the present writing, *The Piano* is the second-highest grossing film in New Zealand's history, and after its acquisition by Miramax, it became an international art-house hit. The film proved especially popular in Britain's former colonial holdings—Canada, South Africa, and the United States, where popular discourse surrounding the film tended to focus on two aspects: the film's eroticism and the nature of its feminism, radical or reasonable.

Two years after *The Piano* broke New Zealand box-office records, Lee Tamahori's 1995 film *Once Were Warriors* attempted to correct the gendered view of New Zealand culture by reminding viewers that gender is not the only social dynamic at work in Aotearoa—there is also the matter of race.

A Polynesian people who settled Aotearoa between A.D. 1000 and 1350, the Maori formed about fifty tribes (iwi) in which social relations were understood in terms of age and genealogy rather than gender. When European settlers began arriving on Aotearoa's shores in the late eighteenth century, the social structure of Maori life changed forever. On February 6, 1840, Queen Victoria's representatives asked a council

Neocolonialist narrative: *The Piano* (Miramax, 1993).

of Maori chieftains to sign the Treaty of Waitangi, an infamously vague document in which the chiefs granted sovereignty to the British, who agreed the Maori should have *tino rangatirantanga,* which translates into something like "full powers of chieftainship." "It seems probable," writes journalist Peter Walker, "that neither side knew what the other was talking about."[9]

Between 1843 and 1860, British settlers, whom the Maori called Pakeha, arrived in quantities so vast that they soon outnumbered the Maori population. Despite the treaty and a long Maori insurgency (the First and Second Anglo-Maori Wars of 1843 and 1861 to 1863; lesser forays well into the 1900s), by the 1940s the tribes had lost nearly all their lands to Pakeha. Through social institutions like the Maori Women's Welfare League, the indigenes were gradually assimilated into the gendered culture of the Pakeha. Today New Zealand is a land of about

3.5 million people, 400,000 of whom are Maori, most of whom live in urban squalor, like the fictional Heke family in *Once Were Warriors.*

Based on a popular novel by controversial Maori author Alan Duff, *Once Were Warriors* attempts to remedy *The Piano*'s Euro- and gender-centric view of Kiwi society, helping to make it New Zealand's all-time highest-grossing film. *Once Were Warriors* contests *The Piano*'s representation of New Zealand from the very first frame, an image of a landscape that might have been snipped from Campion's movie, watercolor mountains with a lake nestling in between. When the camera pulls back, the idyllic landscape is revealed to be a billboard, behind which lies another New Zealand, an ugly urban landscape, crisscrossed by four-lane highways littered with empty beer cans and sprinkled with cigarette butts.

The Brechtian trick that opens *Once Were Warriors* unmistakably positions the film as a postcolonial critique of neo-colonial narratives like *The Piano,* and other "quality" historical films like *Out of Africa,* in which well-born European women in long skirts ramble through lovely alien landscapes. Where *The Piano* imagines nineteenth-century New Zealand from a European perspective, *Once Were Warriors* sees the present country from a Maori point of view. Where *The Piano* paints New Zealand green and blue-gray, *Once Were Warriors* sees Aotearoa in black and red, brown and gray. Where one film suggests illustrations from a book of fairy tales, the other speaks the visual language of MTV.

The subjects of Tamahori's film are the Hekes, a Maori family who live in a dingy Auckland apartment so close to a busy highway that car lights rake the yard at night like search beacons. Jake, the father, has just been laid off, but he is not worried, since the dole pays as much as his job at the fish market. Mother Beth frets, knowing that the possibility of someday owning their own home is unlikely. The Hekes' eldest son, Nig, joins a gang; a younger son, yanked from home by the social services, is confined in a juvenile detention center; daughter Grace, only thirteen or so, shrinks from Jake's mates, who sniff her budding sexuality.

The first reel suggests complicated, historically contingent relationships between indigenes and Pakeha, between Maori men and women, implying that Maori gender conflicts are embedded in larger inequities of race and class. After Tamahori's billboard trick, the camera watches Beth Heke push a shopping cart through an urban wasteland. As cars whiz smoothly by on the freeway, Beth's shopping cart, mostly empty, bumps along slowly, signifying her family's economic double bind: their desire to take part in a consumer society but not having the means to do so.

When the narrative introduces Jake, viewers are allowed to interpret his exaggerated masculinity as a protest against colonial practices that deny the manhood of Maori men, a strategy at work in *The Piano* (notably the scene in which an indigenous Oscar Wilde flirts with George Baines). Though Jake Heke has no job and owns no property, he does possess his own body. Pumping iron, mounting muscle on muscle, Jake rejects colonial ideology mutely even as he recreates white New Zealand's ideals of masculinity.

When Beth prods Jake to find work, he lashes out, saying he is tired of her kind (the ariki, or upper-caste Maoris) telling him and his kind to get to work. Here the film reminds us that Jake bears not only the wounds of colonial subjugation but the stigma of old intertribal slavery. In the film, these stigmata are literally written on Jake's body: his upper arm is encircled by tattoos of barbed wire.

Midway through the film, however, something curious happens. The narrative aperture begins to close, shutting out larger issues of race and class, pinpointing only a local conflict between the sexes. The story comes to a head one night during a drunken party, when Jake tells Beth to fry some eggs for his friends. She hurls the eggs to the floor. He hurls her against the wall. The party guests scatter, and the kids huddle in their bedroom waiting for the hurricane to pass.

The scene that follows finds Jake and Beth in bed the next morning. The camera inspects Jake from above and at a distance; his body, unconscious, unthinking, wraps around his wife's like a lover's. Beth lies wide-awake and ramrod straight. The camera searches her face at close range: one eye is swollen shut, the other stares at the ceiling, and a puddle of dried blood stains the pillow beside her mouth. The positions of their bodies suggest the different strategies by which Beth and Jake will cope with living inside Pakeha society. Jake embraces the solaces the dominant culture offers his people—the forgetfulness of alcohol and the superiority that comes to men who treat women like slaves. Beth, on the other hand, stiffens herself against the dominant culture and stares back into a past when the Maori lived proud and apart.

The camera angles also indicate a shift in the film's politics. Prior to this, the film seemed to be arguing that the difficulties facing the Heke family—unemployment, depression, imprisonment, alcoholism, and interfamily violence—arose from past and present discrimination, but now *Once Were Warriors* tempts viewers to read the Hekes' troubles as springing from the incontestable differences between bad men and good women. Surreptitiously, a symptom of colonialist oppression becomes the origin of modern-day Maori misery.

387

The movie holds Jake responsible for the next eruption of violence against a Maori woman, this time his daughter Grace, though he is neither present at nor aware of the crime. Seizing an opportunity afforded by a riotous party at the Hekes' house, Jake's mate Uncle Bully opens young Grace's bedroom door, climbs on top of her sleeping figure, and rapes her. Grace, unable to voice her rage and shame, hangs herself from a tree.

When the narrative aperture snaps shut at the end, Jake has been transformed into a no-good brute who pummels his wife and causes his daughter to hang herself from a tree. Beth packs up their remaining children, tells Jake she is leaving for good, and walks away, turning toward old values and the sacred tribal land (the *marae*).

While *Once Were Warriors* begins by seeming to reject *The Piano*'s gendered tunnel vision, the movie ends up endorsing just those gender constructions *The Piano* renders problematic: The villain is once again a violently aggressive man who has adopted behaviors of Pakeha culture, and the "good" victim is a light-skinned aristocratic woman who functions as the moral center of the filmic narrative.

Beth-as-embodiment-of-Maori-culture briefly enjoyed a spotlight in international media. The actress who plays Beth, Rena Owen, came to signify "an entire culture," despite having been rejected for a part in *The Piano* for being "too pale and too European-looking."[10] When *Once Were Warriors* premiered in New Zealand and the United States, entertainment reporters rarely asked to speak to Temeura Morrison, the actor who plays Jake, erasing the father from discussions of Maori culture that inevitably arose from the film, effectively reproducing the colonial strategy of feminizing the indigenous culture by concentrating entirely on Beth's character. Director Tamahori admitted feeling uneasy about darkening Jake's character:

> If there is any contrivance in the movie, it is the denouement. . . . When staging the end of the picture, I was very aware of the dangers I was running. The villain of the piece is the father, Jake, but he is a very complex and confused individual, understandable in some ways. I didn't want to make him a one-dimensional villain. . . . I know that I've overstepped the bounds and this is just pure melodrama.[11]

If *Once Were Warriors* sets out to complicate the notion of New Zealand as a culture in which "difference" is marked by gender, Gregor Nicholas's *Broken English* attempts to show that racial and ethnic relations in New Zealand are far more intricate than the simple juxtaposition

Domestic melodrama erasing colonialism: *Once Were Warriors* (New Line Cinema, 1995).

of Maori versus Pakeha that *Once Were Warriors* suggests. Nicholas's film evokes a different social reality: Each year about 30,000 immigrants flood into New Zealand, two-thirds of whom settle in Auckland and most of whom are poor and working class.

In the last few years, the newcomers have been predominantly Asian immigrants from Korea, Taiwan, and Hong Kong, whom many white New Zealanders view with distaste, as evidenced in the rightward shift in Kiwi politics. In the parliamentary elections of 1996, New Zealanders elected their first coalition government made up of representatives of the conservative establishment National Party (whose Jim Bolger was re-elected prime minister) and the New Zealand First Party, whose leader, the rabidly anti-immigration Winston Peters, has been called the Kiwi Pat Buchanan.[12]

Broken English tells the story of Nina, a Croatian girl who emigrates with her family to Auckland in order to escape the Balkan wars. The five-member family live in a multicultural ghetto; their next-door neighbors are a Maori clan. Father Ivan conducts vaguely illegal business from their apartment while the mother cooks and chain-smokes. The couple have a son, Darko, and two daughters, the elder who has borne an illegitimate child and the younger, Nina (Ivan's favorite), who works as a waitress in an Asian-owned restaurant.

One night Nina notices Eddie, the new Maori cook, and they promptly fall in love, like a Kiwi Romeo and Juliet. Nina is mystified by Eddie's reverence for a spindly-looking tree, which symbolizes his family history, or *whakapapa*. Eddie cannot understand Nina's allegiance to the patriarchal Croatian culture. Complications follow: Nina agrees to marry her friend's Chinese boyfriend so that he may legally stay in the country. The two couples cohabitate in a tiny apartment. Nina becomes pregnant with Eddie's child.

As if to correct the popular sentiment, implicit in *Once Were Warriors,* that New Zealand's races are better-off separate from one another, *Broken English* endorses tolerance of cultural cross-pollination. Chinese immigrants who work hard deserve New Zealand citizenship, whatever Deputy Prime Minister Winston Peters of the New Zealand First Party may argue. And Maori men do make good husbands and fathers, whatever *Once Were Warriors* may suggest. As if to underscore this message, Eddie is played by actor Julian Arahanga, who portrayed eldest son Nig Heke in *Once Were Warriors,* while Eddie's wise older brother is none other than actor Temeura Morrison, who starred as father Jake.

The villain of *Broken English* is Nina's father Ivan, a Croatian immigrant who opposes cultural mingling and, like *The Piano*'s Stewart and *Once Were Warriors*' Jake, is a violent man. The film positions Ivan as a dangerously transgressive male who may erect cultural boundaries outside the home, but who fails to acknowledge generational differences within it.

Like the first image in *Once Were Warriors,* the initial scene in *Broken English* disorients, partly because daughter Nina appears to be Ivan's wife. His hands encircle her waist as he displays her to his poker-playing mates, seeking and getting their approval of her womanliness. When Ivan discovers his elder daughter trysting with a young man in a Porsche in front of the apartment, he batters the car and sics his Rottweiler on its owner. Later Ivan and Nina dance together provocatively, and when she proposes venturing outside the domestic arena, he objects fiercely.

The narrative comes to a head when Ivan learns that Nina is pregnant with Eddie's child. Ivan locks Nina in a bedroom and removes the doorknob. Then, in an a scene eerily synonymous with the "nailing-Ada-in-the-house" episode in *The Piano,* Ivan commands his son Darko to nail planks over the windows to prevent Nina's escape. As she screams from her prison, Ivan and Darko go out in the night to kill Eddie.

Unlike *Romeo and Juliet, Broken English* ends happily: Eddie's Maori warrior skills confound Ivan, the young man rescues Nina from her jail, and the two escape to form a perfect nuclear family. But as the film closes with a scene of familial bliss on the seashore, with Eddie holding his daughter and Nina looking on, we hear her voice speaking longingly of her cruel father, whom she has abandoned.

What is going on here? Why do recent films originating from New Zealand return again and again to scenes of savage domestic conflict? Partly it is because attention to the domestic frontier helps prevent questions about the relationship of the national to the global. In *The Piano,* Stewart's final act, severing Ada's finger from her hand, effectively wipes out other acts of violence the film suggests, particularly the damage Old World capital inflicts upon a colonized land and people. In *Once Were Warriors,* the film retreats from considering the plight of Maori living in Pakeha society when Jake turns Beth's face into pulp. In *Broken English,* the war Ivan wages on his daughter drowns out ethnic prejudices the movie has conjured up, as does the film's utopian ending, just to be on the safe side.

It is understandable that the process of reimagining New Zealand social structures should be difficult, given that the roots of a gendered New Zealand are deeply established in the country's colonial past. It is also true that New Zealand cinema takes its formal cues from classical Hollywood movie narratives, which characteristically distill large social issues into a concentrate of character conflict.

However, representing New Zealand society as one in which the overwhelming social conflict is imagined as a brutal masculinity at war with a fragile femininity may have as much to do with present politics as with past history. Conceiving a culture in such terms has at least two reactionary results. First, New Zealand's historically contingent gender differences assume the quality of timeless, immutable biological traits, the age-old, nothing-to-be-done-about-it battle between the sexes. Second, a society riven by sexual difference allows inequitable hierarchies of sex, race, and class to flourish. Even films like *Once Were Warriors* and *Broken English,* which evoke complicated patterns of ethnic and Pakeha relations, end by offering substitute villains and substitute problems, satisfying desires for racial and ethnic justice even as it deflects them.

It is no coincidence that these stories have become popular at home and abroad at this time in New Zealand's history. In this case, cultural practice goes hand in glove with economic politics. The overarching goal of the past three governments—the Fourth Labor Government (1984–1990), James Bolger's conservative National Party Government (1990–1996), and the new coalition government, a combination of the establishment National Party and right-wing New Zealand First Party (1996–)—has been to propel New Zealand from a local agricultural capitalism into global (or late) capitalism, which has disorganized earlier conceptualizations of global relations, especially relations comprehended earlier by such binaries as colonizer/colonized, First World/Third World, and the "West and the Rest," in all of which the nation-state was taken for granted as the global unit of political organization.[13]

This shift to something other than an agricultural mode of production may seem to signal an end of colonization and imperialism, but New Zealand, in fact, is practicing a kind of neo-colonialism, a term that signifies the continuing economic control by the West of a once-colonized world under the cloak of political self-determination.

In order to lure transnational corporations to invest in New Zealand, the state set itself two goals in the late 1980s. First, it needed to restructure itself, an aim largely accomplished. In slightly over a decade, the country's controlled economy and interventionist government metamorphosed into what some call a "laboratory for free-market ideas," shedding trade barriers, industry regulations, agricultural subsidies, controls on interest rates, and a fixed exchange rate. (New Zealand has so far resisted a move from universal to targeted social-welfare benefits.) The country's international credit rating was upgraded twice; the government eliminated its net foreign-currency debt; and the wealthy sector has prospered. The November 1995 issue of *Forbes* advised its readers that "New Zealand is a buy," being one of the most deregulated and least corrupt economies in the world.[14]

The flip side of free trade in New Zealand is not pretty. Maori, Pacific Islanders, and immigrants from Asia are disproportionately homeless or on the verge of homelessness. "It is believed," says a *Social Science and Medicine* study, "that the causes of poor physical and mental health in this inadequately housed population are not due to housing per se, but to widespread socioeconomic deprivation."[15]

392

As its second and ongoing goal, the state needed to prove to multinational corporations that its work force was peaceable. No longer confined to the First World, capitalism has "become porous" and production highly mobile.[16] Native cultures must be colonized all over again—only this time into a capitalist narrative rather than an imperialist one—and immigrant populations must be appeased as well. More subtle than its predecessor, neo-colonialism succeeds by seeming to offer indigenes and immigrants what the first round of British colonialism denied the Maori: visibility, acknowledgment, and respect.

The three New Zealand movies discussed above, while seeming to acknowledge the hidden history of the oppression of white women, the Maori, Asian and Pacific Island immigrants, further this second aim. In each case, an ugly battle between the sexes erupts just in time to prevent the films from becoming dangerously transgressive—representing New Zealand social relations as fundamentally *other* than gender-centric. The gendered culture must be preserved because it sustains the social relations necessitated by a global capitalism.

But if popular New Zealand movies, in narrative content and in sheer dollar power, have helped rather than hindered the free-market designs of the state, it is also true that extra-cinematic voices have been rising in dissent of government policies.

For the first time in New Zealand's history, the parliamentary election of October 1996 was conducted under a Mixed Member Proportional Representation rather than the winner-take-all system of past elections. The MMP, as it is called, provides small parties with improved chances for capturing parliamentary seats. In response to the anti-immigrant New Zealand First Party, two new political parties formed: the Ethnic Minority Party, founded by Malaysian-born Robert Hum, who is Chinese, and the Asia Pacific United Party, which drew support from Pacific Island and Asian groups.

Each year on February 6, the day New Zealand honors the signing of the Treaty of Waitangi (roughly equivalent to the Fourth of July), Maori discontent raises its head. In February 1995, for instance, activists lowered official flags and hoisted Maori banners. When Prime Minister Bolger appeared, the crowd booed. And in March 1997, a young Maori activist took a sledgehammer to the America's Cup, yachting's highest prize and a symbol of New Zealand's majority culture as well as the country's association with the Western power bloc. In a move synonymous with New Zealand's habit of conjuring social unrest only to quell it, after the incident, the America's Cup was sent to its British manufacturer for a prompt repair.

Notes

1. At $1 million per episode, Pacific Renaissance's two gender-specific action series for American-owned MCA TV, *Hercules: The Legendary Journeys* and *Xena: Warrior Princess,* drive money into the local economy and employ scores of Kiwi actors and technicians. In an episode of *Xena: Warrior Princess,* "The Xena Scrolls," the series cheekily demystifies its own means of production. In the last scene, somewhere in Hollywood, a screenwriter pitches the Xena series to Robert Tapert, the real executive producer of the series. Tapert shakes his head, skeptical. Grasping at straws, the screenwriter says something to change Tapert's mind: "It doesn't have to be expensive. We can shoot this thing in a Third World country using the locals!" Tapert's eyes narrow greedily, and the episode snaps to a close.

2. When the British Film Institute commissioned a documentary retrospective of New Zealand cinema to celebrate the centenary of film, director Sam Neill produced a work called *New Zealand Cinema: Cinema of Unease* (1995).

3. Aotearoa is often translated as "land of the long white cloud."

4. See Bev James and Kay Saville-Smith, *Gender, Culture, and Power: Challenging New Zealand's Gendered Culture* (New York: Oxford University Press, 1994; rev. ed.), 16.

5. Ibid., 24.

6. Because the Maori understood social relations in terms of age and genealogy rather than gender, Maori women, especially those of high birth, enjoyed more power and privilege, including the right to possess rights to land and water, to speak at public meetings, and to retain their own names at marriage.

7. For a full discussion of the genesis of New Zealand's social relations see "Creating a Gendered Culture," *Gender, Culture, and Power: Challenging New Zealand's Gendered Culture,* 32–47.

8. For an analysis of recent trends in New Zealand feminism, see Camille Guy, "Feminism and Sexual Abuse: Troubled Thoughts on Some New Zealand Issues," *Feminist Review* 52 (Spring 1996): 154–68.

9. For a journalist's impressions of the rebirth of Maori outrage, see Peter Walker, "Maori War," *Granta* 58 (Summer 1997): 199–228.

10. See Peter Brunette, "In New Zealand This Film Beats 'Jurassic Park'," *New York Times,* February 19, 1995, sec. 2, p. 13.

11. See Andy Spletzer, "Rena Owen Is Maori and Proud: An Interview with the Star of *Once Were Warriors,*" March 10, 1996, http://www.film.com/film/interviews/warriors.interview.owen.html.

12. James Bolger, prime minister at the time I wrote this piece, was ousted in November 1997 by Jennie Shipley, also from the conservative National Party. She has attempted to fashion a coalition between the National Party and the New Zealand First Party.

13. See Robert Sklar, "Social Realism with Style: An Interview with Lee Tamahori," *Cineaste* 21.3 (1995): 26.

14. For an overview of neo-colonialism strategies, see Arif Dirlik, "The Post-

colonial Aura: Third World Criticism in the Age of Global Capitalism," *Critical Inquiry* 20 (Winter 1994): 353.

15. See Steve H. Hanke, "New Zealand Is a Buy," *Forbes* 156.11 (Nov. 6, 1995): 367.

16. Ibid.

17

Woo's Most Dangerous Game: Hard Target and Neoconservative Violence

Tony Williams

We're more capitalistic and cut-throat than the United States. If you survive Hong Kong society, you can survive anywhere.
—*John A. Lent,* The Asian Film Industry

Poor people get bored too.
—*Chance Boudreaux to Fouchon in* Hard Target

In New Orleans's Half Moon Utility Restaurant, the camera pans right, then the shot dissolves to reveal the eyes of Chance Boudreaux (Jean-Claude Van Damme). The waitress inquires, "How's the Gumbo, Chance?" Perhaps in reference to director John Woo's preference for Mandarin rather than Cajun cuisine, Chance replies, "A tragedy." When she asks about the coffee, Chance comments, "Tolerable." Further dialogue reveals Chance's economic circumstances. The waitress tells him the coffee "ain't free, either." Chance understands she discerns his poverty and responds by giving her all his loose change as payment.

This scene introducing the hero of *Hard Target* (1993) is not as formulaic as it initially appears. The setting and dialogue signify both economic hard times and a down-scale environment, features usually absent from contemporary Hollywood films. *Hard Target* is one of the few films that attempts critical analysis of the deadly aspects of neoconservatism and post-capitalism affecting us today. Although promoted as the first Hollywood film made by a Hong Kong director under the "genius of the system," *Hard Target* is more than a movie by a filmmaker whose talents would be crippled by the industry as badly as *Broken Arrow* (1996). Despite being an action film, the movie emphasizes one pernicious consequence resulting from late capitalism, a system in which people face a subhuman existence that sometimes leads to starvation and death in

397

a planned process of capitalist genocide, a process envisioned by Robert Ryan's C.E.O. figure in *Executive Action* (1973). The street people's status as capitalist detritus makes them fair game in the neoconservative political economy whereby victims compete against a system that allows them no chance of success. Read against this background, *Hard Target* is an allegorical condemnation of a new social darwinist contest against impossible odds in a "bread and circus" orgy of destructiveness. It is a vision present in Woo's major Hong Kong films: *A Better Tomorrow* (1986), *A Better Tomorrow, Part 2* (1987), *The Killer* (1989), *A Bullet in the Head* (1990), and *Hard Boiled* (1992). *Hard Target* reveals the deadly results of Western politicians' fascination with the Far Eastern "tiger economy" they initially spawned. As a director caught between two cultures, Woo reveals the deadly implications of this fascination in a cinematically constructed "return of the repressed."

Hard Target is a "tolerable tragedy." Since Universal Studios and the Motion Picture Association of America's rating board resulted in Woo's re-editing his film at least seven times,[1] it is not in the same league as his acclaimed Hong Kong masterpieces such as *A Better Tomorrow, The Killer,* and *A Bullet in the Head.* As with Terry Gilliam's *Brazil* (1985), Universal drastically interfered with Woo's vision after several negative previews by audiences more familiar with Van Damme's mediocre films than with Woo's stylish ones. Although Universal drew the line when Van Damme demanded he take over as editor, it refused Woo a director's cut for the video release. *Variety* insightfully noted the flaws affecting the American version. "The disjointed storytelling, occasional chopped editing and uneven performances undermine what could have been a better picture."[2] While *Hard Target* is undoubtedly not in the same league as such butchered legendary works as Von Stroheim's *Greed* (1924) and Welles's *The Magnificent Ambersons* (1942), Universal's version of *Hard Target* drastically ruined Woo's stylistic rhythms and diminished the expression of certain ideas. In its original form, *Hard Target* is no compromised work by a Hong Kong director eager to break into the Hollywood market. Even the re-edited version retains traces of the original concept as entertained by Woo—a film attempting to critique aspects of contemporary Hollywood's high-tech action movies that "audiences have been *taught* to enjoy" (italics mine).[3] *Hard Target* also comments on America's historical and cinematic fascination with murder and oppression, as seen most gratuitously in works celebrating the serial killer such as *The Silence of the Lambs* (1991) and *Natural Born Killers* (1994).

The major nuance in the scene described above involves Chance's economic plight. Although not on the streets like fellow veterans Douglas

Binder (Chuck Pfarrer) and Elijah Roper (Willie Carpenter), he is precariously near to becoming a homeless person again. The New Orleans setting of *Hard Target* echoes an American society that denies the reality of the growing numbers of homeless people everywhere. It is not accidental that the same society responsible for their plight finds use for its most elite members in a post-capitalist version of Richard Connell's short story "The Most Dangerous Game." This New Orleans resounds with dark elements from America's violent heritage. It is not just the city of Southern gentility, jazz, and culture; it is also a city formerly known for flourishing pre–Civil War slave markets, race riots, and violence (most recently, the publicized murders of tourists). New Orleans is also the diseased and terrible city of Robert Stone's 1967 novel, *A Hall of Mirrors.* Stone opens his novel with an epigraph from Robert Lowell's poem "Children of Light," envisioning New Orleans as a city of Cain linking the spiritual poverty, urban racism, and right-wing movements depicted within the novel with the punitive and genocidal ways of the Puritan fathers. Like Stone, Woo depicts New Orleans as a dangerous environment whose Mardi Gras traditions conceal detritus and spiritual decay, as the concluding graveyard hunt in *Hard Target* reveals. The steel arrows penetrating Binder in the credit sequence parallel the twelve-inch-long totemic "Great American Razor" featured in Stone's novel and aptly described by Robert Solotaroff:

> The razor embodies a good deal of the American illness that Stone located in New Orleans: the harnessing of the immense promise of America— in this case, passion and science, aesthetic vision and technology—for violence and the instruments of violence; the reification of the instruments of violence; the sick blend of Eros and Thanatos, of sexuality and violence.[4]

After Binder's death, Fouchon (Lance Henriksen) speaks to his satisfied customer Lopacki (Bob Apisa), "It's like a drug isn't it. To bring a man down. Was it worth it?" Lopacki replies, "Every nickel." The perverse hunt combines common late-capitalist components of sexuality, eroticism, and money.

Many reviews also recognized Chuck Pfarrer's screenplay as a variation of the most filmed story in American cinema—"The Most Dangerous Game." It first appeared in the October 1930 issue of *Golden Book Magazine.*[5] But this was not a studio-imposed screenplay. Pfarrer stated that John Woo deliberately chose it out of the fifty or so American scripts offered because "he liked the story."[6] Pfarrer is known for scripts such as *Dark Man* (1990) and *Navy SEALS* (1990), and he is also a former Navy SEAL who was injured in the 1983 Beirut bombing. As such, he parallels those knightly heroes celebrated in works such as *Blood Brothers* (a.k.a. *Chinese Vengeance,* 1973), a film directed by Chang-Cheh, a figure revered by Woo both during and after the time he worked with him as assistant director.[7] *Hard Target* is really a composite, multicultural production rather than the American action movie Universal Studios attempted to market. The version recently released in Japan is more visually dynamic than the American release.[8] Comparison of the American and Japanese versions not only reveals more footage, but it also reveals a stylistic and thematic synthesis between American and Hong Kong cinema, one already present in *Hard Boiled.* Although certain stylistic features of Woo's appear in the American print, more appear in the Japanese version. As Lance Henriksen notes, Woo's violent representations resemble more a modern dance, a "balletic" recital, than the type of cynical stylistic approaches common to most examples of American action cinema: "You've got this incredible *dance* movement. And if it was modern dance, it will be the same thing." Woo also draws similar analogies. "When I fell in love with movies for the first time, it was the musical movies. Like *West Side Story* [1961] and Gene Kelly movies, Fred Astaire. The musical movies made me get a strong feeling for the movement, and the beauty of the action, and the beauty of the editing, and the beauty of the visuals."[9] Though indebted to Western and Hong Kong cinematic traditions, Woo's references are far removed from the superficial borrowing of recent directors like Quentin Tarantino. Woo's balletic bloodbaths function more as ritual combats than as Hollywood gore-feasts, often providing important links between past and present values. During one moment in *A Better Tomorrow, Part 2,* Ti Lung refers to his former Shaw Brothers martial arts star prowess by using a sword to dispatch Triad adversaries in the middle of a gun battle. Woo often uses style to complement the specific content of his films, thereby reworking past traditions into a modern framework. The freeze-frame devices stressing male friendship are derived from Truffaut's *Jules et Jim* (1962). But Woo applies these devices into new contexts. While Hong Kong films such as *The Killer, A Bullet in the Head,* and *Hard Boiled* continue the friendship motif by briefly inserting freeze-frames into social and historical contexts where close bonding is difficult, if not impossible, *Hard Target* uses the same device to stress the agonizing death of Binder as the arrow penetrates his back (absent in the American version) and the martyrdom of Elijah. The two characters function as American representatives of Woo's fallen knightly Chinese heroes in a hostile modern world.

Woo's choice of a screenplay modeled on *The Most Dangerous Game* (1932) is not accidental. Familiar with many Western and European movies and often re-working them in his films, the director understands the implications of his source material in its various cinematic incarnations. In the original version of *The Most Dangerous Game* (a.k.a. *The Hounds of Zaroff*), big game hunter Bob Rainsford (Joel McCrea) finds himself confronting his dark alter ego, the Russian Count Zaroff (Leslie Banks) who enjoys hunting humans rather than animals. Hoping that his guest will pursue his interests to their logical conclusions, Zaroff challenges him to join the sport. As Zaroff gazes on Rainsford in close-up, he is lit up in demonic imagery. Although this scene usually evokes laughter from contemporary audiences, it nevertheless represents an ideological American cinematic technique of disavowing dangerous social and historical situations by referring to the mystical realms of the Gothic and supernatural. American horror cinema of the 1980s and 1990s employs fetishistic codes of special effects to deny social and historical realities. In *The Most Dangerous Game*, Rainsford finds himself the hunted rather than the hunter. Prior to his shipwreck, when he finds his way to Zaroff's island as a castaway, he blandly replies to a question asking whether he would ever change places with his prey, "Well, that's something I'll never have to decide. Listen here you fellows, the world's divided into two kinds of people: the hunter and the hunted. Well, luckily, I'm a hunter. And nothing could ever change that." On Zaroff's island, he experiences a reversal of his former situation and later tells Eve Trowbridge (Fay Wray) that he empathizes with his former quarry.

Filmed at the same time as *King Kong* (1933), *The Most Dangerous Game* is usually classified as a horror fantasy far removed from any historical associations. However, both films were made during the Great Depression. Although operating as fantasies, they can not entirely escape the pressing social problems of the day, problems that drove their audiences into the escapist domain of the movie theater. Both *King Kong* and *The Most Dangerous Game* attempt to externalize traumatic social realities into less threatening fantasies. If King Kong functions as an embodiment of destructive Depression-era forces affecting 1930s America (similar to Toho Studio's original conception of Godzilla as representing the atomic bombs dropped on Hiroshima and Nagasaki), Count Zaroff is an externalized scapegoat for foreign aristocratic Old World bankers supposedly responsible for the Great Depression. He is a Dracula/Frankenstein monster figure set in an environment removed from American normality, scheming the destruction of clean-cut, healthy Americans.

Even *King Kong* cannot entirely dismiss the Great Depression. Entrepreneur Carl Denham (Robert Armstrong) discovers Ann (Fay Wray) fainting from hunger in a bread line. Denham's hubris in bringing Kong to America parallels the activities of Wall Street stockbrokers responsible for Black Thursday in 1929. Although Kong does the damage, Denham is ultimately responsible—a fact stressed in the opening scenes of *Son of Kong* (1935). In *The Most Dangerous Game,* Rainsford's fall from security echoes the fate of millions of Americans whom Hoover's market-oriented Republican administration would have left to starve had it not been for Roosevelt's New Deal. Like Paul Muni in *I Am a Fugitive from A Chain Gang* (1932), Rainsford finds himself an outcast from his previously secure position in society. He is now a hunted man.

The *Most Dangerous Game* has several historical resonances absent from Thierry Kuntzel's well-known analysis.[10] Although the film attempts to repress the Great Depression, oblique references occur in the drunken dialogue of Eve's brother, Martin Trowbridge (Robert Armstrong). On meeting Rainsford, the drunken socialite wishes to know all about him, including a curious detail such as "Why I left my last job." This is a peculiar question to ask in the midst of the Depression, when millions lost their jobs, unless we understand it as a veiled reference to the traumatic reversal of fortune that Rainsford now undergoes. By losing his ship, he has lost his former social status distinguishing himself from the animals he once hunted. In any economic depression, the unemployed find themselves bereft of their former status and dignity and are treated as dehumanized objects. They are condemned as convenient scapegoats for the demeaning status capitalism inflicts on its participants. Both Margaret Thatcher's "Victorian Values" and Newt Gingrich's "Contract with America" stress that unemployment is the result of moral and personal failings. Another Depression reference in *The Most Dangerous Game* is Martin's comment that "conditions are bad everywhere these days."

If we understand *The Most Dangerous Game* as more than an R.K.O. fantasy, its connections with a cataclysmic (and reoccurring capitalist) crisis situation become apparent. Within the fictional arena of *The Most Dangerous Game,* Rainsford finds himself sharing the hunted animal mentality affecting homeless and unemployed people. Although the system does not hunt down defenseless people for sport (at least, for the present), it treats them as little better than animals, whether using them as "living statues" in situations depicted in films as diverse as *The Draughtsman's Contract* (1982) and *Roger & Me* (1989) or as objects left to starve once benefits are cut under the "Contract with America." *The Most Dangerous Game* may also be seen as an allegorical representation of the plight of human beings under capitalism. Count Zaroff is an overdetermined demonized representative of a system that will use, abuse, and even murder unfortunate victims whenever it desires. In Britain, America, and elsewhere, many thousands of people have died on the streets, victims of policies coldly executed under late capitalism and clearly equivalent to corporate America's envisaged social genocide, as expressed in a variety of neoconservative state and private sector position papers. Although neither murdered nor hunted like the unfortunate characters in *The Most Dangerous Game* and its subsequent versions, the fates of real-life victims living under capitalism is little different. Once homeless, an individual is unlikely ever to escape the situation, and life on the streets translates into a severely reduced life expectancy.

Most versions of *The Most Dangerous Game* appear in turbulent historical eras and often disavow the real implications within its fictionalized material. Robert Wise's *A Game of Death* (1945) used the same scenario and stock footage from the original R.K.O production of *The Most Dangerous Game*, substituting Edgar Barrier's insane Nazi for Leslie Banks's Count Zaroff, at a time when the American government was dealing with Nazi war criminals and O.S.S. "black operations" against former resistance allies in Greece. Ted Tetzlaff's *Johnny Allegro* (1949) saw George Raft dodging George McCready's silver-tipped arrows on a private Caribbean island. Although depicted as right-wing, effete, and a lover of classical music, McCready is clearly too intellectually "unAmerican" for cold war tastes. In Roy Boulting's Suez-era *Run for the Sun* (1956), Richard Widmark and Jane Greer flee in the Mexican jungle from a wanted Nazi criminal (played by Peter Van Eyck in one of his typical performances in that era) and a British traitor (Trevor Howard's performance is clearly modeled on William Joyce's "Lord Haw-Haw," who was hanged by a vengeful British government after World War II).[11] The film also appeared at the time of the Notting Hill race riots, when the British Nazi Party (protected by the police) attempted an electoral comeback. Ralph Brooke's *Bloodlust* (1961) has sadistic Dr. Balleau hunting his human guests with a crossbow. The theme also appeared in television productions such as *Boston Blackie* (1952) and *Logan's Run* (1977–78), the latter featuring Horst Bucholz as a futuristic Zaroff in one episode.[12]

Woo's intention in making another version of *The Most Dangerous Game* involved a further creative synthesis between Western and Hong Kong cinematic traditions that are characteristic of his films. As many Hong Kong critics have pointed out, that particular national cinema often contains hybrid features borrowing from both Western and Eastern cinematic traditions. Like most directors educated in the various forms of

Western cinema, Woo undoubtedly recognizes colonial allegories present within both *The Most Dangerous Game* and *King Kong*. The former film contains white American victims who become little more than black slaves placed at their master's mercy, while the latter film displays American fears of native revolt both within and outside American spheres. In Woo's film, Fouchon's activities are allegorical representations of the ruthless nature of late capitalism presented as harmless entertainment in a genre film. But *Hard Target* is as important as *The Most Dangerous Game* and *King Kong* when viewed in light of its role at a particular historical and cultural moment of Hong Kong cinema.

Now working in America, Woo often attempts to create a synthesis in his films between the Hong Kong and Western cinematic traditions, both of which are more often than not critical of late capitalist abuses. Like *The Most Dangerous Game, Hard Target* condemns the violence of post-colonialism while making connections, as have others, between the colonial city and the global city. Citing Anthony King, Ackbar Abbas points out that colonialism has "pioneered methods of incorporating precapitalist, preindustrialist, and non-European societies into the world economy and found ways of dealing with ethnically, racially, and culturally different societies." Contemporary politicians such as Bill Clinton and Tony Blair often applaud the methods of the "tiger economy" post-colonial countries as ways of solving their own economic difficulties. More often than not, these methods involve cutting welfare and ending programs such as Britain's formerly free National Health Service. Abbas also states that "*colonialism* in a number of instances is the surprising term that allows imperialism to make the leap to globalism."[13]

Woo's *Hard Target* is a hybrid film like most Hong Kong films. But it is also a warning about the dangers awaiting the Western world as a result of the transfusion of post-colonial practices and ideals into the ailing body of mainstream capitalism. Woo operates as both a Hong Kong director and an American action genre practitioner in directing a film arguing against the fusion of the worst of both worlds, whether "tiger economy" and Western post-capitalism, or exploitative violent special effects techniques existing in both Hong Kong and Hollywood that bolster reactionary belief systems.

Fouchon's biker "dogs" are the violent cyclists from *Hard Boiled* transferred into an American context. Whereas their Hong Kong counterparts are employees of a Triad gang smuggling arms into a hospital, their American partners aid rich capitalists who pay $500,000 for the privilege of hunting unemployed homeless people. As Fouchon explains to one client, his version of the most dangerous game is really a deregulated version of "legal" activities performed by governments around the world:

> It has always been the pleasure of the few to hunt the many. All we do is provide the same opportunity for private citizens like yourself. We pride ourselves on taking combat veterans—soldiers, policemen, fighter pilots. Men who kill for their governments kill with impunity. The same governments who make murder their sole preserve train our targets.

Fouchon's activities are not confined just to America. As he states, "There's always some unhappy little corner of the globe where we can ply our trade," whether Rio during carnival time or former Yugoslavia. Prior to hunting Chance, Fouchon tells Pick Van Cleaf (Arnold Vosloo) about relocating to Eastern Europe. "We can work there for years." The former Iron Curtain territories, now undergoing brutal conversion to capitalism, are ripe for his particular brand of exploitation.

Fouchon provides a service for rich capitalists in this new global economy. Although *Hard Target* contains relatively few of the explicit Hong Kong associations that characterize Woo's other films, there are some. While Hong Kong experiences foreboding about its 1997 return to mainland China in the form of real-life crime and films about cataclysmic bloodbaths, hell is already present in the New Orleans of *Hard Target.*

Woo's Hong Kong films also criticize the decline of codes of honor within the colony's capitalist framework, as *A Better Tomorrow, A Better Tomorrow, Part 2, The Killer,* and *Hard Boiled* all demonstrate. The victims in *Hard Target* face a version of the hellish 1997 scenario already present in Woo's Hong Kong films. The film specifically locates a murderous scenario in America, but it also shows that the malaise is global.

Unlike facile representations of homelessness in Hollywood films such as *Down and Out in Beverly Hills* (1986) and *Life Stinks* (1990), Woo treats the subject with seriousness and sensitivity. During his early childhood in Hong Kong, Woo's family experienced homelessness and was rescued from starvation by Roman Catholic social workers.[14] Although professing Christian beliefs, Woo asserts the importance of social justice actions as well as spiritual values. When Natasha Binder (Yancy Butler) searches for her father, Detective Mitchell (Kasi Lemmons) suggests she try the local missions. At Our Lady of Mission Charity, she meets homeless Vietnam veteran Elijah, who wears the 101st "Screaming Eagles" Airborne Division insignia on his combat jacket. From Natasha's photograph he recognizes her father as a former member of the Marine Force "Recon" unit, the same military group Silver Star veteran Chance belonged to. As Elijah tells Natasha about her father's predicament, Woo inserts three separate dissolves showing street people who are outcasts from the American Dream—an elderly woman, a middle-aged man, and a black youngster. Ironically, despite his elite combat status enlisting him in Fouchon's most dangerous game, Elijah is later demeaned as a homeless person during the last moments of his life by condescending white tourists in the French Quarter. Despite his obvious wounds, one man tells him, "Go, get a job." Another man (played by the brother of executive producer Sam Raimi) ignores Elijah's desperate pleas for help, brusquely yelling at him, "Hey man, I ain't got no change, man." Then Woo intercuts three freeze-frame shots of Elijah's realization of approaching death, matching them with the guns held by Fouchon's men. Elijah stretches out his arms in a gesture of crucifixion, becoming a martyr in the carnivalesque "Mean Streets" of New Orleans.

Chance Boudreaux, Douglas Binder, and Elijah Roper are all former military men who have fallen upon hard times and are living on the streets. Although Natasha helps Chance initially to pay his merchant seaman union dues, he eventually becomes morally and emotionally involved with her quest to find her father. Like Elijah, Chance is caring and sympathetic toward her dilemma. Natasha cannot understand why her father never asked her for help when he became homeless. Chance tells her, "I've been there myself on the street. It's hard. It's hard to put your hand out. Because he loved you so much he didn't want to pull you into it." Binder also refuses charity offered by his former landlady after he loses his job. When Natasha learns about this from the landlady, the scene significantly begins with a foreground shot of a birdcage, before the camera cranes up to reveal both women in an overhead shot. This reference is not accidental. Birds are predominantly associated with Chance throughout *Hard Target,* metaphorically depicting him as a free spirit trapped in a fallen world of late capitalism. The opening shot of the birdcage highlights the major theme of *Hard Target*—the entrapment of human beings by an uncaring and brutal system. Woo suggestively prepares the audience for Chance's second appearance in *Hard Target.* He dissolves from the scene of the birthday cake wish made by Carmine Mitchell (who has decided to work double-duty shifts at her desk during the city police strike, thereby making Fouchon's activities possible) to a shot of a solitary seagull on the shores of New Orleans. The camera then tracks right, revealing Chance gazing at the bird. When Natasha attempts to enlist his help, seagull sounds are prominent on the soundtrack. Later, a seagull flies in slow-motion inside Chance's dilapidated apartment, directing him to two dog tags hanging on the wall. By its action the bird intuitively suggests that Chance return to the scene of Binder's death and search for an undiscovered dog tag penetrated by a deadly steel arrow. A pigeon later perches on Chance's shoulder prior to his battle in the Mardi Gras warehouse. He later avenges a bird shot at by one of Fouchon's "dogs." Chance also descends on a Mardi Gras float, designed to resemble a giant bird, when he fires upon Fouchon's men. Chance's association with birds in *Hard Target* not only evokes the Catholic saint Francis of Assisi (known for his friendship to birds) but also suggests heroic qualities characterizing old Chinese knightly heroes. In his Hong Kong films, Woo regards his heroes, played by Chow Yun-Fat and Ti Lung, as modern avatars of a fallen group of chivalric knightly heroes now existing in inhospitable capitalist hells.

According to James J. Y. Liu, the figure of the Chinese knight-errant differs from Western aristocratic concepts in that they are generally class-less figures who often act for altruistic motives, redressing wrongs and fighting for the poor and distressed. This particular altruism (variously

Violence and the values of late capitalism: *Hard Target* (Universal, 1993).

407

defined as "wuxsia" or "yi hsia," the latter term combining aspects of altruism with knightly values) involved "supermoral" standards combining concepts of justice, individual freedom, personal loyalty, courage, truthfulness, honor, generosity, and contempt for wealth.[15] Tracing the influence of this concept throughout cultural representations in Chinese history, Liu concludes that although "knight-errantry as such has ceased to exist, its spirit has not vanished completely. Even now, though we no longer encounter anyone actually called a knight-errant, we may still hear of men being described as having the spirit of knight-errantry or behaving in a chivalrous fashion."[16]

Chance is a modern representative of this ancient ideal, trapped in a late-capitalist world with its own exploitative version of the "most dangerous game." Fouchon and Pick represent alternative aspects of this tradition. Like Triad "big brothers" in the *Better Tomorrow* films, they have sold out to the dark values of modern capitalism. Although they superficially resemble Jean-Pierre Melville assassin figures, like Chong in *A Better Tomorrow, Part 2* and "Mad Dog" of *Hard Boiled,* they have no redeeming codes of honor. Their dark clothes and behavior patterns mark them as demonic figures. While Binder and Elijah are Vietnam veterans, Fouchon is a former mercenary and ex–Foreign Legion veteran. His silver flask has a Foreign Legion insignia. With his Lucifer-like widow's peak hairline, Pick's imagery has apocalyptic associations. When Chance first sees Pick, Woo matches close-ups of Chance (the first emphasizing his eyes) to those of Pick as thunder ominously booms on the soundtrack. The Japanese version of *Hard Target* emphasizes these sounds, making it clear that Chance has supernatural insights into the nature of his adversary. Pick's surname also evokes Lee Van Cleef's ironically named "Angel Eyes" bounty hunter from Sergio Leone's *The Good, The Bad, and The Ugly* (1966). Before their final gun battle, both Chance and Pick occupy opposite sides of the frame. Separated by a wall, Woo clearly recognizes the twin-brother features characterizing these adversaries. However, unlike Link Jones's (Gary Cooper) regret over his reluctant killing of cousin Claude (John Dehner) in Anthony Mann's *Man of the West* (1958), Chance realizes the necessity of the battle. Both Pick and Fouchon have been too corrupted by capitalist values to have any redeeming features left. Finally, in a scene cut from the American print, Woo matches dissolves of the demonically lit Mardi Gras masks in the warehouse sequence with images of the paranoid Fouchon. Anguished over the loss of Pick, similar to Gig Young's feelings over his friend's death in Sam Peckinpah's *Bring Me the Head of Alfredo Garcia* (1974), Fouchon depicts himself as a satanic presence. "You can't kill me. There isn't any country in the world I've never fought in. I'm on every battlefield." Woo also presents Fouchon as a man of culture. In one brilliant sequence, Fouchon plays Beethoven's *Appasionata* on the piano as he plans his next dangerous game. Woo originally inserted footage of an African safari hunt in this sequence so audiences could easily enter into Fouchon's mind. In Fouchon, Beethoven's Romantic creativity has been perverted into bloodshed and violence, a perversion similar to Alex's musical tastes in Stanley Kubrick's *A Clockwork Orange* (1971). African native hunters spear defenseless gazelles while unseen white hunters shoot down elephants. However, as twentieth-century history amply demonstrates, refined tastes in literature and music do not necessarily guarantee that someone is sympathetic or even human. Pierre Bourdieu states that qualities of good taste are really ideological weapons in the armory of cultural capitalism, no matter how many assert apolitical arguments concerning the salvation-like genius of Mozart, Beethoven, and other figures in the Western canon and their relevance to the human condition.[17] Even though Fouchon plays a refined piano composition, violence and oppression constitute his particular brand of cultural capital.

Although Woo reserves freeze frames for the deaths of Binder and Elijah, he parallels Chance and Fouchon by using similar slow-motion imagery for their appearances in various parts of the film. The device is not merely technical. It emphasizes the supernatural associations both men have. The battle in *Hard Target* also involves a struggle between the forces of Good and Evil. Woo often shoots Chance fighting in slow-motion and then cuts to normal speed. Far from being a showmanship display of technical virtuosity, it presents Chance as a figure operating within different levels of time, befitting his embodiment of old concepts of "knightly" values and his status as modern hero fallen from grace in an inhospitable world. Woo also films in slow-motion Uncle Douvee (Wilford Brimley) retreating from his successful assault on Fouchon's men. Douvee rides away, the arrow quiver on his back an allusion to ancient paintings of Chinese and Japanese warriors, as well as Zen Buddhist monk figures in Hong Kong's popular Chinese Ghost Story films.

Hard Target moves toward its apocalyptic climax in the Mardi Gras warehouse. The building is a graveyard of carnival artifacts left to rot after they have served their purpose in the annual festival. This environment metaphorically represents Woo's employment of motifs from *The Most Dangerous Game*. The gigantic masks (one of which is a huge skull paralleling the small skull seen earlier in the goldfish bowl of Randall Poe) are discarded items. They parallel the disposable status of the homeless veterans Fouchon preys upon. As Ivan Muricy comments, the artifacts embody capitalist detritus.[18] The debris represents castaway items of a consumer-oriented, throw-away economy annually celebrated in a carnival that is little more than a mob-mentality drunken binge in one of America's most violent cities. Facing Fouchon in their last encounter, Chance humorously responds to his adversary's question about his involvement in Natasha's cause, "Poor people get bored too." But the response has other associations. It represents the perspective of exploited homeless people who will eventually turn against their oppressors and move toward a better tomorrow.

Despite its flaws, *Hard Target* is a multilayered work uniting many traditions and motifs in an updating of *The Most Dangerous Game* to highlight the precarious situation affecting everyone in a late capitalist apocalyptic crisis situation. With this film, Woo attempts to combat the type of action movie Hollywood audiences have been "taught to enjoy," whether it be the mindless spectacles of *Speed* (1994) and *Waterworld* (1995), or the derivative productions of Tarantino. *Hard Target* reveals social issues within an action format that duplicates the excessive postmodernist cinematic spectacles of blood and violence. Destabilizing images abound in *Hard Target*. In both the original and the modified credit sequences, the camera tracks to Pick's face. He looks directly into the camera.[19] The Universal and Japanese theatrical release versions insert a shot of Fouchon returning his gaze in a classical shot-reverse-shot manner. Pick's gaze is conveniently sutured into the narrative. However, Woo originally edited the scene so that no character alleviates the audience's anxiety of having Pick staring directly at them. The next shot is a long-shot of Fouchon's "dogs" riding on their motorbikes in pursuit of Binder. In this original version, Woo breaks the rules of classical Hollywood cinema by putting the audience under the interrogating gaze of a character who directly involves us in (or questions our easy acquiescence to) a cinematically manufactured "most dangerous game." Woo attempts to challenge audience involvement in the "blood and circus" arena of American action movies. He hopes that we might consider what the "most dangerous game" now means in terms of direct and indirect corporate murder not just in America but throughout the world.

Notes

This is a revised and extended version of an article that originally appeared in *cineACTION* 42 (1997) and appears here by permission of the editorial collective.

410

I wish to dedicate this article to three people most influential in revealing to me another cinematic world replacing the vacuum left by the death of Hollywood—Craig Ledbetter, Todd Tjersland, and Tom Weisser.

1. See Richard Corliss, "John Woo: The Last Action Hero," *Time,* August 23, 1993, 62.

2. Emmanuel Levy, "Hard Target," *Variety,* August 30, 1993, 19.

3. For this comment and other information about Woo, see the Criterion laserdisc version of *The Killer.* I am grateful to John Roffman for supplying me with relevant material here.

4. Robert Solotaroff, *Robert Stone* (New York: Twayne, 1994), 40.

5. See the special *Midi-Minuit Fantastique* 6 (June 1963) edition devoted to the film and its sequels.

6. See Barbara Scharres, "The Hard Road to *Hard Target,*" *American Cinematographer* (September 1993): 69.

7. For *Chinese Vengeance,* see the review by Tony Rayns in *Monthly Film Bulletin* 41.487 (1974): 172. The film starred Ti Lung and David Chiang. Woo used Ti Lung in his *Better Tomorrow* films after his heyday as a Shaw Brothers star to compare with the newer generation of stars and heroes represented by Chow-Yun Fat. Woo has admitted he directed 60 percent of the uneven *Just Heroes* (1989) as a retirement present for his mentor, Chang Cheh. The film also featured Cheh's Shaw Brothers–era stars such as Ti Lung and John (a.k.a. David Chiang) as well as Danny Lee and Chow-Yun Fat from *The Killer.* The Criterion laserdisc notes to *The Killer* also mention the influence of other Chang Cheh films such as *Golden Swallow* and *One-Armed Boxer* on Woo as well as former stars such as Wang Yu (who appeared in these films) and Takakura Ken of the Japanese *yakuza-eiga* genre, which stresses bonds of loyalty and friendship similar to those in Woo's own films. Woo also admitted that a *yakuza-eiga* Takakura Ken movie (whose title he has forgotten) also influenced *The Killer.*

8. The version is currently available from Video Search of Miami. It represents the cut closest to Woo's original conception, and it contains three important sequences dropped from the Japanese release print.

9. See Harry Allen, "Guncrazy in the Bayou," *Village Voice* 38 (May 25, 1993): 18.

10. See Thierry Kuntzel, "The Film Work, 2," *Camera Obscura* 5 (1980): 7–69.

11. For a subversive contrast to British representations of this figure see David Britton, *Lord Horror* (Manchester, England: Savoy Books, 1990) and the officially condemned *Lord Horror* and *Meng & Ecker* adult comic books. Publisher and editor Britton has served two jail terms as a result of British reaction to his sincere and innovative work in this area.

12. In Paul Landress's February 11, 1952, "The Crusader" episode of *Boston Blackie,* Paul Taylor's Blackie finds himself pursued by a corporate executive "organization man" figure. I am grateful to Francis M. Nevins for showing me this episode. For other possible versions see James L. Limbacher, *"Haven't I Seen You Somewhere Before?": Remakes, Sequels, and Series in Motion Pictures and Television, 1896–1978* (Ann Arbor: Pierson Press, 1979), 143.

13. See Ackbar Abbas, *Hong Kong: Culture and the Politics of Disappearance*

411

(Minneapolis: University of Minnesota Press, 1997), 3. He refers to Anthony D. King, *Global Cities* (London: Routledge, 1990).

14. See the notes presented in the Criterion laserdisc version of *The Killer.*

15. James J. Y. Liu, *The Chinese Knight-Errant* (Chicago: University of Chicago Press, 1967), 1–7.

16. Ibid., 54. Carmine Mitchell also shares these qualities. She does not join her colleagues during the police strike but stays on duty. When Fouchon asks Pick, "Can we buy her?" the latter replies negatively. Like Mark and Kit in the *Better Tomorrow* films, she dies heroically in the line of duty.

17. See especially Pierre Bourdieu, *Distinction: A Social Critique of the Judgement of Taste,* trans. Richard Nice (Cambridge, Mass.: Harvard University Press, 1984).

18. In teaching a film theory class, Muricy has noted Woo's use of Eisenstein's editing techniques, seeing them as evidence of a deliberate strategy in undermining Hollywood's linear time techniques.

19. Woo broke classical editing rules of "crossing the line" in a scene between Danny Lee and Chow Yun-Fat in *The Killer.* In the audio commentary on the Criterion laserdisc, he points out that his breach of the rule intentionally reveals both figures as mirror images. Woo always seeks artistic ways in which to break many rules of film theory.

AFTERWORD

SACRIFICIAL VIOLENCE AND POSTMODERN IDEOLOGY

CHRISTOPHER SHARRETT

You can all go to hell and I will go to Texas.
—*David Crockett upon losing his congressional seat in the August 1835 elections*

We have spent more than two billion dollars on the greatest scientific gamble in history and we have won. Having found the atomic bomb, we have used it. It is an awesome responsibility which has come to us. We thank God it has come to us instead of to our enemies, and we pray that He may guide us to use it in His ways and for His purposes.
—*Harry Truman on dropping the Hiroshima bomb*

The target was there, pretty as a picture. I made the run, let the bomb go—that was my greatest thrill!
—*Captain Kermit K. Beahan on dropping the Nagasaki bomb*

Thanks for the AMERICAN DREAM to vulgarize and falsify until the bare lie shines through.
—*William S. Burroughs*, A Thanksgiving Prayer[1]

FROM THE ALAMO TO ALAMOGORDO

It seems to me that the epigraphs I have chosen offer, in aggregate, a synopsis of many of the key concerns central to an understanding of violence in American culture. They suggest that it would be a mistake to assume, as is the tendency of many cultural critics, that the proliferation of violence within the mediascape of postmodernity is evidence of some new perversity, a breakdown within society, a peculiar aberration associated with some special dependence on the image. This conservative, moralistic approach to violence and the postmodern mediascape looks at postmodernity from an essentially ahistorical perspective. I support Fredric Jameson's notion that postmodernism represents the cultural logic of late capitalism, but I would argue that as we examine postmodernity, with its culture of simulation, its attendant profound alienation, its tendency to inure human beings to all forms of experience, we are talking about questions of degree, and indeed about processes long endemic to the capitalist state. Neither the postmodern condition that increasingly reduces the subject to spectator and consumer nor the destruction of human life in real experience and within the culture of representation necessarily suggests any epistemological or historical breaks when we look at the roots of current assumptions and representational practices in American history and ideology.

The above epigraphs were not chosen arbitrarily and point specifically to themes that have been reflected to various degrees in the contributors' essays. Nevertheless, I could have culled a few dozen similar remarks from American history and folklore. The epigraphs speak to themes rife within discussions of violence in postmodern culture: the aestheticization of violence; the preference for violence over reasoned, democratic discourse; the invocation of divine will as a rationale for violence (that is, the subjugation of others to individual will, or, more generally, the will of state power). I want to separate the Burroughs quote, which obviously has no truck with the other remarks and is used here to suggest that the entirety of the American narrative and its dreams of conquest depend heavily on falsification and simulation—so much for current neoconservative keepers of the canon who argue that contemporary radical postmodernists are "revisionist" in their approaches to history. Burroughs would have argued that the American experience was always about revision, about falsifying a history that would otherwise be too bloody and unpalatable to all but the most barbaric (that is, those who own and administer state and private power) and must therefore be covered by a democratic patina of flag waving and the will-to-myth.

The David Crockett quote is very instructive. Davy Crockett loomed large over my childhood and that of other boys of the postwar boom as the simulational Hollywood/television culture shifted into third gear, complementing a massive military build-up that demanded confrontation as a means of forestalling another economic collapse (the Great Depression and the rise of trade unions haunted the HUAC years and the Truman and Eisenhower administrations). Crockett's image has been reburnished many times in the past two centuries, but never more so than by Walt

Disney (for his 1950s "Disneyland" TV series) and John Wayne (for his superpatriotic epic *The Alamo* [1960]). There are some differences between the Disney and Wayne versions of Crockett. Portrayed by Fess Parker, Disney's Crockett is like an affable and strong older brother, while Wayne's version, though he evokes Crockett as an inveterate joking liar, is basically John Wayne, the standard-bearer of the Sunbelt reactionaries. In the hands of these Hollywood masters of reinvention, Crockett became a staunch archetypal role model for postwar youth, particularly in an obdurate opposition to the Other. Crockett's film and TV battles against Indians and Mexicans reflected the postwar anxieties of communism, "flabby" patriotism (Wayne's concern), excessive domesticity, and the feminine. But the resuscitation of Davy Crockett becomes instructive only when we understand that he was one of many American figures to be reinvented in order to serve the mythification of history, the logical culmination of which is the arena of simulation called postmodernity. The "canebrake congressman" of the 1820s and 1830s donned a linsey-woolsey hunting suit for an official portrait by John Chapman when he felt his "squatter" constituency was slipping from him and as his conflicts with Andrew Jackson were proving fatal to his political career. Although he had little experience in military adventure (contrary to his chroniclers), Crockett was one of the original "Go Ahead" men of early nineteenth-century politics.[2] His motto, "Be Sure You're Right, Then Go Ahead," was emblazoned on many a Southwest town monument and later on coonskin caps and flintlock toy rifles of the 1950s, and was the kind of nonsensical and solipsistic form of self-assurance in keeping with the postwar state's desires to police its vast colonial domain picked up from both enemy and ally after World War II.

The earliest representations of David Crockett included not only a recognition before the fact of Manifest Destiny, but also a sense of the assumptions underneath this inflection of imperialist ideology. In telling his constituents to "go to hell" and lighting out for the territories when he lost his congressional seat to Adam Hunstman, a man with a wooden leg who was berated by Crockett for having "timber toe,"[3] we see a trajectory that moves from Crockett's puffery to *Taxi Driver* (1976) to the valorization of the contemporary serial killer. Reason and parliamentary process were never things that agreed with Crockett. He preferred the proclamation, the tall tale, and above all, the anti-intellectualism undergirding the frontier experience. He preferred the sharp ax and true rifle. But perhaps these, too, were part of his self-created myth of a new Daniel Boone that he and his fashioners wanted to produce for America. In fact, Crockett went to Texas not to fight for a cause but to begin, at age forty-nine, a new political career, as he saw the Anglo-American population converging on Mexico in a movement that coincided well with a Jeffersonian-era state policy to conquer Mexico. Crockett aligned himself with the War Party—the speculators, slave traders, and brigands like William B. Travis, R. M. Williamson, Ben Milam, and James Bowie—men who, in contrast to Stephen Austin's initially more conciliatory and co-optative strategies toward Mexico City, demanded that "settlers" destroy the swarthy hordes of Mexico, whom the War Party frequently characterized as apes. The conciliatory Austin, after his imprisonment by Mexico, declared: "Texas must be slave country."[4] The expansion of the Southern slavocracy was the goal of the Go Ahead men like Crockett.

Crockett's apocryphal Last Stand at the Alamo calamity has no basis in contemporaneous accounts of the siege of the Alamo.[5] He surrendered after the battle and was later executed; his Last Stand, putting aside the ludicrousness of the image of the hero bashing Mexican skulls with a broken flintlock, is an invention of the twentieth-century media. The martyrdom of Crockett, like that of Gen. George Armstrong Custer at the Little Big Horn River forty years later, helped fan racial hatred and provided further rationales for expansionism. The furor over the Alamo and the plight of "settlers" culminated in the Mexican War. The death of Custer (yet another Last Stand)[6], aside from providing a logo for Anheuser-Busch and a whole range of commodity production, was both an 1876 centennial celebration and a diversion from the economic crisis that began with the Panic of 1873, as well as a further call-to-arms against Native Americans, a call much encouraged by mining, banking, and railroad interests. The call would be summoned again in World War II America (Raoul Walsh's 1941 *They Died with Their Boots On*). Steven Spielberg's *Saving Private Ryan* (1998), with its Last Stand that evokes the Alamo, is another sentimental valorization of sacrificial violence within the fractious climate of postmodernity. Spielberg's much-praised film offers a nostalgic image of Norman Rockwell America, with windmills perched on waving fields of Iowa grain, an uncontentious America preserved by the sacrifices of the Good War. The American flag that fills the screen at the prologue and coda is more weathered than the one that opens *Patton* (1970), but the point cannot be missed: While doubt has long since set in about the capitalist system and the state that supports it, we cannot doubt the restorative function of sacrificial slaughter in recasting the national myth and in making us redouble our efforts at keeping things as they are in memory of all who have died for us. The dying Capt. Miller (Tom Hanks) tells Private Ryan (Matt

Damon), "Earn this," earn the right to survive by being a straight-laced American, an admonition fully answered in the military cemetery finale.

There seems no irony in Crockett's telling democracy to "go to hell," with his lasting image one of apocalyptic violence in service of conquest. The journey of Crockett and the Go Ahead men of the last century to the outer reaches of the frontier was always a journey of escape—from bad debts, marriages, failed businesses—always sicklied over with a near-pathological sense of divinely ordained mission, or at least the excuse of such a mission. The journey takes many forms

Crockett's Last Stand in the cold war era: John Wayne in *The Alamo* (United Artists, 1960).

417

in the history of twentieth-century representation. By the late 1960s the journey becomes dissolute and self-defeating (*Easy Rider* [1969], *The Wild Bunch* [1969]). In the 1980s and 1990s the journey becomes much more forthright in its presentation, as *Henry: Portrait of a Serial Killer* (1990) and *Natural Born Killers* (1993) depict the journey of self-affirmation and self-recreation involved entirely in the annihilation of the Other, and finally self-annihilation as the will-to-myth collapses. In these more recent "frontier narratives," the Other is almost exclusively the female principal, as if the demands of discourse and reasonable human interchange have finally been recognized as feminine and designated for destruction at their root. The exceptions, such as *The Silence of the Lambs* (1990), successfully transmogrify progressive feminism into bourgeois feminism, and phallicize the female so as to incorporate her into the dominant order to serve the state apparatus and force her to internalize the myths of journey, recovery, and regeneration through violence.

The Truman and Beahan quotes about the Hiroshima and Nagasaki bombings reiterate something even more disturbing about American bad conscience than Crockett's dismissal of democracy. Shelby Foote has remarked that the great tragedy of the Civil War was the failure of this nation to compromise, when its great genius, in his judgment, is precisely this art.[7] The national experience in the last two centuries would seem to undercut Foote's notion that there was any tragedy to the Civil War, since tragedy requires a sense of waste and individual and collective efforts gone askew. On the contrary, the policies of this country, effectuated by the few against the many, have consistently required bloodletting, with the populace at large encouraged through propaganda to embrace bloodlust even as such violence works directly against public interest. Truman, now valorized as the great "common sense" president of mid-century, inaugurated an entire popular culture focused on nuclear weapons and apocalyptic violence as he invoked the deity and unleashed this inferno against an already defeated enemy, forever changing humanity's sense of self-worth.[8] But this ultimate support of total war doctrine is seen also in Crockett, and in the Civil War, and in the intellectual and political culture spawned by perpetual internecine feuding of American capital.

Capt. Beahan's spectacularization of death, when he noted that his target was "pretty as a picture" before he obliterated it, is also redolent of nineteenth-century America, as total war doctrine and the love of bloodsport became inseparable from ideological ends to the point that ends and means became inseparable. In his masterful study of the Civil War campaigns of Stonewall Jackson and William Tecumseh Sherman,

418

Harry Truman drops the A-bomb.

Charles Royster discusses the ways by which the doctrine of annihilation became basic to the war enterprise, and, vicariously, the national self-concept, from the standpoint of divine ordination for Jackson, and from a hard-bitten posture of instrumental reason in the case of Sherman, but with considerable overlap in both models of explanation. Royster notes the pandemic quality of the call for blood. Speaking just after the first battle of Bull Run, Julian M. Sturtevant, president of Illinois College, remarked that "war would correct the American tendency to object to all government." Even philosophers, he said, "cannot see a political truth until it has been established by conflict and written in blood."[9]

Royster argues that such calls were quite universal. Henry A. Wise, governor of Virginia at the time of the execution of John Brown (Wise was by no means an abolitionist), said, "I rejoice in this war. . . . It is a war of purification. You want war, fire, blood to purify you; and the Lord of Hosts has demanded that you should walk through fire and blood— You are called to the fiery baptism and I call you to come to the altar, take a lesson from John Brown."[10] And Royster notes that Lincoln's second

419

inaugural address is "the best known formulation for a mystical view of war," wherein "atonement sounded quantitative, an exact equivalency of recompense to God for past sins."[11] There is no irony whatsoever, therefore, that the elision of the political dynamics of violence should persist in the mysticism of Truman, or be transmuted into the idiotic banality of Beahan, who seems a perfect product of the twentieth-century image culture, except that Beahan's evil is, while banal, also profound as an emblem of the American condition. It too is redolent of Civil War ideology and the whole climate of romance, including many narratives of the Old West first spawned by that war (the frontier bandit as Robin Hood [Jesse James]; the gunfighter as forged in the furnace of the Civil War [the legends of Wyatt Earp and his brothers, John Wesley Hardin, Cole Younger, and Wild Bill Hickok all have relevance here]). In his discussion of the terrible Kansas/Missouri guerilla conflict, the arena for such legendary berserkers of the Lost Cause as William Quantrill and Bloody Bill Anderson, Michael Fellman notes how for all sides, "Killing was insufficient; one had to complete the dehumanization, 'deface' the enemy, reduce him to mere flesh and bones, obliterate his beauty and the container of his Soul."[12] Fellman also comments how the "male body was a target of these warriors. Everything was done to obliterate the maleness of the enemy fighter."[13] The attack on genitalia within European and American history and representation has its own story, since gender obsession has always been a key locus of violence—William Luhr discusses in this book this obsession in relation to popular narratives like *Braveheart*. I would suggest that the blitheness of Beahan as he talks of his "greatest thrill" is largely a function of the new technocratic state that merges old-fashioned bloodsport with spectatorship, with the most advanced development in this regard to date the video-game complexion of the Persian Gulf War. Beahan's erection (the A-bomb cloud) that brought him his greatest thrill, as so many bodies were erased, contains an aesthetic that comes home to roost in the Persian Gulf attack. In this more recent adventure, by further anestheticizing the subject to bloodshed, and by making murder an aspect of "gaming" (perfectly in keeping with the inurements of postmodernity), state policy could be further accomplished, including the "licking of the Vietnam syndrome," which to state functionaries like George Bush and neoconservative ideologues like Norman Podhoretz had caused a "sickly inhibition" in the populace against armed intervention.[14] The vicarious notion of warfare seen in the Civil War, with the ability of the state to generate images and concepts playing off existing political and religious ideology, finds its best realization in our current postmodern circumstances. But attention must be given to the specific dynamics of this ideology of violence and its function within the context of postmodernity.

APOCALYPSE, CATASTROPHE, POSTMODERNITY

An apparent feature of postmodern criticism is the competition between dialectics and apocalypticism in analyses of politics and culture. The concept of "crisis," as in Habermas's "legitimation crisis" and associated Marxian approaches to history and political economy, is often seen by many post-left critics as an inadequate expression of the postwar situation, particularly that of the last twenty-five years. Neo-Nietzschean postmodernists such as Jean Baudrillard (the most extreme case) or Lyotard distrust all dialectical reasoning, jettison entirely the Enlightenment as it is focused on reason in service of social justice, and reject the notion of contradictions as suggestive of disruptions within the capitalist state with their attendant potential for radical change. This line of thinking is not far from that of neoconservative state and corporate apologists who speak of the final victory of capitalism over socialism, informing us that we have reached the "end of history" in the triumph of liberal democracy, and who seem to agree with seemingly jaundiced pessimists like Baudrillard that we now enjoy utopia achieved.[15]

Apocalypticism seems to be a point of view shared by some of the more audible voices of postmodern theory and the powers whose interests they seem to serve, however unwittingly. The born-again types of the mediascape and state power seemingly intent on creating a theocracy, with an atavistic Puritan reductionist view of human destiny, find their ideas replicated in the comparatively obscure and arcane theories (insofar as the bromides, aphorisms, and proclamations of Baudrillard et al., can be termed theory) of the postmodernists. I suggest that the dismissal of radical and dialectical thinking, the embrace of apocalypticism by dominant culture, and much of postmodern theory (I say "much" to emphasize that there are sectors of radical and progressive activity among postmodern thinkers) become plausible when we see sacrifice as predominant in postmodern culture, and pose a stalemate long discussed by Marxian analysis of capitalist culture, one that accounts for the particular approaches to violence within representation, and perhaps violence within the social sphere.

Postmodernism's catastrophe is the simultaneous affirmation and denial of historical views of reality, the nostalgia for the past simultaneous with its derision, and the constant attempt to prop up mythic readings of history even as they are seen as risible. The catastrophe of postmodern civilization is the need to enforce the will-to-myth, that is, to legitimate false consciousness and to reassert primitive views of human interchange. Scapegoating is a central feature of this process, even as the information culture tends, with its contradictions, to inoculate the spectator, and not just in a manner that we can accept the larger evil by constantly being exposed to the small scandals. We are inoculated from myths of blood sacrifice and patriarchal law by the numerous movies, television programs, and pop narratives that regularly transmogrify myth into critical text, thus destroying myth.[16] We are left with what Peter Sloterdijk terms "enlightened false consciousness," an environment of self-reflexive and cynical (but uncritical) reason.[17] This environment seems to require the time-tested consolations of sacrificial mythologies, of patriarchal rule, subordination, and bloodletting of the Other.

The interpretations of sacrifice derived from various forms of structural anthropology, particularly the work of Georges Bataille, are prevalent in discussions of postmodernity as a society read for its "polymorphous perverse" characteristics, as culture *in extremis,* exceeding the bounds of dialectics with its constant suggestions of implosion or burnout. This is the "ludic" postmodernism much celebrated by contemporary academe that looks also to adversarial gestures associated with early twentieth-century avant-garde modernism for evidence of a challenge to corporate capital and its culture of representation. The great deceit of this quasi-anarchical tendency, with its Bakhtinian preoccupation with "polyphonous" voices (actually complementing very well notions of choice in consumer culture) and multivalent textual interpretation in the wake of failed "master narrative" (the emphasis here is usually on Marxism), is its almost total refusal of an examination of the real dynamics of race, class, and gender in the last part of the century. The bad faith of ludic culture and many aspects of the multiculturalism debate is the idealist status given to sacrificial ideology itself. Most contemporary discussions of figures such as Bataille do not properly situate sacrifice within the confines of a thoroughly depoliticized society that looks self-consciously toward myth (usually in rituals of nostalgia) to validate its political economy and sense of use value. The attempt to survive on the shards of mythic speech while enunciating all aspects of this speech (as deconstruction penetrates advertising culture, etc.), describing it, moving it into the dimension of critical narrative, is a strategy more "fatal" than those described by Baudrillard.[18] This process is a prescription for disaster for the bourgeois view of reality and human life, one all the more catastrophic due to the fact that alternative political instruments are not in place.

422

The key myth that is both deconstructed and resuscitated is the essential conflation of nature and culture, the refusal, in Barthesian terms, to understand human conduct as anything but given and natural, which is to say part of a sacred and preordained order. Flowing from this is the myth of the dichotomy of Self and Other that has driven the process of American civilization. Centered as it is on the opposition to difference, this myth has constituted the basis for most interaction. The cynicism of postmodernity pretends to see through this and associated myths, while refusing to part company with their basic demands even as myth is increasingly demonstrated to be a function of ideology and history.

In postmodern civilization, the hyperreal does not suggest merely the third phase of simulation (in Baudrillard's concept) following the extinction of history and myth, but the schizoid tension created by the vacillation between the two, a vacillation caused in part by the exposure of mediation/myth-making processes in the cybernetic/media era. The self-immolation now confronting bourgeois society is part of Marxist theory: Bourgeois society would rather destroy itself entirely than cross into historical-materialist consciousness, even as its own processes of representation expose its assumptions and their exhaustion. The building of the A-bomb, its presentation by Truman and others, and the pop culture that grew around it is a good emblem of this tendency toward the worship of catastrophe and self-annihilation. But the situation is, of course, complex, with capitalism in its late phase viewing itself as triumphant and socialism considered the experiment gone bad, while amid these facile proclamations capitalism cries out its despair over the death of "community," "common dreams," and the like.

Dialectical analysis has not thus far accounted adequately for the joy not only in the destruction of the Other but also in the suicide that attends sacrificial violence as it becomes a feature of everyday interchange in the last phase of mythic consciousness. Even more important, neither Marxism nor post-structuralist theory has accounted for the ways by which the "adversarial" sacrifice of Bataille and avant-garde modernism have been fully appropriated by late capitalism into free-form ritual mechanisms that not only help support the continued destruction of the designated Other, but also provide legitimacy for postindustrial society's suicidal activity.

SLOTKIN, GIRARD, BATAILLE, AND THE MILLENNIUM

D. H. Lawrence and Frank Kermode have eloquently informed us of millennialism's function in providing a sense of closure to experience primarily as it validates a threatened monadic self.[19] The essential link of these two writers, representative of different phases of dying, reactionary liberalism in Britain, is the apprehension of self-as-text, even as both writers preserve the self. Lawrence's upper-class "paganism" caused him to spurn the Apocalypse as a vengeful wish-dream of the lumpenized self; Kermode sees apocalyptic closure in narrative as the self's answer to collective anguish and its refusal of what mythographers such as Mircea Eliade term the "terror of history."[20] Lawrence sees apocalypse as the response of the "thwarted collective self";[21] in the late twentieth-century environment, apocalypse takes on special significance as a cry for violence within a society that spurns politics and the social, while having a degree of panic in the expression of the sacred (born-again religion, "Promise Keepers," etc.) as the self is totally atomized.[22] Richard Slotkin's work has become especially useful in providing links between millennial consciousness and its apocalypticism and the construction of Self and Other in the social and cultural experience of America.[23]

Slotkin has argued that "regeneration through violence," essentially the will-to-myth (the will to read experience mythically through the apparatus of victimization), is based on the demonizing, destruction, or absorption of the Other (Slotkin focuses on the Indian in American expansionism) due to the Self's construction under millennial and apocalyptic narrative. Of specific relevance is the Puritan "dictatorship of the saints" ideology and its political/religious offshoots over the past two centuries, including the divine contract for conquest, Manifest Destiny, and the discrete narratives these broader assertions generate, such as the narrative of journey and recovery (borrowed from antiquity and medieval culture), the captivity narrative, and the image of sacrifice through the Last Stand. James Fenimore Cooper, Robert Montgomery Bird, the previously discussed death of Custer and Crockett's fall at the Alamo all function as a composite locus classicus for these ideas. Slotkin's work is crucial for its emphasis on the predominance of mythic consciousness in popular narrative and to the formation of ideology; it is especially important for its insistence on the extraordinary primacy of bloodletting in validating mythic assumption and false consciousness. The voluminous evidence in Slotkin's work demonstrates, first and foremost, that there is no need for culture to have a sense of the apocalypse as "revelatory." On the contrary, apocalypse must be read in the full sense of its prevalent misuse as pure destruction and self-immolation when the self dies under the failure of collective mythic belief.

It is the work of René Girard that provides a cohesive theoretical framework for a discussion of sacrificial consciousness on individual

and macrocosmic scales, for understanding the ways by which sacri-
ficial/apocalyptic reasoning begins in the formation of the self and is
recognizable as a form of transpsychical crisis affecting social, political,
and economic institutions. In Girard's early work on the novel,[24] he
developed the notion of mimetic desire, which led to a theory of language
formation and the social function of violence that complements very
well the cultural studies of Slotkin. In the construct of mimetic desire,
desire itself is never direct in the sense that a subject simply wants an
object; an object gains desirability insofar as it is desired by someone
else. While Girard is not a Marxist, this formulation suggests a way of
viewing the origin of exchange value. The object eventually becomes
an abstract principle suspended between two rivals (termed mimetic or
"monstrous" doubles); finally the Self/Other dichotomy established early
in the mimetic process changes as the Self sees the rival's stature as Other
dissolving as the metaphysical properties of the desired object disappear.
The more the Self comprehends the mimetic process, the more the object
loses value, and a crisis ensues because differentiation, earlier sustained
because the Self was entrapped by a mythic perception of interchange,
is suddenly profoundly threatened.

In his discussion of characterization in the novel, Girard also suggests that mimetic desire can occur within individual consciousness
through particular forms of interchange, such as sadomasochistic behavior (which Girard does not speak of as aberrant but as a lawful interchange
in his mimetic law of value). The desire mediating the contract of
the sadist and masochist is power. Thus, the masochist quite readily
acquiesces in a docile and demeaning role as the sign of power remains
dominant (s/he believes eventually the power position will always be
exchanged). On the social level this is easily applied: The worker/soldier
takes abuse from the boss/general since the effectuation of power alone
legitimizes not merely the social formation but the existence of all people.
On yet another level, the mediation of desire does not necessarily require
a specific rival as such. The self's relationship to a social group (or to
society in general) can be predicated on a distorted self-image born of a
perceived transcendent/divine contract functioning as ego ideal (perhaps
the single most important concept at the basis of rivalry and mimetic
desire), through which the self evaluates his/her participation in the object
world in a process not unlike Lacan's discussion of personality locked in
the Imaginary. In a contemporary example (appropriate to this discussion
since its key influence is Dostoevsky's *Notes from Underground,* one
of Girard's models of explanation), the film *Taxi Driver* locates the
protagonist's identity (significantly shaped by media culture, particularly

by media renditions of the American male as regenerative savior) in a divinely ordained errand of "mission." The self, vulnerable under this figuration, fluctuates between self-abasement and violent assertion until a crisis point (apocalypse) is reached, which falls short of revelation, since myth collapses as the mediated self evaporates.[25]

In his later formulations,[26] Girard discusses sacrificial violence occurring as the result of the failure of mimesis. Violence becomes a way of restoring consensus (concerning what is to be valued), totemism, and a language system, all of which are circumscribed by myth through the will-to-meaning. This violence is meant to restore a contractual desire and also prohibition systems (here Girard depends heavily on Freud) that keep mimesis in check and yet support its validity. As sacrificial violence becomes dysfunctional, sacrificial crisis ensues, beginning first with the recognition that social ritual no longer has efficacy (due to excessive enunciation and repetition) in sustaining a language system. The social threat then becomes profound, as the society is faced with the prospect of unchecked violence and pandemonium, a tidal wave of blood. The sacrificial violence Girard sees as most central to the history of mythic perception of reality (which is to say the total history of civilization) is scapegoating, an example of which is the contemporary penal system (a way by which Western society actually *masks* sacrificial violence), but more generally in prosaic forms of interchange where failure is blamed on an individual or group (Other) rather than a structure or process (this would bring society too close to a historical consciousness of interaction). Girard views all human history under the sign of sacrifice. His evidence is easily marshaled, since the mother lode of mythic narrative (Greek, Jewish, Christian) describing civilization's origins begins with the eating of the gods and the gods devouring their own. Connected to this is the *sparagmos,* deconstructed in Athenian tragedy, wherein a salvific hero is torn apart to ensure new vitality and social stability.

Many of Girard's theories help build a theory of violence in the Western world, but much of it is problematical. While a dialectic (myth vs. history) occurs in his work, the dialectic of sacrifice is insufficiently nuanced. Sacrifice has special pertinence to the age of simulation, because postmodern culture is heavily formed around nostalgia and a yearning for origins and coherent truths. This nostalgia, as bourgeois experience has informed us, can be achieved only through blood, through a reduction of the individual and collective self to base matter (chaos), a principle that psychoanalysis has long associated with repetition-compulsion and the death wish (the *fort/da* game is not a bad psychoanalytic emblem for postmodern nostalgia yearnings linked to a suicidal quest for origins and meaning). The avarice of late capitalist society also recapitulates Girard's mimetic desire, the foundation of crisis, wherein "two hands reach for the same object" (a phrase Girard uses in several interviews), as competition and value are exposed as functions of desire. Late capitalism represents a Nietzschean "great awakening" to the paucity of notions of intrinsic value. Value, born of mimesis, falls into a black hole with the collapse of the social, a process faintly diagrammed by Girard. And Girard has insufficiently accounted for some of his precursors on the topic of sacrifice. Although James G. Frazer and Freud are mentioned fairly often (for their interest in the primal lynching and its place in the sacrificial view of history), he has all but ignored Bataille, whose work poses the most direct challenge to Girard's theory.[27]

While Bataille, like Girard, sees sacrificial violence permeating human interchange and functioning as a basic metaphor for experience, he does not see it as reducible to such discrete acts as scapegoating, which could be exposed and overturned, thus providing a path to a non-sacrificial view of history. Bataille is conscious of the problematic position of sacrifice, and he saw that its centrality to culture could not be removed by revolutionary faith or the introduction of dialectical reasoning. Of course Bataille has been criticized for his unscientific, bellettristic approach, encompassed very much by the current of surrealism obvious in both his critical writing and his fiction. Part of Bataille's approach to sacrifice as a function of the polymorphous perverse seems too close to "renegade" surrealism's resistance to revolutionary commitment (particularly as André Breton's politicizing of surrealism caused ruptures among 1930s French intellectuals). Bataille's vision of the "pineal eye" and the "solar anus" applies sacrifice, in a tense, dialectical model, to revolutionary change, since for Bataille sacrifice is not involved as much in propping up sign systems as in disturbing them. Sacrifice for Bataille is an immersion in the destructive element: a site of transgression, a place of taboos. As with Girard, Bataille's view of sacrifice acknowledges the Other, although his sense of the Other is at the heart of his very different view of sacrifice's contradictions. Bataille's sacrifice repudiates the structured notion of political economy that Marcel Mauss assigns to such sacrificial gestures as potlatch. For Bataille, potlatch is merely symbolic of society's tendency toward waste, excess, destruction, and cannibalism, an approach to political economy now very much embraced by certain studies of postindustrial consumer society. More important, Bataille does not believe that potlatch can ensure social stability, but that it indicates merely a repressive gesture geared toward forestalling (but actually fomenting) chaos. Bataille's work is most useful as a "prequel" and a kind of response to Girard when we comprehend the opposite ways by which the two thinkers pose sacrifice as a comprehensive theory of society.

In Bataille, sacrifice is civilization's classic "return to origins" strategy both for dominant and adversarial culture, and it is here that we confront Bataille's nihilism. It is not traducing Bataille too much to say that his work, for all of its anarchical radicalism, evinces the bad faith and moral schizophrenia of bourgeois culture in its disavowal (here in the form of a 1920s French avant-garde intellectual) of organized political action and social transformation. But this is not to diminish Bataille, since his work, as bemused as it often is, may be the baroque skeleton key to the suicidal impulses of Western mythic consciousness. The principal criticisms of Bataille have focused on his sense of ideology as an outgrowth of myth. In his remarks on the Aztecs, Bataille, whose work was always encompassed by the *mal de siècle* temperament of early bourgeois anthropology, shows how the institution of the sacred simultaneously marks the birth and death of a society. The sun god of the Aztecs was the life-giving foundation of chaos to whom human blood was offered as a potlatch, given by the profane world in an attempt to gain the beneficence of the sacred through a homeopathic process. The contradictions of this process are at the center of Bataille's reading, since the waste of human life is simply adjacent to the image of the sun (life) itself. Since the sun's light is a gift freely given, the giving represents nullity in its simultaneous beneficence and destruction. The sun becomes a symbol of entropy and burn out, of light shining to the point that "enlightenment" becomes unbearable. Bataille's reading makes the sacred seem pathetic: The solar anus (death in life) is a parody of humanity's nostalgia for origins and foundations it persistently locates in the sacred.

The difficulties of Bataille's work extend far, since, as a surrealist (at least in temperament and occasional intellectual strategy), Bataille saw the sacred in eccentric terms. For him it is a site of transgression in oppositional hands, a solution to Freud's meditations on repression. The sacred is "good" insofar as it assaults use value through the destruction of goods called for by sacrifice. Sacrifice for Bataille must be recognized as the impulse to destroy, to descend into an orgy of annihilation rather than accommodate repression through the political economy of potlatch that is incorporated into bourgeois civilization. Potlatch serves—in its one-upmanship of "giving more than another giver"—to support hierarchies and class systems.

The release of the irrational is a denial of the profane world and a validation of "heterogenous" (transgressive, socially unacceptable) elements. It is here that Bataille is most problematic in terms of his application to postmodern culture. The introduction of heterogeneity (the Other) can take various and often dangerous forms in the homeopathic contact with the homogenous profane world. Both the charismatic hero and the mass movement can, in modern technological civilization, form the dynamic of the shaman's contact with society. The shaman is powerful because of some primal allure, usually a sense of his power due to his early immersion (through trial or divine will) in chaos, but he is kept at arm's length and called upon only at those times when society needs reinvigoration. This is the realm of "imperial" heterogeneity (as opposed to more elementary forms such as transgressive sexual practices) that allows for Alexander, Caesar, Hitler, Mussolini, Stalin, for the union of eros with thanatos, the collaboration of "fascinating fascism" and the abrogation of the will with the socially taboo.[28] The dangers here are obvious. Fascism has long been studied for its appeal to the unbridled id, and Bataille is aware of the extent to which the pursuit of heterogeneity becomes a link to heteronomy and the surrender of the will to authority. The real difficulty here is not Bataille's concern that the sacred, being not mystical and primordial but involved in humanity's desire to transgress the social order, is easily co-opted by movements such as fascism; rather, it is Nietzsche's sense that the closer one comes to the truth of "origins," the less attractive becomes the whole notion of the sacred realm both dominant and transgressive. This insight is demonstrated in the postmodernist tendency to create anniversaries (the Beatles, Woodstock, the deaths of John F. Kennedy and Martin Luther King) that seem to pose an alternative, progressive notion of history and the sacred, but which merely replicate old formations.

The sacrificial crisis of postmodern experience is, as discussed, grounded in the culture of simulation, recalling that the crisis is indicative of the collapse of language, the consensus from which it originates and the rituals it generates. The culture of the simulacra is not one of "copies" but one of a profound absence marking the demise of lived experience as the will-to-meaning fades with the exposure of myth. The commodity form, the thing desired, is in its most precarious situation in this circumstance, given its evanescence in the realm of simulation. With the new status of money in the cyberspace circuit of exchange, people look for solid "investments to protect them from the terrible oscillations of chance."[29] Mimetic desire will not go away, but it must exist now within the political economy of simulation. The reification, recognition, dismissal, and reification again of the mediator of desire is supported, but operates now within the speed and volatility of the cybernetic era. And as the object desired and the mediation process are constantly debunked and devalued, sacrificial violence is pronounced and continues unabated, until constant repetition of all processes bankrupts scapegoating and other typical attempts to provide cohesion: There is violence "on all fronts."[30] With the collapse of the signifying chain marking the preeminence of third-order simulacra and the demise of the social, Girard's formulations concerning mimesis and the reconstitution of the social (sacred) order seem insightful as to the dysfunction of society under mythic consciousness, but somewhat obsolete as we see them in the current topography. Girard's work becomes central as we see the failure of mimesis and its ritual functions as key features of late capitalist conduct, but Bataille seems to win the critical stakes as sacrificial culture tends to rebuke any nonsacrificial reading of itself and valorizes irrationality. Bataille "wins" not because of his essentialist reading of humanity's impulse toward excess and destruction, but because neither avant-garde culture nor dominant ideology have succeeded in stepping outside myth. His perverse victory may reside actually in academic culture's conflation of culture with politics, and its preference for the individualist excessive gesture over organized resistance, a very American outcome to the late twentieth-century crisis.

In a recent discussion in *Yale French Studies,* Jean-Joseph Goux makes clearer the implications of Bataillean sacrifice for postmodern America.[31] Goux notes that George Gilder's *Wealth and Poverty,* one of the key apologias for Reagan-era supply-side economics, is a postmodern legitimation of capitalism that walks the same terrain as Bataille even if Bataille is not mentioned by name (Gilder does note some related figures such as Marcel Mauss and Claude Lévi-Strauss). In an attempt to construct a "theology" of capital, Gilder offers the bizarre argument that capital formation has never been about the parsimoniousness, frugality, and caution of Calvin, Weber, mercantilism, and the Protestant ethic. Expenditure, according to Gilder, is at the heart of capital, the willingness to spend without real assurance of return—for him this is the relation of sacrifice to potlatch. Although a typical romanticizing of primitive culture (from the right), and a very dishonest reading of the origins and functions of capital, Gilder may be unconsciously exposing, as Goux notes, the heart of darkness at the center of Western capitalist economy. Gilder's argument ignores the fact that the Keynesian state system of the postwar years allowed massive deficit expenditures through state guarantees as the state became linked to the private sector through the mechanism of military manufacture. The "potlatch" and "expenditure" of capital were done by the few at the expense of the many. Gilder's argument becomes, almost unbelievably, a desperate assault by a rightist on Enlightenment reason. It is *almost* unbelievable because it contains within it the lawful outgrowth of capitalist reason—fascism. Right in time with the New Age embrace of return-to-myth strategies, Gilder argues that socialism's real defect is its imposition of instrumental reason on economy. The very precariousness of capital expenditure (again, this is nonsense), according to Gilder, opens humanity to chance and the realm of the sacred. This reads very much like a merger of the New Age outlook with the "ludic" free play of postmodernity that contains the perversity of Bataille's sacrificial gesture. As Goux observes, Gilder is wrong about capital's refusal of rationalism and about the "theology" that capital supposedly permits; at best this religion is a new Calvinism that would look very scornfully on those not "blessed."

Gilder's work seems important, however, as a summary statement on late capitalism at the millennium, and also as a caution for us that avant-gardist notions of sacrifice, with ludic free play and "gaming," need careful reexamination in the postmodern climate. Late capitalism is indeed very much involved in the violence and excess of Bataille's "accursed share," and this fact needs to be associated with Gilder's rationalist validations of postmodern capital's dynamics. The destruction of wealth is apparent enough and not particularly arcane: The use of "gaming" and lotteries as ways of supporting the state as industrial capital migrates; the huge amount of capital focused on speculation against currencies; the continued predominance of the publicly subsidized war economy and its drain on a fragile economic base; and the blatant theft and destruction of resources by officers of state power and capital provide the true evidence and best representation of the "ludic" postmodern climate of chance, polyphony, and fatalistic beneficence. Gilder's supposed assault on the rationalism that previously supported capital seems a keen recognition of the death of the social contract under capital and the new climate wherein all bets are off as the public sector is demolished. A new legitimation crisis has set in that calls for new strategies of inoculation, a new embrace of the public's critical faculties so as to retain our acquiescence. We are therefore offered a validation of capital that turns the worst, most irrational consequences of its essential premises into a blessing through a rewriting of its ethic that conforms to manifestations of a very discordant, manufactured popular culture, itself a manifestation of a disintegrating political-economic order.

With Bataillean economy incorporated into the logic of neoconservatism, postmodern sacrifice looks very much like the suicidal nihilism always implicit in the American millennic vision. Destruction as a validation of power "proves" wealth in the primitive sense as it depends on the magic of regenerative violence. No one believes anymore in the old system of expenditure/reinvestment centered on the expansion of America and its industrial plant; postmodern sacrificial expenditure, waste, and excess looks increasingly like the necessary end game of sacrificial culture to generate meaning. The situation is quite futile. The best representation of this ludic excess and gaming is the consumer's compulsive pursuit of unneeded and unwanted goods that keep the atomized subject from a confrontation with a social, cultural, and political void. These gestures are about assuring the collapse of meaning, not regenerating it, even as blood sacrifice (the Persian Gulf War, the interventions in Eastern Europe, the expansion of NATO) continues as the basic formula for sustaining economy and some semblance of social cohesion. In this context, then, readings of sacrifice by such scholars as Girard seem not very useful as solutions to sacrificial culture simply because such readings posit the notion that society must keep sacrificial gestures and institutions, like all forms of mythic speech, in some sense hidden.

Postmodern America now demands revelry in sacrifice as panicked validation of its already-dead self-concept. Rituals are enacted even as no one believes in the institutions supporting them. Sacrificial bloodletting in particular becomes a vigorously enforced strategy for providing the millennic, suicidal closure once spoken of in rather poeticized terms by the early New England mind, articulated further in the biblically informed political unconscious of Manifest Destiny. The new situation has little concern for, or even knowledge of, the earlier grand schemes and world view at its foundation. The killing of schoolchildren by their own, the slaughter of workers by co-workers, the random revolt of the disaffected white male and the representational culture that follows from all of this are indeed merely the product of a civilization that despises history and any reasonable understanding of material reality and human needs.

Notes

1. William S. Burroughs, "A Thanksgiving Prayer, Nov. 28, 1986," in *Tornado Alley* (Lawrence, Kan.: Cherry Valley Editions, 1989), 7.

2. The "Go Ahead" philosophy of Crockett and his contemporaries is discussed in Jeff Long, *Duel of Eagles: The Mexican and U.S. Fight for the Alamo* (New York: William Morrow, 1990), 100–105, passim.

3. Crockett's speeches are reprinted in numerous sources, including George A. McAlister, *Alamo: The Price of Freedom* (San Antonio: Docutex, 1988), 140,

141. The definitive Crockett biography is James Atkins Shackford, *David Crockett: The Man and the Legend* (Chapel Hill: University of North Carolina Press, 1986).

4. Long, *Duel of Eagles,* 59.

5. Contemporaneous journalistic accounts of the fall of the Alamo for the most part are in agreement that the near-fifty Crockett was executed by Santa Anna's soldiers after the battle. The idea that the middle-aged politician was gratuitously murdered by Mexicans was itself a call to arms in the States. The notion of Crockett's Last Stand is largely an invention of twentieth-century film, yet this version is supported with considerable vehemence by Crockett fans, even in the face of such books as Jose Enrique de la Pena, *With Santa Anna in Texas: A Personal Narrative of the Revolution,* ed. and trans. Carmen Perry (College Station: Texas A & M University Press, 1975). This firsthand account of the Alamo's fall by a Mexican officer was finally translated and released by an academic press in the 1970s, to the consternation of many Alamo fans. Although de la Pena says nothing disparaging of the weary and debilitated Crockett, and even states that he faced his execution with dignity, the diary has been savaged. Some Crockett worshippers allege (with specious evidence) that the diary is a forgery.

6. The death of Custer and its relationship to regenerative violence in late nineteenth-century American political consciousness is a central topic of Richard Slotkin's magisterial *The Fatal Environment: The Myth of the Frontier in the Age of Industrialization* (New York: Atheneum, 1985).

7. Shelby Foote makes this remark in his commentaries in the PBS documentary film *The Civil War* (1989), directed by Ken Burns.

8. The most compelling evidence that the bombings of Hiroshima and Nagasaki were by no means military necessities is offered in Gar Alperowitz, *The Decision to Use the Atomic Bomb* (New York: Random House, 1995). The popularization of nuclear destruction and total war in mass culture is well chronicled in the sardonic documentary *The Atomic Cafe* (1982). I decided to use the Truman and Beahan quotes as epigrams for my afterword after a recent viewing of the movie, one of many since this wonderful film's release.

9. Charles Royster, *The Destructive War: William Tecumseh Sherman, Stonewall Jackson, and the Americans* (New York: Alfred A. Knopf, 1991), 259.

10. Ibid., 266.

11. Ibid.

12. Michael Fellman, *Inside War: The Guerilla Conflict in Missouri during the American Civil War* (New York: Oxford University Press, 1989), 189.

13. Ibid.

14. Noam Chomsky mentions this neoconservative complaint in *Media Control: The Spectacular Achievements of Propaganda* (New York: Seven Stories Press, 1997), 28.

15. This seems the central assumption of Jean Baudrillard, *America,* trans. Chris Turner (London and New York: Verso, 1988).

16. See Claude Lévi-Strauss, "How Myths Die," *New Literary History* 2 (Winter 1974): 269–81.

17. Peter Sloterdijk, *Critique of Cynical Reason,* trans. Michael Eldred (Minneapolis: University of Minnesota Press, 1987), xvii, 5–6, passim.

18. Jean Baudrillard, *Fatal Strategies,* trans. Philip Beitchman and W. G. J. Niesluchowski (New York: Semiotext[e], 1990).

19. D. H. Lawrence, *Apocalypse* (1932; rpt. New York: Penguin, 1975). Frank Kermode, *The Sense of an Ending: Studies in the Theory of Fiction* (New York: Oxford University Press, 1967).

20. Mircea Eliade, *Cosmos and History: The Myth of the Eternal Return,* trans. Willard R. Trask (Princeton: Princeton University Press, 1954), 141–62.

21. Lawrence, *Apocalypse,* 23.

22. The atomization and anti-political bent of late twentieth-century American society is discussed by Noam Chomsky, *Class Warfare* (Monroe, Maine: Common Courage Press, 1996), 83–84, 111, 118–20.

23. Slotkin's *The Fatal Environment,* the second volume of his important trilogy on the representation of violence in American history and folklore, has been mentioned. His first book, *Regeneration through Violence: The Mythology of the American Frontier, 1600–1860* (Middletown, Conn.: Wesleyan University Press, 1973), became of central importance to cultural studies, as did the last book of the trilogy, *Gunfighter Nation: The Myth of the Frontier in Twentieth-Century America* (New York: HarperCollins, 1993).

24. René Girard, *Deceit, Desire and the Novel: Self and Other in Literary Structures,* trans. Yvonne Frecerro (Baltimore: Johns Hopkins University Press, 1965).

25. See my "The American Apocalypse: Scorsese's *Taxi Driver,*" in *Crisis Cinema: The Apocalyptic Idea in Postmodern Narrative Film,* ed. Christopher Sharrett (Washington, D.C.: Maisonneuve Press, 1993), 221–37.

26. René Girard, *Violence and the Sacred,* trans. Patrick Gregory (Baltimore: Johns Hopkins University Press, 1977). A further development of Girard's theories of sacrifice is found in *The Scapegoat,* trans. Yvonne Freccero (Baltimore: Johns Hopkins University Press, 1986), and *Things Hidden since the Foundation of the World,* trans. Stephen Bann and Michael Meteer (Stanford: Stanford University Press, 1987).

27. The essential sources are Georges Bataille, *Visions of Excess: Selected Writings, 1927–1939,* trans. Allan Stoekl, with Carl R. Lovitt and Donald M. Leslie, Jr. (Minneapolis: University of Minnesota Press, 1985), and *The Accursed Share: An Essay on General Economy,* vol. 1, trans. Robert Hurley (New York: Zone Books, 1988).

28. See Bataille, "The Psychological Structure of Fascism," in *Visions of Excess,* 137–61.

29. Andre Orlean, "Money and Mimetic Speculation," in *Violence and Truth: On the Work of René Girard,* ed. Paul Dumouchel (Stanford: Stanford University Press, 1988), 103. On the terror of confrontation with origins flowing from post-modernity's nostalgic yearnings, see Gianni Vattimo, *The End of Modernity: Nihilism and Hermeneutics in Postmodern Culture,* trans. Jon R. Snyder (Baltimore: Johns Hopkins University Press, 1988), 168–70.

30. Girard, *Violence and the Sacred,* 10, 276.

31. Jean-Joseph Goux, "General Economics and Postmodern Capitalism," *Yale French Studies* 78 (1990): 216.

SELECTED BIBLIOGRAPHY

Allen, Robert C., ed. *Channels of Discourse, Reassembled.* Chapel Hill: University of North Carolina Press, 1993.

Alloway, Lawrence. *Violent America: The Movies, 1946–1964.* New York: Museum of Modern Art, 1971.

Alperowitz, Gar. *The Decision to Use the Atomic Bomb.* New York: Random House, 1995.

Artaud, Antonin. *The Theater and Its Double.* New York: Grove Press, 1958.

Bataille, Georges. *The Accursed Share: An Essay on General Economy,* Vol. 1. Trans. Robert Hurley. New York: Zone Books, 1988.

————. *Visions of Excess: Selected Writings, 1927–1939.* Trans. Allan Stoekl, with Carl R. Lovitt and Donald M. Leslie, Jr. Minneapolis: University of Minnesota Press, 1985.

Baudrillard, Jean. *America.* Trans. Chris Turner. London and New York: Verso, 1988.

————. *Fatal Strategies.* Trans. Philip Beitchman and W. G. J. Niesluchowski. New York: Semiotext[e], 1990

————. *Simulations.* Trans. Paul Foss, Paul Patton, and Philip Beitchman. New York: Semiotext[e], 1983.

Bell, Daniel. *The End of Ideology: On the Exhaustion of Political Ideas in the Fifties.* New York: Free Press, 1960.

Best, Stephen, and Douglas Kellner. *Postmodern Theory: Critical Interrogations.* New York: Guilford Press, 1991.

Black, Joel. *The Aesthetics of Murder.* Baltimore: Johns Hopkins University Press, 1991.

Bly, Robert. *Iron John: A Book about Men.* Reading, Mass.: Addison-Wesley, 1990.

Bourdieu, Pierre. *Distinction: A Social Critique of the Judgement of Taste.* Trans. Richard Nile. Cambridge, Mass.: Harvard University Press, 1984.

Brahm, Jr., Gabriel, and Mark Driscoll, eds. *Prosthetic Territories: Politics and Hypertechnologies*. Boulder, Colo.: Westview Press, 1995.

Brown, Robert Maxwell, ed. *Strain of Violence: Historical Studies of American Violence and Vigilantism*. New York: Oxford University Press, 1975.

Burroughs, William S. *Tornado Alley*. Lawrence, Kan.: Cherry Valley Editions, 1989.

Cameron, Deborah, and Elizabeth Frazer. *The Lust to Kill: A Feminist Investigation of Sexual Murder*. New York: New York University Press, 1987.

Caputi, Jane. *The Age of Sex Crime*. Bowling Green, Ohio: Popular Press, 1983.

Chomsky, Noam. *Class Warfare*. Monroe, Maine: Common Courage Press, 1996.

————. *Media Control: The Spectacular Achievements of Propaganda*. New York: Seven Stories Press, 1997.

Clover, Carol. *Men, Women, and Chain Saws: Gender in the Modern Horror Film*. Princeton: Princeton University Press, 1992.

Cohan, Steven, and Ina Rae Hark. *Screening the Male: Exploring Masculinities in Hollywood Cinema*. New York: Routledge, 1993.

Creed, Barbara. "Horror and the Monstrous-Feminine: An Imaginary Abjection." *Screen* 27.1 (1986): 44–70.

Daly, Mary. *Beyond God the Father: Toward a Philosophy of Women's Liberation*. Boston: Beacon Press, 1973.

————. *Gyn/Ecology: The Metaethics of Radical Feminism*. Boston: Beacon Press, 1978.

Dayan, Daniel, and Allah Kate. *Media Events: The Live Broadcast of History*. Cambridge, Mass.: Harvard University Press, 1992.

Debord, Guy. *Society of the Spectacle*. Detroit: Black and Red, 1983.

Derber, Charles. *Money, Murder and the American Dream*. Winchester, Mass.: Faber and Faber, 1992.

Doane, Mary Ann. *The Desire to Desire: The Woman's Film of the 1940s*. Bloomington: Indiana University Press, 1987.

Dumouchel, Paul, ed. *Violence and Truth: On the Work of René Girard*. Stanford: Stanford University Press, 1988.

Eliade, Mircea. *Cosmos and History: The Myth of the Eternal Return*. Trans. Willard R. Trask. Princeton: Princeton University Press, 1954.

Faludi, Susan. *Backlash: The Undeclared War against American Women*. New York: Crown, 1991.

Fellman, Michael. *Inside War: The Guerilla Conflict in Missouri during the American Civil War*. New York: Oxford University Press, 1989.

Fiske, John. *Television Culture*. London: Methuen, 1987.

Foster, Hal, ed. *The Anti-Aesthetic: Essays on Postmodern Culture*. Seattle: Bay Press, 1983.

Foucault, Michel. *Discipline and Punish: The Birth of the Prison*. Trans. Alan Sheridan. New York: Vintage Books, 1979.

Fraser, John. *Violence in the Arts*. London: Cambridge University Press, 1974.

Freud, Anna. *The Ego and the Mechanisms of Desire, Vol. 2*. New York: International Universities Press, 1996.

Freud, Sigmund. *The Standard Edition of the Complete Psychological Works of*

Sigmund Freud. Ed. James Strachey. London: Hogarth Press and The Institute of Psychoanalysis, 1953–74.

Friedlander, Saul. *Reflections of Nazism: An Essay on Kitsch and Death.* Bloomington: Indiana University Press, 1993.

Garofalo, Raffaele. *Criminology.* Boston: Little Brown, 1914.

Genet, Jean. *The Maids and Deathwatch.* New York: Grove Press, 1954.

Girard, René. *Deceit, Desire and the Novel: Self and Other in Literary Structures.* Trans. Yvonne Frecerro. Baltimore: Johns Hopkins University Press, 1965.

————. *The Scapegoat.* Trans. Yvonne Frecerro. Baltimore: Johns Hopkins University Press, 1985.

————. *Things Hidden since the Foundation of the World.* Trans. Stephen Bann and Michael Meteer. Stanford: Stanford University Press, 1987.

————. *Violence and the Sacred.* Trans. Patrick Gregory. Baltimore: Johns Hopkins University Press, 1977.

Goux, Jean-Joseph. "General Economics and Postmodern Capitalism," *Yale French Studies* 78 (1990): 216.

Grant, Barry Keith. *The Dread of Difference: Gender and the Horror Film.* Austin: University of Texas Press, 1997.

————. "Rich and Strange: The Yuppie Horror Film," *Journal of Film and Video* 48.1–2 (Spring/Summer 1996): 13–34.

Groden, Robert. *The Killing of a President.* New York: Viking Studio Books, 1993.

Guehenno, Jean-Marie. *The End of the Nation-State.* Minneapolis: University of Minnesota Press, 1995.

Hall, Stuart, et al. *Policing the Crisis: Mugging, the State and Law and Order.* London: Macmillan, 1978.

Hickey, Eric W. *Serial Murderers and Their Victims.* Pacific Grove, Calif.: Brooks and Cole, 1991.

James, Bev, and Kay Saville-Smith. *Gender, Culture and Power: Challenging New Zealand's Gendered Culture.* New York: Oxford University Press, 1994.

Jameson, Fredric. *Postmodernism, or, the Cultural Logic of Late Capitalism.* Durham: Duke University Press, 1991.

Jay, Martin. *Downcast Eyes: The Denigration of Vision in Twentieth-Century French Thought.* Berkeley: University of California Press, 1994.

Jeffords, Susan. *Hard Bodies: Hollywood Masculinity in the Reagan Era.* New Brunswick, N.J.: Rutgers University Press, 1994.

Jewett, Richard, and John Shelton Lawrence. *The American Monomyth.* Garden City, N.Y.: Anchor Doubleday, 1977.

Kidd-Hewitt, David, and Richard Osborne. *Crime and the Media: The Postmodern Spectacle.* London: Pluto Press, 1945.

Klein, Melanie. *The Selected Works of Melanie Klein.* Ed. Juliet Mitchell. New York: Macmillan, 1987.

Kristeva, Julia. *The Powers of Horror.* New York: Columbia University Press, 1982.

Lacan, Jacques. *Écrits: A Selection.* New York: Norton, 1977.

Lawrence, D. H. *Apocalypse,* 1932. Reprint, New York: Penguin, 1975.

Lehman, Peter, and William Luhr. *Thinking about Movies.* Fort Worth, Tex.: Harcourt, Brace, Inc., 1998.

Lévi-Strauss, Claude. "How Myths Die," *New Literary History* 2 (Winter 1974): 269–81.

Leyton, Elliot. *Hunting Humans: Inside the Minds of Mass Murderers.* New York: Pocket Books, 1988.

Long, Jeff. *Duel of Eagles: The Mexican and U.S. Fight for the Alamo.* New York: William Morrow, 1990.

Marx, Karl. *The Eighteenth Brumaire of Louis Bonaparte.* New York: International Publishers, 1963.

Newton, Michael. *Serial Slaughter.* Port Townsend, Wash.: Loompanics, 1992.

Nietzsche, Friedrich. *The Birth of Tragedy.* New York: Random House, 1976.

Pagels, Elaine. *The Origin of Satan.* New York: Random House, 1995.

Pena, Jose Enrique de la. *With Santa Anna in Texas: A Personal Narrative of the Revolution.* Ed. and trans. Carmen Perry. College Station: Texas A & M University Press, 1975.

Radford, Jill, and Diana E. H. Russell. *Femicide: The Politics of Woman Killing.* New York: Twayne, 1992.

Ragland, Ellie. *Essays on the Pleasures of Death.* New York: Routledge, 1995.

Royster, Charles. *The Destructive War: William Tecumseh Sherman, Stonewall Jackson and the Americans.* New York: Alfred A. Knopf, 1991.

Schlesinger, Arthur. *Violence: America in the Sixties.* New York: Signet, 1968.

Seltzer, Mark. "Serial Killers (1)," *differences* 5.1 (1993): 113.

Shackford, James Atkins. *David Crockett: The Man and the Legend.* Chapel Hill: University of North Carolina Press, 1986.

Sharrett, Christopher, ed. *Crisis Cinema: The Apocalyptic Idea in Postmodern Narrative Film.* Washington, D.C.: Maisonneuve Press, 1993.

———. "The Horror Film in Neoconservative Culture." In *The Dread of Difference: Gender and the Horror Film.* Ed. Barry Keith Grant. Austin: University of Texas Press, 1997.

Shaviro, Steven. *The Cinematic Body.* Minneapolis: University of Minnesota Press, 1993.

Shohat, Ella, and Robert Stam. *Unthinking Eurocentrism: Multiculturalism and the Media.* New York: Routledge, 1994.

Silverman, Kaja. *Male Subjectivity at the Margins.* New York: Routledge, 1992.

Simpson, Christopher. *Blowback: America's Recruitment of Nazis and Its Effects on the Cold War.* New York: Weidenfeld and Nicolson, 1988.

Slotkin, Richard. *The Fatal Environment: The Myth of the Frontier in the Age of Industrialization.* New York: Atheneum, 1985.

———. *Gunfighter Nation: The Myth of the Frontier in Twentieth-Century America.* New York: HarperCollins, 1993.

———. *Regeneration through Violence: The Mythology of the American Frontier, 1600–1860.* Middletown, Conn.: Wesleyan University Press, 1973.

Sobchack, Vivian, ed. *The Persistence of History: Cinema, Television, and the Modern Event.* New York: Routledge, 1996.

Sparks, Richard. *Television and the Drama of Crime: Moral Tales and the Place of Crime in Public Life.* Buckingham and Philadelphia: Open University Press, 1992.

Steinberg, Leo. *The Sexuality of Christ in Renaissance Art and in Modern Oblivion.* New York: Pantheon/October, 1984.

Thornton, Russell. *American Indian Holocaust and Survival: A Population History since 1492.* Norman: University of Oklahoma Press, 1987.

Vattimo, Gianni. *The End of Modernity: Nihilism and Hermeneutics in Postmodern Culture.* Trans. Jon R. Snyder. Baltimore: Johns Hopkins University Press, 1988.

White, Mimi. *Tele-Advising: Therapeutic Discourse in American Television.* Chapel Hill: University of North Carolina Press, 1992.

Willet, John, Trans. *Brecht on Theatre.* London: Methuen, 1964.

Williams, Tony. *Hearths of Darkness: The Family in the American Horror Film.* Cranbury, N.J.: Fairleigh Dickinson University Press, 1996.

Wood, Robin. *Hitchcock's Films Revisited.* New York: Columbia University Press, 1993.

———. *Hollywood from Vietnam to Reagan.* New York: Columbia University Press, 1986.

Žižek, Slavoj. *The Sublime Object of Ideology.* London: Verso, 1989.

CONTRIBUTORS

ILSA J. BICK is a practicing adult and child psychiatrist in Fairfax, Virginia. She has published articles in *Cinema Journal, Postscript, Journal of Film and Video,* and other publications. She has contributed to critical anthologies on *Star Trek* and *The Maltese Falcon.*

JANE CAPUTI taught for many years in the American Studies program of the University of New Mexico and is currently professor of women's studies at Florida Atlantic University. She is the author of *The Age of Sex Crime; Gossips, Gorgons and Crones: The Fates of the Earth;* and numerous pieces for *Journal of Popular Film and Television, Cineaste, Gender and Society, Journal of Communication Inquiry,* and other journals. She is co-editor with Mary Daly of *Webster's First New Intergalactic Wickedary of the English Language.*

SUSAN CRUTCHFIELD is assistant professor of English at the University of Wisconsin at LaCrosse, where she teaches cultural studies and film. Her research focuses on representations of disability in popular film and the depiction of difference in visual culture. She has co-edited a collection of essays titled *Disability, Art, and Culture,* which is forthcoming from the University of Michigan Press, and her essay on the intersection of disability studies and film studies appears in *Disability Studies Quarterly* 17.4 (Fall 1997, published August 1998).

MARK GALLAGHER is a doctoral student in English at the University of Oregon, where he teaches literature and film history. He is writing a dissertation on masculinity and spectacle in the action film and in the contemporary American novel. His work has previously appeared in *Velvet Light Trap.*

BARRY KEITH GRANT is professor of film studies and popular culture at Brock University in St. Catharines, Ontario, Canada. Among his numerous publications are *Planks of Reason: Essays on the Horror Film* (1984), *Film Genre Reader* (1995), *The Dread of Difference: Gender and the Horror Film* (1996), and *Documenting the Documentary: Close Readings of Documentary Film and Video* (co-edited with Jeannette Sloniowski, 1998).

441

WILLIAM LUHR is professor of English and film at St. Peter's College. He is co-author with Peter Lehman of *Authorship and Narrative in the Cinema* and two books on Blake Edwards. He has also written *Raymond Chandler on Film*, and is editor of *World Cinema since 1945* and a critical anthology on *The Maltese Falcon*. He has written a textbook on film language with Peter Lehman titled *Thinking about Movies*.

LIANNE MCLARTY is director of the film studies program and associate dean of fine arts at the University of Victoria, British Columbia, Canada, where she teaches film studies. She has written on Canadian experimental film and popular culture. A recent article on David Cronenberg appears in *The Dread of Difference*, and she has an article forthcoming on the politics of the film sequel to be published in *Take Two: Defining the Sequel*.

KEN MORRISON is an associate professor of sociology at Wilfred Laurier University, Waterloo, Ontario, Canada. His work has appeared in *Cineaction* and in the *Canadian Journal of Sociology*. His most recent publication is a book on the history of social theory titled *Marx, Durkheim, Weber: Formations of Modern Social Thought*.

ANNALEE NEWITZ holds a Ph.D. in English and American Studies from the University of California, Berkeley, and is a freelance writer. She is the co-editor of *White Trash: Race and Class in America* and the author of the forthcoming *When We Pretend That We're Dead: Monsters, Psychopaths, and the Economy in American Pop Culture*. Her articles have appeared in *Film Quarterly, minnesota review,* and *American Studies*. She is also co-founder and contributing editor of the online magazine *Bad Subjects* and writes regularly for *Punk Planet, New York Press,* and the *San Francisco Bay Guardian*.

MARK PIZZATO teaches theater history, play analysis, playwriting, and film at the University of North Carolina at Charlotte. He has published articles on theater and media studies in various journals and anthologies, including *Essays in Theatre, Journal of Dramatic Theory and Criticism, Journal of Ritual Studies, Journal of Popular Film and Television, Spectator,* the online journal *LIMEN,* and in *Ethnologie und Inszenierung: Ansätze zur Theaterethnologie* (1998). He has also written *Edges of Loss: From Modern Drama to Postmodern Theory,* focusing on the drama of Eliot, Artaud, Brecht, and Genet. He is also a published playwright.

ELAYNE RAPPING is professor of media studies and women's studies at the State University of New York at Buffalo and the author, most recently, of *Media-tions: Forays into the Gender and Culture Wars* and *The Culture of*

442

Recovery: Making Sense of the Self-Help Movement in Women's Lives. Her current work focuses on media representations of law and criminal justice. She is a frequent contributor to *The Progressive.*

MARTIN RUBIN was film program director of the New York Cultural Center and an associate director of the San Francisco Film Festival. He has taught at Columbia University, the State University of New York at Purchase, Wright State University, and the University of California at Santa Barbara. His articles on film have appeared in the *Village Voice, Movie, Film Comment, Persistence of Vision, Velvet Light Trap,* and *Film History.* He has contributed essays to anthologies on cinema sound, John Huston, and mass culture. He is the author of *Showstoppers: Busby Berkeley and the Tradition of Spectacle* and a forthcoming book on thriller movies from Cambridge University Press.

CHRISTOPHER SHARRETT is associate professor of communication at Seton Hall University. He is the editor of *Crisis Cinema: The Apocalyptic Idea in Postmodern Narrative Film.* His work has appeared in *Cineaste, Cineaction, Journal of Film and Popular Television, Persistence of Vision, Film Quarterly,* and various anthologies, including *The New American Cinema, Perspectives on German Cinema,* and *The Dread of Difference: Gender and the Horror Film.* He has a bimonthly film column in *USA Today* magazine.

PHILIP L. SIMPSON is an assistant professor of English and humanities at the Palm Bay campus of Brevard Community College in east-central Florida. He also currently serves as area chair in horror for the Popular Culture Association. He has published essays in the *Encyclopedia of U.S. Popular Culture, War and American Popular Culture, The Encyclopedia of Novels into Film, Cineaction, Clues,* and *Notes on Contemporary Literature.* He obtained his Ph.D. in American literature at Southern Illinois University in Carbondale in 1996.

JANE SMITH is a Ph.D. candidate in English at the University of North Carolina, Chapel Hill, where she has taught literature and film. She is currently a film critic for the Durham, North Carolina, *Independent.*

JULIAN STRINGER teaches film studies at Indiana University, Bloomington. His work has appeared in *Film Quarterly, Asian Cinema, Screen, Millennium Film Journal,* and the recent anthology *The Road Movie Book.*

FRANK P. TOMASULO teaches film history and theory at Georgia State University in Atlanta. The author of over fifty articles and essays on film and television, he is currently the editor of *Cinema Journal.*

443

TONY WILLIAMS is associate professor and area head of film studies at Southern Illinois University at Carbondale. His recent books include *Larry Cohen: Radical Allegories of an American Filmmaker* and *Hearths of Darkness: The Family in the American Horror Film.* His work has appeared in *Cinema Journal, Wide Angle, Journal of Film and Video, Film History, Science Fiction Studies, Movie, Cineaction,* and other journals.

INDEX